MW01114437

MAPPING THE COCONSTRUCTION OF MEANING

Regina Rowland

MAPPING THE COCONSTRUCTION OF MEANING

Interactive Graphic Facilitation And Collaborative Visual Mapping In Polycultural Small Group Environments

Lambert Academic Publishing

Impressum/Imprint (nur für Deutschland/ only for Germany)

Bibliografische Information der Deutschen Nationalbibliothek: Die Deutsche Nationalbibliothek verzeichnet diese Publikation in der Deutschen Nationalbibliografie; detaillierte bibliografische Daten sind im Internet über http://dnb.d-nb.de abrufbar.

Alle in diesem Buch genannten Marken und Produktnamen unterliegen warenzeichen-, marken- oder patentrechtlichem Schutz bzw. sind Warenzeichen oder eingetragene Warenzeichen der jeweiligen Inhaber. Die Wiedergabe von Marken, Produktnamen, Gebrauchsnamen, Handelsnamen, Warenbezeichnungen u.s.w. in diesem Werk berechtigt auch ohne besondere Kennzeichnung nicht zu der Annahme, dass solche Namen im Sinne der Warenzeichen- und Markenschutzgesetzgebung als frei zu betrachten wären und daher von jedermann benutzt werden dürften.

Verlag: Lambert Academic Publishing AG & Co. KG
Theodor-Heuss-Ring 26, 50668 Köln, Deutschland
Telefon +49 681 3720-310, Telefax +49 681 3720-3109, Email: info@lap-publishing.com

Herstellung in Deutschland:
Schaltungsdienst Lange o.H.G., Zehrensdorfer Str. 11, 12277 Berlin, Deutschland
Books on Demand GmbH, Gutenbergring 53, 22848 Norderstedt, Deutschland
Reha GmbH, Dudweiler Landstr. 99, 66123 Saarbrücken, Deutschland
ISBN: 978-3-8383-0438-0

Imprint (only for USA, GB)

Bibliographic information published by the Deutsche Nationalbibliothek: The Deutsche Nationalbibliothek lists this publication in the Deutsche Nationalbibliografie; detailed bibliographic data are available in the Internet at http://dnb.d-nb.de.

Any brand names and product names mentioned in this book are subject to trademark, brand or patent protection and are trademarks or registered trademarks of their respective holders. The use of brand names, product names, common names, trade names, product descriptions etc. even without
a particular marking in this works is in no way to be construed to mean that such names may be regarded as unrestricted in respect of trademark and brand protection legislation and could thus be used by anyone.

Publisher:
Lambert Academic Publishing AG & Co. KG
Theodor-Heuss-Ring 26, 50668 Köln, Germany
Phone +49 681 3720-310, Fax +49 681 3720-3109, Email: info@lap-publishing.com

Produced in USA and UK by:
Lightning Source Inc., 1246 Heil Quaker Blvd., La Vergne, TN 37086, USA
Lightning Source UK Ltd., Chapter House, Pitfield, Kiln Farm, Milton Keynes, MK11 3LW, GB
BookSurge, 7290 B. Investment Drive, North Charleston, SC 29418, USA
ISBN: 978-3-8383-0438-0

Dedication

I dedicate this work to my daughter, Sarah Jasmin Rowland. Not only did she witness firsthand the process of completing my doctorate, but she also, inadvertently, lost many hours of personal connection through the time I spent on this that I would have liked to spend with her instead. I beg your forgiveness, Sarah, for my selfishness, and I hope that the experience also serves as an inspiration for you to live your dream as you imagine it.

Acknowledgements

Foremost, I deeply thank my students and their peer mentors for their willingness to participate in this study honestly and cheerfully, for their trust in letting me peek behind their curtains, and for their enthusiasm for my work and the topics addressed. The world is a better place and my life is immensely enriched because of them. Thank you all for sharing yourselves with me! I also thank City College of San Francisco for the many years spent serving the college community, for the learnings I took away from this experience, and for encouraging this research project.

My mentor, Dr. Matthew Bronson, warned me early on about the fact that it takes a village to write a dissertation. He was right (as with so many things). Thank you, Matthew, for your authentic and inspiring guidance, for putting me on the path of your lineage and nudging me along until I could walk on my own feet. You are an amazing human being and I very much appreciate the sharing of your gifts, your heart, and your brilliant mind. It has been a life-altering experience engaging with you at the intersections of linguistics, anthropology, education, intercultural communications, and consciousness studies at this outstanding California Institute of Integral Studies. Thank you, CIIS, for transforming the academic world and for providing a forum that encourages creative and progressive thinking coupled with community action.

Likewise, my other committee members, Dr. Alfonso Montuori and Dr. Lynne Valek, have been extremely influential and generous in sharing their time and wisdom, and left their imprint on my development in ways they will never know. Monty, thank you for introducing me to my own experiences for which you provided a language that made my soul sing. Lynne, thank you for your coaching and the many professional growth opportunities you have provided for me, and for letting me live and work in your personal office during an unforgettable summer in Fresno.

This dissertation would not be what it is without my fearless and highly competent editor, Anna Fitzpatrick, whose time I occupied for an entire year—far beyond what she bargained for, but which she accepted with grace. She gave her absolute best and all to help give shape to this epic; it is her whom the reader must thank for clarity in form and function. Anna, you are the very best editor anyone could ever wish for. You have made the process of sculpting this dissertation a pleasant collaboration, and I am eternally thankful to you for your participation.

Special thanks go to my friends Amy Conger, Julie Gieseke, Natesh Daniel, Melinda Fine, Glen Sebera, Tomi Nagai-Rothe, Brooks Britt, Jamie Cross, and Sharon Till, all of whom propelled me forward in immeasurable ways. Amy, thank you for your friendship and support throughout the years it took to have arrived here. Thank you, Julie, for your selfless and endless support with the many mundane tasks of completing this research project, for sharing your documentation skills, lending your time and ears when needed, and for dissolving some of my self-inflicted barriers.

Thank you, Natesh, for your friendship and for lending your amazing production skills in creating the many diagrams in this work. Thank you, Melinda, for giving feedback on my writing in the last editorial stages when it was most needed (as you had done already for my masters thesis). Thank you, Brooks and Jamie, for your wonderful editorial assistance with the earlier versions of this epic. Glen, Tomi, and Sharon, thank you for offering support in the many wonderful ways that define you and inspire me. Thank you all for your friendship, for feeding my mind, for your shared interest in and admiration of this work, and for giving me joy throughout this process.

Many thanks go to the 2004 Council and Parliaments of the World's Religions where the seed for this project was planted and through which experience my life took a significant turn. Thank you, 2004 CPWR graphic facilitators, for your inspiration and for sharing your inquisitive minds. Thank you, Glen, for inviting me to the CPWR project—who knew, at the time, what a meaningful impact this simple act would have upon my life?

My gratitude goes to all my teachers, to the scholars and the practitioners from the fields of intercultural communication, visual communication, transdisciplinary studies, and integral theory, all of whom nourished this research project with their genius.

Words are not enough to give thanks to my daughter, Sarah Rowland. You are the joy, the pride, and love of my life! Thank you for inspiring me through the beauty of your heart and soul, and for reminding me that life is about living. I am blessed with your presence.

TABLE OF CONTENTS

LIST OF TABLES

LIST OF FIGURES

PROLOGUE

This dissertation project evolved from an interdisciplinary project into a transdisciplinary study, with the correlating investigation of the data from many perspectives and repeated composting of the analysis. Transdisciplinary researchers focus on the inquiry rather than the field and their process is defined as highly creative, positioning the inquirer's subjectivity at its core and pulling from any discipline that can illuminate the phenomenon under investigation (Montuori, 2005; Nicolescu, 2007; Purser & Montuori, 1994). Since the genre of transdisciplinary studies is still rather new to academic discourse and since this work is meant to serve scholars from a variety of disciplines, this dissertation has two distinct parts.

Part one of this case study (Chapters 1–9) presents a mostly traditional dissertation, focusing on staying close to the way the disciplines of intercultural communication and visual communication would each have approached the problem. This first part of the dissertation does answer the research question, offers recommendations from a traditional perspective, and in fact is completely sufficient unto itself as a traditional case study.

The identified gaps and questions that emerged during the traditional data analysis are then investigated further in part two (Epilogue), continuing the inquiry until all avenues are explored, in accordance with transdisciplinary methods and approaches. The process of analysis during part two of this study searched back and forth through the underlying web of connecting roots between the disciplines, the phenomenon investigated, and my personal experience with this matter, engaging the reader in *thinkering* about the thinking (Nicolescu, 2007) emerged during the traditional processing of the data. Integral theory presented the most useful transdisciplinary approach to complement the observed gaps and integrate these disparate aspects into new territory. The unique perspective resulting from this further analysis provided a viewpoint from which to build several interesting concepts and models and make further recommendations.

This unusual two-part dissertation structure is intended to allow both traditional academics and integral or transdisciplinary scholars to benefit from the results of this study. While part one satisfies the doctoral level standards and makes this dissertation accessible to an array of researchers, it is part two that exposes the innovative integral work characteristic of graduates from the California Institute of Integral Studies.

CHAPTER 1

BACKGROUND

The necessity for a dialogue between the disciplines of visual communication and intercultural communication became apparent to me during my participation as an intercultural communication consultant in the 2004 Pre-Parliaments, Assembly, and Parliament of the World's Religions in East Africa, the Middle East, and Southern Europe (CPWR). As part of the leadership team, my responsibilities included lending expertise in intercultural communication to the design of the dialogue process. The graphic facilitators needed clear and concise guidelines on how to visually represent various cultural frames authentically and how to help people from different cultures communicate with each other through visual language. They were sincerely interested in discovering the answers to culture-specific questions such as: how to visually represent a circular, emotionally-engaged communication style versus a linear, emotionally-withheld communication style; how to represent the frame of mind of a collective society versus an individual orientation; how to visually demonstrate the different orientations in regard to hierarchy; or how to visually condition participants who orient themselves purely in the present so they can see themselves acting in the future.

Although I am trained in both intercultural communication and visual communication, I could not supply the graphic facilitators with direct answers because I was not aware of the specific patterns in which cultures express themselves visually, nor is this information readily available within the disciplines of intercultural communication and visual communication. All the graphic facilitators did the best they could, and they did a fantastic job integrating intuitive creative processes with the dialogues, but I felt keenly that the lack of answers and guidelines meant some participants were not authentically represented on the graphic panels.

This experience inspired me to focus this study on the nexus of intercultural communication and visual communication, where I intended to address the visible and invisible components of the coconstruction of meaning. During one class day in the spring of 2007, I thoroughly documented 10 visual literacy students at City College of San Francisco (CCSF) collaborating in two small groups. Each group coconstructed a story of a common experience and represented it on a large-scale graphic panel via interactive graphic facilitation and collaborative visual mapping. *Collaborative visual mapping* is defined here as a process during which participants create a graphic panel together, which involves negotiating content, composition, and design elements and draws upon the skills and talents of the group as a whole. The process is self-guided and may or may not require leadership to emerge from the group. *Interactive graphic facilitation* is understood here as a visual mapping process that is spontaneously guided by a group facilitator who herself is a participant and invites other participants to contribute verbally and visually—literally drawing information out of them and transferring it into visual and verbal forms. This interaction can be considered successful if participants' ideas are represented and depends upon the skills and talents of the facilitator to motivate participation and integrate the information neutrally.

Intercultural communication focuses on cultural aspects of communication—not to be confused with intergroup communication, in which culture is only one of many group affiliations influencing communication (e.g., culture, ethnicity, age, etc., Gudykunst, Lee, Nishida, & Ogawa, 2005). In the data analysis, special attention was paid to the exhibition of information processing modes and the demonstration of intercultural communication patterns. In particular, I was interested in learning how these processing modes and cultural patterns would be represented visually.

A Complex Problem

Neither field (visual communication or intercultural communication) alone could adequately address the meaningful questions graphic facilitators asked during the 2004 CPWR. The closest field that has dealt with the issue of visual representation in various cultures is visual anthropology; however, visual anthropology focuses on the political and social consequences of visual representations rather than on how these representations are structured and deconstructed for visual syntax and semantics by members of various cultural groups. Therefore, addressing the questions raised at the 2004 CPWR required the creation of an interactive relationship between the disciplines of visual communication and intercultural communication.

The fields of intercultural communication and visual communication are two approaches to meaning-making that have distinct genealogies within the human sciences, having begun from different premises and developed within disparate communities-of-practice. Intercultural communication theory evolved out of concern for understanding interpersonal contact across cultures—especially face-to-face and verbal contact within intercultural settings—and therefore has rarely taken into account the visual. The discipline of visual communication is in a figure–ground relationship with intercultural communication in that it has emphasized the semiotics of the visual as a kind of universal symbolic space sealed from the messiness of lived experiences of making meaning in context. Given the enormously rapid and continuous advancements in technology that find immediate application in the graphic field, the absence of culture as a driving force is problematic and disadvantages students who are already living in a highly diverse world. Likewise, the absence of visual language as another form of interacting crossculturally—especially important on the new virtual interaction platforms—leaves the field of intercultural communication and its students disadvantaged vis-à-vis the changing world they are supposed to serve.

3

To mimic the environment of the 2004 CPWR events, a highly diverse participant population was required. When I began this research project I was teaching in a vocational graphic design program at CCSF, one of the most diverse urban community colleges in the US, and my visual literacy class provided an ideal setting. The relationship between culture and how people from different cultural frames learn is being emphasized in the US where the population participating in formal education is shifting significantly, warranting the adaptation of teaching practices to meet the student body. "By 2060 it is estimated that non-Hispanic Whites will represent less than 50 percent of the population, and by 2100 Hispanics alone will represent 33 percent of the United States population and non-Whites 60 percent of the population" (Diller & Moule, 2005, p. 11). The Center for Studies in Higher Education at the University of California (UC) reported, based on an undergraduate experience survey administered at all nine campuses, that

> UC is becoming increasingly racially and ethnically diverse in complex ways that reflect major demographic changes in the state, with Chinese students now representing the second largest identifiable racial group in the UC system, followed by the Chicano/Latino and then Korean and Vietnamese students. Most of these students come from immigrant families....
>
> ...the majority of students are either themselves foreign born or have at least one foreign born parent....Approximately 95% of Asian and 88% percent of Latino respondents reported that either they or one of their parents or grandparents were born outside of the United States. (Center for Studies in Higher Education, 2007)

California, in particular, is ahead of the development in diversifying demographics. What is not obvious from the statistics above is the complexity of the diverse student population. Most of the students in the present study not only have multiple and overlapping ethnic, cultural, and national affiliations but also a rich repertoire of personal experiences that continuously add to the complexity; this observation is consistent with my experience with other classes at CCSF.

I had gained expertise in both intercultural communication and visual communication and was also familiar with graphic facilitation, so I saw this dilemma as an opportunity to lend my skills, talents, and knowledge to solving a problem that was well defined and needed a solution. This particular classroom setting inherently represented an ideal context for intercultural communication dynamics; the content of the research task involved solving visual communication problems creatively and collaboratively. Therefore, this study will be of interest to scholars and practitioners in both disciplines, as well as in graphic facilitation, organizational effectiveness, personal excellence (graphic coaching), and education. The gap between the fields of intercultural communication and visual communication must be closed, given the current trends and developments on the planet as a whole. However, since the fields do not overlap naturally, putting them into dialogue to address the missing links represented a complex research problem.

4

The Research Question and the Research Space

This qualitative case study explored the question: How is meaning cocreated by small groups in a polycultural environment via interactive graphic facilitation and collaborative visual mapping? Discussed in detail below, *polycultural* can be defined as a social structure where (a) cultures are not thought of as separate units but rather as historically interrelated structures, and (b) hierarchies are held flexibly and are not built upon origin or status but upon the needs of a particular task or problem to be solved.

The term *research space* has been defined as an identified gap in existing knowledge and theory that is worthy of further study (Swales, 1990). The present study makes use of the research space concept by visualizing it as a metaphorical hologram. The meaning-making process investigated in this inquiry carried the characteristics of *transclusion* (pointing to multiple positions), as the phenomenon of the cocreation of meaning in polycultural groups is located in the interplay of the perspectives provided by three vanishing points—intercultural communication, visual communication, and myself as the inquirer. Using these three vanishing points, the research space for this inquiry can be represented as a three-dimensional metaphorical hologram (see Figure 1). This visual representation calls attention to the location of the research space in the gap between the fields rather than in the simple overlap or addition of the fields—which defines this study, among other things, as a transdisciplinary inquiry (see Prologue).

Design of the Study

Collaborative visual mapping was selected as a natural touchstone and bridge to begin a conversation between the two fields. Through visual mapping, this study aimed to represent— visually and systematically—the relationship between each participant's meaning-making and the joint construction of meaning by the group. As an attempt to address the confounding variables that attend to how culture may be influencing any given participant's performance in the setting, standard instruments were included in the protocol of this study. These provided background for the review of the data by allowing a *thick case* to be assembled for each participant, a profile of possible factors influencing their performance or meaning-making process in this collaborative setting.

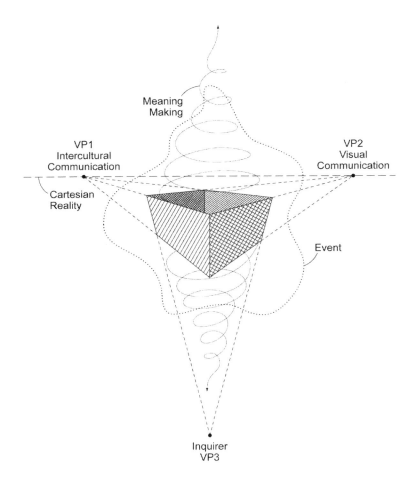

Figure 1. Three-dimensional research space created by this transdisciplinary inquiry, defined by three vanishing points (VP1, VP2, and VP3) and the horizon line of Cartesian reality. The meaning-making act within the observation angles is signified by a vertical up/down movement. The event itself is indicated by an organic shape surrounding the actually observed research space. Author's image.

Visual mapping and diagramming were central to the methodology for both data generation and analysis. The analysis included primary and secondary data sources from dynamic documentation of small and large group processes, various individual assessments (formal and informal), interviews, a member check, and the visual maps the groups produced. Through a

6

process of constant comparison and recognition of significant patterns in the analysis of the body of data, knowledge was constructed that will be recognized as valid by both: the field of visual communication will find the concrete expression of the gestalt in all its ambiguity that it must have as a beginning point, and the field of intercultural communication will find an entrée to its concern with lived meaning and experience as this is expressed in material form. It was my original assumption that I would find intercultural communication theory confirmed and my intent was to apply it to visual communication practice. In particular, I was hoping to observe various cultural frames acted out and represented in visual form so that I could return to the graphic facilitators who originally sparked the need for this case study, and supply them with the answers they had been seeking.

This study was a first tentative attempt to highlight possible points of engagement where these fields can begin to address each other's blind spots. Visual communication scholars and practitioners would benefit from coming to terms with the cultural blinders of their field and the limits of its positivist commitments to a universal truth "out there." Intercultural communication as a field would benefit from extending its theoretical reach into nonverbal visual modalities of expression. Practitioners and scholars in both disciplines need to recognize the leap the world is taking without them and find ways to engage in the present global events—which are dynamic, expand the theories, and potentially require models that allow for collaborative transdisciplinary discourse to solve problems neither can tackle independently.

Largely simplified, "culture is communication" (Hall, 1959, as quoted by Baldwin, Faulkner, Hecht, & Lindsley, 2006, p. 12). The quintessence of the present study, communication as a concept, system, process, function, structure, product, and refinement formed the rich foundation through which the two disciplines were brought into dialogue. Communication is interdependent (between participating parties) and situational (contextual), and oscillates between micro- and macro-positions (in the case of this study, the individual participants and the institution and society at large). The link between culture and communication is meaning (Baldwin et al., 2006) as expressed in (at least) two versions of reality—subjective and objective. Closing the gap between these realities, the fields of visual communication and intercultural communication melted into each other and provided the appropriate space for meaning to emerge from process to product through the form of transdisciplinary inquiry.

The Viewfinder

The aim of this study was to put the disciplines of intercultural communication and visual communication, with their binary Cartesian logic, into conversation with each other. To accomplish this aim, it was useful to construct a *viewfinder* (using integral theory in the form of a four-quadrant approach) that facilitated the reconciliation of subjective and objective perspectives on the individual and collective planes. (In this dissertation, *objective* is used to refer to things that are observable with the five senses and also refers to universalism, in contrast to *subjective* perspectives that are located in a person's inner, nonobservable world and also refer to subjectively constructed reality.) The structure of the integral viewfinder parallels the well trodden path of anthropologists investigating the micro- and macro-levels on the individual and collective planes of the observed phenomena in ethnographic studies—each quadrant contains a different layer of the data considered in standard ethnographic studies.

The viewfinder uses the All Quadrants, All Levels (AQAL) (Wilber 2000, 2005) four-quadrant grid to create a visual representation of the data sources and areas of investigation. The quadrants also represent/incorporate the four aspects of communication (signifier, signified, syntax, and semantics) (see Figure 2), which can be used to connect this model to both communication fields pertinent to this inquiry. The quadrant of the individual exterior (upper right) represents the *signifier*, or denoted objective reality—in this case study, represented by the analysis (or interpretation) of the videotaped event, the coconstructed artifacts, and the assessment results as indicators of the individual experience. The quadrant of the individual interior (upper left) represents the *signified*, or connoted subjective reality—in this case study, represented by analysis of direct expressions during the event and the personal interviews. The quadrant of the collective exterior (lower right) represents the *syntax* of the communication, or the visual grammar or rules of the system within which the event takes place—in this case study, represented by the exposure of the power relationships between participants couched within the structure of the institution and society at large. The quadrant of the collective interior (lower left) represents *semantics*, the socially and collectively cocreated meaning/cultural exchanges—in this case study, represented by the discourse analysis indicative of the mutual negotiation process and the knowledge participants coconstructed during the event.

Considering all the data sources, this record is thick and covers a variety of aspects as would be the case in any ethnographic study. Because I was taking a transdisciplinary approach it was important to me to uncover as many aspects of the observed phenomenon as possible. I chose Wilber's four-quadrant grid structure from the integral theory perspective for its useful method of organizing the disciplines according to the quadrants they occupy and reconciling the disowned parts of both disciplines.

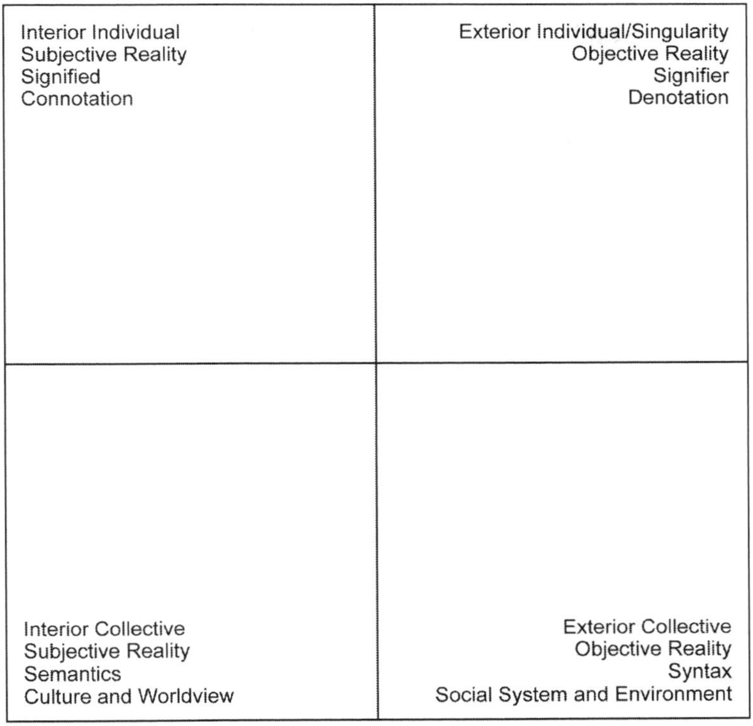

Interior Individual Subjective Reality Signified Connotation	Exterior Individual/Singularity Objective Reality Signifier Denotation
Interior Collective Subjective Reality Semantics Culture and Worldview	Exterior Collective Objective Reality Syntax Social System and Environment

Figure 2. The four-quadrant viewfinder showing the focus of each quadrant and including the four aspects of communication. Author's image; four-quadrant grid based partly on concepts from *The Integral Operating System* [compact disc set and booklet], by K. Wilber, 2005, Boulder, CO: Sounds True.

The four aspects of communication that occupy the four quadrants of Wilber's model provided a conceptual frame common in both disciplines, and function as a "handrail" for the reader. In part one of the dissertation, the four-quadrant viewfinder is important as the frame to hold the literature review together, helping to categorize the parts of the literature review, and later on, the pieces of data, in a logical manner. Figure 3 shows how the metaphorical research space can be considered through the viewfinder, with each field located in the appropriate quadrant. In part two (Epilogue), the viewfinder is investigated in depth as part of the integral theory frame, and developed beyond the structure it provides in the traditional research approach.

Organization of the Dissertation

The creative, complex thinking inherent in transdisciplinary research is extremely lateral and builds connections across multidimensional constructs that are difficult to unfold in the established format of linear logic. The organization of this dissertation into two parts was an unconventional choice intended to create a more readable and more accessible document. In many places, information given in the text is also presented in an accompanying visual diagram. The inclusion of numerous visuals was a deliberate choice meant to offer a second track of information sharing, since this study concerns visual and culturally sensitive communication in an educational setting, and also to address a variety of learning styles—the reader is invited to choose her preferred track and/or take pleasure in engaging with the content on multiple levels. Finally, although the dissertation follows the traditional order of information presentation (introduction, literature review, method, discussion, conclusion), the chapter divisions and titles are uniquely designed to create a more readable document. These choices are expressions of the transgressive writing common in transdisciplinary research.

This case study is an example of transdisciplinary research approaches applied to various disciplines with a heavy focus in intercultural communication dynamics. Chapter 2 concerns vanishing point one of the research space—intercultural communication—which as a field traditionally has focused on subjective realities. Chapter 3 concerns vanishing point two—visual communication—which as a field traditionally views meaning-making through universal perspectives and thus mostly illuminates different parts of the metaphorical hologram than intercultural communication. In Chapter 4, the topic of group dynamics as pertinent to meaning-making in group processes further informs the connections between creativity and group collaborations. Chapter 5 concerns the setting of this inquiry, which provided a particular realm of possibilities, and outlines the research focus through detailed research questions that drove the design of the methodology discussed in Chapter 6. In Chapter 7, the primary data are presented, beginning with the group analysis and ending with participant profiles. In Chapter 8, the results of the traditional data analysis are described, and Chapter 9 offers the main findings, conclusions, and recommendations from that traditional analysis. In the Epilogue, an investigation of the data through transdisciplinary approaches and an integral frame leads to theoretical models matching the complexity presented in this study. Conclusions and recommendations are offered from that enriched perspective.

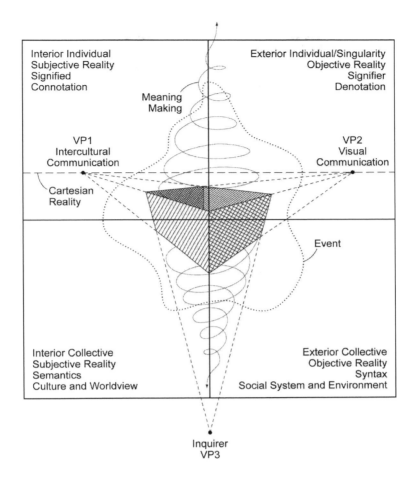

Figure 3. The four-quadrant viewfinder applied to the metaphorical hologram of the research space, showing the intercultural communication focus on subjective reality, the visual communication focus on objective reality, and the inquirer's focus on the gaps in both disciplines. VP = vanishing point. Author's image; four-quadrant grid based partly on concepts from *The Integral Operating System* [compact disc set and booklet], by K. Wilber, 2005, Boulder, CO: Sounds True.

CHAPTER 2

INTERCULTURAL COMMUNICATION AND ITS EXTENSIONS

There are many interpretations and definitions of culture in the disciplines of social sciences and the humanities, to which intercultural communication scholars have also contributed. The discussion of intercultural communication as a vanishing point describing the present study needs to be framed within the larger body of work so that the discipline can be properly sized and situated as part of an extensive canon. Baldwin et al. (2006) consolidated historic and contemporary interpretations of culture from a myriad of scholars and thinkers who defined culture in alignment with their disciplines.

Traditional interpretations of culture described structures of cultural elements and aspects in order to predict behavior. Contemporary views of culture can be categorized into three conceptual perspectives: interpretive (culture as meaning-making), intergroup (culture as membership), and cultural studies (culture as ideology). All three are based on the central idea that culture is a process of constructing social worlds through language and discourse—which implies flexibility and the possibility of change (Baldwin et al., 2006).

Many scholars participating in the canon of the culture discussion continue to create new ways of defining culture, and while consensus is hard to find, Baldwin et al. (2006) decided on seven themes for defining culture: structure/pattern (system of cultural elements), function (means to an end), process (social construction), product (artifact), refinement (aspiration for higher intellect/morality embodied by group/individual), power or ideology (postmodern, postcolonial perspectives), and group-membership (belonging to group or place). Aspects of these definitions interrelate, coexist within disciplines, and cross-reference each other (Baldwin et al., 2006)—a matter of complexity. While the act of categorizing does serve to highlight certain aspects of culture, there is a simultaneous exclusion of other aspects participating in the creation of culture. Holding the complexity of culture at the center while focusing on various aspects simultaneously is a matter of transclusion—a key characteristic of transdisciplinary approaches.

In the present study, various perspectives of culture were highlighted in order to maximize the transclusion process necessary for managing the complexity evoked when polycultural participants interact and cocreate meaning. In honor of this complexity, culture was considered a structure and looked at as a pattern, investigated as a function, and treated as a process in order to produce behavior and artifacts. In addition, group-membership was deconstructed, and moments of culture as refinement were identified. Given that many facets of culture were highlighted, no single definition of culture can be given in this study, and one needs to be prepared for paradoxes to emerge in the enactment of culture—building flexibility to integrate diverse and contradictory aspects of culture.

Focusing on the specifics of intercultural communication represents a narrowing of the many possibilities available to investigate the question of how meaning is cocreated by small groups in a polycultural environment via interactive graphic facilitation and collaborative visual mapping. However, at the same time, narrowing the focus allows a deepening of the research space.

The Location of This Study Within
Intercultural Communication Research Approaches and Theories

Two approaches to intercultural communication research and three categories of intercultural communication theory have been defined. These approaches and categories have historically been kept separate, and the need has been identified to begin consciously combining them to improve the quality of results (Gudykunst et al., 2005). In following the path of transdisciplinary inquiry, the present study used both approaches to research and activated all three categories, offering one small-scale extension of Gudykunst et al. in order to investigate the cocreation of meaning in polycultural groups.

The first category of intercultural communication theory contains theories where culture "is integrated with the communication process of theories of communication… and linked to communication within the theory" (Gudykunst et al., 2005, pp. 3–4). The second category holds theories that "describe or explain how communication varies across cultures" (p. 4). Several theories, instruments, and analysis tools applied and used in this research project (see Chapter 6) were based on theories from the first and second category.

The third category contains theories that clarify communication patterns between people from different cultures, and includes intercultural communication and intergroup communication. The latter is based on the assumption that culture is just one of the many group affiliations that influence communication, resulting in similarity amongst the processes of intercultural, interethnic, or intergenerational interactions. This third category is further divided into five subcategories that can apply to both underlying frames (intergroup and intercultural): theories focusing on effective outcomes, on accommodation and adaptation, on identity management, on adjustment and adaptation to new cultural environments, and on communication networks where the focus is on the relationships between the individuals participating in the communication act rather than on the individuals themselves (Gudykunst et al., 2005). The present study is strongly positioned in the third category as a study of intercultural communication (with cultural aspects as the foci) attempting to describe the patterns of interaction and the underlying structures of meaning-making

13

among participants of various cultural backgrounds involved in creative and collaborative communication acts.

Traditionally, there have been (at least) two pathways in intercultural communication research—*subjectivist* and *objectivist* approaches (Burrell & Morgan, 1979, as discussed by Gudykunst et al., 2005). Proponents of the first assume that there is "no 'real world' external to individuals" (Gudykunst et al., 2005, p. 4), and believe that information about the communication event can only be obtained from firsthand knowledge or from the perspective of the communicating entity, and that people communicate out of "free will" (p. 4). The goals of a subjectivist approach are to analyze subjective experiences and deliver a description of the phenomena. In contrast, an objectivist approach aims to deliver an explanation and potential predictions under the assumption that there is a "'real world' external to individuals" (p. 4) and that the communication act is a direct outcome of the context or even "'determined' by situations and environments" (p. 4). Compared to the many objectivist studies completed in the discipline there is a lack of subjectivist theories, and a need for further integration of objectivist and subjectivist approaches (Gudykunst et al., 2005).

The present research project is thus positioned as a small-scale extension of Gudykunst et al. (2005) because it utilized both subjectivist and objectivist approaches through collecting a thick profile for each participant and investigating their subjective experiences, as well as through documenting, observing, and investigating the entire research event, analyzing cocreation acts and group dynamics, and delivering a thorough description. The integral frame applied in part two of this transdisciplinary study paralleled the layers of investigation of the two approaches and three categories of intercultural communication theory (Gudykunst et al., 2005) (see Epilogue for a detailed discussion).

In addition, this research project extends the work of House, Hanges, Mansour, Dorfman, & Gupta (2004), whose GLOBE study was a collaborative research project involving 170 social scientists around the world and including 62 cultures. The authors attempted to update and expand upon Hofstede's (2001) work on cultural dimensions (the second Gudykunst et al. category) and even developed country-specific instruments in native languages. The authors concluded that there is a need to study mixed cultural groups interacting, because putting more than two cultures in contact complicates the dynamic manifold into a "complex web of multilateral issues" (p. 731). Further, which cultural dimensions are important to keep in mind in such complex webs is critical but not researched. The present case study is thus positioned as a small-scale extension of House et al. offering a first look at polycultural group interactions.

Selecting AQAL as the viewfinder for this study bridges objective and subjective approaches by having all quadrants engaged, in order to fully understand intercultural dynamics through the communication acts. This integral frame holds models expressing the constructivist nature of the individual and the collective consciousness (first category) and includes a system for the various value systems of different cultures (second category). In addition, the collective interior quadrant of AQAL addresses the third category by discussing the cocreation of meaning via cultural exchanges.

Through the variety of instruments and analysis tools selected for this study, the entire spectrum of intercultural communication theory (as defined by Gudykunst et al., 2005) was activated in this study, which also worked to close the subjective–objective reality gap. In this sense, this research project can be considered a metatheory of intercultural communication because it demonstrates how all approaches and categories can be integrated into one whole that is built through transclusion.

The Core of Culture

Much of culture is not visible, and any visible representation can only hint at the complexity underneath; therefore, intercultural communication largely falls into the subjective quadrants of the viewfinder (see Figure 4). In this representation, the upper left quadrant holds the interior experience of individuals and the lower left quadrant focuses on the energetic exchange of interacting individuals. Data obtained from assessment instruments, however, fall also into the quadrants of objective reality (upper and lower right quadrants), as they attempt to measure and predict observable behavior.

Intercultural communication as a field traditionally focuses on face-to-face and verbal interactions between people of culturally diverse backgrounds. Historically and ironically, intercultural communication dynamics have largely been defined through researching cultures in isolation rather than in moments of interaction (House et al., 2004) and by studying individuals. Communication patterns between cultures have been simulated, theoretically, by comparing scores for cultural dimensions (Hofstede, n.d.a) and cultural styles (Peterson, 2004), usually for only two cultures.

Located at the heart of a person's subjective interior, but shared with a group of people, culture partially defines how experiences are organized and how meaning is constructed. Culture is built through a series of every-day *dilemmas*, the solutions for which vanish from consciousness once applied but continue to operate at the core (Trompenaars & Hampden-Turner, 1998). Cultural maps are installed during one's formative years as *mental programming*—a self-perpetuating system that directs behavior (a *social game)* through cultural norms and distinguishes cultures from each other (Hofstede, 2001). The three levels of mental programming can be represented by a pyramid in which human nature (inherited and considered universal) forms the bottom level.

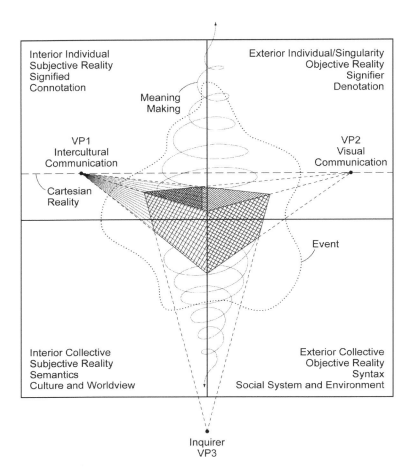

Figure 4. The metaphorical research space seen through the four-quadrant viewfinder, with the focus on the areas contained within intercultural communication (largely in the subjective quadrants). VP = vanishing point. Author's image; four-quadrant grid based partly on concepts from *The Integral Operating System* [compact disc set and booklet], by K. Wilber, 2005, Boulder, CO: Sounds True.

Culture (learned and specific to a group) is the middle layer, and personality (inherited, learned, and specific to an individual) forms the peak (Hofstede & Hofstede, 2005). This model implies that personality emerges as a combination of both the innate (nature) and the cultural (nurture).

Intercultural communication scholars are in agreement that there is a core to culture that contains the (invisible) motivational factors for (visible) behavior, although they have different entry points to the depth of the core and different ways of defining the core's elements. In general, there has been acceptance in the intercultural communication community that value structures are positively correlated to behavior. One scholar determines the deepest element of the core to be worldview constructions, which emerge from language structures and precede the forming of basic assumptions (Bennett, 2003). Those same basic assumptions are presented as the deepest element of the core in another model in which they precede the forming of norms and values, artifacts, and products (the *onion layers* model, Trompenaars & Hampden-Turner, 1998). Another onion layer model determines values to be the deepest element of the core followed by the formation of practices (symbols, heroes, and rituals) (Hofstede, 2001).

Visual metaphors are widely used to indicate the relationship between different aspects of the invisible core of culture and what emerges in objective reality. For instance, the tip of the iceberg shows only a very small portion of the much larger invisible complexity of culture underneath. Another commonly used metaphor is the map, which is not be confused with the territory.

The Status Quo of Intercultural Communication

Intercultural communication as a field is largely concerned with providing theories and models for practitioners to advise, teach, and train for and/or facilitate communication across cultures. In this effort it has been deemed important to identify various cultural frames, with the goal of predicting the gap between cultures and helping to close that gap during communication acts as well as predicting the effect of developing intercultural sensitivity and cultural intelligence. Intercultural sensitivity (Bennett, 2003) involves having a high level of self-awareness, knowledge about cultures other than one's own, the ability to take the perspective of other cultural frames, the flexibility to shift behavior and switch codes authentically to meet other frames, and the freedom to move between cultural frames one has integrated. The concept of cultural intelligence includes, likewise, knowledge about cultures, awareness of self and others, and specific skills demonstrated in culturally appropriate behavior (Peterson, 2004).

Intercultural communication scholars and practitioners participated in moving the world from monocultural frames into multiculturalism, a significant step forward in growing awareness and appreciation of cultural differences. *Monoculturalism* refers to a culture that is homogenous and without diversity, and implies that immigrants to such a culture would be asked to assimilate to the cultural norms of the dominant monoculture. *Multiculturalism* is a social structure that is composed

17

of different cultures where each cultural group is preserved as autonomous and a compartmentalized part of the whole. Multiculturalism implies an attempt to move out of monoculturalism yet still upholds a binary construct in that multicultural groups are often defined as not belonging to the dominant culture. Identifying cultural differences and measuring them was an integral part of the shift to multiculturalism. Hofstede (2001) is the pioneer of such work and his research was superb for the timeframe during which it was conducted.

Culture is shaped by people interacting, and pivotal to determining the patterns of further interaction—in other words, a dynamic relationship between events and participants.

> Culture is a result of the lived experience (praxis) of participating in social action. Part of our experience is "languaging" about our experience, which generates the "explanations" about our lived experience that we can call "culture". In other words, culture is a construction, but culture is not purely a cognitive invention. It is both the explanation and the essence of our lived social experience. Our cultural behavior is an "enactment" of our collective experience, and, through this enactment, becomes yet more experience. (Bennett, n.d., p. 2)

This perspective of culture underpins worldview construction, with language structures as the most basic element of meaning-making. Further, the exchange between language and meaning is determined to be reciprocal.

Several current global trends affect how we might or should define culture, including the shifting from isolated cultural groups that were slow to change, to a more dynamic and faster-paced pattern of interaction and intermingling between cultures virtually and face-to-face. This shift inherently may generate a more complex set of experiences and expectations and, consequently, may provide more flexibility in how to interact in such a dynamic space.

Intercultural communication theory has largely been based on the idea of cultural groups existing autonomously (multiculturalism), and the focus has been upon cultural differences. However, an increasing number of people shift cultural frames across geographical and virtual borders, between home and school, school and work, or one set of friends and another. While the world has flattened in regard to global interaction and exchange of services and products (Friedman, 2005), not to mention virtual communication across the globe, intercultural communication theoretical frames have not kept up with these developments. Even the most recent and laudable study (House et al., 2004) did not examine the possibility that culture may have become more dynamic and contextual than traditional theory indicates.

If culture is in fact dynamic and contextual, then intercultural communication theories and practices may need to develop new metaphors to reflect and describe the mutable nature of culture (see Epilogue).

Identity and Culture

Identity refers to membership in social categories (Chandra, 2006), and many misinterpretations are possible once labels are given for any category of belonging. Labels operate on the level of signs, setting up expectations of *signifying* certain meanings and expected behaviors consistently, which is inherently problematic (Kulick, 2000)—not even a handwritten signature a person may write thousands of times during a lifetime can ever be exactly the same twice (Derrida, 1972, as discussed by Kulick, 2000).

When questioned, intercultural communication practitioners usually agree on the idea that identity (inclusive of cultural aspects) is not a fixed state of being but a flexible and contextually dependent phenomenon. The concept of culture as a shared space inherently requires that generalizations are made; otherwise, the conceptualization of culture would not be possible. The danger of stereotyping versus generalizing is usually mentioned when identity, values, and behaviors are discussed. However, intercultural communication theory, models, and instruments indicate and thus set the expectation that culturally determined behavior is definable, measurable, and predictable. As a field, intercultural communication is about describing and the predicting cultural frames of groups and resulting behavior as it was originally researched in individuals, most often not during times of interactions.

In fact, intercultural communication theorists who have developed instruments to measure cultural orientations or styles (Hofstede 2001; Peterson, 2004) offer opportunities for the public to compare statistical information (averaged measurements) between two defined (national) cultures in order to predict what kind of communication dynamics, synergies, and problems may arise from this particular duo of interacting people. In addition, the fact that these categories are listed as "national" indicates (at least to a novice of intercultural communication) the assumption that behaviors of people from the same country are consistent and that nationality indicates homogeneity. Such a position is largely absurd vis-à-vis the developments in the 21st century, and has been heavily critiqued in the more current literature (Uleman, Rhee, Bardoliwalla, Semin, & Toyama, 2000, as discussed in Baldwin et al., 2006). The conditions of globalization provide a platform for culture to be produced, circulated, and consumed all over the planet, offering a multitude of "cultural repertoires" (Baldwin et al., 2006, p. 122) from which each group and individual can supply themselves freely. These cultural repertoires are the foundation for building syntheses anew as information is updated.

While trained intercultural communication experts may have the wisdom and experience to take any such two-dimensional statistics at face value and only use them as a vague starting point, the problematic inherent in these kinds of predictions is not clearly referenced except in very rare instances. Even when the paradox of culture is pointed out by determining assessed behavior to be contextually fluid (Rosinski, 2008), the basic concept of bipolar systems is kept intact as a measuring device, thus delivering the same result—*unipositionality* on a continuum between two opposite orientations.

Scholars of social psychology and social and cultural anthropology have been discussing identities as shifting and changing experiences of the self for years. "Identity can be viewed as a more flexible resource in verbal interaction....identities change as interaction proceeds, that is, how contextual variations shift identity claims" (Howard, 2000, pp. 372–373). Identity can also be described "as multilayered, with different identities activated at different times" (pp. 375–376). In today's world, participants hold "multiple identities, multiple allegiances and affinities" (Podur, interviewed by Albert, 2003). In other words, "identities are points of temporary attachments to the subject positions which discursive practices construct for us" (Hall, 1996, as quoted by Howard, 2000, p. 386).

> Key principles underlying this approach stand in marked contrast to much of the traditional literature. Fragmentation emphasizes the multiplicity of identities and of positions within any identity. Hybridity is also key, evoking images of liminality and border-crossings in which a subaltern identity is defined as different from either of several competing identities. (p. 386)

This form of constructing identity includes the concept of "no-man's land" as a space to construct new alterations of identity in the gap provided.

Intercultural communication as a field does not easily contain the idea of drastically shifting cultural identities. Although in practice many interculturalists certainly acknowledge and expect that individuals will, most likely, not behave directly as is described in the theory, there is little or no acknowledgement of the need to reassess the basic theories of culture and identity in terms of the lived experience.

If identity shifts, then cultural interactions cannot be as consistent as has been traditionally assumed. When societies were more stable, identity was to a great extent assigned rather than selected or adopted. In current times, however, the concept of identity carries the full weight of the need for a sense of who one is, together with an often overwhelming pace of change in surrounding social contexts. Changes are constantly underway in the groups and networks in which people and their identities are embedded as well as in the societal structures and practices in which those networks are themselves generated and activated (Howard, 2000).

Judging from the literature and formal discourse, neither intercultural communication nor visual communication scholars and practitioners acknowledge the paradigm shift toward flexible identities as part of the current global events. Both disciplines seem to ignore the consequences of a world that continues to complexify and may spin traditional cultural concepts into the next level of development.

Cultural Competence

Traditionally speaking, closing the cultural gap includes raising self-awareness and being able to take the perspective of other cultural frames and consider them as valid as one's own even if one does not agree (morally) with the practices of other cultures. Such capacity falls in the area of cultural competence (Bennett, 2003). The capacity for cultural relativity is an important aspect of the Developmental Model of Intercultural Sensitivity (DMIS) (Bennett, 1986b, 1993), which has a strong practical and theoretical base. In this model, *cultural relativity* is the ability to include more than one worldview in one's perceptual frame, thus experiencing one's own culture in relation to others.

A grounded theory, the DMIS is a six-stage model of cognitive development that begins from a position of *egocentrism*, in which others are perceived only from the position of the self. A person evolves from egocentrism to *ethnocentricity* (in which cultural differences are avoided) and then to *ethnorelativity* (in which they are accepted with increasing capacity to hold them simultaneously) (see Table 1). In the ethnorelative orientation, behavior is understood within its cultural context. Cultures other than one's own are construed as equally complex and as equally real, and are seen as relative to one another. The definition of intercultural sensitivity thus can be summarized as the ability to "transcend ethnocentrism and establish effective, positive relations across cultural boundaries both internationally and domestically" (Hammer & Bennett, 2001, p. 6). The result is that, eventually, one can experience another culture as equally real and valid compared to one's own. In fully realized ethnorelativity, individuals actually construct an identity that is inclusive of other cultural frames and leads to intercultural sensitivity—the ability to step back and forth between different cultural maps (Hammer & Bennett, 1998).

Because the DMIS allows growth through stages, it offers the possibility of expansion to meet a changing world. Development through the DMIS stages is described as gradual and most often happens naturally through immersion into cultures other than one's own, and sometimes through cultural sensitivity training. In this model, developing one's intercultural sensitivity requires making finer distinctions in increasingly more complex ways, a notion that parallels current events on the planet.

Table 1

Stages of the Developmental Model of Intercultural Sensitivity (DMIS)

Stage	Behavior
Ethnocentrism—cultural differences are either not recognized, avoided, defended against, or minimized, and one's own culture is the exclusive definer of reality	
Denial	Differences are either not noticed or not experienced through vague categorization (ignorant, naïve observations).
Defense	Differences are recognized but evaluated negatively (us vs. them thinking, negative stereotyping).
Minimization	Superficial differences are accepted while believing that all humans are the same (focus on similarity and commonality) from an ethnocentric orientation (own worldview frame). Represents transition between polarized positions and nonjudgmental acceptance of cultural differences.
Ethnorelativism—cultural differences are accepted with increasing capacity, and many viable constructions of reality become possible	
Acceptance	Appreciation of cultural differences (behavior and values). Growing ability to interpret phenomena within context (but sometimes moral dilemmas vis-à-vis opposing cultural norms).
Adaptation	Growing ability to shift cognitively and behaviorally and to enact alternative experiences authentically. Capable of empathy.
Integration	Internalization of multiple cultural frames, experience of encapsulated or constructive marginality.

Note. Author's table; data from Bennett (1986b).

Defining and Measuring Cultural Difference

In intercultural communication theory, cultural differences are defined, at a basic level, as different solutions to everyday dilemmas (Trompenaars & Hampden-Turner, 1998)—a reflection of multiculturalism's focus on the differences between cultures. These differences are then described through the concept of cultural dimensions—individualism versus collectivism, neutral versus emotional, and so on (see Table 2 for examples). Each cultural dimension is measured on a bipolar continuum on which individuals or groups occupy one single position that is assumed to reflect a more or less permanent value position likely to be expressed in a certain behavioral pattern characteristic of that position on the continuum. In other words, an individual or a culture falls either more on the left or more on the right of each continuum. This binary thinking may be the natural result of our dual physical structure (two hands, eyes, ears, legs, etc.) and is also reflected in the means of measuring positionality on such a bipolar continuum (e.g., the Likert scales used in most instruments of this kind). Dichotomies and dualism seem to be more native to Western thinking compared to other available options such as holistic processing and the ability to hold paradoxes (Osland & Bird, 2000). It is, however, questionable whether such bipolar systems are capable of capturing shifting identities.

Peterson, for example, does not deny that a range would be more reflective of the "qualitative and unpredictable messiness of interacting with people from other cultures" (personal communication, December 6, 2007).

Well, it's *good* to think in ranges, rather than aiming for precise number points....I tell people that you may be somewhere to the (say, left) of a scale, and the people from (China) may be somewhere to the right. I tell them that the precise number for (China) is not knowable, that anyone who tries to claim having a precise and authoritative number for (China) on a given scale is a charlatan (or a misguided researcher)....The precise number of where they are doesn't matter. And of course there are exceptions to every general rule, so they may surprise you. But at least know how to anticipate differences. (Peterson, personal communication, December 27, 2007)

Nonetheless, the chart generated after taking Peterson's (2004) inventory (the Peterson Cultural Styles Indicator[tm] or PCSI) results in one-dot positions for each of the five cultural dimensions his instrument measures (see Chapter 6 for descriptions of his dimensions). One person's (or culture's) dot on each continuum can then be compared to those of one other culture of choice in the same manner (Across Cultures, 2007a). Peterson recommends that the issue of unipositionality be addressed when discussing the results (personal communication, December 27, 2007), but most participants receive their score online immediately after finishing the questionnaire, without needing to speak to an administrator who could help them interpret those single points into the possibility of a range. And there is no communication of the consideration that the range may be contextual.

Table 2
Sample Traditional Cultural Difference Scales

Pole 1	Pole 2	Scholar(s)	Description
Individualism	Communitarianism	Trompenaars & Hampden-Turner (1998)	Whether people consider themselves as autonomous individuals or as belonging to a group (whether to support the individual so she can contribute to the community, or the group that then can help individuals succeed)
Individualism (Individualism vs. collectivism)		Hofstede (2001); House et al. (2004)	How people live together—whether their family structures are extended or nuclear—but the consequences influence every action, for instance how people prefer to work, learn, and make decisions.
Linear/sequential Monochronic Clock time	Circular/synchronic Polychronic Event time	Trompenaars & Hampden-Turner (1998); Hall (1976, 1998); Levine (1997)	Linear/clock time/M-time: performing tasks sequentially, future-oriented, or achievements from the past/present. Circular/event time/P-time: multitasking and interrupting tasks often, eventually completing them all but usually giving preference to quality human interactions over accomplishing tasks on time.
Neutral	Emotional	Trompenaars & Hampden-Turner (1998)	Whether interaction should be experienced objectively (neutral) or whether expressed emotions are acceptable (affective).
Specific	Diffuse	Trompenaars & Hampden-Turner (1998)	Whether areas of life such as business and family are kept separate (specific) or overlap (diffuse). Diffuse cultures focus on relationship-building over task mastering (specific and efficient).
Power distance (Hierarchy vs. equality)		Hofstede (2001); House et al. (2004)	Measuring interpersonal power (hierarchy vs. equality), e.g. of a superior as it is perceived by those he supervises. Both maintain the power distance voluntarily as part of their cultural norms.
Uncertainty avoidance (Avoiding certainty vs. tolerating ambiguity)		Hofstede (2001); House et al. (2004)	Uncertainty avoidance addresses how comfortable people are when it comes to ambiguous future events.

Pole 1	Pole 2	Scholar(s)	Description
Achievement	Ascription	Trompenaars & Hampden-Turner (1998)	Whether someone is judged by their (recent and recorded) accomplishments or by the circumstances of their social status reached by birth, kinship, gender, age, education, networking, etc.
Universalism	Particularism	Trompenaars & Hampden-Turner (1998)	Whether to apply absolute rules in life (universal; right/wrong, good/bad), or to pay attention to relationships and circumstances of a situation (particular; no abstract societal codes).
Inner-directed	Outer-directed	Trompenaars & Hampden-Turner (1998)	Whether the cultural group looks within the person as the center of gravity (inner-directed) or attributes more power to the exterior world or nature (outer-directed)
Gender egalitarianism (Masculinity vs. femininity)		Hofstede (2001); House et al. (2004)	How societies manage differences between gender roles; whether men and/or women are supposed to be assertive and success-oriented or relationship-focused and concerned with quality of life, or both.
Long-term/future orientation (Long-term vs. short-term orientation)		Hofstede (2001); House et al. (2004)	Whether societies orient themselves around virtues of the past/tradition in short-term orientations (wanting results NOW—Western approach), or orient themselves around future-oriented virtues of frugality, persistence, or education (with more flexibility regarding HOW to accomplish the goals—for instance some Asian frames).
Humane orientation		House et al. (2004)	"Related to few retail outlets per capita. People…tend to use extended, warm greetings. Hospitality is very important. People show empathy and are very high in satisfaction" (House et al., 2004, pp. xv-xix).

In contemporary society, where shifting identities are acknowledged and maybe even expected, individuals and groups may inhabit more flexibility about where they choose to reside on the continua depending on context. Trompenaars and Hampden-Turner (1998) consider the opposite poles of a cultural dimension as complimentary rather than opposing since integrated processes are possible. I term this possibility *multipositionality*, or the holding of multiple noncontiguous positions. Trompenaars and Hampden-Turner's recommendations refer to holding those multiple points simultaneously, and provide an excellent foundation for the possibility of reshaping traditional cultural dimensions to reflect contemporary perspectives of shifting identities.

Examples of this multipositionality can be found, for instance, in individuals who have inherited an orientation of universalism (absolute social rules) versus particularism (rules to match the context). Such individuals can learn the limitations of universalism from "particular instances" (Trompenaars & Hampden-Turner, 1998, p. 53) where the application of established norms could not solve the problem and therefore norms needed to be loosened or abandoned. Or, individuals with an orientation toward individualism may voluntarily address "the needs of the larger group" (p. 53) in order to make progress on the issue to be solved. In a business context, organizations can pursue reconciliation between the opposing poles of inner-directed and outer-directed—feeding the market with the right dose of innovation and leaving the system open enough to allow both inner- and outer-directedness to flourish (Trompenaars & Hampden-Turner, 1998).

The next step in rethinking cultural difference vis à vis life in the 21st century may be to add the possibility that locations on the scale shift contiguously and noncontiguously depending on the context of the interaction—*contextual multipositionality*. Cultural distance may depend on context, rather than being symmetrical as is assumed by traditional theory (House et al., 2004; Osland & Bird, 2000). Cultural differences may have different levels of impact given certain circumstances, and could be taken advantage of in different ways in various scenarios in order to solve culturally bound problems; however, this concept has not yet been researched. I would restate this idea to say that in contemporary societies, cultural difference may manifest differently depending on which culture holds the power in that particular interaction under investigation, and add that the manifestations of cultural exchanges may even depend simply on a person's mood on that day under those circumstances.

Critical voices are emerging and new language is being coined to point to the limitations of established intercultural communication theories and models. For instance, the term *sophisticated stereotyping* (Osland & Bird, 2000) refers to the danger of reducing entire nations or groups into unipositionality on the continua of cultural dimensions. In spite of this limitation, the dimensions are still found valuable as a beginning point for understanding that differences in cultural behavior do exist, sometimes even within the same individual; however, it is recommended that the limitations of these traditional practices be clearly defined in any conversation. Knowing the limitations of these assessment methods of cultural behavior provides the possibility for flexibility when faced with the paradoxes of culture. Paradoxes are likely to emerge when observing contextually different situations. In addition, scores on the cultural dimension continua might relate to ideal values that may never translate into actual behavior, as values in themselves are interrelated and may be expressed differently when evoked in certain combinations (Osland & Bird, 2000).

Polyculturalism, Transculturalism, and the Challenges of Culture

Intercultural communication theories and practices were originally constructed within the concept of multiculturalism and thus were part of sensitizing the world to paying attention to cultural differences. The practice of cultural dominance was largely still upheld in multiculturalism, and ethnic groups (renamed to "cultures") were acknowledged as autonomous, given resources, and, over time, no longer asked to assimilate to the dominant culture. If culture is to be understood as a system of solutions to everyday problems, multiculturalism solved the problem of moving people and the world from ethnocentric to ethnorelative worldview orientations, into the last stages of what is called adaptation and integration in the DMIS.

The new concept of *polyculturalism* (Podur 2003; Kelley, 1999; Kureishi, 2005; Prashad, as interviewed by Frontlist, n.d.) represents the next step—moving the world out of the assumption that cultures function as autonomous units. Polyculturalism implies a social structure in which cultures are considered interrelated and therefore cannot be compartmentalized, yet also are not flattened and simplified into one universal culture. A polycultural environment represents a system that strives for equality across a diverse population, and fosters the authenticity of *cultural hybrids* with shifting identities.

Cultural hybrids are individuals who carry multiple cultural frames inside themselves—"porous, fuzzy-edged, indeterminate, intrinsically inconsistent, never quite identical with themselves, [with] their boundaries continually modulating into horizons" (Eagleton, 2000, p. 96). Traditional intercultural communication theory indicates that only face-to-face lived experience (even in the form of a simulation) can lead one toward incorporating additional cultural references in one's system. In contemporary society, the experiences and cultural exposure of cultural hybrids include virtual interactions (Lee, 1999; Goodfellow & Hewling, 2005), which also help to expand their cultural repertoire and cause them to move toward ethnorelativity.

Polyculturalism is concerned with the welfare of all—an environment that erases, by default, concepts of cultural dominance. The overarching goal of polyculturalism is that wellbeing for all humanity is met without focus on a particular region or group of people. The welfare of all is understood by radical polyculturalists to be accomplished through abolishing all political borders and establishing a world federation that is led by representatives from the various diverse constituents. A new kind of leadership is required to manage a new system of distribution, in which goods and services are freely distributed as needed. In the current, multicultural era, the dominant culture leads the world and reaps most of the benefits while the rest of humanity is struggling to survive. In polyculturalism, the wellbeing of all breathing creatures and the planet itself is everybody's business (Podur 2003; Kelley, 1999; Kureishi, 2005; Prashad, as interviewed by Frontlist, n.d.); thus, polyculturalism is a response to a world in crisis that has not yet solved the problems it is now facing. These present challenges are unsolvable within the existing paradigm and warrant, consequently, a paradigm shift.

Pushing through to polyculturalism requires the concept of hierarchy to be restructured. A polycultural system does not include a nonhierarchical structure or a uniform culture, but it does imply a hierarchical structure through which universal problems can be solved collaboratively and under consideration of diverse ideas—a structure that is not based on origin (ethnicity, race, nationality, etc.) or social status. Proponents of multiculturalism, in their conviction to level all hierarchies and experience each culture as distinctly unique, different but equal, will bring forth one or both of two objections to the new frame of polyculturalism. Hard-core multiculturalists may respond by protesting the re-establishment of hierarchy—any hierarchy. Hard-core ethnorelativists may respond negatively, or at least cautiously, to any notion remotely resembling universalism that could push the world back into the minimization of cultural difference. Both responses are a positive sign in that strong responses show more density in the current development, implying that we are near completion of the challenges of multiculturalism; they could also be seen as one aspect of the new challenges arising from that completion, challenges that may become the task of the potential new paradigm.

Another term in use for discussions of power relationships and tensions between social groups is that of *transculturalism*, which is used in several contexts. First, transculturalism refers to the reality of merging ethnicities in cosmopolitan areas where the dominant culture is diminishing greatly in numbers, and where transcultural youth (post-baby-boomers or echo-boomers) are conscious of diversity but do not perceive it as a challenge (Tseng, 2003). Some references to transculturalism in this context border on commodification by referring to trendy urban youth culture (mixed races used in "hip" commercials or as marketing strategies).

Critical transculturalism discusses political-economic issues of concern for an international platform and includes a conversation about cultural hybridity as a new concept for the core of human identity (Marwan, 2006)—not unlike the principles of polyculturalism, but slightly different.

In this context, the presence of transculturalism can be seen as a transformative opportunity that carries potential and flexibility (Lewis, 2002).

Transculturalism is also used within discussions about transdisciplinary frames. For instance, Nicolescu (2007) defines it as designating "the opening of all cultures to that which cuts across them and transcends them...a new *transcultural...attitude*" (p. 14). Polyculturalism engages the challenges of integrating cultural differences with the experience of a metaconsciousness that nurtures the human bond across cultures; transculturalism is the sense of transcending cultural differences by not holding on to frames that do not fit the current circumstances and by freely integrating those aspects of cultures one has access to (virtually or face-to-face) that either match the current lifestyle or create a new desired style (Tseng, 2003). Both new concepts, polyculturalism and transculturalism, thus represent a potential paradigm shift changing how we may perceive culture to be established and nourished. (This discussion describes how these terms are being used by other scholars; in the Epilogue, I define both terms as they are best suited to this study.)

Moving Forward

Both polyculturalism and transculturalism developed out of the observation that culturally mixed groups are becoming the norm rather than the exception. This shift points to a gap in intercultural communication research, namely the study of highly diverse groups interacting. Observing these interactions puts the focus on commonality and negotiation of bonding rather than on difference; cultural hybridity may render static measurements irrelevant, obsolete, or impossible. Intercultural communication models and instruments would need to be rethought to measure or even to observe from that perspective, and contextual multipositionality offers a foundational building block for that rethinking process.

The GLOBE project scholars concluded, "what is probably important is not how a culture is objectively measured but how it is subjectively perceived by those from another culture" (House et al., 2004, p. 730), and suggested that polycultural or transcultural environments are much more complex. The present study is a first, small-scale effort to address this new and important area of concern.

CHAPTER 3
VISUAL COMMUNICATION

Visual communication as a field is largely focused on objective reality (see Figure 5); in particular, visual communication scholars and practitioners concern themselves with the principles and elements of design and only partially touch upon the experience created for an audience in regard to culture. How audiences perceive visual messages is taught under the assumptions of universal truths. The question of how meaning is cocreated in small polycultural groups through interactive graphic facilitation and via visual mapping can thus only be partially addressed through this lens; conversely, the question cannot be addressed without this lens.

Historically, visual communication dates all the way back to early cave paintings. On a large scale, words and images became two separate forms of communication in Western history, with separate skills, practitioners, syntax, concepts, and tools—even different departments in universities. Under these circumstances, a hierarchy developed with text ranking first and visuals second, which caused an emphasis on linguistic/verbal intelligence versus visual/spatial talents in the education system. Western society returned to a visual culture with the inclusion of television during the second half of the 20th century and nowadays also the Internet in people's daily lives. Likewise, the business world includes more visuals and creativity in their daily operations—to the extent that practices in Western culture have moved toward preferring iconic representations over words (Horn, 1998). We are, however, still recovering from that separation between visuals and words and are in the midst of awakening multiple intelligences in order to solve our current problems. As the world becomes more complex, the need for a visual language increases.

The Status Quo of Visual Communication

Visual communication is an umbrella term for a variety of practices that convey ideas, generic information, and targeted messages in visual formats. The terminology used in this field is not consistent and largely not agreed upon; however, it can be assumed that communication aspects are involved. This assumption can be a distinguishing factor when visual communication is compared to fine arts, where personal expression can be the sole objective. The visual communication field has evolved from two- or three-dimensional representations to also include communication in the virtual space.

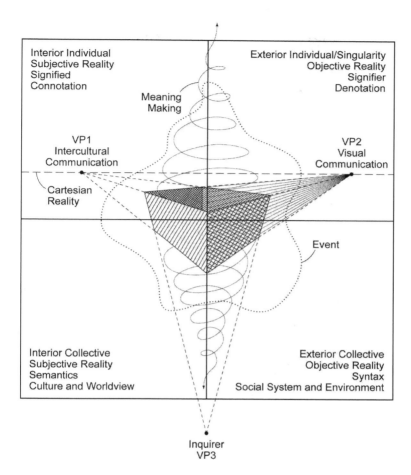

Figure 5. The metaphorical research space seen through the four-quadrant viewfinder, with the focus on the areas contained within visual communication (largely in the objective quadrants). VP = vanishing point. Author's image; four-quadrant grid based partly on concepts from *The Integral Operating System* [compact disc set and booklet], by K. Wilber, 2005, Boulder, CO: Sounds True.

Given the history of visual communication, it is not surprising to find cutting-edge designers, educators, and schools continuing the canon of "universal truths" even when culture is, in fact, considered and studied as an aspect of successful design merged with business efforts (e.g., Stiller, Shedroff, & Rhea, 2005; Making Meaning, 2005). The universalist underpinning of visual communication and the business world's strong preference for reliable, fixed expectations combine to create an environment that effectively ignores the culture debate.

This lack of cultural knowledge and awareness in the visual field consequently affects the quality of information that is passed through visual forms by designers even if they are interested in encoding messages into visual formats for diverse audiences. For example, the newest design book used in the Visual Literacy class that was part of this inquiry (Evans & Thomas, 2008) describes the principles and elements of design and gestalt, but does not consider culture as a variable in meaning construction. If an instructor wants to talk about culture in relation to visual communication, the only recourse is to bring in sources from outside the discipline and then collaborate with the students to fill in the gaps. This method actually has its benefits if the students are culturally diverse and the instructor practices critical pedagogy, but is not possible if the instructor is not adequately informed or not flexible in sharing power. A classic sample textbook does mention that the meaning of certain signs is culturally bound to the "visual and verbal currency of its culture" (Meggs, 1989, p. 40), but contains no further guidance or information for designers about resources.

While there are different terms for similar principles, the visual communication community largely agrees on the core of the design principles and elements used to create, discuss, and analyze design. However, the field traditionally lacks not only cultural information but also formal academic intellectual discourse, caused by a lack of doctoral-level programs available for studying the field. Since there is little high-end research in the field itself, areas that apply directly (e.g., the meaning-making process) are therefore borrowed from whatever designers can find at the time when they need the information—a creative, but eclectic pastiche of often-outdated information or information with a heavy focus on the Western frame that comes so easily in this context.

These limitations in available resources translate into a limited perspective. For instance, designers in the Western world are familiar with the Gestalt principle stating that the whole is greater than the sum of the parts. Nonetheless, they still tend to focus on the elements (positive space) in their communication efforts and sometimes on the inter-relationship between them (object-orientation and figure–ground distinction). The relationship between foreground and background (figure–ground relationship) as a whole, interlocking unit is usually not considered in the gestalt discussion from the perspective of field-dependency (focusing on the intertwining relationship aspects). If figure–ground relationships are discussed, they are usually understood as the negative space merely defining the positive space (focusing on objects again). Holistic perception would be more characteristic of an Asian frame (Nisbett, 2003) referring to field-dependence.

Lacking both information regarding culture and the necessary research skills, designers default to discussing syntax (design elements in objective reality, neutral) rather than semantics (interpretation in subjective reality, indirectly assumed to be equal to the designer's interpretation by the lack of cultural discourse)—hence design books void of cultural information. If designers do address semantics, they usually speak to it from positions of incomplete, Western-oriented, or incorrect information (e.g., Tufte, 2001). Robert Horn, for example, is the only academic and published theorist of visual language who is also a visual mapper and graphic facilitator. Horn admits to a lack of expertise in cultural studies (personal communication, September, 2007), and his book largely avoids the subject.

Information designers and graphic facilitators tend to reference Tufte as their model for good information design, defining graphical elegance as the simple design of complex data (Tufte, 2001). Some guidelines for this elegance are properly chosen formats and designs; integration of words, numbers, and drawings; relevant scales in correct proportions; accessibility to complexity of detail; narrative quality or data expressed in a story; technically correct and meticulous details; and avoidance of decoration or "chartjunk" (p. 177). These are appropriate items upon which to place judgments. However, nowhere is it considered that these kinds of judgments are value-based and thus inherently cultural—what may be considered elegant by some audiences may be perceived as junk or kitsch by others.

Visual Communication Theory

In visual communication theory, a number of qualities of *visual language* imply culture as an important aspect of meaning-making, but nowhere is culture openly acknowledged or discussed from other than a universal perspective. The language of visual and mental images has a *grammar*, a set of principles that mediate the external and internal worlds. A visual language is formed through nonlinear experience and speaks on intuitive and emotional levels. Reading visual language is more demanding and engaging but supposedly immediately comprehensible. Visual language is a full integration of words, shapes, and images into a single communication unit that forms a gestalt, follows a syntax, and invites the building of semantic relationships. Design principles (syntax) and elements (signifiers) form the objective reality of visual communication. Its combined elements and flexible structures provide opportunities for different context-dependent interpretations (Horn, 1998).

The meaning of visual language is not private, because as a language it must be understandable by the community of users. A visual language must lend itself to be learned by non-native speakers and must have its own distinct history that separates it from other languages; therefore, visual language is inherently culturally bound. The elements of a language must be combinable and lend themselves to different interpretations depending on context. A visual language needs to have enough ambiguity to allow for these interpretations but also hold together congruently. Visual language facilitates cross-cultural communication because of its ability to expose underlying assumptions that otherwise would not be expressed (Horn, 1998). It is also important to give guidelines for how visual language differs in various cultures—a need that is essentially not addressed.

Graphic language communicates via *signs* such as sounds, visuals, gestures, and marks. Terms to describe different forms of signs are borrowed from the discipline of linguistics. In the graphic language, distinctions are drawn between denotation (objective reality) or signifier, connotation (subjective reality) or signified, syntax (objective), and semantics (subjective).

This transdisciplinary case study used a viewfinder as a framework to bring the fields together, through which it is possible to separately investigate and later reintegrate objective realities and subjective experiences on the individual and the collective levels. This AQAL-based viewfinder (Figure 2 in Chapter 1) also overlaps with the four aspects of communication (signifier, signified, syntax, and semantics) that provide a map upon which to examine the visual communication (and intercultural communication) aspects that pertain to this study.

Signifiers are located in the upper right quadrant of objective reality on the individual level (or thing), represented by isolated elements of design (object-orientation) and/or the gestalt of a design perceived as a single image (field-dependence).

Signifieds belong to the upper left quadrant of subjective reality on the individual level, represented by the meaning that is created by the interpreter of the information individually. Signifieds are thus interpreter-dependent because if there is no interpreter there can be no signified. The meaning created by the interpreter is not visible unless she is asked to bring it into objective reality through feedback that can be shared and observed through the sensory world.

Syntax represents rules and structures on the lower right quadrant of objective reality, in this case visual grammar, represented by the principles of design and the relationships that constitute a visual system (i.e., visual language). Syntax incorporates multiple ways of gestalting including the perspective of considering elements carved out of the background (figure–ground distinctions) and relationships between foreground and background (figure–ground relationships).

Semantics reside on the lower left quadrant of subjective reality and refer to the meaning cocreated by interacting individuals and groups of people during a shared experience. Semantics in this study is represented by energetic exchanges that cannot be seen unless they are brought into the shared space of objective reality through, for instance, the cocreation of an artifact that can be shared and observed through the sensory world. Visual communication theory, as with signifieds, refers largely to ethnocentric interpretations when considering subjective reality on the semantic level.

Designers think quite a bit about how to encode messages upon elements and build structures that create meaning in the subjective realm. However, because of the lack of cultural information in visual communication fields, the act of encoding matches the frame of the designer rather than the frame of the audience. If the audience and the designer occupy a similar cultural map, there is no problem, but if the audience is from a different culture, the message may get distorted or misinterpreted in the transmission. While this has always been a problem in visual communication, it has been less of an issue within a society controlled by a dominant culture (Caucasians), where that dominance extended to the profession itself. With the expected drastic shift in population and power, this issue can be expected to become increasingly problematic.

Culture is a more common buzzword in recent design books but the discussion is limited to surface-level statements about culture, such as "Cultural awareness is vital for the modern designer and most designers are culturally aware people" (Shaughnessy, 2005, p. 19). No concrete suggestions are given as to what cultural awareness means, let alone how to gain cultural awareness. In addition, it is dangerous to assume that most designers (or any people) are culturally aware without concrete evidence. Nor does a thorough search of available design education books locate information about how the construction of visual language or the encoding of messages might change from culture to culture, let alone what mixed cultures might look like.

This is not to say that individual educators have not taken on the responsibility of involving their students in learning about culture. Many probably do, regularly, on their own account and by pooling sources in their communities and the resources they have access to. For example, a collaborative project between four university design professors and their students led to a public exhibit accompanied by a printed catalog (Sticks and Stones, 2006). Throughout the semester students collaborated on uncovering their own layers of culture and investigating acts of stereotyping, working with each other as research subjects and also addressing the public. It is safe to assume that most students and educators are interested in participating in issues of culture and creating meaningful work.

What is being critiqued in this chapter is the failure of those who lead the discipline in progressing the profession to provide designers with the necessary information to grow into culturally sensitive designers in service of the public. Visual messages are powerful aspects in the social fabric, and the privilege of participating in creating public messages comes with the responsibility to enter this sacred space with knowledge about social and cultural dynamics. The responsibility is larger for designers and educators who publish, and the damage is greater if they continue to gloss over culture, which is central to the design process and the dissemination of information.

Designers use a form of rhetoric for visual communication through signs. These terms refer to the fact that signs have the power to connote beyond their original meaning, thus manipulating various aspects of comprehension with the effect of entertainment and enrichment. Concepts are best understood metaphorically and often represented in mappings that enable humans to think of complex issues, called *target domains*, in familiar ways, called *source domains*. Source domains can stand for more than one idea. In visual language the metaphor can be carried with an emphasis on verbal or visual elements, or carried by both equally. There are simple and complex metaphors as well as metaphors for passing time, which is described as a generally linear element that can be segmented from left to right on a graphic panel (Horn, 1998).

Other forms of representation to consider are emotional expressions, typographic expressions, mixtures of verbal and visual messages, spatial relationships, and cropping of frames (Horn, 1998). Universally oriented theorists often minimize the question of culture by hinting at the possibility that different cultures may have different norms for expressing emotions but then quickly defaulting to the proposal that all humans have emotions, which redefines the issue of emotional expression, again, as universal for them.

Graphic design theory, as virtually all visual communication fields, does not easily make connections between subjective and objective realities even when the concept or need is recognized. To communicate more authentically and/or more accurately, designers would need to study the culture(s) of their audiences to understand how visual messages might be decoded in that cultural context. Decoding is subject to cultural and personal variance and to context in meaning-making, but this level of complexity is not included in the designer's education and thus hardly enters the practice.

Significant to this study, words, shapes, and images form a visual language only when considered together—meaning is lost if the gestalt principles are violated in the syntactic structure. The form of an arrangement (or *topology*) interconnects to meaning independent of context or content by its mere structure. Topologies, which can manifest in a variety of conceptual and stylistic compositions, need text to clarify meaning. The syntax of topologies is context-dependent. Dimensionality in topologies adds more complexities and can direct the intended interpretation (Horn, 1998). Although cultural difference is not mentioned as a factor in the creation of meaning connected to form, Horn does point to the possibility of different people making different associations to the same form, and the need for more research in the way different people associate certain meanings with certain forms. However, in Horn's definition of visual language the negative space is not even mentioned as a variable.

The semantics of visual language require the analysis of the cocreation of meaning by words and visuals used in combination. When confronted with visual language, the human brain goes through a process that includes semantic fusion and percept–concept integration. *Semantic fusion* is the tight integration of words, images, and shapes (e.g., words inside upward-pointing arrows may mean "of higher quality"), and fosters the use of visual language as an efficient communication tool. *Percepts* are impressions of objects perceived via the senses, *concepts* are mental ideas, and visual language mediates the two. An example is information landscapes (another term for visual maps)—large panels that demonstrate ideas via visual language. On those large panels there is often a horizon line that may be intended or perceived as global ideas. Mountains in the background may be designated as big issues, and rising sun in the distance may stand for future events. Temporal relationships, voice (speech bubbles), and mood setting add other dimensions (Horn, 1998). Intercultural theorists would agree that meaning is created via percept–concept integration, but would disagree with the notion that horizon lines, rising suns, and mountains transmit the same meaning across cultures. Again, negative space is omitted from Horn's definition, and neither is culture brought up as a variable in meaning-making.

This universalist underpinning is a significant obstacle to awakening cultural awareness in the discipline of visual communication. For example, Tufte (1990), who is widely read and admired by visual practitioners (including graphic facilitators) as an expert information architect, claims that "the principles of information design are universal—like mathematics—and are not tied to unique features of a particular language or culture" (p. 10). Horn's explanation of percept–concept integration does at least imply the involvement of the viewer's culture/worldview in the meaning-making process, and offers a possible starting point for discussion. It is hoped that this study may initiate some growth of cultural awareness and understanding in this field.

Visual Communication Practice

In this dissertation, the term *visual practitioner* is used to refer to a variety of subdisciplines within visual communication, such as photography, illustration, drawing, typography, graphic design, information design, graphic facilitation, fine arts (if the art is meant to communicate), and so on. The areas most of interest to this study are graphic design, information design, and graphic facilitation (including visual mapping).

Graphic design refers to a theory, a process, and a product. Graphic designers organize information and prepare messages in the form of communication pieces for defined audiences and on behalf of their clients. They communicate in the form of a visual language and through a variety of media. Their main goals are to solve problems for their clients and to establish effective communication (Poggenpohl, 1993, reprinted by AIGA, 2008) by translating messages into visual form (encoding) to be channeled from the sender to the receiver with as little noise interference as possible (Morgan & Welton, 1992).

Information design is the manipulation and efficient presentation of quantitative and qualitative information in a variety of media, including murals and visual maps. Inherent in the teaching and practice of this field is a strong bias for the dominant cultural frame. For example, information design theory refers to the usefulness of applying colors as they exist in nature.

> A grand strategy is to use colors found in nature, especially those on the lighter side, such as blues, yellows, and grays of sky and shadow. Nature's colors are familiar and coherent, possessing a widely accepted harmony to the human eye—and their source has a certain definite authority. (Tufte, 1990, p. 90)

However, no distinctions are made between different geographical areas around the planet. A desert with many shades of beige, greys, or browns and a lack of green during much of the year would certainly evoke different color schemes than a jungle with many different greens and bright vibrant colors. Which scheme to choose certainly would need to match the frame of the intended audience, in order to carry the desired associated meaning. For example, Imhof's first rule for using colors in creating Swiss maps states, "pure, bright or very strong colors have loud, unbearable effects" (Imhof, 1982, as discussed by Tufte, 1990, p. 82). This value judgment is probably true for snow-covered Swiss alps, but is hardly an acceptable absolute guideline.

Another example of the distribution of incorrect information from a Western frame can be found in a design book for studying color theory, where it is determined that socioeconomic aspects affect choice of color hues (property of light, shade or tint) and values (lightness or darkness of a color). The higher the status, the more likely a preference for "darker, less saturated, complex hues" (Bleicher, 2005, p. 40). The lower the status, the simpler, brighter, and purer the hues. The only exception given to this "rule" is the group of young urban professionals who choose the color choices of the "next higher economic bracket" (p. 41). These "rules" simply cannot be true for cultures in which bright colors are valued by people with high socioeconomic status (e.g., expensive, hand-painted Iznik tile in Turkey).

With the following definition, the leading authority in the field of information design places himself in the Western frame where time is measured and used efficiently and where truth is defined as absolute. He defines graphic excellence as

> the well-designed presentation of interesting data—a matter of substance, of statistics, and of design….which gives to the viewer *the greatest number of ideas in the shortest time* [italics added] with the least ink in the smallest space. Graphical excellence is nearly always multivariate…and requires telling the truth about the data. (Tufte, 2001, p. 51)

Time-series are another important aspect of information design generated from a Western frame. The tracked item flows up and down and across the chart, and time is depicted in a linear fashion flowing from left to right. Time-series do not lend themselves to demonstrating causal explanations; however, including the spatial dimension with the time dimension helps this issue tremendously. A famous historical example is the French engineer who mapped the fate of

Napoleon's army on its march to Moscow in the early 19th century. This map had a political impact because it exposed the cruel intentions of a commander (Napoleon) to continue waging a war that was impossible to win (Tufte, 2001). Maps based on linear time flow work well for those cultures who experience time as linear, but much of information design does not acknowledge and thus does not investigate non-Western frames of reference. It is therefore difficult for visual practitioners to obtain accurate information about non-Western frames in order to imagine different mapping structures that might be more authentic for non-Western cultures.

In instances where culture plays a role in communicating via a visual language, it is noted that it is best to involve representatives of that particular culture in the visual communication process to assure authentic representation (Tyler, Valek, & Rowland, 2006). The process of collaborative visual mapping can be helpful in assuring authentic representation, as it is a dynamic, self-directed group visualization process unfolding in real time. In other words, the group participants themselves negotiate and create the visual map. Interactive graphic facilitation is a process in which a participant-facilitator collects and consolidates input from other participants, with their acquiescence. In *noninteractive* facilitation, the facilitator who translates the information graphically is not a member of the group. Where authentic representation is the goal, interactive graphic facilitation is preferred to noninteractive.

Visual mapping is used in group processes and graphic facilitation. Various structures and templates of visual maps have been developed by and for graphic facilitators. Visual practitioners in this genre identify as an "emerging grassroots network of diverse practitioners who use visual methods to assist learning and communication between groups and individuals" (International Forum, 2003). The professional space for this type of visual work carries several names (Rowland & Valek, 2005) and there is no agreed-upon definition for the practitioners in this field, which is also true for the activity itself. Visual mapping, metaphor mapping, visual mindscaping, information muraling, information landscaping, wall scrolling, information chunking, visual practice, graphic recording, graphic facilitation, and graphic reflecting all support group processes by working on large-scale graphic panels attached to the wall.

Graphic facilitation uses visual mapping in order to assist group and learning processes. A graphic facilitator guides the group and records the information flow on a large-scale graphic panel attached to the wall. A *graphic recorder* collaborates with a group facilitator in leading the group through a process in the same way, but focuses on creating the visual map. Information designers also "use graphic facilitation during the initial design stages to develop ideas collaboratively with clients" (The Grove, 2007b).

While visual mapping processes have been used ever since humanity scribbled on the walls of caves (Margulies & Maal, 2002), the profession of graphic facilitation in support of group

39

processes began developing in the 1970s, around the same time that intercultural communication began to grow as a field. "The process has evolved to include many varieties of visual mapping and has spawned entirely new career fields called graphic (or visual) recording and graphic facilitation" (p. 10). Background is lacking on this genre of visual communication—there are few publications available to the public, and informal information is hidden away on blogs that are primarily visited by specific communities who already know the basics of graphic facilitation/recording.

Benefits of Graphic Facilitation and Visual Mapping

Benefits of incorporating graphic facilitation into group processes and group dialogues are increases in clarity and comprehension that allow participants to "see what they mean" (International Forum, 2003), depth of learning for visual and kinesthetic learners, levels of thinking enabling deeper levels of dialogue and discussion, time efficiency, and quality of decisions and understanding of commitments and accountabilities. In addition, benefits include lower rates of misunderstandings and the diminishing of potential conflict. Graphic facilitators consolidate key information emerging in the group process without interrupting it. The presence of visual maps in a room expands retention of key information and themes, and helps build group memory and a gestalt of the event (Ball, 1998).

Visual note-taking/mapping is an old form of influencing processes and of supporting communication "...that allows you to see the parts and the whole and notice the relationship between them" (Margulies & Valenza, 2005, p. 8). Diagrams and visual maps work well for representing complex relationships. They make the abstract concrete and show changes in time and branching, plus external, internal, and conceptual structures. Diagrams come in many types and are considered superior to verbal descriptions because they can synthesize information and facilitate computation of information (Horn, 1998).

Graphic facilitation is, potentially, a transformative process that produces both a graphic record and a measurable effect on the group itself. The knowledge base and skill set required to perform graphic facilitation includes deep listening, synthesizing information, structuring information into cohesive wholes, creating information systems, and acquiring cultural competence, as well as design sensitivity including image banks, group facilitation, organizational dynamics, and, at times, content-specific knowledge (Rowland & Valek, 2005). Graphic facilitators perform their tasks in real time, similar to the process of simultaneous translation and interpretation.

Graphic facilitation is "more than just a fancy way to take notes; it's a technique for helping groups reach consensus and resolve disputes" (Ball, 1998). Graphic facilitation has been defined as "a type of 'explicit group memory'" that assists in managing complexity of group discussions. It reflects back the expression of multiple perspectives, makes connections between thoughts, provides a way to store information, describes complex flow of activity, energizes the group, helps a group maintain sufficient focus to work together, and provides an explicit structure of thinking. (Ball, 1998)

This structure of thinking is largely supported by a form of feedback loop, as participants can see what they mean on the large graphic panel and also remember what they meant by referring back to the map as a parking lot. If produced well, large-scale graphic panels reflect the relationships between different aspects of the communication all laid out on one surface. In conversations that are in danger of turning into conflicts, the large graphic panel could also function as a buffer zone that allows for different opinions to be seen and acknowledged by the group—often the first step towards deflecting or ending the conflict (Rowland & Valek, 2005).

Visual Communication and This Inquiry

At the 2004 CPWR events, graphic facilitators asked important questions about how to translate intercultural communication concepts into visual maps to the benefit of polycultural groups in process and dialogue. There is little to no information documenting the processes and benefits of graphic facilitation. There is also little to no information available for practitioners to learn how to work crossculturally within their field, or to learn interactive practices that involve the clients in their preferred modes of information processing. Through this inquiry, I hope to help fill these gaps in visual communication theory and practice.

In addition, the present study is an extension of the work of Horn (1998), who proposed that visual language facilitates cross-cultural communication because of its ability to expose underlying assumptions that otherwise would not be expressed, but did not indicate whether or how visual language would differ in various cultures. Driven by that very question and based on Horn's hypothesis, this study investigated collaborative visual mapping as the logical method of bringing visual communication and intercultural communication into dialogue. Specifically, this study focused on meaning-making through interactive graphic facilitation and collaborative visual mapping as activities that inherently merge visual and intercultural communication.

CHAPTER 4
THE NEXUS: MEANING-MAKING

The fields of visual communication and intercultural communication overlap in the nexus of meaning-making. Intercultural communication theorists and practitioners focus on the subjective reality quadrants, and within those mostly on the level of the individual, while visual communication theorists and practitioners (those whose writing is available in English) focus on the objective reality quadrants, and within those choose to look at phenomena and build theories from the perspective of universalism through a Western lens. Yet, meaning-making (as all events analyzed through the AQAL frame) happens on all four quadrants of the viewfinder simultaneously. Therefore, investigating the meaning-making process from all four quadrants through those disciplines provides a more complete picture of the actual construction of meaning. This study focused on the events observable through the quadrant of subjective, collective cultural exchanges (the coconstruction of meaning), because this lens has been the least investigated in both fields.

This chapter presents what scholars and practitioners have found when looking at the meaning-making process from within the boundaries of their individual disciplines, exploring some of the ways individuals, cultures, and groups in creative play perceive and process information, and thus structure the meaning-making process. This exploration of the different aspects of meaning-making shows how they are interrelated to a great extent and are difficult to separate into discrete parts. In Figure 6, the spiral rising through the center of the research space represents the meaning-making process, bound in this inquiry by the perspectives of the fields of visual communication and intercultural communication and of the inquirer herself, within the event of this research project.

In psychology, the meaning-making process has been described as a form of building relationships in which portraits of reality are created through the interaction between visual and mental images (Barry, 1997). On the level of the individual, the meaning resulting from that interaction is not found in the parts that make up the whole but in the relationships between them. On the level of groups—in particular, groups engaged in creative activities—meaning is cocreated not by the interacting individuals directly but by the energetic exchange between them (Sawyer, 2006).

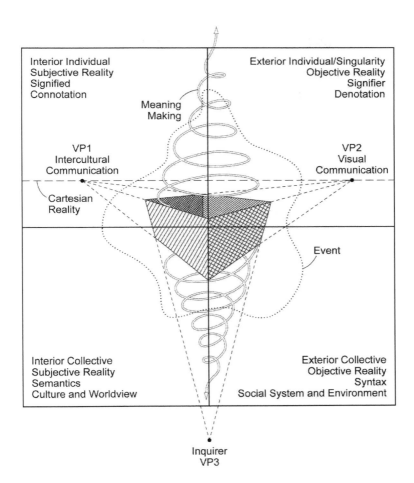

Figure 6. The research space seen through the four-quadrant viewfinder, with the focus on the meaning-making spiral running through the vertical axis of the viewfinder (dependent on the inquirer's perspective). VP = vanishing point. Author's image; four-quadrant grid based partly on concepts from *The Integral Operating System* [compact disc set and booklet], by K. Wilber, 2005, Boulder, CO: Sounds True.

Each discipline has its emphasis in regard to the basic elements of meaning-making. Visual communication scholars focus on vision as the driving influence on perception and therefore on meaning-making, while intercultural communication scholars focus on culture and language as most important. Both fields recognize that perception is a process in which meaning is made from the gestalt of current perception and past templates (or mental maps). Some scholars claim that language structures are at the base of it all (Bennett, 1998; Barthes, 1977; Whorf, 1956; Pearce, 2005). Others insist that imagery (Barry, 1997), the environment (Tuan, 1974), or bodily-physical experience prior to language (Lakoff & Johnson, 1999) engrave meaning upon the neural networks of the brain and structure experiences as meaningful. However, none of these scholars look outside their own focus to consider other possible inputs to that gestalt; in reality, meaning-making may receive input from all these areas and probably many others.

Visual literacy has been defined as the ability to understand and to express oneself with images (Barry, 1997). It includes the skills of understanding, producing, manipulating, and communicating through the logic, emotions, and attitudes suggested by visual representation. Visual language formed through nonlinear experience speaks on a basic, intuitive, and emotional level—perception, visual language, and visual intelligence are all aspects of meaning-making.

Visual communication theorists and scholars often place greater emphasis on images than on words. "What visual images express can only be approximated by words, but never fully captured by them" (Barry, 1997, p. 75); images "dominate the written or spoken word when they appear together" (p. 78). Although we cannot avoid using words to discuss visual constructions, it is problematic to impose the terminology of a linear, written language onto a nonlinear visual experience. This assumed hierarchy of images over words is based on cognitive theory. Written and spoken language must be processed cognitively before they can reach the emotions, but an image is processed differently and more directly, and "is therefore capable of reaching the emotions before it is cognitively understood" (p. 78). The described dynamic between words and images may be slightly different when considered from a non-Western frame. Alphabetic and syllabic sound-based writing systems (for instance, English) may be closer to the linear, while a logographic writing system (for instance, Chinese) is visually based and may be closer to Barry's concept of the immediacy of visual imagery.

Eyesight sends information to the nervous system quicker than any other sense, but what the eyes see and send to the brain is not necessarily real in an objective sense. The visual data is synthesized with past experiences and those detected by other senses, which creates a representation—a *mental map*—unique to the person who perceives. The construction of this mental map is a repeated action that results in humans seeing what they expect rather than what can be confirmed in objective reality, a filling-in of what's not perceived at all (Barry, 1997). In this way, beliefs are created and confirmed in the human mind. In this thinking of constructed reality, visual intelligence correlates directly to intercultural communication's theoretical foundation of socially constructed worlds (see Bennett, 1998, and Pearce, 1999, 2005).

Perception and meaning-making are inextricably linked. In the absence of sight, such as in the case of blind individuals, the other senses construct the world with similar templates. In this understanding, if there is no template, there is no experience—what is not seen or sensed through those templates cannot be put together in a meaningful way (Barry, 1997). This conclusion overlaps with the claim that people can only construct realities that emerge from some reference in their internal systems (Bennett, 1986b), and with the theory that meaning can only be made where a physical experience has preceded the construction of the metaphoric meaning (Lakoff & Johnson, 1999).

Besides visual intelligence, the bodily/kinesthetic and naturalist intelligences are of importance when considering a body-driven perspective of meaning-making. From this perspective, humans categorize (make meaning) and build a worldview (which is at the base of values, beliefs, and cultural practices) through bodily/kinesthetic experiences in their environment. In order to imagine something, at least the first contact with that something (or a similar concept) would have had to be a physical contact through one's body in order to lay the template for the imagination to occur (Lakoff & Johnson, 1999). Along these lines a comparison can be made to quantum physics, where the results of an event can be measured (in this case the ability to recreate that holographic image back into a physical sensation), but the event itself cannot be brought into observable reality. A similar relation has been made to culture as a wave (function or process) and a particle (structure) (Talbot, 1991, as discussed in Baldwin et al., 2006). In order to examine the function and process of culture, the structure has to be frozen into real space so that the other aspects of culture can be examined and tested against something tangible.

It seems thus that one aspect of meaning-making may need to reside in the objective realm while the other(s) occupy subjective realty, and closing the gap between those two is the task of making meaning. This understanding of meaning-making would lead to a definition of culture as a meaning-making process closing gaps between outer and inner realities through a "shared understanding of the world" (Baldwin et al., 2006, p. 47).

It is widely believed among graphic designers and typographers that words produced in a sound-based writing system (such as English) are read as images first by scanning the outline of the overall shape. This concept is supported by some research in psychology and cognition (see Mayall, Humphreys, & Olson, 1997, and Reicher, 1969) though results are not entirely conclusive (see Pelli,

Farell, & Moore, 2003, and Perea & Lupker, 2003). The designer who works with typography counts on the human system to scan words also by the modalities in which they are designed, thus influencing the meaning-making process. This understanding of reading as a nonlinear experience brings "linear" writing closer to the realm of images.

In the perception process, the brain first perceives the boundaries of objects and then fills in the interior of that object by averaging out sensory data. This form of gestalting makes the perceptual process a form of hypothesis testing. Perception can thus be described as a flexible system of patterns that compensates for fluctuations and change over time. It is a transformative process that fuses separate and discrete parts from present and past stimuli into cohesive wholes, moving linear concrete information into the amorphous, nonverbal realm of the feeling world (Barry, 1997).

Visual intelligence interprets direct recordings from the environment into internal representations called "images," which are then efficiently broken into manageable units stored in different places in the brain. Images remain available for later recall when they merge with new information in a process called "learning." What humans perceive through sight is thus an interaction between new and old information, where personal experience and cultural conditioning meet in constructing social worlds (Barry, 1997).

The combination of cognitive distortions and this type of perception leads to inner logic, which intercultural communication correlates to the construction of worldviews (Bennett, 1986b), basic assumptions (Trompenaars & Hampden Turner, 1998), mental programming (Hofstede, 2001), and the onion model (Hofstede, 2001). The patterns perceived—a pulling together of parts into meaningful wholes—determine both perception and abstract thinking. While this task is performed by deriving meaning out of disparate elements and is an important skill for survival, it also needs to be recognized that we thus act according to what we believe we see rather than what is actually there (Gregory, as discussed by Barry, 1997).

The research discussed in the following paragraphs correlates to intercultural communication theories that grew out of constructivist theories (e.g., Bennett, 1986b, 2003, and Pearce, 1999, 2005) and provides a direct link between the visual and intercultural worlds. Worldviews are built from incessant experience, categorization, memory, and reconnection. Reconnection happens by matching the current vision against templates in long-term memory; those that match the closest are considered accurate representations of the remembered images. As gestalts, both visual and mental images work together to paint portraits of constructed reality reconciling inner needs with outer realities (Barry, 1997).

The construction of social worlds and worldviews is of interest and shows up as a theme across several disciplines—for instance, in research describing worldviews as dependent on people's social settings and natural environments. An environment-driven perspective of meaning-making states that worldviews depend on people's social settings and natural environments, and that meaning is made through our understanding of our setting, or physical environment. The visual field is the widest of all the fields of the human senses—the human eye can see even in the far distance. This sense of distance is often overlaid even on objects that are close to the viewer. All senses are applied in perceiving the world and culture determines certain preferences for certain sense organs; for example, modern cultures demonstrate a strong preference for sight (Tuan, 1974).

The visual impact upon communication is estimated to be as high as 93% (Barry, 1997). However, it has been observed in brain imaging that visual images, verbal thoughts, and mental representations—although hemispherically and neurally processed differently—are experientially related but cause different behavioral consequences. Neurologists agree with gestalt psychologists that images do not reside in any particular part of the brain. Rather, they exist as patterns permeating the whole system and determine behavior, which is not a response to a stimulus but rather a response to internal images.

> As the individual interacts with the world, random images from life and from media are registered and tested continually against an overall sense of how things really work. General acceptance of the image by others, its relation to already ingrained sets of values, including a value ordering of potential acts and their consequences, and knowledge gained through experience or assimilated through the culture—these become some of the elements that interact within the turbulence of perception. (p. 101)

With this statement, the individual is identified as a system that is relatively constant but open to change depending on the exchange of incoming and outgoing messages in the form of visuals. The quality of abstract thought depends on the ability to grasp the form of ideas and combine the forms into more complex gestalts. When humans find the image relevant to their lives, they differentiate finer details that influence their worldview, which is at the basis for behavior. "In this way, whatever we see will be measured, remembered, and interpreted against the background of self-image and worldview" (p. 102).

Neurologically speaking, all images are gestalts because they are composed of fragments seen in the environment and processed together with pre-existing and stored mental constructs (Barry, 1997). As already mentioned in Chapter 3, people with a predominantly Western frame may tend to understand gestalt as relationships between objects in the foreground (object-oriented, figure–ground distinction). People with a predominantly Asian frame, on the other hand, may not distinguish between positive and negative space but rather see all the elements as relational and interdependent (field-dependent [Nisbett, 2003] or figure–ground relationship). A similar distinction that has been researched and named is that of Western minds working digitally and

Japanese minds working analogically or holistically (Hayashi & Jolley, 2002). While the digital processing method is about analyzing, defining, and categorizing objects logically and sequentially, the analog method leads to feeling the object and ground as an inseparable unit intuitively.

This is not a new idea—related to these basic differences, two main schools of thought discuss perception: holistic and analytical. Based on gestalt theory, the holistic strand describes perception as an interpretation of the environment with an emphasis on relationship. The analytical strand describes meaning as built from separate pieces of information directly received from the environment (Barry, 1997). Perception is probably all of these theories combined and possibly more, but cultural focus on one way over another may have influenced the West in solidifying the belief that analytic perception is the only way. One challenge of contemporary society may be to bring these two ways of perceiving together to increase our resources in facing the current global challenges.

The Learning Process as Meaning-Making

In this inquiry, the student-participant groups cocreated meaning together, raising the question of how people influence each other in their way of meaning-making or learning. Meaning-making is an inherent part of learning, because if the student cannot make any meaning from the material studied, no learning can occur. Investigating the learning process as meaning-making provides a link between individual and group meaning-making, because learning is an individual process that occurred, in this case study, in a group setting where differences in learning preference often manifest.

In understanding and possibly assessing learning preferences, educators can choose from various models and bodies of knowledge. Two models used in this inquiry are the Kolb (1984) Learning Phases and Learning Styles (LS) and the Gardner (1999) Multiple Intelligences (MI). Both models involve identifying an individual learner's meaning-making preferences, with the goal of enhancing the learning process for that individual. Since this inquiry focused on learning in a group setting, this discussion of learning preferences has relevance for both individual and group meaning-making and was used as form of intervention in this class.

Meaning-making in LS theory means that information is taken in through thinking or feeling, and then processed through observation or doing. The LS presents learning phases and styles in a circle (the Kolb Wheel) bisected by two axes (see Figure 7). The vertical axis depicts how information is taken in, and has feeling at one end and thinking at the other. Each person's learning phase falls somewhere between those two poles. The learning process can be entered anywhere on the wheel, but logically may begin with the preference between thinking and feeling,

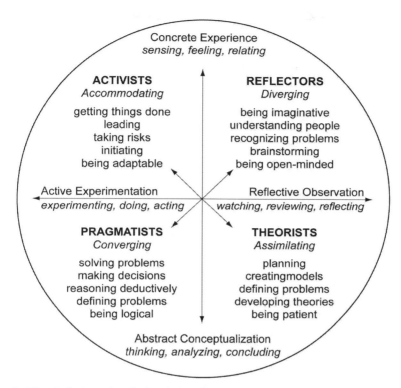

Figure 7. The Kolb Learning Styles (LS), shown as a "learning wheel." Author's image; consolidated and adapted from Clark (1999), Hay Group (2005), and Bennett and Bennett (2003).

and is completed through the horizontal axis activities of doing and observing (which concern information processing preferences). To complete the learning cycle (i.e., the meaning-making process), the learner must move through all four quadrants of the circle.

Four distinct learning styles are formed by the pairs of learning phases bounded on the Kolb wheel. *Accommodators* focus on "*acting skills:* committing oneself to objectives, seeking and exploiting opportunities, influencing and leading others, being personally involved, and dealing with people" (Kolb, 1984, p. 93). *Divergers* focus on "*valuing skills:* being sensitive to people's feelings and to values, listening with an open mind, gathering information, and imagining implications of ambiguous situations" (p. 94). *Assimilators* focus on "*thinking competencies:* organizing information, building conceptual models, testing theories and ideas, designing experiments, and analyzing quantitative data" (p. 94). *Convergers* focus on "*decision skills:*

creating new ways of thinking and doing, experimenting with new ideas, choosing the best solution to problems setting goals, and making decisions" (p. 94).

These four ways of learning (experience, perception, cognition, and behavior) contrast with each other at times and result in creative tensions and conflicts between different ways of being in the world—learning happens as a form of resolution to these conflicts (Kolb, 1984). This description of the learning process is similar to the definition of culture as the result of the resolutions to daily problems that societies invent collectively (Trompenaars & Hampden-Turner, 1998).

In another view of learning preferences (and therefore meaning-making preferences), Gardner (1999) has identified eight intelligences with a ninth under consideration and several more under discussion. Linguistic and logical-mathematical intelligence are highly valued in traditional Western education settings. Musical, bodily-kinesthetic, and spatial intelligence (from the visual communication skill set) have usually been improperly labeled as "talents" rather than intelligence. Interpersonal and intrapersonal intelligence are aspects of intercultural sensitivity as defined by Bennett (1986b). Naturalist intelligence is the latest edition to the set and correlates to pattern recognition.

For both theories, the influence of culture on learning preferences has been recognized. Kolb (1984) is clear about the assumption that "no account of human learning could be considered complete without an examination of culturally accumulated knowledge," (p. 99) and suggests that there is an isomorphic relationship between the structure of social knowledge and the structure of the learning process. Deciding how to deploy one's intelligences is a "question of values, not computational power" (Gardner, 1999, p. 46) and thus a question of culture. In MI theory, a distinction is made between culture, which leads to certain value judgments and is considered a "socially constructed human endeavor" (p. 82), as compared to intelligence, which is considered "biopsychological" (p. 82).

Cultures tend to prefer some intelligences over others—"each of us is equipped with these intellectual potentials, which we can mobilize and connect according to our own inclinations and our culture's preferences" (Gardner, 1999, p. 44). Due to socialization experiences in communities such as family, school, and work, individuals emphasize some learning processes over others (Kolb, 1984). This would then result in some social groups (cultures) leaning more toward feeling while others draw more from thinking, and some groups being more involved in practical application while others orient themselves through observation.

Useful correlations have been found between cultural dimensions and learning styles (Yamazaki & Kayes, 2005, as discussed in Yamazaki, 2005), and the results aligned with sophisticated stereotypes (culturally informed assumptions about groups) (Osland & Bird, 2000).

For example, Japanese demonstrated a preference for a divergent learning style, which was correlated to their high-context culture, strong uncertainty avoidance, analog processing, collective orientation, and field-dependent style. In comparison, Americans (who were categorized as low-context culture, weak uncertainty avoidance, digital processing, individual orientation, and field-independent style) demonstrated a preference for a convergent learning style. In another study (Fridland, 2002, as discussed in Yamazaki, 2005), Chinese were also more oriented toward reflective observation compared to Americans. Field-dependent styles have been linked to concrete experience and field-independent to abstract conceptualizing (Murphy, 1993, as discussed in Yamazaki, 2005).

These and other research results linking aspects of culture to LS or MI preferences (Barmeyer, 2004, Auyeung & Sands, 1996, Hoppe, 1990, all as discussed in Yamazaki, 2005; Auyeung & Sands, 2003) represent important complementary information regarding LS and MI applications. However, it must be noted that this research inherently worked with the same limitations pointed out in the discussion of intercultural communication in Chapter 2: the core of culture may not be fixed, behavior may not be predictable, and bipoloar models may not be complex enough to match the current situation in which people find themselves (in the era of globalization in the information age).

Innate or cultural learning preferences can change over one's lifetime (Kolb, 1984). Thus, learning (and therefore meaning-making) is not only a process of adapting to the world, but also of cocreating the social worlds we are part of, a process described in constructivist theories of intercultural communication. Cultural preferences for certain learning phases or intelligences are most strongly observed in the education system, which often has no room for students with nonmainstream preferences.

The Socialization of Culture

While the opinions of scholars are not consistent in the sequencing of the meaning-making process, there is a general consensus among researchers with a constructivist orientation that individuals construct meaning from a repertoire of cultural concepts that are themselves the product of sustained collective experience and (re-)interpretation over time. Intercultural communication theory supports the notion that language creates culture, and that through language we construct worldviews that construct our realities, but this may be another case where certain disciplines only look at partial truths. Linguist Dan Moonhawk Alford (n.d.) states, "for a relativist, language and worldview—ways of speaking, thinking, perceiving and being—reciprocally influence each other in a hermeneutic spiral." In Bennett's (1998) view, language is a "system of representation" (p. 13) that carries verbal categories that assist the conceptualization and categorization of objects. In other words, language provides a structure through which experience turns into meaning and as such language participates in creating culture rather than being formed by it. Language and language structures predispose which distinctions are being made in a particular culture because "language encourages habitual patterns of perception" (p. 15).

Language and culture guide how people distinguish between figure and ground. "What we think exists—what is real—depends on whether we have distinguished the phenomenon as figure [digital gestalting]. And since culture through language guides us in making these distinctions, culture is actually operating directly on perception" (Bennett, 1998, p. 16)—by means of all stimuli. Bennett suggests, "the perceiver is assumed to respond to culturally influenced categorizations of stimuli. Like the assumption of linguistic relativity, this assumption of perceptual relativity lies at the heart of intercultural communication" (p. 16). If there were no difference in the perception/ construction of reality, only one view or one truth could be correct, while all other interpretations would need to be false.

It is also important to consider how people construct reality on a social level. If we build worldviews from language structures, and worldview is the basic structure to build values, then out of values comes deontic logic, which is the focus of Coordinated Management of Meaning (CMM) (Pearce, 2005; Cronen, 1995). CMM is a theory and process with a focus on making social worlds coherent by managing the many meanings people make on a daily basis while interacting with others. CMM theory, discussed here, helps explain how meaning is created by individuals participating in group experiences. (The process tools of CMM used in this inquiry are discussed in Chapter 6.)

CMM has a strong foundation in Wittgensteinian philosophy, which makes the assumption that a particular language presupposes a particular form or way of understanding life, and that in order to know the meaning of any event things need to be investigated in the context of a variety of other issues that influence a particular event. Investigating the context includes investigating *deontic logic* (what one should do, must do, and must not do) in communication episodes, which exposes various aspects of social worlds (Pearce, 1999). Culturally speaking, these "oughtness" differences shift in different ways, as prescribed by the particular context and the social worlds of particular groups and languages. These shifts can be explored when looked at from several perspectives simultaneously. With this acknowledgment of individuals shifting their underlying assumptions in context, CMM supports the possibility of culture not as a fixed frame but rather a flexible structure.

A person's understanding of the deontic logic of the situation or context drives the meaning they make from the experience, the coding of the experience as positive or negative, and the reasoning behind that coding. CMM focuses on story-building as the backdrop to how meaning-making occurs in group experiences. Specifically, there is a gap or "a tension between the stories we 'tell' ourselves and others and the stories we 'live' with others" (Pearce, 1999, p. 12). CMM describes two solutions to the daily dilemmas that arise out of this gap (similar to the understanding of the core of culture as solving daily problems, to the essence of learning as solving the dilemma of the four ways of being in the world, and to the act of gestalting in perception as closing the gap between internal and external realities). Either a person adjusts the told stories so they match the experience, or she lives in a way that leads to congruence with the told stories (Pearce, 1999).

The concept of *coherence* refers to the stories told in order to create meaning in one's life and is "the process by which we tell ourselves (and others) stories in order to interpret the world around us and our place in it" (Pearce, 1999, p. 12). Stories are told about oneself, either individually or collectively, about philosophical issues and about the world one lives in. In a world that has stories as its main substance, people are meaning-makers and simultaneously actors. While meaning-making and acting are not the same thing, they are also inseparable. *Mystery* is "the recognition that the world and our experience of it is more than any of the particular stories that make it coherent or any of the activities in which we engage" (p. 12). Once a story is told in a particular way through a particular language, it is also narrowed in that it is seen only through that expression rather than in all the other ways in which it could have been interpreted. Therefore, life is not about resolving anything but rather about exploring its mystery in a coherent way. In this way, the *management of meaning of coherence and mystery* describes the management of the meaning created in the social interaction.

As with the other theories about meaning-making and learning mentioned above, CMM is based on the belief in a human need to close gaps in psychological landscapes as a form of gestalting, and the belief that the meaning is created and cocreated exactly in these gaps. The CMM stories Lived, Unknown stories, Untold stories, Unheard stories, stories Told, and storyTelling (LUUUTT) model (see Data Analysis in Chapter 6) provides a process through which to surface the unknown, untold, and unheard stories from an interaction as well as possible future observations—all of which may not be tellable at the time of the episode (Pearce, 1999). This bringing together of known and unknown elements in the gap between the two is a form of gestalting, and also synonymous to the core essence of this transdisciplinary research method. The goal of the present inquiry is to integrate the untold parts of intercultural communication and visual communication in order to construct a hologram of the whole inclusive of the missing parts—to create meaning about this meaning-making process, to close the gap between realities, and to construct a map to begin to see the unseen and experience the unknown.

As mentioned above, this study focuses on culture as the main variable (intercultural communication) in group dynamics. *Group creativity* is defined here as polycultural individuals engaging in creative play that results in the cocreation of meaning; this process may have been different and may have yielded different results if the same individuals interacted at a different time, or if they had worked alone.

People also make meaning out of group experience through the CMM concept of coordination. CMM defines *coordination* as weaving the patterns of one's own actions with those of other people. Mastering the skill of coordination in this sense means the ability to coordinate the whole gestalt of one's communication, including the refusal to coordinate if that was the original intention (Pearce, 1999). Group creativity and meaning-making in groups was of primary importance to this study. Unfortunately, the majority of research concerning creativity has focused on the individual rather than the group—intercultural communication research has a similar bias. Among available research, psychology and education provide one emphasis (group creativity research) while organizational development provides another (group dynamics research). Although they use different language, these two general approaches to group creativity and meaning-making are somewhat complimentary, examining the same phenomenon from different perspectives.

One focus of group creativity research is the concept of group flow. While flow theory (Csikszentmihalyi, 1990) refers to a certain consciousness in the individual, *group flow* refers to the "property of the entire group as a collective unit…in interactional synchrony" (Saywer, 2006, p. 158) and emergence. The best work is done when groups perform in this flow state, because it results in participants performing at their individual best. Group flow requires "parallel processing" (p. 159), which means paying attention to one's tasks while also paying attention to what others in the group are doing, and responding to each other in synchronicity. Graphic facilitators, for example, must be skilled in parallel processing so they can scribe the previous conversation while listening closely to the current conversation and planning the layout of their maps for the future conversation. While diversity is an important element of group creativity it is also necessary to have a common ground of "cultural knowledge and practices" (p. 156) so that group flow can occur, even if it is as simple as chemistry in that moment. Groups in the flow state have described their experience as "a timeless feeling [that] seemed to take over. The group just flowed. We were more at ease and patient with each other. People really seemed to be listening" (Purser & Montuori, 1994, p. 27).

Group dynamics (as in organizational development) present a related concept in the idea of groupthink, which differently frames the state in which group members agree. A *groupthink* mentality "is promoted when the group is highly cohesive, when it is insulated from outside criticism, when the leader is directive and dynamic, and when the group does not search for and critically evaluate alternatives" (Johnson & Johnson, 2005, p. 296). One characteristic of groupthink is "the collective striving for unanimity" (p. 296), in which group members are highly motivated to agree and therefore tend to inhibit discussion, emphasize agreement, and avoid disagreement or argument. Groups may display "direct pressure on dissenters: Anyone expressing doubt is pressured to conform" (p. 297) and each group may have mind guards, "certain group members [who] try to prevent dissenters from raising objections" (p. 297). Rationalization may occur, in which "group members invent justification for whatever action is about to be undertaken, thus preventing misgivings and appropriate reconsideration" (p. 297). Rationalization, mind guards, and pressure on dissenters may create the *illusion of unanimity* dynamic of groupthink, in which "each member assumes that everyone (except oneself) is in agreement. There is a state of pluralistic ignorance where members falsely assume that the silence of other members implies consent and agreement," (p. 297) which describes a Western lens. In the self-censorship dynamic of groupthink, "each member minimizes any doubt about the apparent group consensus." CMM offers one solution to group dynamics' concern with the way a groupthink mentality may prevent dissenting ideas or opinions from being heard, through the LUUUTT model (Pearce, 1999) that encourages investigation of that which was not heard or said in a particular group interaction (see Chapter 6).

In group dynamics, attribution theory stipulates that individuals form hypotheses about other people's behaviors in order to make events predictable. Attributions are defined as inferences about the reasons for someone's behavior and are significant factors in conflict situations. If these perceptions are accurate, they may help the group to find mutual understanding, but if they are inaccurate they lead to alienation and make conflict resolution more difficult (Johnson & Johnson, 2005). Here the description of mutual understanding versus conflict closely parallels flow states versus nonflow states in group creativity. Attribution theory also overlaps with group creativity's concept of the habitual behavior of each participant that is recognizable and somewhat expected by other participants. Perhaps flow is possible when those habitual behavior attributions are accurate, and less (or im)possible when they are inaccurate.

According to group creativity research, group flow is sometimes negatively influenced by "self-oriented behaviors" (Purser & Montuori, 1994, p. 29) caused by fear. Such negative influence can result in individuals wanting to leave or fight the group, both of which are defensive reactions based on assumptions/beliefs that may cause the group to spend energy on defending opinions rather than getting into the flow state.

Conflict often plays a vital role in group processes for effective decision-making by utilizing the resources and varied positions in a group. Controversy is defined as "conflict that arises when one person's ideas, information, conclusions, theories, and opinion are incompatible with those of another person and the two seek to reach an agreement" (Johnson & Johnson, 2005, p. 326). Many factors may contribute to groups avoiding controversy in favor of concurrence, including "group norms [that] may block group members from engaging in intellectual conflicts" (p. 330).

Groups in creative activities share leadership and pass it back and forth between each other. Often, ignoring the leader in favor of paying attention to the behavior of other participants, groups reach intersubjectivity—a space of coconstructed shared meaning that fosters playful interpretations through interconnectivity (Saywer, 2006). Group dynamics' distributed-action theory of leadership (Johnson & Johnson, 2005) is in alignment with this idea, stating that "each group member provides leadership by having the diagnostic skills to be aware that a given function is needed in the immediate situation in order for the group to function most effectively" (p. 191). *Task leads* focus on directing, synthesizing, and providing insights and ideas, while *social–emotional leads* focus on relationship-building and balancing the harmony of the group (Johnson & Johnson, 2005). Task mastering results in telling other people what to do, and relationship-building results in delegating and negotiating. Which style is most effective depends on the level of power or authority held by the leader, on the leader's relationship with the other participants, on the type of task at hand (whether or not it is highly structured or more ambiguous), and on the maturity level of the group (Hersey & Blanchard, as discussed by Johnson & Johnson, 2005).

According to group creativity research, the product of group creativity cannot be attributed to any single member's contributions. Improvisation, collaboration, and emergence are three categories of group creativity (Saywer, 2006). Improvisation refers to the unpredictability of groups involved in creative activities. The concept of improvisation refers to actions that are not scripted, yet there is a structure to improvisation that comes from the habitual behavior of each participant (recognizable and somewhat expected by other participants) or from repetitive scripts played in life that are familiar to all participants. Given this structure in a particular context, tasks are completed collaboratively with each participant bringing various parts to the activity/ product created that contribute to the whole—"an emergent group-level phenomenon" (p. 153). Group dynamics may be less predictable in polycultural groups than in homogenous groups as there are many more variables to consider and the context is much richer and may shift during the event.

This chapter examined the meaning-making process in the nexus of this study—the gap between visual communication and intercultural communication—and exposed the tension between various beliefs about the most fundamental aspects of meaning-making. While some hierarchy can be imagined—for instance, images and physical experiences as primal, language as secondary—it is most likely that all theories carry a piece of the puzzle. Looked at as a whole, all of these different perspectives together provide a fuller spectrum of the ways one creates meaning. This inquiry involved all three levels of meaning-making discussed in this chapter: by individuals, in an educational setting, and interacting in a social group.

CHAPTER 5
SETTING AND CONVERGENT RESEARCH FOCUS

Many aspects of the phenomenon of this inquiry have been touched upon so far; when the viewfinder is used to organize the information, significant gaps are apparent. Two vanishing points (intercultural communication and visual communication) and the meaning-making nexus where they meet have been explored, forming the outline of the metaphorical research space (see Figure 8) as seen through the four-quadrant viewfinder (showing subjective and objective reality on the individual and collective planes). Intercultural communication theory concerns mostly the upper left quadrant (individual subjective experience, as in signifieds) and makes inferences into the lower left quadrant (collective subjective experience/cultural exchanges between individuals/groups, as in semantics) by making gross assumptions from investigations of the subjective experience of individuals. Visual communication theory largely occupies the upper right and lower right quadrants (design elements as in signifiers and design principles as in syntax), and the only superficial attention given to the left quadrants is through the individual designer's own lens. Neither discipline investigates the lower left quadrant on the collective level directly. This study is an attempt to observe the phenomenon from all four quadrants authentically in order to integrate various aspects and arrive at a holistic perspective, while paying special attention to the collective subjective quadrant (networks).

In this chapter, these various aspects pertaining to this research are fused together through an investigation of the context and an outline of the convergent focus of the research. This tighter focus emerging from the initial intent and literature review results in a restatement and refinement of the research questions pertaining to this inquiry.

Setting

With its highly diverse student body, CCSF provided the ideal environment for this inquiry into meaning-making in polycultural groups. The primary data were collected in week 12 of a CCSF visual literacy class, during a Saturday class meeting from 10:00 a.m. to 2:00 p.m. (*data collection day*). The visual literacy class allowed an organic mixture of visual and intercultural communication during the observed research project, as the class was already studying and practicing visual communication techniques. This section describes the setting in greater detail through an institutional profile, department profile, and class profile, and concludes with an overview of class content, learning, and participation up to data collection day.

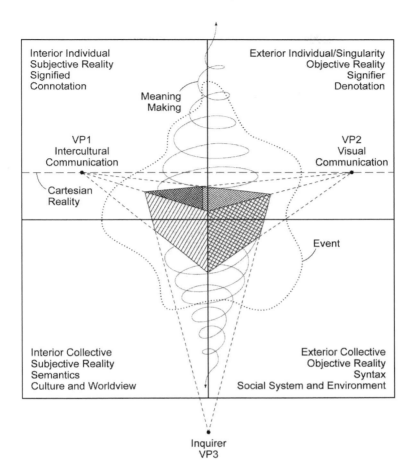

Figure 8. The metaphorical research space as explored and defined through the literature review, seen through the four-quadrant viewfinder and dependent on the inquirer's lens. VP = vanishing point. Author's image; four-quadrant grid based partly on concepts from *The Integral Operating System* [compact disc set and booklet], by K. Wilber, 2005, Boulder, CO: Sounds True.

City College of San Francisco (CCSF)

Founded in 1935, CCSF is an accredited, public two-year community college guided by California state laws. With more than 700 full-time and 1,100 part-time faculty, CCSF serves over 98,000 students annually at 12 campuses and nearly 200 sites, and offers non-credit, credit, and not-for-credit classes. Students can choose among 11 majors, 130 certificate programs, and 34 awards of achievement, and earn associate degrees, receive vocational training, or prepare for transfer to a four-year university or college. CCSF is comprised of the following schools: Applied Science and Technology, Behavioral and Social Sciences, Business, Health and Physical Education, International Education and ESL, Liberal Arts, and Science and Math (CCSF, 2006). In 2007, tuition was $20 per unit for California residents and $170 for nonresidents or international students (CCSF, 2007). Although tuition is considered affordable, the number of students receiving financial aid is steadily growing, with 13,995 students receiving aid in the 2004–2005 academic year (CCSF, 2006).

CCSF has an adult participation rate of 8.2 percent (the highest among state community colleges), as reflected by a June 2005 poll stating, "over one third of [San Francisco] residents have taken classes at CCSF, and 72 percent have friends and family who took classes through CCSF" (CCSF, 2006, p. 13). Eighty percent of CCSF students are from the City and County of San Francisco with the rest commuting from San Mateo, Marin, Alameda, and Contra Costa counties. The average student age is 33, "slightly younger for credit students and older for noncredit" (p. 30).

CCSF has evolved into a polycultural, multicampus community college that is one of the largest in the country. In 2004, 42% of full-time and 39% of part-time faculty were non-Caucasians (CCSF, 2006). The CCSF vision addresses diversity and multiculturalism in several sections.

…Through the outreach to and inclusion of all populations, the provision of an unparalleled learning experience for students, and the enhancement of a supporting and caring environment that sustains and leads them to the successful completion of their educational goals, we are motivated by a compelling and authentic vision…

We will continue to reach out to all neighborhoods, ethnic populations, and economic segments of our service area…and foster informed participation of our students and employees in community life.

We seek to build an inclusive community, where respect and trust are common virtues, and where all people are enriched by diversity and multi-cultural understanding; a responsive environment in which student needs are met in a friendly, caring, and timely manner; and a working environment for all faculty, staff and administrators in which everyone is valued and the climate is supportive, positive, and productive. (CCSF, n.d.)

The CCSF community certainly strives to follow these ideals. As can be expected from an institution of this size and high degree of diversity, these ideals are interpreted in many different ways. Some departments, schools, and faculty within the institution manage to be more successful in creating the supportive environment described above.

CCSF culture can be described as extremely diverse with a strong left-wing political orientation and a deep conviction in social justice issues across all the layers of the college community. The school maintains an open-door admissions policy. Diversity is celebrated at CCSF on all levels with meetings, discussions, hiring practices, curricular issues, diversity institutes, and a thriving multicultural infusion project (a professional development program for faculty). The Multicultural Resource Center provides opportunities for students, faculty, and staff to appreciate diversity through informal dialogues and structured programs. In 2004, CCSF received the MetLife Foundation Community College Excellence Award for its "accomplishment in the areas of innovation, institution-wide commitment, and improved outcomes based on careful assessment of strategies that promote access, retention, and completion for students from underserved populations" (CCSF, 2006, p. 4) including the city's immigrants. Its demographics were last measured in the school year of 2004–2005:

> The ethnic demographics of students in credit and noncredit programs includes a plurality of Asian students (35 percent), 20 percent non-Hispanic White, 20 percent Hispanic/Latino/a, 7 percent African-American non-Hispanic, 5 percent Filipino, and smaller numbers of other Pacific Islanders and Native Americans, as well as other non-identified students (approximately 10 percent). (p. 102)

The demographics of CCSF are in fact more complex than what is described above. Ethnic backgrounds are often multilayered and are difficult to represent in the official forms used to collect such information. Student satisfaction is high as measured by CCSF surveys: 75-94% of students rated CCSF as having "supportive faculty, supportive staff, and supportive administrators" and "would recommend CCSF" (p. 38).

The Department of Graphic Communication

The Graphic Communication department's vision statement addresses diversity and communication:

> Passionate and supportive faculty provide an inspiring and structured environment that invites diversity, encourages collaboration, and challenges the individual…

While there is a focus on visual communication, during their course of study students participate in classes that allow them to examine and practice multiple forms of communication including client relations. (CCSF, 2005)

Capacity to bring culture to the center of the learning experience, to teach multiple forms of communication, and to facilitate learning experiences from a position of critical pedagogy varies greatly among the faculty in this department. Since this is a vocational program the teaching faculty are not required to have completed graduate education, although some have. The design faculty largely carries the same blind spots as the discipline in which they were trained, visual communication. As a whole, the graphic communication faculty span a wide range of experiences and interests that they bring to their teaching practices—which provides diversity of a different kind.

The mission of the CCSF Department of Graphic Communication is to provide entry-level job skills for individuals desiring to enter the design, production art and print production professions, provide additional technical training and skills upgrades for individuals currently employed in graphic communications industries, provide a two-year foundation in graphic design for individuals desiring to transfer into a four-year university design program, provide job skills for re-entry students, design and produce informational and promotional materials for the college community. (CCSF, 2005b)

My design of the Visual Literacy class used in this study was intended to fulfill this vision statement.

To meet its mission goals, the department offers credit and noncredit classes, leading to a variety of options for the completion of a program, including a production art certificate, press and finishing certificate, digital printing and publishing certificate, A.A. degree in graphic design, and an A.S. degree in print production. The classes are designed to be taken in sequence and it is possible to graduate within two years. The department also provides a variety of opportunities for students to engage in their communities with community projects, service learning opportunities, internships and work experience, peer mentoring programs, and access to professional organizations—all organized by faculty.

During the last few years I have observed a shift in the typical Graphic Communication student from day students to working students who have a need for evening and weekend classes and online options. Working students have many other obligations to take care of, such as family and multiple jobs. It is therefore sometimes difficult for them to manage both life and school, and a large portion might drop out early. This is especially true in the online forum, which students often enter with false expectations that online classes will be less work than face-to-face classes. More often than not, they experience the opposite, especially when taking their first online class (due to the steep learning curve involved for students who are new to the virtual experience).

The Visual Literacy Online Hybrid Class

This class in particular was chosen for this research project because both the content of the Visual Literacy Online Hybrid (GRPH 21) class and the fact that the class is populated by a highly diverse group of students made this context ecologically and conceptually appropriate for this inquiry. Offered through the Graphic Communication Department, Visual Literacy fulfills general education requirements as well as satisfies a prerequisite for further study in the department. There are no prerequisites for this class, and the open enrollment policy attracts a wide range of levels of student skills, college preparedness, professional experience, enthusiasm, and availability to accomplish the coursework. Attrition rates have been high for this class traditionally, as students enrolling in this entry-level survey are often either still shopping around to find their passions or are not quite ready for college work (when they first enter college, re-enter academic rigor, or have to attend to other pressing needs in their lives).

As with all classes at CCSF, the students in this class were highly diverse, with several individuals carrying multiple cultural frames. While such a diverse population provides a rich fabric of intercultural experiences, I have observed that this type of environment can also raise levels of anxiety for participants as they need to learn to appreciate each others' gifts and adjust to a variety of ways of participating and communicating. This need represents an enlightening and welcomed experience for many students, while it is also a source of frustration for some. We experienced some of both in this class.

Students worked mostly online and met physically on 11 Saturdays throughout the 16-week semester. Based on my experience teaching this class since 2003, it is vital to focus on team-building in order to retain students in an online learning environment. Therefore, during the first month I tend to focus on team-building through the tasks, after which time we focus on the tasks while continuing to nurture team effectiveness and relationship-building within the teams (online as well as during face-to-face meetings). This focus on team-building requires my leadership and frequent presence online. Paid design peer mentors serve as role models both in the online discussions and in the face-to-face meetings.

Of the 36 students officially enrolled in this class prior to the beginning of the semester, 19 attended the first day of class and 12 were still enrolled during data collection. While this rate of attrition may seem high, it is within the norm for this type of class at this urban community college.

Possible reasons for dropping the class include life circumstances, levels of college preparedness, ability, and comfort level with the online learning environment.

Ten students participated in the research project—one student chose not to participate in the research aspect of the class, and another student was absent on data collection day. In general, the 10 participants were enthusiastic about their learning experience and serious about their work. They were diverse in regard to culture, demographics, age, gender, and professional and academic background. Most worked a full-time job and had already earned a college degree.

Team Development

The participants had undergone significant team development over the 11 weeks of class prior to data collection, moving through the team development stages of orientation and established purpose, team identity, and membership. A certain level of trust had been established through collaboration on weekly tasks. Team goals and commitment had been under weekly investigation through their management of the assigned tasks and self-assignment of roles. Moderators led the teams through the week, and students took turns as moderator throughout the semester. The teams had developed and were, for the most part, accustomed to clear processes, goal alignment, and disciplined execution of their assignments. In general, students were supportive of each other in this class, and each team pulled through as much as possible with the resources available.

Although team composition shifted around during the first half of the semester, approximately two weeks before data collection day the class settled into a configuration that was maintained on data collection day and for the rest of the semester. Virtual team-building activities had been conducted throughout the semester. By data collection day, participants had become familiar with each other, worked successfully in teams through weekly tasks, been exposed to mind mapping processes, and created visual maps for their collaborative midterm exam. It was appropriate and useful to leave participants in their accustomed teams on data collection day in order to provide an opportunity to further deepen their team-building efforts.

Participation

Class participation depended on personal and cultural styles, levels of enthusiasm, and priorities placed on the class and on teamwork. Online class participation scores were automatically consolidated within WebCT, the online learning environment used at CCSF at the time (see Appendix B for participation figures). Most students only participated in their own team forum. I participated in all forums, and the peer mentors were each focused on one team to provide maximum support.

My classes have had a comparatively high total number of postings compared to some other online CCSF classes. This class posted a total of 2,739 times and some of my classes have posted more than 6,500 times with a record of 10,000 postings in one semester (that class had twice as many students as this one). This high volume is due to the vigorous teamwork interaction facilitated in my online classes but not controlled by me. At some point in the first half of the semester, interaction in the teams becomes self-generated and organic.

Class Content

Class content in the first eight weeks focused on practical activities: learning how to draw and becoming familiar with design principles and elements via reading, discussing, and completing formal design exercises. In the second half of the semester, the focus was on analytical activities: critiquing, evaluating, and improving existing work. Students analyzed and discussed content, form, design concepts, principles and elements in design, audience, messages, and quality of work (see Appendix C for the syllabus and other course information).

Discussions about cognition, perception, and the processing of information in different cultures were always central to the coursework. Since culture-specific information is not readily available in the design world, we used each others' references and brought each others' lived cultural experiences into the learning environment. This not only validated the importance of each student and their willingness to share what they were experiencing, seeing, and valuing, but also expanded the class content in ways that were lively, inviting, and personally meaningful to students.

This research project was conducted during the midterm interlude between the practical activities of the first half of the semester and the analytical activities of the second half. During the interlude, students usually engage in a variety of creative group processes that introduce them to brainstorming and problem-solving techniques and allow them to activate the group mind during different kinds of activities. This process also provides opportunities to literally see the differences in each others' ways of processing, managing, and sharing information. This research project engaged participants in group processes that were typical of the midterm interlude.

Students in this class had also become familiar with navigating and nurturing a virtual professional community space, engaging in virtual team-building across cultures, collaborating on tasks with well defined outcomes and tight deadlines, and observing how classmates structured information. Teams worked on weekly tasks with a weekly group submission, and moderators lead the teams through the week. Students took turns as moderator throughout the semester—some accepted the role willingly and with enthusiasm, while others shied away from the responsibility. Three peer mentors supported the class by cofacilitating face-to-face activities, working with students online and individually, and modeling graphic recording during class. Face-to-face meetings happened in a highly interactive manner with learning activities often disguised as game structures and many opportunities to observe different cultural and communication styles.

Due to the highly diverse population at CCSF, the class content, and the fact that the students I worked with were interested in both visual communication and intercultural communication as well as were creatively engaged, this scenario was an ideal ecology for the research questions I wanted to address.

Convergent Research Focus

My visual literacy class with a focus on visual communication at CCSF with its polycultural population provided an ecologically valid setting to investigate the questions raised by the CPWR event. In the class, visual communication and intercultural communication converged organically and the questions I had uncovered about the cocreation of meaning in highly diverse groups could be addressed through lived experience. In addition, the class provided an ideal context for observing different cultures interacting and for studying the dynamics of group creativity.

The research space was further defined as a result of the literature review, through which the roots of the problem were identified for each field. Visual communication theories and practices are focused on objective reality, and several culturally significant factors are overlooked through the assumption that visual communication can be defined and practiced universally. Intercultural communication theory and practices focus on the subjective experience of individuals, from which inferences are made into the collective realm. Objective reality is then constructed through assessment scores that are collected and processed in limiting ways, while areas that could describe objective reality better (e.g., artifacts) for this discipline are ignored as viable variables constructing the whole.

These blind spots affect both disciplines internally. Visual communication as a field assumes a universalist position (translating into the viewpoint of the dominant culture) in regard to audience. Intercultural communication as a field makes assumptions that flatten the human experience by assuming the validity of measuring cultural dimensions as fixed points and by predicting behavior from the study of individuals in isolation. The effects of these blind spots external to the disciplines are excavated in a project like this one, where the two disciplines could complement each other but are highlighting two different halves of the problem (subjective/objective) and thus generate incomplete if not incorrect conclusions.

This inquiry began from the basic research question: How is meaning cocreated by small groups in a polycultural environment via interactive graphic facilitation and collaborative visual mapping? Based on the background and context discussed above, the main research question for this inquiry can be specifically defined as:

> How do two polycultural groups of five students each enrolled in a beginning college-level visual literacy class coconstruct meaning when given the task of collaborating on telling a story and representing it visually by assembling a visual map of their own choosing?

The following four subquestions can then be identified as part of this main research question.

1. What can be noticed or learned about the group dynamics of these two polycultural groups engaged in group creativity?

2. How will culture be represented visually in the products of these 10 participants?

3. If instruments developed by intercultural communication experts are used to account for cultural factors, is it possible to tease out the cultural variables? Do the participants act in alignment with the cultural values and worldview orientations identified by the instruments?

4. How is culture evoked in this process? What are participants' conceptions of how the innate (nature) and the cultural (nurture) are at play during such an event?

CHAPTER 6

RESEARCH METHODOLOGY

This research was a case study exploring, in depth, the event of culturally diverse participants cocreating a story and representing it visually. In particular, two diverse groups of students in a basic design class in the polycultural environment of CCSF collaborated on telling a story addressing a familiar issue and representing it on a large-scale graphic panel with the elements of visual language (images, words, shapes) and via interactive graphic facilitation and collaborative visual mapping. This event was a typical class activity scheduled at this time in the semester, namely creative processes for designers. Groups received minimal instructions and largely self-organized the activity, worked consecutively, and came back together for a gallery walk and a class debrief, which ended the research activities on data collection day. Thus the project described a particular moment of collaborative meaning-making in a community college class that was bound in time, location, choice of participants, and context, was therefore framed and conducted as a qualitative case study. In such a moment, the participants' world was socially constructed as a series of experiences and interactions, leading to a research study that was largely interpretative, richly descriptive, and inductive in nature.

Pilot Study

I first conducted a pilot study asking a similar research question about the meaning-making process of international individuals (rather than groups), with the intent of refining the methodology for this dissertation project. Analysis showed that the confounding variables made it difficult to define cultural patterns, and the results of the pilot study informed a different design for this research that was more expansive and included a variety of data sources. The pilot study was conducted at the Summer Institute of Intercultural Communication at Pacific University in Forest Grove, Oregon, from July 24, 2005 through August 1, 2005. This well-attended series of workshops brings together an international community of scholars and practitioners to learn from each other and exchange their professional experiences. As a global community they share the belief that "education and training in the areas of intercultural communication can improve competence in dealing with cultural difference and thereby minimize destructive conflict among national, ethnic and other cultural groups" (Intercultural Communication Institute, 2008).

For the study, 18 participants from various cultures, of different ages, genders, and sexual orientations, were asked to visually represent five items/concepts on sheets of paper. I was interested in investigating the differences in the visual representations and whether any culture-specific patterns would appear. The five items/concepts were: family, love, school, procedure, and highlights in one's life. (See Appendix D for images from the data set as well as the participant instruction and consent packet.) Unfortunately, due to the many confounding variables it was impossible to draw any conclusions in regard to cultural preferences.

While participants did not express any feelings of discomfort or frustration, several hindering factors were observed. Participants might have felt embarrassed by being asked to draw in my presence and thus might have been more inhibited, which would have distorted the authenticity of the data. Participants might have exposed their personal preferences rather than their cultural conditioning due to the difficulty of separating the innate (nature) from the cultural (nurture) in such an observation. Participants worked individually and the data demonstrated a focus on personal information that turned out to be difficult to identify as an indicator for cultural preferences. Participants' varying drawing skills may have distorted the data—for instance, I interpreted a particular spatial arrangement as a preference when it was actually the inability to draw perspective that caused the participant to arrange elements on the page in a particular way. In addition, the five elements of the research may not have been connected enough to the participants to fully engage with the task.

These hindering factors identified through the pilot study were addressed in the design of this study by: including a variety of data collection methods and instruments that assisted with clarifying some of the confounding variables, asking participants to work in groups rather than by themselves, reducing the amount of focus on personal issues by asking for a story instead of personal feedback about particular concepts, and reducing the potential for feelings of embarrassment by providing prepared objects and visuals for the participants rather than relying on participants' own drawing abilities.

Research Design

The chosen environment for this study (a diverse CCSF Visual Literacy class) and the research design were intended to largely replicate the environment of the CPWR event that inspired this research. The timeframe chosen for this case study was one particular learning unit in the semester with the topic of creative processes for designers, which was chosen because it provided an ecologically valid scenario for addressing the research questions. The process for this observation was designed to provide an open frame for participants to self-organize how they were going to solve the problem. However, from the instructions and the materials provided it was clear that the outcome needed to be a collaboratively created visual map that told a story addressing the topic given.

Participant Selection

Participants were CCSF student volunteers from the basic design class Visual Literacy Online Hybrid (GRPH 21) during the Spring 2007 semester. A few weeks into the semester, I presented my research proposal to the students and invited them to consider participating as part of the class activities. I made it very clear that participation in the research project would have no effect on their grades, and that students would be neither rewarded nor penalized for participation or nonparticipation. There were no exclusion criteria. The class as a whole was very interested and excited to become part of this project. Only one student chose to decline.

Procedure

Much of the data were collected on April 14, 2007 (data collection day), a class day dedicated to the topic of creative processes for designers. A research assistant (Julie Gieseke) was responsible for videography and photography on data collection day, and also assisted with transcribing the videos and with the analysis. I gave the participants all pertinent forms, instruction sheets, and debrief questions in the form of a participant packet (see Appendix E) prior to the administration of the first instrument (a few weeks prior to data collection day), and readdressed the packet on data collection day.

At the start of data collection day, I briefed participants on the events of the day and reminded them of their rights. All participants took the Team Performance Indicator (TPI) (Forrester & Drexler, 2005) individually, and results were not discussed. I then confirmed the two existing teams as *Group A* and *Group 1* for the purposes of data collection day. The two groups worked through the research process in rotation. A second facilitator (faculty member Amy Conger from the CCSF Department of Graphic Communications) led the rest of the class through a variety of other creative processes that were in sync with class objectives for that day; the class was thus not interrupted in its routine and easily met the objectives of the day with or without the research aspect. Providing various activities in addition to the research activities also allowed the one student who opted not to participate in the research project to have alternative learning experiences that were aligned with the content of the class.

At the beginning of each group's process, I gave the group instructions (see Appendix F) for the assigned task, namely coconstructing a story about the CCSF experience. First, participants were to collaborate on the story they wanted to tell and then use prepared materials for constructing a large-scale visual map of their story. I required them to collaborate because I was interested in observing the coconstruction of meaning as modeled in the CPWR process rather than in discovering what individuals would create by themselves. I gave no other instructions, as it was up to the group how they arranged themselves and their processes. Next, the group was introduced to the materials and image set I provided for their use.

Each group was given a total of 40 minutes to complete the process, and I encouraged them to move to the image set 10 minutes into the process to begin creating their visual map. At the end of the mapping activities, we took a lunch break during which snacks were provided.

After lunch, all participants visited both visual maps in the form of a *gallery walk* that included a presentation by each group during which the other group could ask questions. The final activity of data collection day was the *class debrief*—a question and answer session in which all participants debriefed their experiences of the process, guided by a debrief question frame (see Appendix G).

All three phases of data collection day (the process of the cocreation, the gallery walk, and the class debrief) provided transformative learning opportunities for the participants to increasing degrees—which defined this case study also as an intervention (Wagner, 1997). The cocreation activities were designed as an opportunity to gain self-awareness and learn something about the other people in the class through exposure of beliefs and values, and as a teambuilding activity. The gallery walk was intended to facilitate sharing between the two groups regarding their different working and presentation methods. The class debrief frame was selected to bring beliefs and values onto the table and elicit useful discussions around these issues.

Strategically chosen individuals from each group were invited for a *personal interview* (see Appendix H) about the process and their experience in order to fill potential gaps from the class debrief. These interviews were conducted during May and June of 2007. I chose four individuals because they were quieter than others during the class debrief; the other two were directly involved in a critical incident (stereotyping) during the class debrief.

Last, a *member check* was conducted at CCSF on September 15, 2007, during which I presented the preliminary results and findings to all the participants (all 10 attended) and asked them for feedback.

Materials Provided

Providing preselected visual language components streamlined the process and eliminated the possible danger of data distortion due to potential lack of drawing skills. Basic shapes for tracing were provided in the form of toys and interestingly shaped sticky notes. Markers and press-on letters were provided for maximum flexibility when creating words. The *graphic panel* (a 4 ft x

6 ft sheet of white paper) was hung on a wall, and a variety of basic art materials were supplied (pastels, crayons, erasers, tape, and cotton balls).

Images were provided by a VisualsSpeak(tm) image set composed of 200 diverse images of life, nature, people, and things. I provided two identical sets, one for each group. The VisualsSpeak(tm) set was used in this study for engaging participants intuitively, and in order to avoid the need for drawing images (in case drawing was not a strength that individuals brought to the group). As recommended, the time for choosing and grouping images was limited to avoid turning the visual intuitive process into a thought process (VisualsSpeak, 2006).

A single-framing task of "Collaborate on creating a story of the City College experience" introduced the objective of the activity and thus included what participants focused on when choosing images. As recommended, the framing question was precise but open-ended enough to allow for multiple interpretations that are free of assumptions and inherently meaningful for the group (VisualsSpeak, 2006).

Each of the four categories in the set includes three sub-categories:

1. Life (activities, concepts, spirituality);
2. Nature (animals and birds, country, plants);
3. People (adults, children, groups); and
4. Things (cities and structures, household and personal items, tools and machines) (VisualsSpeak, 2006).

VisualsSpeak(tm) is recommended for activities or trainings in the areas of team-building, strategic visioning and goal setting, conflict resolution, career and life coaching, and intercultural communication, and thus was very appropriate for this setting. In this sense, the use of the image set added opportunities for personal and team development and thus enhanced the intervention aspect of the participant experience.

I had previous experience with the VisualsSpeak(tm) set and find it a very useful tool to help groups work intuitively and also effectively share the essence of their communication through the visuals—despite the strong dominant culture bias in image choice and composition. The VisualsSpeak(tm) team is working on creating a variety of sets to focus on and be photographed by various nondominant cultures (Christine Martell, personal communication, December 14, 2006), but their updates were not available at the time of this research.

Tangible Product: Coconstructed Visual Maps

The product of the research activity was one visual map for each group. Visual maps were appropriate and congruent with the course curriculum because students in this class were learning about visual literacy and communication. Specifically, students were studying how visual materials are perceived by an audience and learning to construct visual messages through the use of visual language elements. By the time of data collection, students were familiar with mindmapping strategies, both small- and large-scales, as they had been consolidating reading content into mindmaps and also worked on large-scale group maps together for their midterm exam. Space for the maps was provided on an area on the wall as is customary for graphic recording and graphic facilitation, allowing each participant a good view of the visual product and space to interact with it and with the other participants. Visual maps were coconstructed in the form of interactive graphic facilitation by using the three components of visual language (Horn, 1998): images, shapes, and words.

Data Sources and Instruments

The primary sources of data were collected through observing each group's process as well as the class debrief. Primary data sources including the visual maps were videotaped, transcribed, and thoroughly analyzed. Secondary sources of data were comprised of formally and informally administered instruments (to provide background information on the individual participants), personal interviews (to validate the initial findings), and a member check in which preliminary results were presented to the entire group of participants for feedback. Table 3 provides a complete list of data sources, processing tool, and analysis tools.

The formally administered instruments informed different aspects of the study and were intended to contribute to the thick profiles for each participant with the goal of accounting for the confounding variables. Participants' perceived stage of team development was measured via the TPI. It is useful to identify one's repertoire for various communication styles (Peterson, 2004), as well as one's positions on the scales of basic cultural dimensions and orientations (Hofstede, 2001; Trompenaars & Hampden-Turner, 1998; Peterson, 2004). Accordingly, cultural profiles of the participants were constructed through the Intercultural Developmental Inventory, version 2 (IDI-2) (Bennett & Hammer, 2002) and the PCSI. The PCSI indicates cultural styles, and the IDI-2 provides information about individuals' capacity for and development of intercultural sensitivity (the "capability to shift cultural perspective and adapt behavior to cultural context," M. Hammer, personal communication, April 6, 2008).

Table 3

Data Sources, Processing Tool, and Analysis Tools

Description	Organization of participants
Primary data sources	
Group process[a]	
Group profile	Group A, Group 1
Group analysis	
Episodes	Group A, Group 1
Gallery walk[b]	Group A, Group 1
Visu2al map	Group A, Group 1
Class debrief[a]	Entire class
Visual map	Group A, Group 1
Secondary data sources	
Participant profiles	Individual
Formally administered[c]	
Intercultural Developmental Inventory, version 2	Individual
Forrester/Drexler Team Performance Indicator	Individual
Peterson Cultural Style Indicator(tm)	Individual
Informally administered	
Kolb Learning Styles	Individual
Gardner's Multiple Intelligences	Individual
Personal interviews[d]	Individual
Member check[e]	Entire class
Processing tool	
VisualsSpeak(tm) image set	—
Analysis tools	
Coordinated Management of Meaning (CMM) concepts Coordination; Management of meaning; (coherence and mystery); Deontic logic	Individual, Group A, Group 1, entire class
CMM stories Lived, Unknown stories, Untold stories, Unheard stories, stories Told, and storyTelling (LUUUTT) Model	Group A, Group 1
CMM Serpentine model	Group A, Group 1

[a]Videotaped and transcribed. [b]Presentation of the group's visual map. [c]Taken at different times. [d]Six of the ten participants were interviewed separately; interviews were audiotaped and transcribed. [e]Group meeting after the first phase of data analysis.

In training or educational situations, and in order to begin a conversation about cultural dimensions/development and team performance, it is useful to create profiles for individuals and the relevant cluster of participants working together. Both individual and group profiles were completed for this study and provided some interesting insights. However, it must be acknowledged that all the instruments available for this type of assessment measure individuals' specifics in isolation and not in interaction with others—which was the nature of this entire event. Vis-à-vis the lack of alternatives, the instruments were used and critiqued regarding this missing aspect.

The Intercultural Developmental Inventory, Version 2 (IDI-2)

I selected the IDI-2 (Bennett & Hammer, 2002) as the best means of investigating participants' stages of development of intercultural sensitivity, since the study involved a diverse group of participants collaborating with each other and since version 2 aligned with the DMIS closely. Originally based on the DMIS, the IDI-2 captures the individual's experience vis à vis cultural difference within the range of ethnocentricity and ethnorelativity. The IDI-2 (and the new version 3, Hammer, in press) uses 50 questions/statements on a Likert scale of 1 to 5, and scores are intended to provide insights into what significance cultural difference plays during interaction with people from cultural groups other than one's own (Hammer & Bennett, 2001). There are several articles and book chapters to choose from (Bennett, 1986a, 1993, 2003, 2004; Hammer et al., 2003; Bennett & Hammer, 2002, Hammer & Bennett, 2001) in order to fully understand what the model and the tool are designed to accomplish. Currently, some aspects of the IDI-2 are being revised, and version 3 is described as assessing "how individuals and groups construe their social interactions with people from different cultural communities" (Hammer, in press, p. 253). Hammer indicates that—unlike the IDI and IDI-2—the IDI-3 is not a measurement of the DMIS (or the integration stage), but an indicator for intercultural competence (Hammer, in press).

I formally administered the IDI-2 (the latest version available at the time) on March 17, 2007 (prior to data collection day), to collect background information, and the results were not disclosed to or discussed with the groups or individual participants. (As is customary for a certified IDI administrator, a personal information session is required if and when a participant requests information about their results.) In the analysis, the qualitative information obtained from the observed behavior and comments made by participants during the group interaction were compared with the quantitative data obtained from the IDI-2 scores.

It is important to note that, contrary to previous versions and previous ways of encouraging the usage of the IDI, Hammer (codeveloper of the IDI and IDI-2, and sole owner of the IDI-3) disqualifies the IDI, in general, from measuring the stage of integration, identity construction, or even positions on the DMIS (Hammer, in press). However, I considered the observed behavior and comments made during the class debrief as qualitative information and compared that qualitative data with the quantitative IDI-2 scores as indicators for the DMIS stages participants occupied, in order to learn something about participants' capacity for intercultural competence during group interaction in the midst of cultural differences. As Hammer himself has suggested,

> The IDI can be used to assess a group's capability to deal with cultural differences. When used in this way, the IDI becomes a blueprint of the group's overall capabilities and can help identify the struggles the group will likely encounter as they attempt to work together to accomplish tasks that involve bridging across cultural difference. (p. 255)

To do complete justice to what the IDI-2 actually measures it would have been necessary to conduct a personal interview with each participant relating to their experience of cultural difference; I did not take that step because I was mainly interested in group communication patterns during interactions, and not in researching the instrument itself.

The Team Performance Indicator (TPI)

The Drexler/Sibbet (2004) Team Performance Model (TPM) (see Appendix I) and its accompanying performance-based diagnostic instrument, the TPI (Forrester & Drexler, 2005) were chosen for this project because they provided a unique opportunity to put the visual world in contact with group dynamics in action. The TPI asks team members to evaluate how the team is meeting the challenges of the fundamental issues that each team faces in the process of team development. The data relates only to on-the-job performance and allows team members to measure team performance across the seven dimensions. The TPI is a 21-item instrument in the agree–disagree format with seven 10-item scales. It represents a range of typical behaviors exposed during certain stages of team development. It also assesses leader performance and the level of interdependence the team needs in order to succeed (The Grove, 2003).

The TPI was developed for the corporate world and thus follows the protocol of the dominant culture (often male-dominated), which translates into a format that, stereotypically, could be described as linear, focused, results-driven, and forward-looking. Validity or reliability information is not available for the TPI as used in academia and U.S. corporate culture (R. Forrester & E. Claassen, personal communication, December 1, 2006), much less across cultures. However, as far as I know there are no alternatives available to this unique work that is visually based, and the tools seem to work very well in the world for which they were crafted. Because of its correlation to graphic facilitation, I included the TPI in my secondary data sources. The TPI was administered on data collection day before the group process.

The Peterson Cultural Style Indicator(tm) (PCSI)

Peterson (2004) developed the PCSI in an effort to provide a profile for an individual's cultural styles, in a language that can be understood by a general audience. The PCSI measures cultural differences on five dimensions. *Equality versus hierarchy* measures whether social structures are built on equality or are hierarchical, and determines distribution of tasks and responsibilities. *Direct versus indirect communication style* measures whether people communicate in a direct or indirect manner during face-to-face verbal and nonverbal interactions. *Individual-versus group-orientation* measures depth of affiliations to groups, flexibility of moving in and out of groups, and loyalty to group(s), as well as whether one defines oneself as independent or belonging to a group/family. *Task- versus relationship-orientation* measures whether relationship-building and trust take priority, or whether tasks/business are more important. *Risk versus caution* measures whether people are comfortable with change and risk-taking, or prefer to plan and weigh their options before acting (Peterson, 2004). This instrument is based on national cultures; however, it is not the result of empirical research but rather of a broad but thorough literature review and the author's interpretation thereof to arrive at the national scores.

The PCSI uses 25 questions on a Likert scale of 0 to 10, and is intended to be a simple and clear tool that can be used easily and quickly in basic crosscultural and intercultural training, even without an administrator. The PCSI focuses on demonstrating participants' profiles in comparison to other cultural maps from various different nationalities, and provides results in the form of one point on a bipolar continuum for each of five cultural dimensions. The PCSI has an accompanying book (Peterson, 2004) written by the developer on cultural intelligence that amplifies the value of the tool. In addition, Peterson provides information about validity and reliability on his website (Across Cultures, 2007b).

As Peterson himself describes, the scores for different nations are a professional estimation made by him based on a thorough literature review. The results as a one-point position for each cultural dimension indicate that cultures live on bipolar continua (an individual or a culture falls either more on the left or more on the right of each continuum) (Across Cultures, 2007b). Peterson confirmed that a range of experiences described on a continuum is more authentic in his experience, too, and that is how he would portray it to a client rather than giving one particular point, which is the limitation of the measuring system (Likert scale) used on the PCSI (B. Peterson, personal communication, December 27, 2007). However, the fact remains that the result is one-dimensional and points to a concrete spot in a range of possibilities, as well as forces the individual to make very concrete choices on the questionnaire.

All in all, the PCSI scales and results are a useful way to open a discussion about cultural styles in an educational or training situation, and also give participants a language to use when expressing their own feelings or reporting their observations. I chose to use the instrument in spite of its limitations—bipolar dimensions assessed on a Likert scale—and the problematic underlying assumption that one can answer the questions in a clear or definite way. The PCSI was taken online by each participant independently during the week following data collection day, and the results were then discussed during the class meeting on May 5, 2007.

Kolb Learning Styles (LS) and Gardner Multiple Intelligences (MI)

Both the LS and the MI instruments were self-administered by participants as part of the class events during the second half of the semester. This is a regular occurrence in my classes, and I always use the informal tools (see Appendices J and K) due to the cost involved in using the formal instruments themselves. It is my experience that people find this kind of information about themselves fascinating and are willing to engage in this discussion.

Learning styles and various intelligences as defined by Kolb and Gardner encompass both innate and cultural preferences. Since I teach design, this material also relates to audience studies and is therefore of interest to the students for that reason. I prefer to have this discussion after midterm as by that point participants have had a chance to get to know each other and thus can give feedback about someone's profile. This way, participants have three anchor points to draw a picture of themselves: their own perception, the feedback from other people they have worked with, and the scores themselves.

I used these tools to collect more background data about the participants to help illuminate some of their innate and cultural preferences. The results served as background information for the study and as an opportunity to further discuss innate and cultural preferences with the class.

Data Analysis

To begin the data analysis, I first built a foundation of participant profiles by consolidating the personal information and the scores from the instruments in diagrammatic form onto a personal information sheet for each participant that allowed me to see their entire profile at a glance. I also created group score diagrams for each instrument to surface patterns in the group compositions.

Transcripts (of which I had 293 pages) exist in linear language format and I first attempted to perform open coding on them to find themes by color coding repetitive instances. Then I looked for themes that the instruments suggested, such as the different poles for the PCSI continua, the stages for the IDI-2 and the TPI, and issues of group dynamics, leadership, and intercultural communication themes. This linear coding activity led to a very colorful pattern that my mind processed as texture rather than a meaningful dissecting of the data.

The frustration of working linearly through the transcripts led me to follow my personal preference for processing information intuitively through all my senses by watching the videos and mapping the events visually, rather than sequentially following a linear order. I watched the video of the event without taking notes, and sensed the significant moments instead of marking them on my transcripts. Then I watched them many times over, together with my research assistant, backwards and forwards, until we had a clear idea where to break the event into smaller parts, which I called *episodes*. An episode is defined here as a series of communication acts that are grouped together thematically—a unit in the narrative structure. The duration of an episode was chosen based on natural breaks in the process of dialogue such as a change in the setting signified by the group moving to a different task or changing direction or mood within a task. An episode ended when a conclusion could be defined. Thus, episodes had different lengths and each group's process was not divided into the same kind or number of episodes.

Graphic facilitation techniques were applied for defining the exact sequence of these communication acts and to mark significant moments on large graphic panels on the wall and in diagrammatic format (see Figures 9 and 10 for samples). From these graphic records it was then easy to begin describing each episode in its entirety and drawing significant observations for each. Through this process, I experienced the power of diagrams as a superior means of synthesizing information (Horn, 1998), as the key findings were illuminated through diagramming rather than linear processing of the transcripts.

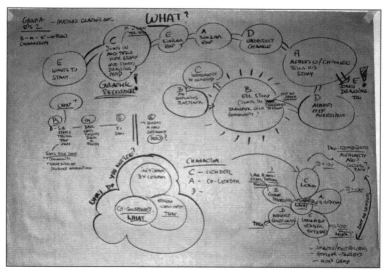

Figure 9. Sample graphic panel from data analysis, Group A episode 2. Author's image.

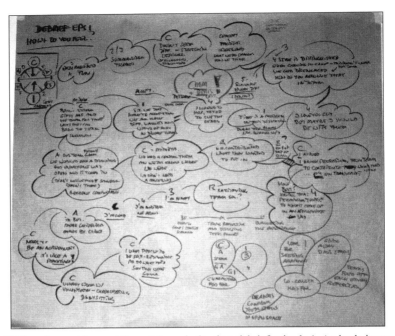

Figure 10. Sample graphic panel from data analysis, class debrief episode 1. Author's image.

Using this method, I thoroughly reported on all the episodes for the entire event (including each group's process, the gallery walk, and the class debrief). Benefits of the visual mapping activity included being able to see the relationships between the elements and the communication patterns. In addition, I listed significant observations for all the episodes, each group's process, and the groups in comparison, and investigated the visual maps for syntax and semantics using the principles and elements of design.

After this phase of the data analysis, I performed a member check to collect feedback from the groups directly, to which all participants were invited. The member check was an informal meeting in order to double-check my first impressions and interpretations of the data. Having collected information about context, participants, and events, and solicited feedback from the participants, I was ready to report on the results and consequently move to the findings.

This study generated a thick case of multiple forms of data that were folded into several layers (institution, class, groups, individual participants, event, and products) most of which were then further subdivided. The primary data sources (group process, visual map, gallery walk, and class debrief) provided the main data, which was framed by the class profile (average class scores obtained from the instruments) and group profiles (demographic data, instrument results, and participation figures for the participants in the group).

Each videotaped group process (groups in group dialogue, working on their map, in the gallery walk, and during the class debrief) was divided into sequential episodes similar to storytelling frames. Each episode was given a title and introduced by listing the main characters and a short description of the scene. Descriptions of significant observations analyzing the specifics of the episode are supported with participants' own statements. The gallery walk and the class debrief were intended to expose some of the subjective reality as perceived and shared by participants in a facilitated process (see class debrief questions, Appendix G).

In general the primary data concerned the research space of cocreation and group interaction, which were the main focus areas of this study, while much of the secondary data provided background information about the individual participants and groups and was therefore only pulled into the equation when needed. Secondary sources (formally and informally administered instruments, personal interviews, and the member check) were used for clarifying variables and potential gaps. Secondary sources reflected participants' subjective reality into the objective realm; the resulting data were then mixed with my interpretation (professional opinions) of the scores and thus also my biases. Overall, primary and secondary data sources integrated both subjective and objective approaches as suggested by Gudykunst et al. (2005) in order to understand the intercultural event of this study more fully.

In addition to the methods described above, I also used the VisualsSpeak(tm) processing tool and several CMM analysis tools that complemented the generation and analysis of the visual maps and further clarified some aspects of the event. When analyzing the visual maps themselves, I counted the VisualsSpeak(tm) images chosen from each category and also consulted Christine Martell, the developer of the set, for her feedback concerning the VisualsSpeak(tm) elements in the maps.

I applied two CMM analysis tools (the Serpentine model and the LUUUTT model) and two CMM frameworks (deontic logic and the key concepts for mastering CMM: coordination; and the management of meaning—coherence and mystery) in the data analysis. CMM provides flexible tools that can be combined with other forms of analysis. Its power as an analysis tool lies in its diagrammatic form, which allows for meaning to emerge that may not make itself known in other, more linear methods. In this diagrammatic form, CMM is additionally aligned with the rest of the study. Therefore, CMM bridged intercultural communication and visual communication by functioning as a theory and process simultaneously that exposed the study's dynamic play on several levels, conceptually, visually, and relationally.

Theoretically, the entire event could have been underpinned by CMM theory and analyzed through CMM processes via the full array of CMM tools, and it would have been a complete analysis that would have uncovered the deeper structures of the communication acts. As a transdisciplinarian, however, I wanted to look at the event from various different angles, and used a mixture of methods and tools to look at the matter through different lenses. Therefore I only chose four of CMM's tools and frameworks that filled a space not covered by the other methods.

CMM Serpentine model diagrams were created to sequence each group's map construction process. The Serpentine model is a time series diagram that maps the pattern of reciprocal processes of act and interpretation, which results in another act (oughtness), and continues in a serpentine pattern until the episode is over and or shifts into another episode. Through the CMM Serpentine model diagrams, the leading elements that built the groups' visual maps could be made apparent and then could be compared. This model had the potential to surface the different strategies each group utilized in sequencing the elements and confirm the underlying assumptions that constructed the communication patterns displayed by the groups.

The LUUUTT model is designed to surface the untold, unheard, or unknown stories—components of the interaction that may otherwise go unnoticed. The LUUUTT also considers how future experiences and observations might change the story though they cannot be known at the time, and provides a place on the diagram for that future context as a framing element. The LUUUTT can be applied as a form of intervention if used and discussed with a group. Or, this model can help an educator or researcher to recognize their own bias in terms of what they delete from the whole story. The LUUUTT highlights to the knower all the things she doesn't know and calls for the invisible to be seen.

While the Serpentine model is a linear sequencing of events that can also demonstrate cause and effect, the LUUUTT model builds from the inside out. The told and lived stories are depicted in the center, circumscribed by the mystery of untold, unheard, and unknown stories, which are believed to be part of the whole. Both models attempt to uncover further the dynamics involved.

CMM's two key concepts of (a) coordination and (b) the management of meaning—coherence and mystery, were also used to scan the entire event for moments of highly functional patterns of communication acts. A few epiphanies could be highlighted by analyzing them through these key concepts. In addition, deontic logic was used as a framework to investigate each group and uncover the group's expectations. Deontic logic was helpful in noticing how group expectations were confirmed throughout and/or shifted the groups at times.

When I finished this traditional data analysis, I was able to answer the research questions on a surface level. In the spirit of transdisciplinary inquiry, however, peeling away the first layers brought up more questions, which then motivated me to compost the data again and continue my inquiry, as described in the Epilogue.

Limitations

This case study was limited to volunteer participants in my visual literacy class at CCSF during the Spring 2007 semester. The scope of the research was thus limited to 10 participants in this particular context within an urban higher education institution that is largely composed of a diverse west coast population. The small sample size limits the generalizeability of the findings.

Since this study was of a qualitative and interpretive nature, there was no intention to compare the results to any quantitative approach.

It is important to note that the models and instruments used in this study are from the dominant culture, and thus inherently may reflect a Western (male) bias. The models and instruments were also limited in that they are based on bipolar cultural dimensions that produce static patterns and positionality, and were developed through studying cultures in isolation. These limitations must be kept in mind when interpreting the data and findings.

Another limiting factor was the initial intent to look mainly through a traditional cultural lens, which was my bias as an interculturalist (see Appendix L for a more complete discussion of my personal biases).

Because my focus was on interaction patterns, all methods used to collect and analyze data fulfilled their main purpose in defining significant points in the research space that helped to map the territory, clarify confounding variables, and provide various viewpoints from which different aspects of the coconstruction of meaning could be observed and contextualized. For instance, it was not my intent to create complete case studies of the individual participants, but rather to use the scores obtained from the inventories to further clarify certain behaviors or reactions in an attempt to tease out the cultural. Thus, no assessments were undertaken to expose personality or motivational sensitivities, which I did not consider as culturally significant at the time I designed the study. It was also not my intent to test any of the instruments for their validity or practicality although some limitations were discovered in the analyses and are commented upon. A study intending to produce a manual for educators, facilitators, visual practitioners, or intercultural communication specialists would have taken a different approach.

Validity

With regard to the discipline of visual communication, validity was enhanced through the selection of processing tools such as VisualsSpeak (TM), the consulting of other experts in visual facilitation (e.g., Christine Martell), and the application of multiple analysis methods for the visual products and process of creation (a visual record via videography and photography, the CMM Serpentine model for sequencing, map analysis in accordance with standard critiquing techniques for design principles and elements, and art therapy for another form of interpretation).

With regard to the discipline of intercultural communication, validity was enhanced through the selection of a variety of instruments and tools (the IDI-2, PCSI, LS, MI, CMM LUUUTT model, and CMM Coordination of Meaning concepts), and through the collection of a thick record for the individual participants and the group interaction (personal interviews, class debrief, member check, videography of event, and transcripts) to investigate each category and approach defined by Gudykunst et al. (2005).

This inquiry took the objectivist approach to intercultural communication research through observation and documentation of the event in the space of shared reality, assuming that the communication acts emerged from the context and could be further clarified through delivery of an explanation for cause and effect. This explanation was delivered through (a) comparing personal actions to scores on various instruments (the IDI-2, TPI, PCSI, LS, and MI), (b) investigating actions contextually to each other, (c) investigating each group's products for significance in pattern, (d) focusing on group dynamics, (e) using the CMM processing tool of the Serpentine model for sequencing acts, and (f) using the CMM processing tool of the LUUUTT model for including excluded stories, (g) using CMM's key concepts to identify moments of mastering the coordination and management of meaning, (h) using the CMM concept of deontic logic to uncover intergroup basic assumptions, (i) applying the four-quadrant viewfinder, and (j) making predictions about human behavior.

The subjectivist approach to intercultural communication research was pursued through the collection of information from the personal viewpoints of participants (e.g., the class debrief, member check, and personal interviews) and by applying the lenses of the upper left and lower left quadrants of the four-quadrant viewfinder. In addition, the application of the four-quadrant viewfinder in both approaches lent the opportunity to integrate the two.

Constructivist theories were represented through CMM theory (Pierce, 2005) and some of its processing tools, DMIS theory (Bennett, 1986a, 1993, 2004), and the IDI-2 (Bennett & Hammer, 2002). Theories of cultural difference were represented by consideration of a number of theories of cultural dimensions (Hofstede, 2001; Trompenaars & Hampden Turner, 1998; House et al., 2004; Peterson, 2004). Additional second category theories and tools include the PCSI, theories of variances in meaning-making (learning) as outlined by Kolb (1984) and Gardner (1999), the LS and MI, and the VisualsSpeak(tm) image set. The focus of the study was on observing interaction patterns and relationships between interacting participants amongst themselves and the group mind, and thus occupied the third category—communication patterns and communication networks. In addition, AQAL's quadrant of collective subjective reality (cultural) and the TPM and TPI also fall into the third category.

The frame of the four aspects of communication applied to both disciplines and to the viewfinder and provided greater assurance that multiple viewpoints were included in the investigation. Addressing all four aspects simultaneously integrated objective and subjective realities on both the collective and the individual levels as outlined in AQAL.

Since this transdisciplinary study is also a qualitative study with the assumption that results and findings must include the experience of the participants, the design included opportunities for individual interviews, a class debrief, and a member check, all of which contributed to the many layers of information gathering. The nature of transdisciplinary methods is based on transclusion and assures that various touch points connect to various parts of the participating disciplines, thereby confirming their validity through triangulation.

Ethical Considerations

Ethical considerations were especially important since this study involved not only human participants but students who were in a learning–teaching relationship with me. All possible measures were undertaken to communicate my intensions clearly and to ensure that students felt free to volunteer or decline participation without any positive or negative relation to my evaluation of their performance in class.

This case study fully complied with the regulations and recommendations of the California Institute of Integral Studies Human Research Review Council. Proper forms to satisfy the formal aspects of the council's review were generated, approved, and used as intended. Such permissions were granted by both the California Institute of Integral Studies and the hosting institution, City College of San Francisco (see Appendix M). Procedures were followed as outlined and data has been securely stored and will be properly destroyed within three years.

Research Question Array

Given this methodology, it is now possible to define each specific research question further. The main research question,

How did these two polycultural groups of five students each enrolled in a beginning college-level visual literacy class coconstruct meaning when given the task of collaborating on telling a story and representing it visually by assembling a visual map of their own choosing?

was addressed through the investigation of all the data sources with a focus on interaction. The subquestions were defined as follows.

1. Through investigation of the data sources, what can be noticed or learned about the group dynamics of these two polycultural groups of five participants engaged in group creativity?

2. Through analysis of the visual maps cocreated by these two groups of five participants, what can be learned about how culture is represented visually in the products of these 10 participants?

3. If the PCSI, IDI-2, LS, and MI are used to account for cultural factors, is it possible to tease out the cultural variables? Did the participants act in alignment with the cultural values and worldview orientations identified by the instruments?

4. If the cocreation instructions are designed to elicit participant sharing of values and beliefs and negotiation of such among the group, what can be learned about how culture was evoked in these two particular cocreation processes? Through investigation of the data sources, what can be learned about participants' conceptions of how the innate (nature) and the cultural (nurture) were at play during the event?

CHAPTER 7

RESEARCH EVENT

This chapter presents the results and findings woven into the unraveling of the events on data collection day: Group A's cocreation process, Group 1's cocreation process, the gallery walks, and the class debrief. (This nontraditional presentation of intermingled results and findings is a deliberate strategy to enhance readability.) A short class profile and group profiles help to set the stage for the research event itself. Significant moments relating to the research questions are described and supported with excerpts from the transcripts. While I would have liked to illustrate each point with complete excerpts from direct speech, length concerns required me to limit reported participant speech to those quotes that best illustrate the arguments further elaborated on in the following analysis (Chapter 8). Next, the new insights that arose from the member check (performed several months after data collection day) are added to the fabric of the data. The focus of this study was on the group interaction and cocreation of meaning; therefore, detailed profiles on the individual participants are provided after the significant moments from the group interactions have been fully described.

For the purposes of this chapter, *class* is defined as the 10 students who participated in the research project. Aliases were chosen by participants to protect their anonymity. Group A's aliases begin with the letters A–E: Aiden, Bella, Caroline, Dianne, and Eugene. Group 1's aliases begin with the letters M–R: Michelle, Nick, Olive, Paige, and Rusena. To conserve space in the figures, two-letter codes are used beginning with P (for participant). To create a simple visual distinction between the groups' codes, Group A's codes are the letters PA (Aiden), PB (Bella), PC (Carolina), PD (Dianne), and PE (Eugene), while Group 1's codes are the numbers P1 (Michelle), P2 (Nick), P3 (Olive), P4 (Paige), and P5 (Rusena). Each figure lists the names and codes used in the figure caption, for easy reference.

Occasionally I needed to refer to a participant's background in order to further qualify my comments. As part of the demographic profiles, I asked the participants to self-identify their ethnic background, cultural identity, and nationality, and they responded with a rich plurality of identifications. To create short parenthetical references for each participant's background, I chose from this colorful palette, attempting to match each participant's most often and most consistently demonstrated identity. Because my interpretation of their behavior was the determining factor in this choice I did not change their own words in order to keep some aspect of their authenticity intact. This decision resulted in references to participants' backgrounds that do not match in categorical indexing but are consistent throughout. These parenthetical designations, indicated on the demographic table for each group, are not intended to represent the complexity of the participant's background and identity, but to call attention to large-scale themes in the interactions.

Conventions for Reported Speech and Writing

Since the focus of this study was on the emerging patterns of group interaction (analog) rather than on the details (digital), a full discourse analysis was deemed unnecessary to investigate the research questions. Only three conventions are used. First, (words in parentheses) are used to give contextual clues or other extra-contextual commentary. Second, [...] (ellipsis in brackets) indicate that a segment of the speaker's utterance has been omitted. Third, when dialogue is quoted sequentially, if a speaker has been skipped to keep the focus on other speakers, the first initial of the missing speaker(s) appears between bracketed ellipsis, as in [...A...] or [...A,B...]. This notation is given at the end of the utterance before the missing turn(s) in the dialogue. I use both my initials [...RR...] to refer to myself, since my first initial is identical to the first initial of one of the participant aliases.

When participants' writing is quoted, as in personal e-mail communications or written feedback forms, "[sic]" is not used to mark each irregularity, since such irregularities are numerous enough that using [sic] would render the passages unreadable. All participant writing is reproduced exactly as written, with all punctuation, spelling, or other language irregularities as originally rendered, to communicate some the characteristics of a highly diverse classroom.

Class Profile

To create a profile of the class as a whole, this section provides an overview of the instrument results for the entire class; complete data tables for the PCSI, TPI, LS, and MI as well as class participation figures are provided in Appendix B. The class as a whole fell right in the middle of minimization on the DMIS (see Figure 11), which would be an expected result in a very diverse group. However, individual participants occupied each stage of development with the exception of integration, with six participants in ethnocentric stages and four in ethnorelative stages. Working with a group of individuals who occupy diverse stages of cultural competence development presents challenges for the facilitator, as this would indicate a wide range of worldview constructions— potentially requiring negotiation.

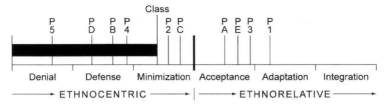

Figure 11. Class average and individual participants' scores on the Intercultural Developmental Inventory, version 2 (IDI-2) with class score determined as Minimization. P5 = Rusena; PD = Dianne; PB = Bella; P4 = Paige; P2 = Nick; PC = Carolina; PA = Aiden; PE = Eugene; P3 = Olive; P1 = Michelle. Author's image.

Comparing the class results on the PCSI to average U.S. scores, participants across the board were uniformly more oriented toward equality than hierarchy, more toward group orientation than individualism, and more toward relationship- than task-orientation (see Figure 12). The class operated more from a direct than indirect communication style; in fact, only a few participants communicated indirectly. More participants were more risk-friendly than cautious. Participants with a more Western lens deviated significantly from the average U.S. scores, indicating that these participants, as a whole, were more relationship-based and more group-oriented than could be expected from a diverse group.

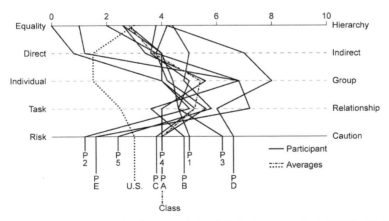

Figure 12. Participant scores on the Peterson Cultural Style Inventory (tm) (PCSI) with U.S. and class averages. P2 = Nick; PE = Eugene; P5 = Rusena; PC = Carolina; P4 = Paige; PA = Aiden; PB = Bella; P1 = Michelle; P3 = Olive; PD = Dianne. Author's image.

The TPI scores demonstrated that the participants did not perceive any significant issues that needed to be resolved in the teams, but scores varied widely within the medium range. Five participants scored high in a few of the areas of team performance, and only one participant gave a low score.

The MI scores were very diverse, and participants' highest three preferences are listed in their personal profiles below. On the LS, eight of the ten participants scored as accommodators, one as a diverger, and one as an assimilator.

Group Process

For each group, this section provides an initial description of the participants and the group, and describes the group behavior during the coconstruction process, class debrief, and member check. Before each group's process description, a group profile is provided that includes demographic data, class participation figures, PCSI scores, and DMIS stages for the group's five participants. Additional explanation is then provided in the text where necessary to understand the events, and full profiles of each participant are provided at the end of this chapter.

I divided the group process into four episodes (introduction, storyline coconstruction, completion of the sketch or image selection, and visual map coconstruction), which are followed by analyses of the visual map and gallery walk. I closely examined each episode's characters (participants in action) and scene, and reported significant observations of the coconstruction of meaning. I used two of the traditional CMM tools (the Serpentine model and the LUUUTT model) to diagram and analyze the construction of the visual maps themselves. Each layer of investigation brought new insights and added to the rich fabric of data.

The following character descriptions were developed from observations of the data collection day video recordings, and are used as defined for the purposes of this dissertation. *Lead* is defined as the participant who directed the group and focused on the task rather than on relationship-building. *Colead* is defined as the participant who supported the lead and jumped in when the lead handed off control. *Supporter* is defined as a participant who supported the lead, colead, other supporter(s) in the group, and sometimes the outgroup participant(s); supporters focused on relationship-building rather than task-mastering. *Questioner* is defined as a participant who directed group activity through questioning. *Thought stimulator* is defined as a participant who did not actively join in the group activity, but directed those who did from the back. *Observer* is defined as a participant who watched the other participants but did not engage. *Independent participant* is defined as one who participated by herself at times without checking with anyone for a while. An *outgroup participant* is defined as a participant who could not or did not step into the group rhythm, was not accepted by the group, and/or was ignored by the group. *Antagonist* is defined as a participant who acted against the group norm and whose ideas were openly rejected. *Timekeeper* is defined as a participant who took responsibility for tracking the time elapsed and informing the group about time remaining. *Mediator* is defined as a participant who functioned as the glue for the group, for example, bringing focus or resolution after contentious discussion; mediators occasionally ascended to the role of group/class *healer*. *Presenter* is defined as the main speaker during the gallery walk, and *copresenter* as someone who assisted the presenter during the gallery walk.

Group A Process

In this section, a group profile sets the stage for the events of data collection day. Group A's coconstruction process is then described with a focus on the group dynamics and roles and how they developed. Group A's visual map is presented with an analysis based on the principles of design. The last section describes how Group A presented their visual map during the gallery walk and how Group 1 responded.

Group A Profile

Group A's aliases begin with the letters A–E: Aiden (PA), Bella (PB), Carolina (PC), Dianne (PD), and Eugene (PE) (see Table 4 for demographic data). Parenthetical background designations are indicated in italics in Table 4.

Cultural styles varied among this group (see Figure 13), but all team members scored higher in group orientation than the average U.S. scores on the PCSI.

IDI-2 scores for this polycultural group indicated that three participants were operating from ethnocentric perspectives (defense, minimization) and two from ethnorelative positions (acceptance) (see Table 5).

Group A participants were very active online, with four participants above average (108-127%) and the fifth at 82% of the class average (see Appendix B for participation data table).

TPI scores indicated that Group A was in agreement prior to the research process that there were no pressing issues to resolve with regard to team performance. Regarding the LS, four team members identified as accommodators and one as a diverger. MI preferences were very diverse.

Table 4

Demographic Data for Group A Participants

Demographic	Aiden (PA)	Bella (PB)	Carolina (PC)	Dianne (PD)	Eugene (PE)
Age	46	18	55	22	40
Gender	M	F	F	F	M
Nationality[a]	Irish, US	US	*US*[e]	Filipina American	Korean
Cultural identity[a]	*Irish*[e], European, Western, US	Hispanic, *Latina*[e]	Female, professional, family, teacher	American, Filipina, Japanese pop culture	Socialist, green, democrat
Ethnic background[a]	*White*[e]	Hispanic	*Caucasian*[e]	*Filipina American*[e]	*Korean American*[e]
Countries lived in (no. of years)[b]	**Ireland (19**[d]**)** Germany (2) US (25)	**US (3.3)** El Salvador (14.7)	**US (55)**	**US (22)**	**Korea (2**[d]**)** Argentina (7) Spain (1) US (30)
Formative years	Western Europe	Central America	North America	North America	South America
Years in the Bay Area	7	1.3	22	0.5	16
Language(s)[c]	**English** Irish Spanish	**Spanish** English	**English**	**English** Tagalog	**Korean, English** Spanish Italian Russian
Education	College graduate	High school graduate	Some college	College graduate	Master's degree

Note. [a]In participants' own words. [b]Country of origin is listed first in bold. [d]Number not specified by participant, but deduced from other figures given. [c]Native language(s) are shown in bold. [e]Parenthetical background designation used in discussion, shown here in italics.

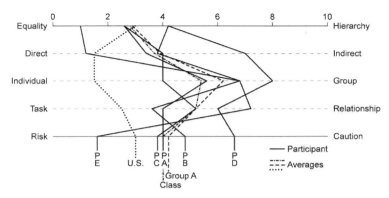

Figure 13. Group A participant scores on the Peterson Cultural Style Inventory (tm) (PCSI) with U.S., class, and group averages. PA = Aiden; PB = Bella; PC = Carolina; PD = Dianne; PE = Eugene. Author's image.

Table 5

Group A Participants' Developmental Model of Intercultural Sensitivity (DMIS) Stages with Associated Learning Opportunities

Stage	Participant(s)	Learning opportunity
Ethnocentric		
Denial	—	Recognize the existence of cultural differences
Defense	Bella, Dianne	Mitigate polarization by emphasizing "common humanity"
Minimization	Carolina	Develop cultural self-awareness
Ethnorelative		
Acceptance	Aiden, Eugene	Refine analysis of cultural contrasts
Adaptation	—	Develop frame of reference shifting skills
Integration	—	Resolve the multicultural identity

Note. Author's table; stage and learning opportunity data from Bennett and Bennett (2003).

Episode 1: Introduction

  Main characters Carolina—lead, Aiden—colead.

  Scene. All five participants were seated around a U-shaped table with Carolina at the head of the table.

  Course of events. Carolina and Aiden set the groundwork for stepping into their leadership roles by being the first ones to double-check the task and ask questions for clarification.

  Aiden   So it's the group's story, like one story for the whole group. [...RR...]

  Carolina   Okay, now state what it is you're creating a visual representation of.

  Regina   You don't need to write the story.

  Carolina   I know. What are we, what is the story about? (Group A process, p. 1)

Besides the fact that the lead and colead spoke up first and stepped into their leadership roles immediately, it is noteworthy that they responded with clarifying questions in spite of the written directions they had just received and my verbal introduction to the tasks—confirming that communication in a polycultural environment cannot be taken for granted and needs to be patiently and repeatedly addressed.

  The seating arrangement is noteworthy also. Carolina, the lead, sat at one end forming the head of the table with the other four sitting at the sides. The group member(s) at the head of the table participate more and are "seen as having more influence on the group decision than members seated at the sides" (Johnson & Johnson, 2005, p. 164).

Episode 2: Storyline Coconstruction

  Main characters. Carolina—lead, Aiden—colead, Eugene and Dianne—supporters, Bella—outgroup participant.

  Scene. All five participants were seated around a U-shaped table with Carolina at the head of the table.

  Course of events. The conversation was initiated by the lead, Carolina, who also gained respect and power by immediately creating visual notes of the conversation, drawing a sketch of her understanding of what people shared and how she understood the sharing in context of all that was said.

  Eugene   So, so I see we're gonna (unintelligible) all right?

  Carolina   So, I can tell you what, I can tell you visually what my experience was (sketching while talking) that you have this whole of CCSF [...] (Group A process, p. 3)

Carolina jumped in enthusiastically, which was accepted by the group. In this role as visual note-taker, Carolina fulfilled the task of a graphic facilitator. At times, the activity moved into interactive graphic facilitation, as other group members were invited to draw onto her map directly (see Episode 3).

Carolina's story expressed her satisfaction in connecting and building community with her classmates in different classes, and included her feeling a lack of connection to the larger CCSF community. Eugene (supporter) agreed, saying, "My experience, is, is similar to that" (Group A process, p. 3). Aiden (colead) concurred, saying, "Mine is similar to that, too, yeah. There is no kind of community here, just a kind of transience, you know" (p. 3). Carolina's personal experience and visual representation remained central to the group's coconstructed story, as they worked off of Carolina's initial sketch.

Bella, who has a language barrier, jumped in at a moment that was out of sync with the rest of the group and began telling her story. The group did not quite understand what Bella was saying. Carolina asked several clarifying questions that did not seem to bring out Bella's real story, but Bella's answers were quickly accepted and adopted by Carolina as Bella's contribution.

Bella My (unintelligible), uh, I'm studying like a ESL student, uh, so I have, uh, four classes here. Um, the graphic design, uh, my counselor say that only Saturdays able to meet. I say, "Wow, that's, that's really, uh, a little difficult because I have never have, I never, I have ever have a class on Saturdays." But (unintelligible) now is not so difficult, uh, uh, I share with my, other class, uh, we do like a team but we are all the class one team, so we share what our experience, um, why, uh, we are taking classes is because we have to improve our skill language? Um, uh, something like that, um.

Carolina So for you, (sketching while talking) you're taking three classes.

Bella More classes.

Carolina That are, sort of together? And then this class is sort of, a separate class, is that what you're saying?

Bella Um, I—

Carolina —Or, or, you share what you're doing with all the classes with what you are doing in the ESL class?

Bella Um, no. I, uh, I taking classes, uh, like a student, I'm studying? So, graphic design is my major, um, I will still study more so I will get, uh, out of here, (unintelligible), I will finish, um, study to, transfer to the US, to the university.

Carolina So for you, you're creating more of a community in your classes, okay? (Bella nods) (Group A process, pp. 3–4)

This was the only time during the entire data collection process that Bella offered any verbal participation. After her attempted input was appropriated by Carolina, she did not speak again. While this moment could easily be misinterpreted as the moment when Bella became the outgroup participant of Group A, it is important to acknowledge that Bella played this role consistently throughout the semester. She often agreed when it was clear that her meaning was different, making it difficult to gain more clarity about the point she was making. In addition, communication with her included long moments of silence, and her classmates were used to this dynamic and had developed a pattern of moving on without her when communication could not be established.

The lead roles were taken by two Caucasians (U.S., Irish) who were also the oldest students in the group. Eugene, who has leadership skills but did not take a leadership role, is of Asian origin (Korean American) and had the highest level of education in the group.

Episode 3: Completion of the Sketch

Main characters. Aiden—lead, Carolina—colead, Eugene—supporter, Dianne—questioner, Bella—observer.

Scene. All five participants were seated around a U-shaped table with Carolina at the head of the table.

Course of events. Aiden initiated this episode and contributed significantly, with Eugene and Dianne adding more thoughts. Carolina continued to summarize and clarify what everyone was saying, while adding their thoughts to her sketch. Eugene offered his own sketch to describe his ideas about the story.

Aiden	But how are we gonna represent the story, I mean, I think an idea that, if we take somebody comin' in like this (pointing to Carolina's sketch) into, City College a whole and then connecting out in different directions, like, (Carolina moves her sketch to the middle of the table) say you try different classes, and stuff like that. Just, I'm trying to think how we're going to—(pointing to Eugene's sketch) is that what you're thinking?
Carolina	(smiling and pointing to Eugene's sketch) There you go.
Eugene	(pointing to his own sketch) Like a circle for the community. CCSF is a part of the community. You were talking about classes going like that, I draw a star,
Carolina	Great.
Eugene	Then the squares represent each place within the community outside of City College and the circle represents […] (Group A process, p. 5)

Carolina established her leadership role through her function as the graphic facilitator for the group, drawing the map. Managing the information for the group gave her power in that role, which was accepted by the group without any noticeable resistance.

As Aiden jumped in and discussed his points on Carolina's sketch (which was four times as large in size as Eugene's), they decided on a structure of arrows coming in and out of CCSF into different neighborhoods spread throughout. Eugene withdrew his sketch from the middle of the table when Aiden continued to point to Carolina's in the center of the table, saying "It really is connected to other businesses around the city, so if somebody comes into City College it connects them with the whole. They can find new ways and directions to go anywhere" (Group A process, p. 5). Because Aiden and Carolina were so excited about their ideas, nobody may have noticed that Eugene's contribution got lost in the midst of this discussion.

Aiden pulled in Bella's idea even though she hardly had spoken, saying "for Bella too, she's coming in here and she's making a community over there" (p. 5). Here, Aiden managed to bring Bella's point of view into the picture without making it awkward. The group seemed to be satisfied with the dynamic and indirectly agreed with how and where things were going.

Carolina   Yeah, so do you see these as the outside of City College, the hotels and stuff?

Eugene   Yeah, they're all kind of linked to City College [...] the connections going through City College to whatever place outside of it, they're all interconnected through City College. (Group A process, p. 5)

Participants genuinely took turns and quickly found ways to agree and move the process forward.

At this point, the group had moved from the storyline to the structure of the story, then began discussing the characters in the story. Carolina, in her enthusiasm, sometimes interrupted both Dianne and Eugene to make her own points. Dianne was successful in entering the conversation several turns after her first attempt.

Aiden   Maybe if we try to take [...] one person, who is a typical City College student [...] if we wanted to show a person going in [...] obviously it's not [...] a kid, it could be someone [...] our age or it could be somebody [...] these guys' age.

Dianne   I think—

Carolina   Well, could we do like one of these for people coming in? You know, this looks like there are all sort of different goals for someone going out, how about coming in—

Eugene   I mean—

Carolina   Like an arrow to go into the college—

Dianne   I think there are two types of students, one whose college experience is like this for the first time, and someone who has already gone through other education systems. (Group A process, p. 5)

Aiden and Carolina matched each other's communication style and speed and were sometimes insensitive to the other cues in the conversation. At times, it seemed as if they had their own conversations going on while the other two were trying to break in.

Carolina maintained her lead role through approval of other people's ideas.

Aiden   But not really coming out with the same experience. [...] I think if we had an arrow going in, maybe if we found a photograph over there of a person we could agree on represents [...] maybe they're not like 19 years old [...] not a white male, maybe they're not typical. Just going in and coming out in all different directions and different people and stuff.

Carolina   Okay. (Group A process, pp. 5–6)

Carolina was not hung up on details and easily agreed if the established direction was generally upheld.

Then Eugene was able to enter and brought up the issue of needing to decide on an entry point for the story, to which Aiden replied that students coming to CCSF had different entry points but could be represented by one type of student exiting the college. Dianne again asked for more than one representative. Carolina and Aiden finally decided that students came into CCSF from different locations and returned to different places after completing their goals at CCSF, and that it would be all right to show different personalities to be more inclusive of the different kinds of people coming through CCSF. Eugene and Dianne approved. The following dialogue demonstrates the typical decision-making dynamic of this group.

Eugene   We should have a point of entry somewhere—

Aiden   It doesn't really matter where the point of entry is, 'cause it would be different for all of us—

Dianne   Would we have to use just one person or could we use like a few people for the entry?

Carolina I think we have people coming in from different places like radii—

Aiden   And coming out as one.

Carolina Coming out as one? It's like that pie machine in Chicken Run.

Eugene   Yeah, I guess we could do that. Actually I got this idea from yours.

Dianne   That sounds like City College. (Group A process, p. 6)

While Aiden and Carolina were, more often than not, the driving forces of the conversation in a direct manner, Eugene and Dianne carefully steered the direction. If something was really missing Dianne often brought it up indirectly by questioning.

At this point, I entered the conversation to tell the group that 10 minutes had passed, and it was the lead who reacted immediately and directed the group to move to the VisualsSpeak(tm) image set.

Aiden   How long do we have to do— [...RR...]

Carolina (standing up) We got it.

Dianne   I think we're ready. (Group A process, p. 6)

Again, Carolina's leadership was confirmed when other participants agreed to her directions. When the group stood up to move to the next task across the room, the issue of who would represent the CCSF student body was unresolved.

Episode 4: Coconstruction of the Visual Map

Main characters. Carolina—lead / independent participant, Aiden—colead / independent participant, Eugene and Dianne—supporters, Bella—observer.

Scene. Participants chose images and walked back and forth between the graphic panel on the wall and the images.

Course of events. At the beginning, Carolina led as observed in the previous episodes. After I explained the materials, Carolina directed the group to the image set and all five began searching through the images.

Carolina	So maybe the five of us could pick out a picture that represents ourselves or someone— [...D,C...]
Aiden	Are we trying to represent ourselves, or—
Dianne	How about like entry points and— [...C...]
Eugene	Like a salad—
Dianne	Like a big salad, that could be the end result.
Carolina	I think we should definitely put the chocolate in.
Dianne	Definitely, yeah.
Carolina	How 'bout a candle because we're all so bright?
Eugene	All right. [...C...]
Dianne	How about this one?
Carolina	That's cool, it's kind of representing what we're drawing.
Eugene	Are these all entry points?
Dianne	I think some might be entry points and middle points. (Group A process, p. 7)

Carolina's lead role is reflected in this example through her approval of image suggestions. Dianne and Eugene asked questions indicating their preference for a more linear logic, which was ignored.

Aiden then asked Carolina whether he should go to the graphic panel and start drawing the structure of the map they had sketched earlier. Carolina encouraged him to go ahead, but checked on him shortly after that and followed him over to the graphic panel to participate in building the basic structure of the visual map. Aiden was clearly following what he thought they agreed upon in the sketching phase, but his beginning the drawing sealed the nonlinear structure without including Eugene's and Dianne's preference for a more linear representation.

Aiden	Should we draw the inner circle for City College and then an outer circle? Would I do that?
Carolina	Yeah, yeah, go for it. (Group A process, p. 7)

Here Carolina was clearly the lead—even Aiden (the colead) asked her initially before every step he took—which was notable because he had such a strong voice during the brainstorming phase.

The other three participants quickly interrupted their task of sorting images and moved to the graphic panel also. Again, Dianne and Eugene asked for items that would lead to a more linear representation. Both Carolina and Aiden disagreed and continued to build their predetermined structure based on nonlinearity, a way of showing that people come in and out of CCSF in an organic manner best represented by the nonlinear visual they had sketched earlier. Carolina later called this "stream of consciousness" (Carolina, gallery walk, p. 6).

Carolina   [to Aiden] This is CCSF? Right here?

Aiden   CCSF, yeah, should I make it bigger?

Carolina   I think we had the inner circle, then the outer circle can be encompassing.

Aiden   I think I am just going to leave that for the moment. I have San Francisco here, the districts here—

Eugene   Yeah, except that North Beach should be north—

Aiden   Oh yeah, it's…my bad spelling you know.

Eugene   Should this be the entry, or like—

Dianne   I think maybe that should be the middle—

Eugene   The middle? Okay.

Dianne   So where does end result go? [...RR,A,RR...]

Carolina   I think what's interesting is that any of the entry points could also be the exit points. You know you could come in from the Marina and then end up over in the Mission, or you could…it doesn't have to be like a linear process.

Eugene   We could have like a grid, criss-crossing lines—

Carolina   Or just things going in, things going out.

Aiden   Put some pictures here, like different programs, like—

Carolina   Yeah, yeah.

Aiden   Like culinary, for example.

Carolina   Yeah.

Aiden   People coming in from like North Beach and ending up in Potrero Hill or—

Carolina   Yeah, yeah, yeah. Let's do that.

Dianne   Okay. (Group A process, pp. 7–8)

Since Eugene and Dianne kept bringing their ideas back for a linear map, Carolina finally had to comment and steer them back to the planned version. Aiden backed her up, and together they were too strong to be resisted; their enthusiasm was also contagious. Dianne gave up on her preconceived notion and agreed to go with the flow.

Once the main structure was established, Carolina released power and immersed herself deeply into drawing shapes on the map. At this point, about 30 minutes into the entire process, the group quickly fell into a calm rhythm of working peacefully next to each other—what could be called the flow state (Sawyer, 2007). Aiden and Carolina had already bonded and released each other into individual work that did not need much conversation, and were focused on the tasks they had chosen. Carolina let the group make decisions without her direction and even asked other group members about color choices on the arrows she was working on, which may have been an attempt to share leadership (Sawyer, 2007).

The established hierarchy, however, was continued by the group—the other group members kept asking Carolina for design direction. Occasionally, Dianne and Eugene checked in with Carolina about image placement. Carolina was deeply immersed in her task and less available for directing, so Dianne and Eugene started to follow Aiden to the images and engaged him in a conversation instead. When they didn't get much direction from either leader, they began making their own decisions and bonded during this phase.

Dianne and Eugene were building relationship, working as the image crew with Bella helping them by preparing the tape loops needed to attach the images to the graphic panel. Bella did not participate much in constructing the map, nor did she talk. She helped pick images and prepare tape loops, and the group used her images largely because Eugene kept including her, at least on the level of asking her where to put the images she had picked.

Eugene   Where do you want these—these are yours. Right there?

Bella   [nods]. (Group A process, p. 15)

While she did not answer these questions, Eugene and Bella seemed to be successful in their nonverbal communication that included nodding and smiling on Bella's part while Eugene kept asking questions to confirm his understanding of her opinions.

After all the images were up, Carolina and Aiden completed the visual map by adding embellishments. Judging from the group's relaxed mode at the end of this episode, the group seemed satisfied with their work.

Visual Map

Group A created a nonlinear but structured and very colorful organic map that placed CCSF at the center of all events and showed movement into and out of the center (see Figure 14). The visual map represented the energy of the group. Its organic structure allowed elements to flow into each other effortlessly, looking like a dance rather than a sequenced representation of a story on a

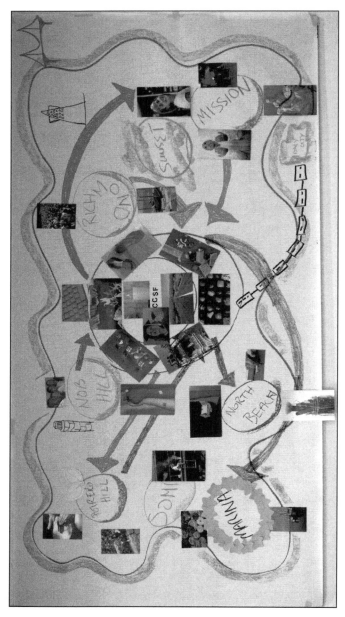

Figure 14. Group A visual map. Photograph by author.

timeline. The entire map represented San Francisco with various neighborhoods that were identified by images and drawn elements. Carolina and Aiden created the structure and finished the map with embellishments, while Eugene and Dianne chose and placed the images. Bella observed the action, chose a few images, and helped Eugene and Dianne with taping the images to the visual map.

There was little contrast in this rather harmonious piece. Elements of both positive space (drawn items and pictures) and negative space (white spatial elements) were mostly the same size and were evenly spaced as well as grouped, indicating integration and an emphasis on democracy in this group (Rosen & Mayro, 1995). The composition was characterized by circular movements contained in a wide organic frame, indicating group cohesion, as well as by horizontal emphasis alluding to harmonious interaction (Rosen & Mayro, 1995). There was no linear alignment, but the pieces seemed well connected through a natural flow. The piece had a rhythmic quality to it and flowed in and out of the center, which was also the entry point and depicted the most important part, CCSF. The story was told with very few words. Many colors were included and some embellishments were used, such as sticky notes shaped into stars and leaves. Due to the materials and techniques used, the map looked flat and without depth, and floated horizontally on a single plane like a cross-section. This lack of anchoring in the piece possibly indicated that the group may have represented something ideal rather than grounded in (objective) reality (Rosen & Mayro, 1995).

Out of the VisualsSpeak(tm) image set, the group chose 13 images from the life category (3 spirituality, 6 activity, and 4 concepts), 1 image from the country subset of the nature category, 4 images from the people category (2 adults and 2 groups), and 7 images from the things category (3 household and personal items, 3 tools and machines, and 1 cities and structures).

The developer of VisualsSpeak(tm) noted that Group A's map demonstrated a strong preference for verticals inside their horizontally oriented composition, which might stand for "things reaching, moving upwards, trying to go somewhere" (C. Martell, private communication, December 27, 2007). A repetition of similar elements throughout several images was also noted in the box of chocolates, the keyboard, money, and heads of people grouped together which formed a similar texture, possibly alluding to group orientation. In addition, there was a theme of deflecting something from outside the circle, seen through the negative space in the images which formed holes like a filter controlling what could come in from the outside. This deflection and use of negative space also alluded to the potential of group cohesion and focus on the in-group experience (C. Martell, personal communication, December 27, 2007).

Gallery Walk

Main characters. Carolina—presenter; Eugene—copresenter; Michelle, Nick, and Paige—questioners.

Scene. Carolina and Eugene stood on either side of Group A's map. Carolina spoke while Eugene pointed to the pertinent areas on the map. They presented in a humorous way with Eugene playing Vanna White from the television show *Wheel of Fortune*.

Course of events. After Group 1 had finished the presentation of their visual map, Carolina and Eugene presented Group A's visual map together. The presentation was humorous and calm, and expressed the way the group had worked through the process itself.

Carolina explained that their map represented a "stream of consciousness" (gallery walk, p. 6) rather than a linear flow. Carolina referred to many of the images and stated that they represented individuals from all walks of life coming into CCSF from all kinds of directions and neighborhoods to which they return in the same organic manner. Carolina explained that they had first shared their own experiences and observations during which time she drew a sketch of what was being said:

> The structure came about because—bum, bum, bum—there was a circle when we were first talking about how we wanted to do this. I was just drawing as we were talking because I talk better with a pencil in my hand, and we had CCSF as the unifying element to all of us because we came from so many different places. Then and how to me, my experience, and then everybody sort of agreed, not everybody, but most people agreed. You came in, you took a class, there was this little community, temporary community, and then you went out again and that community was gone. It was like an in-and-out kind of thing. And then Eugene included how the community around CCSF is actually very much involved in what we're doing here, and then drawing in what was around us as well. (p. 6)

Carolina's sketch had become the base for the group's collaborative visual map.

It was striking that the group could not answer questions about the choices they made. They explained that they were following intuition rather than rational thought and did not need any further planning to act—an improvised flow state.

Regina   […] so what do the colors mean?

Carolina   Aiden has a very complicated formula for why he picked the colors, as do I with the arrows, it's just too complicated to go into right now. Right?

Aiden   It's a trade secret.

Regina   Which means you chose them for some sort of emotional value?

Carolina   Yes, that's exactly what we mean, right? (gallery walk, pp. 6–7)

Michelle   I have a question about the neighborhoods, because you sort of have neighborhoods that aren't necessarily together on the same different sides. So was there like a process for how you were writing the neighborhoods, or?

Carolina   It's alphabetical (pause) I don't know.

Eugene   It's a trade secret.

Carolina	Those complicated things.
Aiden	We couldn't put every neighborhood in so—
Paige	Did you pick your own neighborhoods?
Carolina	It's all representational rather than accurate. (pause) Okay? (gallery walk, pp. 7–8)

Carolina and Eugene played humorously through this piece, while Group 1 asked their questions from a more serious frame.

Group 1 Process

In this section, the profile of Group 1 sets the stage for the events of data collection day. Group 1's coconstruction process is then described with a focus on the group dynamics and roles and how they developed. Group 1's visual map is presented with an analysis based on the principles of design. The last section describes how Group 1 presented their visual map during the gallery walk and how Group A responded.

Group 1 Profile

Group 1's aliases begin with the letters M–R: Michelle (P1), Nick (P2), Olive (P3), Paige (P4), and Rusena (P5) (see Table 6 for demographic data). Parenthetical background designations are indicated in italics in Table 6.

IDI-2 scores for this polycultural group indicated that all participants occupied a different stage of the DMIS. Three participants were operating from ethnocentric perspectives (denial, defense, and minimization) and two from ethnorelative positions (acceptance and adaptation) (see Table 7).

TPI scores indicated that Group 1 was in agreement prior to the research process and that there were no pressing issues to resolve with regard to team performance. Regarding the LS, four team members identified as accommodators and one as an assimilator. MI preferences were very diverse.

Cultural styles varied among this group (see Figure 15), but all team members scored higher in group-orientation than the average U.S. scores on the PCSI.

Three of Group 1's participants were less active online than Group A's, with overall participation scores of 66%, 68%, and 94% of the class average. One participant had the highest participation in the class (145%), and one participant's data cannot be compared as that participant did not complete the class.

Table 6

Demographic Data for Group 1 Participants

Demographic	Michelle (P1)	Nick (P2)	Olive (P3)	Paige (P4)	Rusena (P5)
Age	33	25	33	26	25
Gender	F	M	F	F	F
Nationality[a]	American	*US*[e]	Vietnamese/Chinese American	American	Ukrainian
Cultural identity[a]	American, African American, female	Male, college graduate, returning student, professional, Buddhist, sober, gay	Vietnamese American, heterosexual	American[e], female, heterosexual, white, blond/redhead	Eastern European, post Soviet Union
Ethnic background[a]	*African American*[e]	*Caucasian*[e]	*Vietnamese/Chinese American*[e]	*White*[e]	*Russian-speaking Ukrainian*[e]
Countries lived in (no. of years)[b]	**US (28)** Japan (5)	**US (25)**	**Vietnam (6)** US (27)	**US (26)**	*Moldova*[e] **(24.75)** US (0.25)
Formative years	North America	North America	North America	North America	Eastern Europe
Years in the Bay Area	5	1	22	26	0.25
Language(s)[c]	**English** Spanish Italian, Japanese	**English** Spanish	**Vietnamese** English	**English**	**Russian** English Ukrainian, Romanian
Education	College graduate	College graduate	College graduate	College graduate	College graduate

Note. [a]In participants' own words. [b]Country of origin is listed first in bold. [c]Native language(s) are shown in bold. [d]Number not specified by participant, but deduced from other figures given. [e]Parenthetical background designation used in discussion, shown here in italics.

Table 7

Group 1 Participants' Developmental Model of Intercultural Sensitivity (DMIS) Stages with Associated Learning Opportunities

Stage	Participant(s)	Learning opportunity
Ethnocentric		
Denial	Rusena	Recognize the existence of cultural differences
Defense	Paige	Mitigate polarization by emphasizing "common humanity"
Minimization	Nick	Develop cultural self-awareness
Ethnorelative		
Acceptance	Olive	Refine analysis of cultural contrasts
Adaptation	Michelle	Develop frame of reference shifting skills
Integration	—	Resolve the multicultural identity

Note. Author's table; stage and learning opportunity data from Bennett and Bennett (2003).

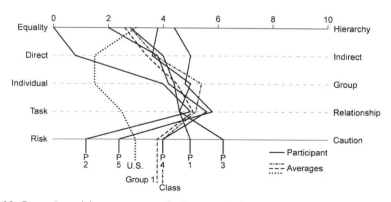

Figure 15. Group 1 participant scores on the Peterson Cultural Style Inventory (tm) (PCSI) with U.S., class, and group averages. PA = Aiden; PB = Bella; PC = Carolina; PD = Dianne; PE = Eugene. Author's image.

Episode 1: Introduction

    Main characters. Paige—outgroup participant.

    Scene. All five participants were seated around a U-shaped table, with Rusena at the head of the table.

    Course of events. Paige asked questions, which is important because tensions arose around Paige's different viewpoints and interpretation of tasks (a not unusual occurrence in this class, as discussed below).

Regina	(explains instructions) Any questions?
Paige	So, we should concentrate on one character, or a big group of characters?
Regina	It's up to you. You as a group need to collaborate within 10 minutes to come up with that story. (Group 1 process, p. 1)

In Group 1, the antagonist was the first one to make herself heard.

Episode 2: Storyline Coconstruction

    Main characters. Michelle—lead, Olive—colead / thought stimulator, Nick and Rusena—supporters, Paige—outgroup participant.

    Scene. All five participants were seated around a U-shaped table, with Rusena at the head of the table.

    Course of events. Michelle emerged immediately as the lead by spontaneously taking notes and synthesizing and summarizing information for the group. Michelle took her notes in words and in a linear fashion, which fulfilled the role of a graphic facilitator. Her notes became the roadmap for the visual map and also dominated the structure of the storyline as well as the conversation. Michelle was joined in leadership by Olive, who was a strong thought stimulator and supporter throughout the entire process, and who switched back and forth between task-leader and relationship-builder. In this episode Michelle was the taskmaster, while Olive built relationships and led the group in driving the conversation forward.

Olive	Flexible, encouraging, very positive—
Nick	—diverse—
Olive	—diverse. (pause) I feel it definitely builds my skills. (pause) Um, you guys can jump in. (Group 1 process, p. 2)

Group 1 began by sharing their personal experiences at CCSF, and then expanded to the larger CCSF community and discovered that nobody had any contact beyond their classes. Michelle consolidated the information shared and clarified by repeating what she heard people say, "I think one thing we all have in common is that we all are coming from [...] we're older students. It's not like we're out of high school" (Group 1 process, p. 2). They decided to share their common experiences as a narrative story, which led to discussing their life paths, their aspirations, and the desire for career changes. They acknowledged that they all had earned a college degree before coming to CCSF. Michelle summarized, "So, kind of what I have so far is […] older, who have life experience, older students trying, we came to discover our life path, our potential, a fulfilling career. In the process we've met new people" (p. 2). This conversation allowed them to get to know each other better and also to find their commonalities.

They compared work life to school life, and agreed that school was a safer place where they experienced no fear of exploring and sometimes failing, and where they felt supported. Michelle continued to consolidate and synthesize the information shared, at times asked for clarification, and thus drove the conversation. In this dialogue, Nick provided an important statement that other participants immediately picked up on.

Olive	I feel I am very different here than at the workplace. Like I feel like in my workplace I don't wish to lead, but here if we need a leader, I don't mind it at all, I enjoy it. But in my workplace I refuse to, I was just thinking it's so—
Michelle	So it's bringing out new skills that are maybe roles that you didn't fulfill in your other part of your life.
Olive	Yeah, I thought it was kind of interesting and I was wondering if you guys feel the same thing.
Rusena	School is very different. Actually I don't like to be a leader here and at work also.
Nick	It's safe here.
Olive	Yeah, I think you hit it right on the head […] here it's a safe environment and I like that. (Group 1 process, p. 3)

While other participants often had to talk themselves through their own thinking, Nick tended to listen, consolidate in his mind, then offer a concise short statement that summarized what the rest were thinking and feeling.

Nick also never spoke into other participants' communication acts. He found the right moment to say important things that either brought the group back on track or influenced where the group went next.

Michelle	I think the story is that we all come for practical reasons, but basically it is to find out what we want and sort of go—
Olive	—Exploration—
Michelle	—exploration for what we want to do with our lives […] and in the course of that we met new people, learned, participated in different social experiences, and learned different ways of thinking. We've learned new roles in other parts of our lives, so to me the theme is: you come in thinking one thing, and now you sort of realize that there is more than we thought.
Nick	Change of perspective

Olive	Change our perspective, to me that's the story. Yeah, okay. (Group 1 process, p. 5)

This exchange exemplifies Nick's listening and communication skills.

Michelle continued to consolidate and synthesize the information shared, at times asked for clarification and thus drove the conversation. Olive usually took the conversation to a deeper level.

Rusena	(regarding the school vs. work environment discussion) Very supportive.
Olive	Yes, very supportive. You can do wrong, there's room for errors and growing from your errors.
Paige	And accepting, and that—
Olive	No judgments. And then I like to observe when you guys do something really well, it becomes an inspiration for me and I think I want to do that. And then sharing each other's art and each other's skill set, it generates creativity and ideas like oh, I didn't know you could do something like that. Like when I did my self portrait I didn't know what to do, and then I looked at yours and I'm all, oh, that's pretty cool. It kind of break me away from my fear and I start doing it. Anyways, I hope I am not off track with that.
Michelle	No.
Paige	No, that's exactly it. (Group 1 process, pp. 3–4)

Paige was agreeable at the beginning when the group created the storyline, but began to show disagreement further into the process.

One of the questions they asked addressed how they felt about the larger community at CCSF. Since most participants were working full-time, they quickly established that they did not have much contact with the rest of the college community. Michelle summarized the outcome of the conversation, and was officially acknowledged as the group's leader.

Olive	(regarding Michelle's summary of the storyline) That works. Good job—she's such a natural leader.
Rusena	She likes it.
Olive	Yes, she likes it.
Michelle	I don't think I do so well.
Rusena	Actually you do. (Group 1 process, pp. 5–6)

With this dialogue, Group 1 confirmed Michelle as task leader as defined both in situational leadership theory and via the interaction-process analysis (Johnson & Johnson, 2005).

Despite their harmony through Episodes 1 and 2, from this moment forward Group 1 looked like a group frequently on the verge of conflict, played out in Paige wanting to move differently than the rest of the group who often ignored her pleas or shut her down. The dynamic between Paige and the rest of the group may have started prior to data collection day, due to Paige's ongoing confusion and difficulty with following the classwork and thus sometimes had contributed negatively to this team's online performance (see Paige's Participant Profile for a detailed discussion).

Episode 3: Image Selection

Main characters. Michelle—lead, Olive—colead (from the back) / timekeeper, Nick—supporter / mediator, Rusena—independent participant, Paige—antagonist.

Scene. Participants chose images from the image set and then grouped around the images on the floor to categorize them.

Course of events. The leadership roles of Michelle and Olive were reinforced in this episode, while the independent role of Rusena and the supporter/mediator role of Nick solidified. Olive started the action. Michelle hung her notes on the wall to the left of the graphic panel. Olive joined Michelle in task mastering in this episode, asking for and keeping track of time.

Regina   (gives instructions)

Olive   Let's move over (to the image set)—a picture's worth a thousand words.
           [...RR...]

Olive   So we have 10 minutes on this? [...RR...] (Group 1 process, p. 7)

Olive kept the role of timekeeper throughout the process and was successful in moving the group forward. They all went to the image table and started to choose from the VisualsSpeak(tm) image set. Michelle directed the group, and Olive chimed in.

Michelle   I think we should just pull out (images) as they strike us as appropriate.

Olive   Then we can explain them to each other. (p. 7)

Michelle and Olive worked in tandem leading the activities.

Group 1 started with a linear verbal description and with images that were categorized according to the verbal sketch. Rusena was the first one to walk to the graphic panel with an image in her hand, but then she returned and asked, "So, Michelle, where is our story?" (Group 1 process, p. 7)—acknowledging that they would be working off Michelle's notes. Michelle suggested the group review her notes, and they all walked to the graphic panel area. Michelle acted as task leader, saying, "Why don't we look at what we have first" (p. 8), and Olive acted as relationship-builder with her addition, "Yeah, see what we agree with, too" (p. 8). It was Olive who held the focus on agreement for the group.

In the middle of this episode, Olive declared that she would be available for assistance, saying, "Why don't you guys let me know what I can help?" (Group 1 process, p. 7)—indirectly declaring that she wouldn't be participating in the action. From then on Olive mostly directed from the back. This provided great support to the group in that she kept the group on schedule and paid attention to the design principles we had learned in class, such as similarity, balance, and attention to white space.

Paige suggested that they could work as they had done earlier in the day in a brainstorming game that included categorizing. Michelle agreed and Olive suggested that they put the images on the floor and work from there. As they began categorizing, the energy of the group rose spontaneously at times, with much overlapping talk. In the following sample of this communication pattern, overlapping utterances are aligned vertically and [enclosed in brackets].

Paige	So, this is, you know, learning stuff. [People working together].
Nick	[Here's a building]. Learning.
Rusena	Building—
Olive	—Let's sit on the floor.
Paige	Graduation I guess can be like learning—
Michelle	—Okay—
Paige	—and this can be people working together.
Michelle	Okay.
Rusena	[Some sort of] social interaction (hands image to Michelle).
Paige	[Okay, so, working] Social interaction stuff, um, [What the, I thought this was like art.]
Rusena	[Unintelligible crosstalk] Art? Uh (noise indicating uncertainty)
Paige	Yeah, art.

(Rusena, Michelle, Olive, and Paige speak simultaneously, unintelligible crosstalk)

Rusena	[…] Periods, for example—
Paige	—and this is like challenges—
Olive	—Yeah, challenges—
Paige	(talking over Olive and Michelle, whose words cannot be distinguished) Challenges or tasks or mental thinking.
Nick	This is like results. (everyone laughs)
Paige	Results.
Olive	(group overlapping, unintelligible crosstalk) Then there's goals—
Paige	—goals, and like that was—
Olive	—challenging, too.
Paige	(talking over Olive, Rusena, and Michelle) And like, style.
Nick	Where's emotions?

Rusena	Emotions?
Olive	Put it under culture.
Paige	So I think, probably, maybe like. I thought that these things, like [sky], [and like the mountain can be]
Michelle	[Which one is open-ended.]
Nick	[That can go with the results.]
Michelle	[Yeah, that can go with results.]
Paige	[Can be results related.]
Olive	Results (Nick and Olive laugh). (Group 1 process, p. 8)

It seemed as if they were in competition to make sure their images were picked for the story. They defined the following categories: challenges, results, emotions, journey, examining, multicultural, goals, culture, life path, social interaction, beginning, and searching for something or looking for signs as to which class would support their goals.

Although the categorizing activity was Paige's idea, the process showed Paige clearly that her ideas were different than those of the group. Paige continued to try to join the group's thinking, but wasn't able to convince them of her ideas. It also seemed that she was getting frustrated with the group for not letting her provide a lot of input. In turn, they were getting irritated with her attempts to take them off the path they had decided on.

Michelle	(to Paige) What's that?
Paige	I don't know, I just thought like signs and this is like examining stuff. And then that, contemplative.
Nick	The journey, here's the journey (pause) that could go under creative or like actions.
Michelle	Here?
Paige	Um, that's multicultural right there.
Michelle	This is more like examining.
Paige	Yeah, that's examining.
Olive	So that's a separate category.
Paige	So this is goal-oriented, or tasks, or what? (Group 1 process, pp. 8–9)

Paige had agreed to the storyline, but early in the process it became clear that she would have represented the story completely differently than the rest of the group. At times it seemed as if she was actually really confused about making the connections from the storyline to the categories to the representative images, and at other times she demonstrated clarity about her thinking. She suggested several images that were not chosen by the group because the image did not support the storyline the group had in mind or because they felt the image would misrepresent the group's ideas.

Olive	All these are people and this one is a very different design.
Nick	This could be like looking for signs, because I've have like taken different classes and having varied results, so then that could kind of tie in with the fish and you're searching for something and looking for signs—
Paige	—Or you're stuck with stinky old fish, things you want to change.
Nick	Or they're not the results you're looking for.
Paige	Okay, so maybe in the beginning, say if we were going to have it spaced out like a story.
Rusena	For me it's not very obvious.
Paige	Well for me it's, the sign is that your life is getting corroded and it's rusting and you're not in the right spot, you know, change your direction.
Michelle	I don't think we should use that, because if we're going to tell the story visually, that is going to throw people off. (Group 1 process, pp. 9–10)

Paige saw the story representation in abstract terms (one could say more through the eyes of an artist or a creative person thinking laterally), while the rest of the group was interested in communicating ideas more literally and linearly.

The following exchange around multiculturalism exemplifies the misfit between Paige's worldview and the rest of the group, a difference that may have brought about the tensions during this process. Paige's statement minimizing the importance of culture in the midst of a very diverse group was shut down immediately by Michelle, who then led the rest of the group on with their discussion as though nothing had happened.

Paige	I don't know about the multicultural thing, is that really important to you guys? I mean, to me it's not really important.
Michelle	It's part of that, learning different social experience, so many different people—
Olive	—We're so different right now, I mean it, emphasize—
Michelle	I mean, we don't have to use them all, but.
Rusena	Why not?
Nick	I think this should be at the end and so should the eagle and so should the graduation (Group 1 process, p. 10)

Michelle shut down many of Paige's ideas in this same way. Paige's thinking style was nonlinear, intuitive/experimental, and completely different from the rest of the group, as was her way of expressing herself visually.

Paige	Why don't we just arrange, like, what's the beginning (of the story).
Rusena	Our path.

Paige	The beginning is—
Michelle	—Lost or—
Paige	—Not so much lost but wanting to—
Nick	—This is like the beginning.
Paige	The beginning is having the desire to change.
Michelle	I think the beginning should be a person, because this is like a story, so we should have the older student.
Paige	Okay, so this will be our main character? The old guy? So old guy says, "It's time for me to go back to school. I want to learn graphic design"?
Michelle	So then, trying to get the right path, would that be the theme. (Group 1 process, p. 11)

In this segment, Paige finally succeeded in finishing her suggestion on her fourth attempt, only to have Michelle totally ignore her input. Throughout the episode, the final decisions were made and monitored by Michelle, who was accepted as the leader by everyone except for Paige, who kept challenging Michelle's decisions.

Episode 4: Coconstruction of the Visual Map

Main characters. Michelle—lead, Olive—colead (from the back), Nick—supporter / mediator, Rusena—independent participant, Paige—antagonist.

Scene. Participants began by working on the floor with the images and then quickly moved to the graphic panel to create the visual map.

Course of events. Michelle, Nick, Olive, and Rusena were in sync with each other and formed the ingroup (participants experiencing solidarity and common interests) that determined the flow of the process, with Michelle taking the lead and Olive providing backup. Olive took on a dual role, both task-mastering with Michelle and relationship-building with Nick. Paige was the outgroup—she tried to come in, and went with the flow many times for short periods, but was mostly out of sync with the ingroup.

Rusena placed the first image on the left side of the graphic panel, indicating a linear flow. She was immediately joined by Michelle, who put up the second image following movement from left to right across the graphic panel. The group continued to work in this manner across the graphic panel from left to right.

Disagreements between Paige and the rest of the group arose in this episode also. Paige walked up to the image Michelle had just placed and took it off to move it around for a different composition; this action occurred while Michelle had her back to the graphic panel, which may have been unintentional. Michelle moved the image back to its original position and reminded Paige of the linear flow of the story.

> Paige   (walks around behind Michelle, reaches up and places images on the graphic panel) So how 'bout with the crowds, we can put his friends—
>
> Olive   I thought that space was for CCSF?
>
> Michelle   That space is for CCSF (removes images placed by Paige), sorry. (Group 1 process, p. 13)

While Michelle made the final authoritative call, the other group members and in particular the colead, Olive, watched for Paige who repeatedly acted on the graphic panel when Michelle had her back to Paige. This sequence of events happened several more times, almost as if Paige were trying to sneak her ideas in while the boss wasn't looking—without success. For example, Paige tried to bring in an image for challenges (a mountain image), placing it on the map in an empty spot. Michelle pointed out that they already had a challenges image in a different location, and moved Paige's image to that location. Paige argued her point, explaining that she was "thinking of using these things as more like imagery to balance the thing out" (Group 1 process, p. 15). Michelle replied with disagreement, saying, "To me, I'd rather have something that means something then," (p. 15) and moved both the group's challenge image and Paige's mountains to Paige's chosen location. Then Nick entered the discussion with an idea about having different places for positive and negative outcomes, and moved the two challenge images up so he could place other outcomes below them. Paige gave up, saying "Just put it wherever you want" (p. 15).

Paige's actions raised the energy of the group and caused the rest of the group to verbally shut down Paige's ideas. In addition, Paige mocked the group's chosen image for the protagonist, saying "I'm in the classroom with all these stupid kids" (Group 1 process, p. 12). Paige often did not understand the thinking of the group and vice versa. Paige's behavior may have been an example of self-oriented behavior based on fear and played out in fighting the group, defending her opinions (Purser & Montuori, 1994). At this point, Paige had become the antagonist of the group.

> Michelle   (outlining on the graphic panel with her finger) So, if CCSF is here, something can sprout up here and something can sprout down here and then... [go—] [come back].
>
> Paige   [I have a question.]
>
> (Michelle looks at Paige)
>
> Paige   Sorry, go ahead.
>
> Michelle   Literally, go (gesturing across the graphic panel) through here.
>
> Olive   Balance. We're trying to go for balance.
>
> Michelle   Yeah, everything is sort of together. (to Paige) What was your comment?

Paige	Oh no, I was just going to ask what, (pointing to the visual map) why do we have the cranes with the, people?
Michelle	'Cause it's like meeting new people, new experiences.
Paige	Oh—
Olive	—Diversity, culture—
Michelle	—Diversity, yeah.

(Olive and Michelle talk simultaneously, unintelligible crosstalk)

Paige	Oh, like multicultural? I see.
Olive	It's just art.
Paige	(stepping away from the graphic panel to the back of the group) Wow. Okay. (Group 1 process, p. 14)

Paige's tone in her final statement seemed to indicate amazement at the logic of the group's image placement.

Thirty minutes into the process, Group 1 finally fell into a rhythm in which everyone except for Paige had a job that they seemed to enjoy doing, which moved the project along. This rhythm approached a flow state, but was consistently interrupted by Paige's actions. Michelle and Rusena worked independently, with Rusena drawing different elements and Michelle labeling the different categories.

Olive continued her role as timekeeper and colead from the back, saying, "So, if we only have 15 minutes left, let's divide how we want to—" (Group 1 process, p. 14). In his role as healer, Nick encouraged Olive to join the active creation process and make a mark on the panel, and they both completed the placement of the images and started coloring the graphic panel.

Michelle	What do you want to do?
Olive	I don't want to draw, I just want to help, so if you guys want to tell me what to do, then I will do it. I don't want to mess up the thing. How do you want to divide up the tasks for the next 15 minutes? I know you got a good—
Michelle	Well, we still need to finish the rest of the story, do you want to work on that?
Olive	Yeah, what do you want me to do with it?
Nick	Do you want to do the happy ending?
Olive	Okay, but you have to instruct me on what that means.
Nick	Well, we have the eagle and the graduation. (pause). So you don't want to draw anything?
Olive	No, you have to tell me what to draw.
Nick	Do you want to draw some fireworks? Like some bursts of color? (Group 1 process, pp. 14–15)

During this activity Nick and Olive bonded quite a bit.

Paige kept trying to bring in her ideas, but was not in sync with the group's rhythm and never really found a way in. At times, she stood around with nothing to do, and the group ignored her completely.

Judging from the video record, in spite of being on the verge of conflict at many times, the group seemed very satisfied with their product in the end—as they expressed during the class debrief. Even Paige defended it later when its strong linearity was critiqued by Group A's members.

Visual Map

Group 1 created a linear map that clearly showed its progression from left to right across the graphic panel (see Figure 16) but also demonstrated vertical up and down movement. Horizontal movements may suggest participants cooperating, while vertical emphasis may indicate "a need for hierarchical structuring and concerns about rank and authority" (Rosen & Mayro, 1995, p. 137). Elements placed high on the composition may relate to ideals (in this case CCSF, teamwork, ideas, and graduation), while those placed low on the surface may relate to less glamorous experiences (in this case, previous experience, challenges, and results) (Rosen & Mayro, 1995). Colors moved from dark on the left side (the beginning of the story) to very colorful, vibrant, and warm on the right side (graduation), indicating a bright future. A hybrid of participants' shared experiences, the map represented the story of an older student moving through his experiences of going to CCSF. These experiences were both good and bad, challenging and rewarding, and occasionally diverted the protagonist from the direct path but always brought him back on track as he completed his goal of graduating from a CCSF program.

Visually speaking, the last part of the story (the graduation) became a focal point because of the use of color. The bright color of graduation was partially balanced by the black cloud depicting the beginning of the story when the character was still confused about his future. The character's story developed from left to right across the map and up and down in the composition, and his experiences along the way were grouped. These isolated moments were separated by white space, which extended beyond the border of the paper into infinite space and represented the biggest contrast in this composition. Remarkable was the absence of a boundary to the piece, as if it were a slice of something larger that extended into infinity. There was little or no interaction with the negative space, indicating a composition focused on the details (Rosen & Mayro, 1995) created by the positive space rather than on the whole (integration).

Figure 16. Group 1 visual map. Photograph by author.

The groups of items were aligned horizontally from left to right in a timeline fashion, and easy to follow although they moved up and down a bit in order to expose the path of the character through his story in a serpentine-like motion. With these aspects, Group 1's map somewhat resembled a time-series diagram as described by Tufte (2001), with causal explanations made through color (moving from the metaphor of a black cloud on the left that stood for a confused state to a firework of intense color depicting a happy ending and celebration on the right side of the map).

In addition to images, the map included illustrations of the character in motion, buildings, embellishments such as fireworks, and shapes. The piece had a bit of a choppy quality to it—while the story flowed clearly from left to right, there was little connection between the highlights of the character's experiences, which represented isolated moments like objects stuck onto space rather than interacting with space. Words were used to label the moments. Color was used sparingly but was intense wherever it was applied, and provided depth to the map (which was otherwise flat).

Out of the VisualsSpeak(tm) image set, the group chose 8 images from the life category (1 spirituality, 3 activities, and 4 concepts), 5 images from the nature category (3 country, and 2 animals and birds), 9 images from the people category (2 groups, 6 adults, and 1 children), and 1 household and personal items subset of the things category.

The developer of VisualsSpeak(tm) noted that Group 1's visual map was very structured and linear, and that it emphasized drawings. Another clearly distinct feature was noticed in its movement from left to right, with the right side showing more diagonals, bringing a bit of rhythm to the otherwise disjointed piece, as if things started to become more expansive. The piece also moved from dark to color indicating a positivist approach (C. Martell, personal communication, December 27, 2007).

Gallery Walk

Main characters. Olive—presenter, Michelle—copresenter.

Scene. Michelle and Olive stood to either side of the visual map. Olive began to reveal their story and process with Michelle taking over about halfway through their presentation. Rusena occasionally gave a cue from the back if they forgot to mention a significant point. It was Group 1's choice to present their story before Group A did.

Course of events. The lead and colead presented the visual map, and were clear on the fact that they were image-focused. It is also significant to notice that they thought of themselves as "we" in spite of having just experienced tensions in the process. None of these tensions were brought up by the presenters as they explained their process.

Olive explained that their story was based on their own experiences and what they found in common with each other, such as that they were all college graduates and that they all worked full-time. She pointed to different images on the visual map that represented the narrative, and took us through the plot of the story, linearly, explaining the metaphors depicted in the images.

Michelle stepped in and discussed that they had worked independently on the shapes, which were there to further clarify the direction of the journey. She expressed that the group had relied on the images to tell the story rather than movement. Rusena assisted Michelle in explaining that the color theme moved from dark to bright and warm, interjecting "color, color" and "in the beginning color, in the beginning" (gallery walk, p. 1). Rusena did not speak much while she was working on the panel independently during the process, seemingly lost in her own world; it was therefore surprising that she could remember the details of discussions about various topics that she did not participate in, such as the color discussion.

Michelle and Olive explained that the story was on a timeline and therefore linear with some sidetracks that ended up in the same direction eventually.

Regina   What about direction?

Michelle   It starts there and (laughs) and up here.

Olive   We're kinda of linear—

Michelle   —linear this way.

Olive   Yeah, timeline wise, that was our flow.

Michelle   Yeah, and then we have different, you sort of break off. You do still start in one place and kind of ends in another place even though you move off, and that sort of represents also how maybe you came in thinking one thing, like we talked about how we came into this class and be about one thing and realized it's sort of not exactly as you thought, and so we kind of deviate from a straight line but you do still come back where you want to end up. (gallery walk, p. 2)

It almost seemed as if they were apologizing for their linear preferences.

Olive and Michelle explained the categories that sketched the themes addressed in their story: culture, diversity, art, challenges, achieving goals, teamwork, learning, friendships, good and bad results, graduation cap, toasting, and celebration. Michelle explained their process, saying, "We kind of looked, we kind of, when we started, we had these sort of buzz words and we tried to find photos to kind of fit that, I guess" (gallery walk, p. 2). This group had a strong preference to lead with words, and the images came as an afterthought.

To the question of how agreements had been made, Michelle and Olive explained that there was some sort of majority voting/filtering process for accepting images onto the map. It was also important to them that the images were clearly communicating.

Michelle	We all sort of just picked images that we thought would work, and then we came and sat on the floor and spread them out and grouped them into where we…thought they all kinda went, like the exercise in the other room, and then we just—
Olive	And when we decide as a group, like, if the majority thinks that this is what should be here and what should be left out. Because we don't wanna put too many stuff and just do […] be agreeable with everybody—it has to be a consensus. So we do end up filtering […] things out that […] as a group we probably don't like.
Michelle	Also, if something was unclear to everybody, then we kinda stepped away from it just because.
Olive	Yeah, it leaves too much room for interpretation.
Michelle	Yeah, it left too much room for interpretation and thought it was a waste of space. (pp. 2–3)

Both omitted that Paige was not included in these group decisions.

It was interesting that the Group A participants who asked questions chose questions stemming from their own concerns, which they had raised in their own group. Carolina had a need for nonlinearity, intuition, and stream of consciousness, and said, "Um, I'm just amazed at how linearly you organized all that" (gallery walk, p. 4). Olive agreed that it was surprising, and then Michelle spoke up to take partial responsibility for the linearity and to express appreciation for the input of the other group members.

Michelle	And I think it may be part my influence, because I—okay, I'll own up to that— because that's how I visually saw it as having a beginning and an end, and to me having a beginning and an end means one line 'cause that's the way my brain thinks so, um.
Olive	Kinda like a timeline.
Michelle	But then other people, they sort of make it so it went a little off the linear path, but it was I think a lot of my influence. (p. 4)

This raised an interesting question about Michelle's motivation to dominate the group's work to the extent she did, and created an opening for Paige to voice her frustration about the process. Paige first distinguished herself from her more linear-oriented group members and openly exposed Michelle as having shut her down.

Paige	[…] I was trying to […] kind of spread things out and […] have different ideas, like in different corners and sort of imagery and stuff like that, and [Michelle] said something like, "Oh no, I want to have the things that go together, go together," or something like that and it was like, "Okay, fine."
Michelle	I don't think I said it like that, but— [....P…] (gallery walk, p. 4)

In the gallery walk, Paige demonstrated a pattern I often observed in Paige's behavior—she was on both sides at the same time, defying her group in the example above and supporting it in the excerpt below. The rest of the group remained strongly united and some of them disclosed in their personal interviews that they did not appreciate what they had interpreted as Paige's "disloyalty" to the group during the class debrief.

Dianne asked, "How do you think the timeline would change to incorporate like first-time college students?", raising her concern that there are at least two types of students, those with previous college experience and those without. And Paige jumped in to support the group and defend the original storyline, even though

she had mocked the group's choice of protagonist with her intonation when calling him "old guy."

Olive	[...] We wouldn't have an old man here for sure. We would have a very naïve, young child.
Michelle	It would probably, wouldn't necessarily be linear.
Paige	Yeah, that's sort of like the point of our whole story, that we weren't first time [...] (p. 5)
Michelle	To answer her question about if it was, it probably wouldn't be linear, because a lot of times when you are like 18 and you're trying to figure out what your life is going to be, you go off in all directions. You might start and stop, especially common here at a school like City College, so it could completely go off in different areas.
Paige	But we wanted to focus on the older students as the one thing we all had in common.

Here, Paige was willing to defend the group to outside critique, while in other instances she used the opportunity of class discussions to expose her group for having shut her out.

Class Debrief

The class debrief was the last phase of data collection day, and elicited reflection on participants' experiences during the various activities. After the gallery walks, the groups assembled around a large table for the class debrief. I gave no instructions regarding seating arrangements, simply asking participants to sit down at the table for the class debrief activity. Figure 17 shows the seating arrangements and participants' roles.

The question frame used in the class debrief (see Appendix G) was designed to elicit deepening reflection about the group activity just completed, in this case the cocreation process. The resulting discussion among the participants was very fruitful and free-ranging, and responses spoke to a number of the specific research questions identified at the end of Chapter 5 and specified in Chapter 6. The data are organized around the themes of culture evoked, expected patterns versus observed behavior, nature versus nurture, group dynamics, and transformative learning experience.

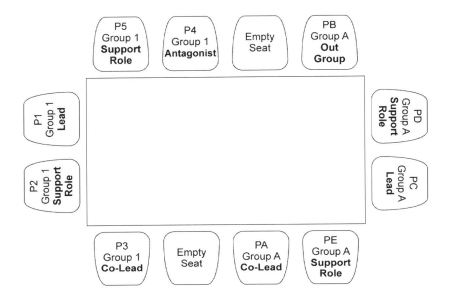

Figure 17. Class debrief seating arrangement. PA = Aiden; PB = Bella; PC = Carolina; PD = Dianne; PE = Eugene; P1 = Michelle; P2 = Nick; P3 = Olive; P4 = Paige; P5 = Rusena. Author's image.

During the class debrief, participants' intercultural developmental stages, worldview orientations, and cultural styles became noticeable as they disclosed more of their beliefs and observations. As the following discussion reflects, in many cases participants' PCSI and IDI-2 scores were confirmed by what they shared in the class debrief, while in just as many cases statements fell outside of what would be predicted by their scores. Participants demonstrated behavior that was not captured by the IDI-2, and showed a lot more flexibility than is classically described in the DMIS stages upon which the IDI-2 was based.

Group Dynamics

Participants showed awareness (or metacognition) of the differences between the styles of the two groups. Dianne named the difference between the two groups' process and visual maps, saying, "I am wondering if there was another group who did this project how theirs would turn out as well. Because ours seems pretty different—the linear and the stream of consciousness" (class debrief, p. 2). Carolina also noticed the different approaches of the two groups.

> It seems to me that the two different groups just approached the assignment in very different ways. Like it sounds like you started from words, text you know, and we really started from pictures and imagery and the words are kind of an afterthought. And for you it's like the words were like a whole basis of how you put the stuff together, so I find that very interesting. (p. 8)

Here, Carolina noticed that the different processes led to different outcomes. However, when I pointed out that Group A's process was shown in the structure of their visual map, Carolina and Aiden expressed surprise.

Carolina   Huh.

Aiden   That's what we look like?

Carolina   I told you I was worried. (class debrief, p. 7)

Group 1 was much more in tune with the fact that their visual representation demonstrated, in its structure and sequencing, the exact process the group went through. Group 1 did not acknowledge or recognize, however, that the visual "tightness" of their map may have represented the sometimes-challenging dynamic they had experienced in their process. Olive spoke up to state that Group 1's map was also representative of their process.

> I feel ours still reflects our process, like theirs reflects theirs. Ours was like that too because we came with a story we organized about what we want the storyline to be and our storyline was focusing back on how did we get here. (p. 7)

Group 1, and Olive in particular, took a defensive tone at times when discussing their map, without being prompted.

Paige was aware that her style better matched the other group's, "I mean, I love you guys, but maybe I should be over there (motioning to Group A)?" (class debrief, p. 3). In the class debrief, Paige again took both sides, criticizing her group in one exchange and supporting it in the next. When Group A's process was under discussion, Paige took the opportunity to voice some of her disagreement with Group 1's process.

> I think our group would have benefited from maybe doing a draft or something, drawing something out first like a general idea, instead of just going straight to the board and putting stuff, it might have made it more visually interesting. (p. 7)

But when Group 1's process was the focus, Paige chimed in with a supportive statement that could also have been understood as criticism depending on one's preferences around structure. When Olive said, "I mean, visually maybe it isn't the most beautiful. I feel it," Paige interjected, "It's structured," and Olive continued, "I feel it is structured, it really tells a storyline" (p. 7).

The deontic logic of agreement, the deontic logic of learning from the experience, strong groupthink, trust-building, and inclusion were themes in both groups. Both groups demonstrated a strong preference for agreement when making decisions, in congruence with the class scores on the PCSI showing more preference for equality, group, and relationship orientations than the average U.S. scores. Paige described her struggle to contribute to the group despite her different instincts.

> Yeah, I tried to just sort of stop. […M…] I do disengage just a little bit, but then I try to figure out […] got to get it done and what can I do to […] help you guys […]. I tried to switch gears at least. (class debrief, p. 4)

In spite of not having had her contributions accepted, it was true that Paige had not given up on the group and had continued to participate. However, rather than doing things in a different way or asking the group for help, she had continued to follow her same pattern with the same result of not being able to step into the flow of her group. Carolina's conclusion to the discussion of bringing outsiders into the group reflected the desire to include and the belief that everyone has a gift and strength that helps out a group, and that the group ought to find a way to resolve their differences.

> Well, I'd say in a situation like that you would find out what that person's really strong gifts are and what they individually can bring to the group that no one else can and you use them for that. Like [Paige] might be an excellent drawer or something. Then, "Paige, would you draw this and draw this?" and something like that. That would be my solution to it. So that you're still included. That's how I would do it. (p. 4)

In fact, Carolina demonstrated her skills in pulling people in throughout the semester and especially supported Bella in helping her make unique contributions in spite of Bella's communication limitations.

Both groups described aspects of the deontic logic of agreement, Group A in a discussion of their cocreation process.

Aiden	We talked about how our experience were similar to relate to that and we started contributing in a group from there. […P, A…]
Paige	So did you have everyone in your group in the beginning drawing on individual paper?
Aiden	Just Carolina. […RR…]
Dianne	Um, because what we were saying for going was expressed. […RR…]
Aiden	I think we went around the table first, each one of us spoke for a minute or two, I think you started first, then I think I, the five of us spoke and we agreed, okay, that's where we're coming from and then we had the circles and then we just kind of discussed then about we knew what kind of materials, we had the pictures and what the pictures represent. (class debrief, p. 6)

It was interesting to notice that both groups were convinced that they had made their decisions from a place of group agreement. Olive described Group 1's deontic logic of agreement, saying, "[…] in that story line there was definitely a common understanding of that we have this experience and we agreed on this experience" (p. 7). Group A did not acknowledge that silence was accepted as agreement, and Group 1 did not acknowledge that dissent was oppressed.

Another aspect of deontic logic exposed and named by both groups was that one ought to trust the group to succeed in the task without one person controlling the process.

> I think we learned to just trust each other more and we put something on there, we would work around it and work with it and just build on it. One example is I know at first Eugene was trying to find an image depicting an entry or something that represented one of the locations like Potrero or Nob Hill. He would put another image for the end results on where people come out of CCSF but then it just became more of trying to describe the locations themselves and we just […] tried to define the images. (Dianne, p. 9)

Certainly, the group had worked together before this event, but this description leads to the interpretation that the group entered a deeper layer of trusting each other that resulted from this activity.

Nick described his feeling that everyone added to the process, saying, "I feel like that everyone had an idea kind of that they wanted to incorporate and it happened" (class debrief, p. 15). Aiden felt that the group energy freed him from his usual pattern of overthinking his choices and learned that giving in to the group could be a good thing.

> […] If I had done it on my own, I think I would have been overthinking it. I might have come up with the idea, I might have overthink it, "Should I go into the neighborhoods?" or "Is this right or is that right?" As everyone else was contributing, I think it kind of gave me a freedom to say […] okay, I can do this 'cause it's going to be diverse anyway. But if I was doing it on my own, which I do a lot of stuff on my own, I tend to get totally into it and overthink it like perfectionist kind of stuff. But this was kind of liberating to just be in the group. (p. 11)

Each group discussed more or less indirectly a desire for commonality in the coconstruction process, a desire to agree with each other in various aspects of the task.

> […] it's okay to relinquish control sometimes and let the process happen, and you'll end up with the results. My instinct is to want to piece it all together myself and micromanage to a certain extent. It was nice letting everybody participate and […] see how we worked as a group to […] create this thing together. (Nick, p. 21)

Even though the experience of the group process was very different for each group, deep learning connected to the benefits of working in a group was a key element participants mentioned as a take-away from this activity.

Nick noted that this experience and these principles would apply to any area in life, "I can't really separate this experience from working with people in general. I mean, you could really apply it to any area of your life if you wanted to, in interacting with other people, the same principles there" (class debrief, p. 21). His statement here referred to the benefit of simulations as a learning tool.

Carolina noticed in both groups that there were times when everyone checked in with the group as to whether what they were doing was aligned with the collective thinking of the group, which would help her in her work supervising volunteers.

[…] it sounds like for each of our groups there were times when there were a personality kinda misplaced […] the person that really felt like, "Well, this group is going very linear and I am sort of more associative," and vice versa […]

(In our group) there was a lot of nonverbal communication […] everybody just kind of went ahead and did what they felt comfortable doing, but at one point at least everybody would stop and say, "Is it okay if I do this?" […] I think […] for a moment they didn't feel they were a part of the collective […] they had to find permission to come back in and that moment of uncertainty. […]

And that helps me when I am working with these groups of volunteers that at some point there's going to be a person who is kind of the odd one out and at some point everybody is going to bump into something they're not certain of. (class debrief, p. 22)

The debrief process assisted participants to stimulate these connections for themselves and in each other.

Both group leaders described a level of discomfort with leadership positions.

For me this is still a new team, so at some point in my life I let go of having to manage everybody doing what I thought that they should be doing, and I think I have a lot of permission for people to just contribute how they can contribute. Possibly what I do best is just having that permission there for it come out the way it is appropriate to come out. (Carolina, class debrief, p. 4)

Carolina, in fact, led in every team she participated, but stepped back more and more as the semester progressed. At one point, Carolina openly relinquished her leading of the conversation, saying, "Someone else needs to talk" (p. 6). Aiden immediately stepped in to describe Group A's process, demonstrating his position as Group A colead. Michelle described her discomfort with taking on the role of leader, and Paige spoke up to praise Michelle's leadership style.

Michelle   […] I don't really like to be in a leadership role, I really don't, but […] I like results and I like to get things done and so if there's sort of like a vacuum or waffling […] I have to sort of marshal people together and […] let's just get it done, because I am an end results kind of person.

Paige   That's what I really like is that you like sort of take on leadership roles, not like you're a reluctant leader, but you know what I mean. Not, like, it's a power trip for you at all—it's just sort of more of an "Okay, let's move it forward," and […] I like that a lot about you. I think that's what you're saying. (class debrief, p. 13)

Here Paige supported the leader who had shut her down repeatedly during the cocreation process.

Group A participants eloquently described their experience of a flow state during the coconstruction process, in the following discussion of the decision-making process. Olive's question showed her awareness of the differences between the groups.

Aiden   I think it's interesting how our group kind of formed. You started drawing and we just kind of just fed off that and it just kind of all came to everyone put in what they wanted to put in, and we felt comfortable with that, no one was really like 'don't put that in' 'you got to put that in' everyone was really open […C…]

Aiden   I felt everybody contributed what they wanted to contribute, when I look at it I can see all different people, like what they put into it.

128

Olive	Is that why there's so many trade secrets?
Aiden	That's it, yeah.
Carolina	Well, it was unspoken, we really just trusted that we knew what we were doing and to let everybody do it. It's just different, just a different way of doing it. (class debrief, p. 4)

Group rapport was certainly a key element supporting Group A's ability to step into the flow state so easily. At another moment, Eugene and Aiden described the flow state itself and Group A's experience of rapport.

Eugene	I think our group just worked as a unit. We didn't say much, we just started doing things and everyone worked around each other's ideas and it came together really well.
Aiden	[...] It was definitely fun [...] [...C...]
Aiden	[...] I think we were all on the same page, there's no right or wrong way to do this. Just do it and just do whatever we want. (p. 9)

Aiden's sharing of the enthusiasm about his experience was unusual (compared to other face-to-face class meetings he participated in during the semester) and contagious.

Even though Group 1 experienced conflict and had a harder time reaching the flow state, they did experience moments of flow and their rapport was also confirmed by caring about each other. In the class debrief, Olive set herself apart from Group 1 by self-identifying as a noncreative member who did not contribute to the group—each of the other four members spoke up to contradict her, with the effect of drawing her back into the group.

Olive	[...] I see what I can put together, I know what I like no problem. That's part of visual, that's part of design why am I comfortable there. But when it comes up there, I can't reflect myself, I don't know what myself is up there and that upsets me because it seems inconsistent. [...]
Paige	You are a little self-defeating, because it's almost as if as soon as you start, you automatically go into a little tirade "I don't know, I can't do this"—you know what I mean. But you totally, I mean, you can. You contributed just as much as everybody else all of what's up there.
Michelle	One of the first things you said when we were on the floor looking at pictures was, "I can't draw, you guys do it." Well you just defeated yourself by saying you can't draw, and I experience the same thing and I tell myself that I can't draw but if you tell yourself you can't do it then you're not going to do it...
Rusena	But you (Olive) added color in it. [...M,R,O,R...]
Nick	But the stars, that's where I got the idea for that.
Olive	Thank you. (class debrief, pp. 12–13)

Again, the debrief process provided unique opportunities for the participants to support each other and confirm mutual caring, which are usually not available to that extent in the normal class routine.

The groups discussed the question of whether Group A's flow-state process would be a valid approach to a professional assignment, and openly expressed their different perspectives of the task. Group A's comments indicated that they perceived Group 1's map as closer to what a professional client might want.

Aiden   [...] I think in a situation where somebody would be paying you or something you'd probably have to be a bit more like—

Carolina —more like them (Group 1).

Aiden   Yes, exactly. (class debrief, p. 9)

Group A had a hard time connecting the fun aspect with which they had labeled their experience to professional responsibilities. Later on, Aiden stated, "I think we could come up with something pretty useful if we had to (out of Group A's visual map) [...] I think there are ideas there" (p. 19). Dianne described Group A's visual map as "more unfiltered, I guess, as opposed to how (Group 1) filtered what they put up [...] eventually ours could probably look like (Group 1's visual map)" (p. 19). Carolina considered the fact that the research process was ungraded, "so it was fun [...] like sandbox" rather than her usual class performance anxiety (pp. 19–20). In spite of brief moments spent questioning the validity of their work, Group A returned to the essence that dominated their experience and connoted it as fun.

Olive pointed out that Group 1 took the project as seriously as if it were classwork, even checking their design for balance and other design elements and principles, partly due to her influence.

Dianne   [...] for instance, today we didn't keep stepping back and say "Where's the balance in this?" [...] "Are we covering the white space?" [...]

Olive   We did that in ours, we stepped back and go, "Where's the balance? Is there too much white space?" I mean, we tried to incorporate. I kind of looked. Even though this was a fun day, I wanted the results to reflect all the principles, especially now that we're going into critiquing, so trying to apply that. So I am probably better at asking those questions than trying to get that to where we should be. (class debrief, p. 20)

At times, the debrief questions encouraged some competition between the groups, which resulted in each group sharing their successes.

While Group A did not experience any time pressure (a characteristic of flow states), Group 1 was always highly aware of time running out. Nick voiced his opinion that Group 1 focused on the structure because of the time pressure, saying "but with the time deadline made it sort of challenging" (class debrief, p. 8). Michelle spoke up in favor of Paige's suggestion that a preliminary sketch would have been a good idea and helped with the time pressure, but "we kind of had run out of most of our time" (p. 8). While Group 1 noticed that the quality of their product might have suffered because of the experienced time pressure, they did not seem to make any connections between potential loss in relationship-building opportunities because of the focus on task.

Culture Evoked

The cocreation process evoked multiple cultural frames, because participants had to expose values and beliefs in order to agree upon the storyline and complete the task. The reflective mode of the class debrief evoked culture more strongly, and also brought up a critical incident about stereotyping.

When invited, participants easily generated stereotypical images of national cultures. For instance, when asked what a map would look like that was created by Germans, Michelle said it would be "more linear" (class debrief, p. 14). Aiden described a group of Irish, saying, "there'd be, like, much more arguing and stuff, more like, in your face" (p. 25). Paige (a White American and native of San Francisco) brought up the belief that there is more cultural competence in San Francisco:

> [...] it's always multicultural, it seems that's just such a big part of what American culture is to me, it is a multicultural culture, you know, so I mean, I even thought it was sort of funny that you guys wanted to have that stuff about the multicultural thing, because for me it's so much a part of just the air it wouldn't even be a subject that I would even think about because it's so much just around. (p. 26)

Carolina (U.S. Caucasian) made a similar statement, "Being in San Francisco, it's exposed me to so many different cultures and thought processes. There's a level of acceptance here that after awhile you're just like 'okay'" (p. 23). While Carolina minimized cultural differences, Paige actually denied them, demonstrating a regression.

Dianne brought up Filipino culture as, "[...] more [...] comfortable in the way that you could say something and you would understand what they meant. [...] a lot more joking around but with coming from the same topics" (class debrief, p. 25). Dianne also pointed out that,

> I had to do a lot of explaining to my parents about what graphic design was, because it's not something a lot of traditional Filipino parents are familiar with. They're familiar with routes for [...] nurses and doctors and dentists, because of other family members. (p. 25)

When asked further about this comment, Dianne referred to her culture as high-context, meaning that it is taken for granted that one either knows the protocol or has to be properly introduced to the way things are handled (Hall, 1959, as discussed by Trompenaars & Hampden-Turner, 1998).

Shortly after this discussion, I drew attention to the fact that the African American population was not adequately represented in the design community, including our class. This statement produced a rich but uncomfortable discussion.

Olive That's because they are good at singing and athletic stuff, they can't be good at everything, they have to save some for us. [...] I'm sorry, I'm stereotyping completely. But seriously, I feel like African American people are born with those two gifts, singing and sports.

Michelle I'm not good at athletics.

Rusena (looking at Michelle) But you sing better.

Michelle Yeah, well, there's a lot of people that sing.

Olive They're definitely born with a gift. (class debrief, p. 24)

Culture was evoked in this comment in the form of a serious violation that surprised Olive (in the DMIS stage of acceptance) herself and many other participants. The conflict was addressed publicly and privately, and both participants managed to recover from this incident fairly quickly. Their ethnorelative positions may have been a reason for the capacity to forgive and move on. This incident was one of those perfect teaching moments, which I took advantage of by discussing the group's PCSI scores and cultural styles during the next face-to-face meeting.

Expected Patterns Versus Observed Behavior

In the critical stereotyping incident, both Olive and Michelle backtracked to the DMIS defense stage briefly (polarization, us-vs.-them orientation), but caught themselves in the act. Eugene confirmed his DMIS stage of acceptance by offering a statement of empathy:

I think that's socialization. That is how people see them, so that is the path that they take. It's not that they are necessarily good at it, but they become good at it because that's what society expects of them. And I think in most societies, that's how people grow up. What you expect from them is what you give to that. That's what you want to be, you want to fit in in any type of society and if you want to fit in that's what you're going to do. (class debrief, p. 24)

Eugene handled this situation well and also provided some learning for the rest of the class in that moment. Michelle was understandably still upset, saying,

[...] If people feel you're not supposed to do that because no one ever expects you to do it, then you're never going to do it and it doesn't mean that you don't have educational [...]. I don't know, I'm getting emotional. (p. 24)

It only took a few minutes for Michelle to notice that she had slipped into an emotional space that was not helping the situation. Her recognition and naming of that fact in the midst of a very stressful situation demonstrated a form of coordinating the meaning-making she was part of. Olive, on the other hand, needed about twenty minutes to realize the full scope of the event, her part in it, and the potential consequences.

I decided to take the heat off of Michelle (the only African American participant) when she shared her emotional state because we had almost reached the end of the classtime and I needed some time to close this wound. I stated that there were stereotypes for all cultures. Olive (Vietnamese/Chinese American) replied, "Oh yeah, we can't drive" (p. 24). Several participants then contributed stereotypes of their own cultures.

Michelle showed a typical response of being re-stimulated (triggered vis-à-vis a "well meaning" attack against her race and ethnic group in regard to academic achievement). Concerning the issue of academic achievement in African American communities, it has been described that "when blacks are placed in achievement situations, the negative stereotypes are activated and black students become more self-conscious and work less efficiently" (Steele & Aronson, 1995, as quoted by Johnson & Johnson, 2005, p. 456). Michelle had all the signs of being successful in school (quick comprehension, academic competence, accuracy, timely completion of tasks, leadership skills, and excellent communication skills) and was especially offended by Olive's comment.

When the American or U.S. Caucasian/White participants joined the discussion of stereotyping, Carolina said that people come to San Francisco because they don't want to be with their "natural" cultures, so that they can gain other perspectives and experience other aspects of life. Paige said that she was born in San Francisco and that, to her, all she knew about the US was multiculturalism. Then Nick made a statement that demonstrated his depth of awareness.

> But I do think there's a certain amount of American culture that is homogenized...But basically that there's a whole world out there [...] it is a feeling of [...] being really isolated in a bubble [...] to what extent am I imposing my own kind of context on the world around me. I feel like there is a lot out there that is sort of sucked into this like American culture that when it's spit out we're all just kind of from my own personal experience it gets kind of glossed over. (class debrief, p. 26)

Nick did not speak much during the class debrief, but when he made a comment it was usually indicative of a sensitivity beyond his DMIS score of minimization.

Expanding his role as group mediator to the entire class, Nick shared an amazing epiphany about his comfort zone that provided a beautiful uplifting closure for the group—a healing moment that was much needed at this point. Significantly, this healing moment was provided by a participant who occupied the DMIS stage of minimization.

> I think it's getting outside of the comfort zone, at least, for me, getting outside of my comfort zone and I don't know why, for whatever reason I am aware of this kind of black and white mentality about life and not accepting uncertainty for this gray area that as I try and, like, compartmentalize any part of my reality that that inherently restricts my experience and the way that I interface with people. (class debrief, p. 28)

133

With this comment, Nick demonstrated high density in minimization through his self-awareness and movement (leap, even) into ethnorelativism through his ability to take perspectives outside of his own frame.

Olive raised the question of Paige's disharmony with the group in a very indirect way that implied her sensibility for keeping the relationship intact and also expressed her concern for equality. In all three aspects she falls somewhere in the middle of the PCSI continua or slightly to the left, meaning that her behavior could fall to either side of the orientation.

> I'm sorry, in my opinion, Paige's style is very distinguished, so when we came together as a group to do this, when your style is so distinguished that when you come together as a group, she was mentioning it's hard if she has a certain way to do that, then she gets a little bit disengaged right? (class debrief, p. 3)

With this statement, Olive may also have been making an attribution error, in which causes of another participant's behavior are attributed to his or her personality while one's own behavior is considered contextual.

Michelle's contribution to this discussion showed her preferences for task-orientation, direct communication style, and linear time:

> I felt that you (Paige) kind of were having problems, like, with how it was sort of going but it was, like, the clock was ticking and we have to get it done so that's hard to try to play (class debrief, p. 3)

It would be interesting to know how Michelle would have handled the situation without the perceived time pressure and whether this factor also influenced her stronger preference for a direct communication style or task-orientation than her PCSI scores indicated.

Asked what a map based on Dianne's work would look like, Dianne answered,

> It would look more linear. At first our sketch looked pretty linear, there was an end result and entry type of person or people and CCSF as something that would help people from the trajectory. But what I noticed what was happening up there wasn't what matched the picture. I was a little scared at first but I learned to work with it and it came out nice in the end. Not as linear, but... (class debrief, p. 9)

Dianne had the highest score on group orientation, as reflected by her compromising her personal preferences to stay with the group. Her group orientation preference showed up consistently, and Dianne was highly conscious of her need to seek approval before placing images because of her desire to maintain what the group had decided, saying, "I would ask 'What represents this location?' and then go look for a picture that helps out. Because if I were to randomly stick pictures up it probably wouldn't relate to the group's thinking" (p. 10). Dianne had excellent rapport with all students in the class, and her group-oriented behavior was consistent throughout the semester.

In contrast to Dianne, Aiden and Eugene operated from confidence that they would do the right thing and did not seek approval of their choices. Aiden said, "I just stuck it (an image) up," and "I was trying to do the right thing, so I kind of felt confident" (class debrief, p. 11). This level of independence is supported by Aiden's PCSI orientation toward task but may stand in tension with his preference toward group orientation. Eugene said, "I did the exact same thing Aiden did. I just started sticking pictures up there based on what I'd learned here from 16 years" (p. 11). However, Eugene's independence contradicted his PCSI scores that leaned toward both relationship and group orientations.

Bella's overall silence and nonparticipation throughout the entire experience did not match her strong group orientation. However, her description of learning how to speed up the process when there was time pressure did align with her PCSI preference for being part of a team while still being task-focused.

> How to share our own experience with each other, and how to make the work, how to done the work faster when we only have 30 minutes. [...RR,B,RR...] I will apply that in my job, in my work. [...R...] I have to work faster, so in the store I have to put the produce when it's over and the people go and produce go faster, so I have to go faster before the store is closed. (class debrief, pp. 20–21)

Bella also demonstrated her learning preference in this comment by expressing that she learned from observing.

The Innate (Nature) and the Cultural (Nurture)

The issue of innate versus cultural came up multiple times but could not be clearly separated. For instance, a question about a direct communication style was initially coded as dominant personality by Dianne, who had the most indirect communication style and highest score on group orientation on the PCSI of the entire class. Regarding whose ideas were represented on the visual map, Dianne stated, "because whoever was more vocal personality-wise, well, that could go for culture and personality but they had more of a way to put what they wanted up there" (class debrief, p. 10). Behavior resulting from a direct communication style and orientation toward individualism could easily be (mis-)interpreted as a violation by a culturally inexperienced individual. Because Dianne practiced indirect communication it is not clear from this comment whether she was actually criticizing the behavior or simply making a point about the innate (nature) versus the cultural (nurture).

Overall, participants agreed that the cultural and the innate could not be separated. Dianne expressed that a map made by a group of Diannes would be more linear; asked whether this choice is due to cultural conditioning or personality, she said, "I think both play a part" (class debrief, p. 9). When asked why some people are more verbal than others, she said, "to be more verbal (pause) both personality and culture (pause) it's hard for me to distinguish between the two" (p. 10).

Carolina took the issue a step further when she expressed that she did not feel that culture was an isolatable variable in the group process.

> I would say that I don't know that you can separate (personality and culture) in this situation […] I think you have to take into account personality, environment, expectations, experience—all these sorts of things come together at once […]. Dianne can be a very associative person that's been forced into a very linear "You should be this way," and Bella's got things going on that we will never know about, and all of a sudden they come out in this little package […]. (p. 22)

With this comment, Carolina showed her interpretation of Dianne's behavior as culturally driven (deviating from what Dianne might prefer innately) and Bella's behavior as an indefinable mix of innate and cultural. It also needs to be noted that she brought in the situational dimension as a variable, which indicates a rather sophisticated understanding of the dynamic relationship between the innate, the cultural, and the contextual in a person's interiority.

During the class debrief, Olive shared that for her it was still hard to live in two cultures, the one her family was from and the one she currently lived in. She also described her personal conflict about two types of personalities, the "assertive" one and the "shy" one. While this is a perfect example of the identity confusion characteristic of people with multiple cultural frames at some point in their development, it is also an example of Olive's confusion as to whether these traits are cultural or innate.

> […] I feel I have two very distinct personality. One is very assertive about certain things I am not shy at all and in other aspect I am so shy I feel like I can't think or break through things and have that assertiveness […]. (class debrief, p. 12)

> […] I feel like I am such two different people […]. (p. 18)

> […] I feel like I am living in two worlds and trying to find a balance, trying to straddle the Asian culture and American life because I have my parents' thinking and that they will force upon me, and then I have the American culture thinking. So living in two worlds is very hard actually. I feel that way still. (p. 27)

This issue of internal conflict came up several times in Olive's comments, and exemplifies the complex reality of people with multiple frames if they have not been integrated into a constructive frame of multiplicity.

Group 1 also discussed the question of how it would have been different in a homogenous group. Michelle didn't think that culture had any impact on how the group interacted with each other or created the map.

> I don't really see how we are, in this particular task how our cultures came into it. Maybe a little bit with the pictures, but I am trying to remember the whole picture section—I think we mostly agreed on the pictures. I don't think, I know I was a sociology major so I know you can never separate those things from yourself from your experiences, but I didn't see how it directly impacted how we worked together on this assignment. (class debrief, p. 14)

This inability to recognize the presence of culture, at least partially, was surprising for an ethnorelative individual scoring in adaptation, the highest DMIS scores in the class. One has to wonder whether other variables influenced what Michelle could notice or not, such as the fact that she was the only African American in her group and in the class. It as also interesting that she coded culture as a significant variable only if it caused disagreement.

Michelle did say that a visual map produced according to Michelle's style "would probably have less color" (p. 14). Paige said a map in her style "would probably be much more all over the place, definitely" (p. 14), to which Rusena added that her own map would have "more drawings, I guess" (p. 14). Asked if it was "a personal thing or a cultural thing," Rusena answered, "No, it's personal" (p. 14). Except for Paige, Group 1 expressed satisfaction about their cocreation. Hearing that many of them would have created the map differently had it been their choice also confirms that this group, in spite of the conflict moments, was able to close the gap between their personal preferences and what emerged in the group.

After the stereotyping incident, Aiden suggested that the polycultural nature of the group affected the communication dynamics by allowing more flexibility, because a group of Irish would definitely act differently.

> […] I think if there were six Irish people […] we'd know each other much more, there'd be […] much more arguing and stuff, more like in your face, maybe that's because we're Irish too. I think there would be more competition among people because they're all the same or something. I think here [San Francisco] is more we're allowing each other more space than if we were all the same. (class debrief, p. 25)

His last comment implies that a diverse group of individuals such as the ones in the class or in San Francisco in general would be more flexible in their interactions in a way that a monocultural group of Irish people would not.

Transformative Learning Experience

As discussed above, this research process was also an intervention for the participants, intended to evoke new understandings of cultural and communication issues. The data collection process related directly to the class content and provided not only an additional avenue for learning to the students but also a transformative experience for all participants, myself included. "All forms of cooperative educational research have the potential to alter the social life of individuals and institutions….as it provides those individuals with opportunities for new or revised forms of social life" (Wagner, 1997, p. 9). As Carolina expressed during the class debrief, "my reception of new information keeps changing as we keep doing different exercises and different approaches" (p. 2)— showing her satisfaction about her learning experiences in this class and tracking her experiences.

Many comments during the class debrief revealed the transformative nature of the experience, particularly in response to the two debrief questions asking what participants learned. The fourth debrief question (see Appendix G) set up the deontic logic (inspired by the wording of the question) that one ought to take some learning away from this experience and apply it to other areas of one's life. All but one participant (Paige) identified something they had learned through this process.

In response to the question " How do you feel?", Dianne answered, "I feel great. I learned something new today as in the classes we've had […]" (class debrief, p. 2). Carolina said, "A little exhilarated, a little fuzzy on the edges like I haven't processed it all, it's kind of swirling around waiting for me to work with […]" (p. 1). Both expressed excitement about the content, but they also brought up the learning from their groups. Dianne stated her main learning as trusting the group, "I think we learned to just trust each other more […]" (class debrief, p. 9). Aiden felt that the group energy freed him from his usual pattern of overthinking his choices. When asked, "So the group helped you do that?", he answered, "Just let it go" (p. 11). Olive mentioned more than once that she learned from her team.

> […] I learn from my team because they are not shy in general I think actually they are all a lot of strength because they really have a vision of what they see. I don't have a visual of what I see. I can tell what I don't like or what I like and I make opinion. I tend to be scared and I don't like that. (p. 12)

For someone who voiced the experience of being scared, Olive was rather engaged and vocal throughout the semester—not to diminish her experience of her limitations. She also described her two different personalities between work (subordinate, fear of judgment) and school (equal, safe experimentation).

> When I am in the professional world I don't feel safe and I kind of play more of the "I am at the bottom, you're at the top." Here I feel as equal and like Michelle I don't want to be a leader, but I like results and if we're not meeting results it concerns me, and I will jump in and try to get results […] it's just a safe environment. I feel if I do some wrong it's okay, judgment is not big. I am not afraid of things, whereas in the corporate world, I kind of play more of "I'm just a little girl who doesn't know a lot." They're very two different personalities. (class debrief, p. 18)

Olive clearly defined her CCSF environment as one of equality that she could step into, while she considered herself in her work environment as leaning toward hierarchy (another example of her identity confusion).

Nick learned that he could trust the team to pull it together even if he couldn't see that happening at first, and that he would take this confidence back to his workplace.

> It was kind of cool for me just sitting down initially and not really understanding where we were going or what was going to happen. Like, mostly when we were selecting the pictures and seeing what everyone was choosing. We all kind of were together on that and really had this vision. But for me seeing it up there and having it all make sense to me compared to

what we started with, it makes sense, and just the fact that we could do that and it helps me to, like, trust more and trust the team. (p. 14)

[…] it's okay to relinquish control sometimes and let the process happen, and you'll end up with the results. My instinct is to want to piece it all together myself and micromanage to a certain extent. It was nice letting everybody participate and […] see how we worked as a group to […] create this thing together. (p. 21)

Participants' ability to recognize and articulate the learning points so well was striking, and not just about Nick. The ability to take the learning to the next level and find applications to one's professional life was another sign of participants' high level of coordination of meaning, but may also have spoken to the effectiveness of the facilitation.

Both groups experienced this process as freeing in ways that they had not in their work lives or in their various classes. Both groups declared the class experience a safer and more fun place than their workplaces. Dianne described the group process as "something for us as a team" (class debrief, p. 18), which Carolina supported, and also "sort of a bonding experience, just having fun with it" (p. 18). Michelle learned from Dianne's discussion that it's useful in the work environment, "sometimes when you are so serious all the time at work sometimes it's fun to do something just for you guys just sort of not wacky, just sort of to let go" (p. 21). The sense of belonging to a group was very important to the participants, and was mentioned many times.

Eugene agreed with Olive that the class environment was safer and stated that he learned, "I think we can work without speaking" (class debrief, p. 16). He found Group A's process agreeable to his nonlinear learning style, and described the sketches he created for work as more planned and linear than the group process.

I wouldn't work like this professionally […] I think it's because we're in a class setting, it's a different kind of environment. It's safer and […]. I just kind of let myself go start putting things up […]. So it's more structure, more linear. That's how it would look at work. (p. 18)

While some people saw a lot of correlation or opportunities to take their learning back to their professional life, Eugene was somewhat skeptical. He finally decided he would take brainstorming activities away as a useful tool for his work environment, saying, "I would try to think outside of the box and see if I can get everything done more efficiently and quicker" (p. 19).

After the critical stereotyping incident, Olive openly named her discomfort:

It started out as something fun, but as we started sharing and analyzing, I am feeling anxiety […] having thoughts that are spoken so honestly, and also just thinking about your own behavior and what you can do better, and I don't know I just have this not warm-fuzzy feeling any more. (class debrief, p. 28)

The fact that Olive could express her feelings so freely in a sensitive moment spoke to her level of competence in coordinating the meaning emerging from her experience. Dianne's response reflected on the class debrief as an intervention, bringing the participants to a new place.

I thought we were working well as a team because we were getting things done and it might just be because we are afraid to cross those boundaries and right now that's kind of what we are doing and that's very uncomfortable. (p. 28)

With this statement, Dianne disclosed her preference for group- and relationship-orientation that would imply a focus on group harmony rather than personal needs.

Then Nick brought up the fact that U.S. culture was somewhat homogenized, that Americans lived in a bubble compared to other parts of the world, and that he noticed his own boundaries as a false sense of security—observations placing him beyond his DMIS stage of minimization. He named his anxiety in his role as mediator and healer to the class.

And that, yeah, I do feel a little anxious after talking about it, but having those feelings of security and comfort I've really come to find that those aren't really real, that it's kind of false. Inherently, there's always going to be this unknowing. As soon as I start trying to define things, is when I stop looking at them for what they really are. (class debrief, p. 28)

Nick's comfort with suspending himself in liminality demonstrated, more than once, his capacity for ethnorelativity and possibly beyond. After his closing statement, I ended the class debrief because we had run out of class time, but made myself available for anyone who wanted or needed more closure.

Member Check

Toward the end of my data analysis (several months later), I met with all the participants again to double-check my initial interpretation of the data and get their feedback on my findings. Participants were largely in agreement with the results. Groups acknowledged that they were aware who the leaders were but that they did not recognize the coleads (including the coleads themselves who did not notice that they had played that role). All four supporters acknowledged that they were aware of their supporting tasks, which they identified as relationship-building. While the leaders were working onstage, the supporters were consciously working in the background to make sure everyone was included and consensus was reached.

Both groups had an outgroup participant and according to the feedback of the outgroup members, they had been highly aware of their role and confirmed that this was, in fact, a familiar experience for them personally. It was acknowledged by the less verbal participants that those who were dominant in the planning stage and during the process got their ideas represented more so than others. We found that there was a noticeable similarity between the seating choices made for the class debrief and how participants arranged themselves for the member check.

Participants brought up two points that deserve attention. When discussing the LS results that identified 80% of the participants as accommodators, they suggested that the design and facilitation of the class favor project-based learning over lectures, group- orientation over individualism, and active experiential participation over observation, all of which would be very comfortable for accommodators. Participants suggested that the students who withdrew from the class may have inhabited other positions and may therefore not have been enthusiastic about continuing the class. This possibility is worthy of consideration for the future design of the class, although I very rarely get such lopsided scores on the LS—the majority of my classes have had a much wider distribution of learning styles. Hypothetically it is also possible that participants shifted toward group- and relationship-orientations because of their positive experiences during the semester.

Another interesting point was brought up by the supporters, who questioned the definition of leadership. Supporters felt that participants who worked behind the scenes to make sure relationships were nourished should be included in the group leadership, rather than only the dominant participants whose engagement was more noticeable. This feedback strongly supported leadership in both groups as a shared responsibility, as described in the distributed-action and interaction-process theories of leadership (Johnson & Johnson, 2005).

Participant Profiles

Using both primary and secondary data sources, I compiled a thick profile for each participant. These profiles cannot be considered exhaustive, since my focus was on the interaction between the individuals. However, investigation using the profiles was helpful in the analysis of the instruments and their effectiveness for this type of inquiry. Profiles include participants' own offerings about their age, gender, origin, residence(s), education level, culture, ethnic background, and language skills. In addition, the profiles include each participants' results from the IDI-2, TPI, PCSI, LS, and MI as well as their class participation figures. The MI scores were very diverse, and participants' highest three preferences are listed in their personal profiles. Where a participant's score was identical for two or more intelligences, all are included. (See Appendix B for complete data tables for the TPI, PCSI, LS, and MI as well as class participation figures.)

Aiden

Aiden is a 46-year-old male who identifies his nationality as Irish and U.S., and his ethnic background as white. His country of origin is Ireland. His native language is English. He also has what he describes as a "fair" knowledge of Irish and Spanish. He lived in Germany for two years, and has been living in the US for 25 years, and in San Francisco for the past seven years. Aiden spent his formative years in Western Europe. He is a college graduate. Culturally, he identifies as

Irish, European, Western, and American. On data collection day, Aiden acted as colead and as an independent participant.

Aiden's IDI-2 scores placed him in the DMIS stage of acceptance with an overestimation of his intercultural sensitivity by one stage (see Figure 18). Aiden demonstrated his occupation of acceptance consistently throughout data collection day. There were no signs of his denying, defending, or minimizing any culture including his own. He corrected my background as Austrian when I made a reference to a Teutonic cultural heritage (class debrief, p. 23)—a sign of ethnorelativity. On another occasion, he gave a neutral account of how Irish would solve a particular problem (p. 25). Both statements demonstrated his ability to create detailed categories of cultural references.

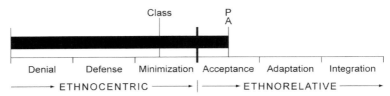

Figure 18. Aiden's (PA) score on the Intercultural Developmental Inventory, version 2 (IDI-2). Author's image.

On the TPI, Aiden scored within the medium range for almost every stage of team performance with the exception of low scores for implementation (clear process, alignment, and disciplined execution).

Compared to the U.S. average scores on the PCSI, Aiden was more oriented toward equality, more oriented toward an indirect communication style, significantly more oriented toward group orientation, slightly more oriented toward relationships, and more oriented toward caution (see Figure 19). However, in his actions during the map coconstruction he demonstrated strong tendencies toward individual orientation and risk taking—possibly pointing toward multipositionality in his cultural styles. While he described his group experience very much as a collaborative effort, he acted as an individual many times. For instance, when asked whether he considered anybody else's opinion when placing items on the map Aiden responded, "No, I just stuck it up" (class debrief, p. 11).

Aiden self-identified as an accommodator on the LS; intrapersonal intelligence is his highest preference, followed by linguistic and musical intelligence.

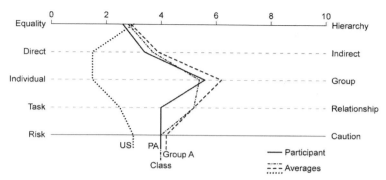

Figure 19. Aiden's (PA) score on the Peterson Cultural Style Inventory (tm) (PCSI), shown with Group A, class, and U.S. averages. Author's image.

Aiden is a very talented professional musician and songwriter who struggled with the fact that this class required a lot of group interaction. His total for online participation was 108% of the average, but he had the second lowest number of postings in the class (58% of the class average). On many occasions Aiden expressed frustration with the (online) group process. In his final reflection he wrote,

> The group experience was not much fun for me. […] Significant moments were when I stopped taking responsibility for what others were not doing and started taking care of what I could control. […] Beyond the classwork, I learned how to work in a virtual group, however awkward and alien I found it. (final reflection, May 19, 2007) (see Appendix N for the final reflection form)

As for many other students, getting used to the online environment represented a learning curve for Aiden. In addition, it usually takes teams about half a semester before they fall into a productive pattern as a group in spite of a focus on team-building during that time. On data collection day, however, Aiden was most engaged and group-oriented compared to his otherwise more withdrawn style that matched his preference for an intrapersonal orientation.

Bella

Bella is an 18-year-old female who identifies her nationality as American and her ethnic background as Hispanic. Her country of origin is the US. At the age of two she moved to El Salvador where she lived until 16 months before data collection day, when she came to San Francisco. Her native language is Spanish, and she considers English a foreign language. Bella spent her formative years in Central America. She is a high school graduate. Culturally, she

143

identifies as Hispanic and Latina. On data collection day, Bella acted as an outgroup participant and as an observer.

Bella's IDI-2 scores placed her in the DMIS stage of defense with issues in reversal and an overestimation of her intercultural sensitivity by two and a half stages (see Figure 20). However, in a private e-mail her description of not feeling as if she belonged to a particular culture could possibly indicate a position in encapsulated marginalization (integration). Bella wrote, "No. I'm not more Salvadorian even American. I'm out of those two different cultures" (personal communication, May 16, 2007). In her personal interview, when asked what her culture was she answered, "I think I have many cultures because I interact with a lot of different cultures" (p. 8).

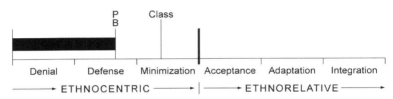

Figure 20. Bella's (PB) score on the Intercultural Developmental Inventory, version 2 (IDI-2). Author's image.

Regarding her contact with Chinese students in her San Francisco high school, Bella expressed,

> [...] Maybe sometimes it is difficult because they are Chinese people and they have another culture and we speak and they misunderstand me and you have to be more clear. [...] I just try to learn their language. Show myself interested in their culture so they say, she wants to learn what we do and they come close. [...] because I like to learn how they live and how they act to people. (personal interview, p. 5)

These statements demonstrated Bella's strategies for communicating across cultures, and her genuine interest in the Chinese she met at school—not the characteristics of someone in defense. While Bella was certainly still learning how to be effective in U.S. culture (her chosen current residence), and thus may very well have inhabited positions of ethnocentricity at times, she also demonstrated a capacity for ethnorelativity that was not captured by the IDI-2.

On the TPI, Bella scored every stage of team performance within the medium range.

Compared to the U.S. average scores on the PCSI, Bella was more oriented toward hierarchy, more oriented toward an indirect communication style, dramatically more oriented toward group orientation, more relationship-oriented, and more cautious (see Figure 21). Bella compared her PCSI profile to the El Salvador profile, and her curve was mostly very similar to the

El Salvador profile in structure but slightly shifted toward a Western frame. The only exception was in the direct versus indirect orientation, where she exactly overlapped with her Salvadoran community. When asked about this interesting similarity, Bella responded by demonstrating no clear identity for her cultural experience:

> When I was in El Salvador, my friends, teachers, people around me asked me where I come from because my thoughts, and behavior are different from them. For example, They like to be one hour late for meetings even if it is important, I don't like to be late (I really hate that), and when I have an important meeting I even arrive half hour early. They like to hide their thoughts, but me when I want I say what I really I'm feeling. [...] USA culture, I guess that be so far where I real belong to makes me feel stranger. They like to talk, and I see they are more social, but I don't like to talk too much. (personal communication, May 16, 2007)

Bella was consistent in her behavior throughout the semester—quiet, withdrawn, yet attentive. She communicated vigorously by e-mail and was seeking connections with others in her own way, but hardly spoke.

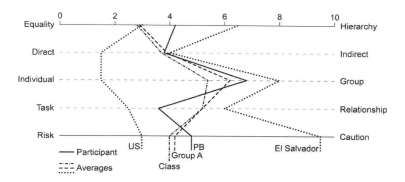

Figure 21. Bella's (PB) score on the Peterson Cultural Style Inventory (tm) (PCSI), shown with Group A, class, Salvadoran, and U.S. averages. Author's image.

Bella's PCSI score showed a strong group orientation, expressed in her personal interview response about how decisions were made in her team, "When they asked me something just say, 'Yes, I agree'" (p. 11). She confirmed this notion many times during the interview. When asked again how that influenced her sense of self, she consistently confirmed that she would always agree instead of expressing her own feelings, "Maybe they did not want to know my different opinion. I did not want to be outside the group" (p. 11). When asked whether she experienced any internal conflict about this issue she said, "I just ignore that" (p. 11). Her response confirmed a strong preference for group orientation and possibly a symptom of voluntary assimilation, but one also needs to consider the possibility of her feeling alienated in both of the cultures she participated in (El Salvador and the US).

Bella self-identified as a diverger on the LS, the only one in the class, and confirmed this position throughout with a heavy emphasis on observation; linguistic intelligence was her highest preference on the MI, followed by intrapersonal and musical intelligence. From another context I am aware of the fact that Bella writes poetry in Spanish and enjoys getting lost in her creative world, which would confirm her preferences for evoking linguistic and intrapersonal intelligences.

Bella was challenged by her English language skills, and was, by far, the quietest student in the face-to-face meetings and in the online forum in spite of her vigorous online reading. Bella had a low participation score in postings (55%) but a relatively high score for reading pages online (118%). While she was the quietest student in the class, her scores indicated that she was always present, observing and participating in her own way. Some of her peers informally mentored Bella through the online forum and assisted her in the leadership role as moderator, which she reluctantly accepted only once during the semester. Many Spanish online postings went back and forth in Bella's team—meant for those who spoke Spanish (Eugene fluently, Carolina enough to connect with Bella)—to encourage Bella with her tasks.

Bella was conscious of the fact that the role of observer (outsider) is a comfortable one for her, in the classroom and in other areas of her life. After the member check, Bella wrote in an e-mail:

> You're right with the things that I was the outsider, and observe person in the group. I also know that I play that roll since we start the class. I wish you could tell me something that I don't know of myself but, I think I know myself so well that you can't tell more than you can see. Be the Outside of the group doesn't feel strange for me it is so natural. I like to observe people's act and their conflict and bad or good ideas. I only share a emotion or my thinking if someone ask me for my point of view. And also I only answer is I have something to say. (personal communication, September 17, 2007)

Bella's preference for silence was striking, and would certainly confirm her learning style of observing the world rather than interacting with it verbally. Bella was silent during the coconstruction process after her first attempt to participate verbally was co-opted. During the class debrief, she did not volunteer any information, but when asked, communicated that she selected images for their colors and content.

The following exchange exemplifies how Bella was a quiet participant, difficult to draw out for various reasons.

Regina   How did you do it, Bella? Did you pick out a picture?

Bella   Yes.

Regina   And how did you decide which picture?

Bella   I just decide the pictures that attract me.

Regina	So you go for your own reference?
Bella	No.
Regina	How did you decide what attracted you?
Bella	Colors, what the image was.
Regina	So you made that judgment from what you liked? The color that you like?
Bella	Yes. (class debrief, pp. 11–12)

Many times communication was difficult not because Bella was not willing to participate in the conversation, but because the turns she made required her conversation partner to think how to connect the parts of what Bella said (usually in an unexpected composition), and then figure out how to reenter the conversation because Bella usually did not leave a connection thread hanging. In the meantime, long moments of silence passed that Bella seemed to be comfortable with but that required patience and willingness by her conversation partner, to sit with her in silence while she held a very focused eye contact.

The following statement in her final reflection, again, demonstrates a metacognition atypical for someone in the DMIS stage of defense:

> If this was a traditional face-to-face class, probably I would choose a desk from the back so the teacher couldn't ask me what I think. If this were a full online class, I could hide my feelings from my team because they never could see my facial expressions....I would like to take an online class again because it's a great opportunity to know people from different perspective 'without judging on the bases of appearance (gender, race, and attractively). (final reflection, May 19, 2007)

Bella's online communication was even harder to follow than the face-to-face interactions. She often posted short, disconnected thoughts that did not seem to relate to any other conversation that was going on in the forum. These stand-alone postings were hard to follow, similar to the example above. Her team never complained about this; Carolina's statement during the class debrief, "Bella got things going on that we will never know about" (p. 22) demonstrated their typical patience and care in spite of the difficulty with communication.

Carolina

Carolina is a 55-year-old female who identifies her nationality as U.S. and her ethnic background as Caucasian. Her country of origin is the US. Her native language is English. She has been living in San Francisco for 22 years. Carolina spent her formative years in North America. She has some college experience. Culturally, she identifies as female, as a professional, with her family, and as a teacher. On data collection day, Carolina acted as the lead, an independent participant, and the gallery walk presenter.

Carolina's IDI-2 scores placed her in the DMIS stage of minimization with an overestimation of her intercultural sensitivity by one and a half stages (see Figure 22). She confirmed this position at times, for instance, in this comment that demonstrated her underlying assumption that her experience is reflective of everyone else's, "and at some point everybody is going to bump into something they're not certain of" (class debrief, p. 22), or in this comment:

> Well, we were on a different process. We got a central idea and then everybody kind of individually contributed to it, but we didn't have a group consensus about everything that was going in it. It was just kind of trusting that we all knew where we were, what the central theme was, and we just kind of let it go from there, so it was not a real control. (p. 4)

This minimization statement assuming everyone was on the same page may have come out of the real experience of the flow state in her group, but was also confirmed by other such comments during the class debrief that were not connected to a conversation about flow. However, Carolina also made a comment indicating movement beyond minimization when she recognized and named cultural relativity:

> Yes (it would be different with a homogenous group) [...] pick anything, pick the educational system, and it's going to be very different from culture to culture. You can pick (pause) Bella brought a religious aspect to our picture [...] she brought a very different spiritual base to stuff [...] I think we all brought our own stuff. (p. 23)

Carolina offered broad themes in this conversation but also demonstrated her ability to make distinctions and appreciate various viewpoints. For instance, she said,

> [...] we don't want to be with our natural culture or whatever so you're talking to people that have separated themselves from whatever that distinction is so that they can see other aspects of life and other viewpoints and other perspectives. (p. 26)

This statement implied ethnorelative distinctions and a desire to grow by exposing herself to other cultures. Usually people will demonstrate characteristics of the next stage when they are ready to move; Carolina's next stage would be acceptance, which could match this statement.

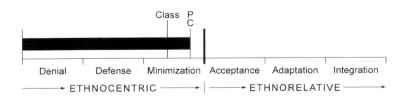

Figure 22. Carolina's (PC) score on the Intercultural Developmental Inventory, version 2 (IDI-2). Author's image.

On the TPI, Carolina self-identified no significant issues to work on in any of the stages of team performance. She scored rather high in the last three stages—higher than in the earlier stages and much higher than her zero in stage one (orientation).

Compared to the U.S. average scores on the PCSI, Carolina was slightly more oriented toward equality; significantly more oriented toward an indirect communication style, group orientation, and relationships; and close in her score in regard to risk versus caution (see Figure 23). Her PCSI scores were largely confirmed in what could be observed of her behavior. In fact, Carolina became group leader in the activity and got along well with her group and the class, as would be expected from her PCSI chart (similar structure in the curves).

In his personal interview, Eugene complimented Carolina on her leadership skills:

> [...] she wasn't oppressive about her leadership, she was more like these are ideas that I have and she would throw it up on the table and then she would go, are any of these good. And I think just by doing that she takes on a leadership position because she takes the initiative. And then we would say, that's good, that's good, and that's good. And she would take that and go, okay, and then go, here's the next step. How about this? And everyone would react to that. (p. 19)

Carolina was an excellent facilitator in her team and, as can be seen here, was appreciated for her abilities to move the ball forward by including the group in the decisions that needed to be made.

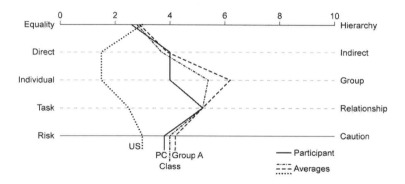

Figure 23. Carolina's (PC) score on the Peterson Cultural Style Inventory (tm) (PCSI), shown with Group A, class, and U.S. average scores. Author's image.

Carolina self-identified as an accommodator on the LS; musical intelligence and visual/spatial intelligence were her highest preferences on the MI, followed by bodily/kinesthetic and intrapersonal intelligence. Carolina was ambidextrous, as she demonstrated by drawing the same image with her left and right hand simultaneously.

Carolina started off as a strong leader and informal mentor but decided to step back from these positions about halfway through the class. Her online participation scores were 86% of the class average for number of hits, 65% for pages read, and 139% for postings. Her overall participation average was third lowest in the class. In her final reflection she wrote, "It's been good for me to poke at my self-imposed limitations, share my knowledge and ham it up during presentation time" (final reflection, May 19, 2007). It was interesting to watch Carolina take this turn outside a leadership role during the second half of the semester, a conscious choice acted upon consistently.

Dianne

Dianne is a 22-year-old female who identifies her nationality and her ethnic background as Filipina American. Her country of origin is the US, and she has never lived abroad. Her native language is English, and she describes herself as having "some" knowledge of Tagalog. She has been living in the San Francisco Bay Area (in the town of Daly City) for six months. Dianne spent her formative years in North America. She is a college graduate. Culturally, she identifies as American, Filipina, and Japanese pop culture. On data collection day, Dianne acted as a supporter and a questioner.

Dianne's IDI-2 scores placed her early in the DMIS stage of defense with some issues in reversal and an overestimation of her intercultural sensitivity by approximately three stages (see Figure 24). However, her description of where cultural influences begin demonstrated more sensitivity than her defense stage would indicate.

> [...] it is not something people choose, like you kind of get born into it. And then that is what you know, so that's normal only when you observe someone else doing something differently, is when you go, hey, wait a moment, there is another growth out there that I didn't know about. (personal interview, p. 4)

This statement implied ethnorelative thinking and an interest in other cultures that was not captured by the IDI-2.

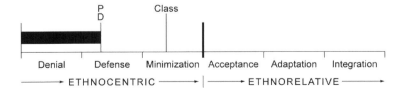

Figure 24. Dianne's (PD) score on the Intercultural Developmental Inventory, version 2 (IDI-2). Author's image.

On the TPI, Dianne self-identified medium scores for most of the stages of team performance with the exception of extremely high scores for orientation (purpose, team identity, and membership).

Compared to the U.S. average scores on the PCSI, Dianne deviated greatly in all five cultural dimensions with the exception of equality where her personal scores were a little bit closer to the U.S. average (see Figure 25). Her behavior matched her PCSI scores. While not identical, her PCSI chart curve is similar in structure to the class average and her group's average—as that similarity may predict, Dianne got along very well with everyone in class.

Dianne self-identified as an accommodator on the LS; visual/spatial intelligence and intrapersonal intelligence were her highest preferences on the MI, followed by linguistic intelligence, all of which were confirmed by her way of working the class assignments and interaction with her peers.

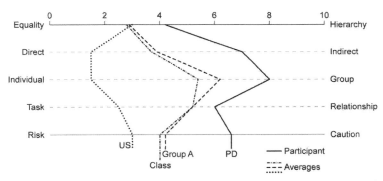

Figure 25. Dianne's (PD) score on the Peterson Cultural Style Inventory (tm) (PCSI), shown with Group A, class, and U.S. average scores. Author's image.

Dianne demonstrated high capabilities with the classwork; in fact, she had the best portfolio and binder in the class, completed her tasks as promised, participated rigorously, and took a sensitive leadership role. Dianne's online participation scores were 120% of the class average for number of hits, 122% for pages read, and 122% for postings—her overall participation average was third highest for the class. When taking a leadership role, she always checked with the others before she made any decisions, but did step forward to act when others didn't. In her final reflection she wrote, "If this was a traditional face-to-face class I would really want to work alone" (final reflection, May 19, 2007). Even though this message is consistent with one of her preferences (intrapersonal intelligence), this note came as a surprise to me as her behavior did not once indicate that she did not enjoy working on her team. She was consistent as an indirect communicator.

Eugene

Eugene is a 40-year-old male who identifies his nationality as Korean, and his ethnic background as Korean American. His country of origin is Korea. His native languages are Korean and English. He also speaks Spanish, Italian, and Russian. He lived in Argentina for seven years, and in Spain for one year. He has been living in the US for 30 years, and in San Francisco for the past 16 years. Eugene spent his formative years in South America. He is a college graduate with a master's degree. Culturally, he identifies as a socialist, a green, and a democrat. On data collection day, Eugene acted as a supporter and as gallery walk copresenter.

Eugene's IDI-2 scores placed him in the DMIS stage of acceptance with an overestimation of his intercultural sensitivity by one stage (see Figure 26).

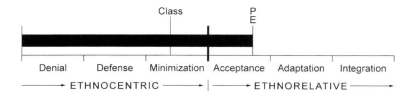

Figure 26. Eugene's (PE) score on the Intercultural Developmental Inventory, version 2 (IDI-2). Author's image.

In his personal interview, Eugene expressed a strong opinion about educational strategies as well as a rather sophisticated understanding of his own cultural background as it relates to his education when he said, "[…] in Argentina education was taken seriously. Since higher education is free and your parents do not have to pay for it—it has a European base—it is all up to you." Asked about the cultural background of his parents, he shared,

> […] Korean, Korean American. I guess they crossed over. They are not completely Korean, they are not completely American, so they get the hybrid immigrant, first generation immigrant mentality and I think it comes from that, because they really emphasize education because in their mind, they were the outsiders, and to be accepted as an outsider, you have to succeed or even do more than what the regular people are within that society. So they were always pushing us to study more, to learn more, to be better, in their minds, a better person, by actually getting straight As. To them grades were a reflection of part of your personality. (personal interview, p. 8)

Eugene demonstrated deep self-awareness about his complex background that he could communicate fluidly and clearly. When asked whether this belief is due to their Korean background or their immigrant status he answered:

> I would say it is because of a combination. But I think it is mostly because they are Korean, because in most of the east Asian countries like China, Japan, Korea, even southeast Asia too, those countries—there is a heavy emphasis on education. Kind of expect on making yourself a better person, not by just being moral, but by giving back to society that gave you all that. So you had a responsibility to the people who gave you the education in the first place so if you never succeeded in getting the education you would never get that. (p. 8)

With this comment he also demonstrated his PCSI preference toward group orientation, which he reinforced when he described his experience of American students complaining about the amount of work in some of his CCSF classes.

> They basically become part of the dominant paradigm, I guess that is the word, and here in the United States, it is not about respect, it is all about what you can take from the system and what you can do with that for yourself. (p. 9)

In these and other comments, while Eugene expressed sophistication in regard to cultural knowledge, he also demonstrated more or less neutral judgmental thinking about individualism. Eugene's judgmental statements could be misinterpreted as ethnocentric (judging cultural norms), but for a person with an ethnorelative worldview beyond the DMIS stage of acceptance, there would be clarity about what he is willing to accept because the moral confusion characteristic of the acceptance stage would have been transcended. It is thus possible that Eugene's judgments are honest and true to his personal morals and that he was comfortable with being critical of any frame that looked opportunistic to him. Eugene never brought up anything that looked like an internal conflict.

When asked to identify his cultural background, Eugene demonstrated a depth that goes beyond acceptance but was not captured by his IDI-2 scores.

> I guess racially, genetically, I am Korean or of the Mongoloid super family, so Mongoloid, Mongol descent Korean, and if I am getting more exact—it is more of North Korean because my family before the war came from the North. And it is culturally and ethnically different so I have to make a difference. So, that's it. Genetically, I am a Mongoloid North Korean. Ethnically, I would say that I am mostly American because—well, that is not ethnically, I think. Ethnically I think I am Korean American because I grew up in a Korean American society. Not strictly American and not strictly Korean, but a hybrid combination [...]. I also grew up in Argentina and I have this affinity for Hispanic, I mean Spanish speakers. (personal interview, p. 14)

Again, this statement (which went on for several more paragraphs) demonstrated a deep understanding of his own background readily available to be translated from his experience into language that was sophisticated and expressed clearly.

> But, even now, if you go to China I don't think someone from Shanghai would say they were Chinese—they would say they are from Shanghai and someone from Beijing would

never consider themselves associated with the Cantonese. And the same thing in Korea— even now, North Koreans are North Koreans. South Koreans are South Koreans. There is no real tie except for the fact that we all consider ourselves Korean but I think ethnically speaking, I mean genetically, we are all probably related and similar, but ethnically the North Koreans are a different people. (personal interview, p. 14)

With this statement, Eugene also demonstrated characteristics of a polycultural worldview. He gauged the unleashing of his intellect and knowledge very carefully.

I never observed him overwhelming anyone with sharing something he did not think they could hold. He had deep knowledge in every area that was discussed, from language to culture to computer science, and could engage with everyone on their level of interest and sophistication. While he spoke English most of the time, he also used his other languages to connect with people on a more personal level. For instance, he spoke Spanish with Bella, and German with me at times.

On the TPI, Eugene scored every stage of team performance equally, within the medium range bordering on high.

Compared to the U.S. average scores on the PCSI, Eugene was more oriented toward equality and slightly more oriented toward a direct communication style. He deviated highly in group-orientation over individualism and relationship-focus over task-orientation, and was also a higher risk-taker (see Figure 27). His chart was a bit unusual in that it jumped back and forth, radically, between the left and right poles. Eugene was far beyond even the U.S. curve in regard to equality and risk-taking, and matched with Asian and Hispanic frames in regard to relationship-building and group orientation. With his DMIS stage of acceptance and capacity to build relationship in groups, Eugene was able to build deep rapport with Bella (Latina) and thus functioned as her support system at times. He also connected to Dianne (Filipina American), while staying in deep rapport with other frames in the room that matched some of his other scores.

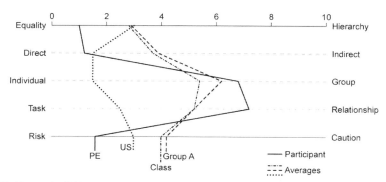

Figure 27. Eugene's (PE) score on the Peterson Cultural Style Inventory (tm) (PCSI), shown with Group A, class, and U.S. average scores. Author's image.

I have seen similar curves from other individuals with a mixed cultural background, which would indicate high flexibility in behavior and potential multipositionality, and this was certainly confirmed by Eugene's adaptability to different scenarios and people throughout the semester. While his deep understanding of his own and others' cultural backgrounds would certainly put him into acceptance on the DMIS, his ability to carry three frames inside himself comfortably (Korean, Latino, and U.S.) may also indicate capacity in integration (which the IDI-2 does measure).

Eugene self-identified as an accommodator on the LS; logical/mathematical intelligence was his highest preference on the MI, followed by intrapersonal, linguistic, and naturalist intelligence. Eugene's scores in online participation surpassed all other participants in hits, pages read, and postings, for an overall participation of 187% compared to the class average. Given Eugene's high level of cultural sensitivity, it is not surprising that in his final reflection he wrote,

> I learned more about cooperation within a diverse group, how to harmonize my perspectives and preconceptions with those of my team mates. The online group exercises, I believe, taught all of us some humility in what we believed was the correct course of action when confronted with diversity....It demonstrated in a microcosm the 'real' world of the working place: an employee can't expect all other employees to hold the same world views as she or he does. Creating this atmosphere of cooperation and camaraderie enabled us to learn the skills to successfully work in a diverse environment. (final reflection, May 19, 2007)

Statements such as this one indicate Eugene's role as a supportive resource for his teachers in polycultural classrooms.

Michelle

Michelle is a 33-year-old female who identifies her nationality as American and her ethnic background as African American. Her country of origin is the US. Her native language is English and she also speaks some Spanish, Italian, and Japanese. She lived in Japan for five years, and has lived in different U.S. metropolitan areas. She has been living in the San Francisco Bay Area (in the town of Alameda) for the past five years. Michelle spent her formative years in North America. She is a college graduate. Culturally, she identifies as American, African American, and female. On data collection day, Michelle acted as a questioner, lead, and gallery walk copresenter.

Michelle's IDI-2 scores placed her early in the DMIS stage of adaptation with a slight overestimation of her intercultural sensitivity by a half stage (see Figure 28). When asked about flexibility regarding code and cognitive frame shifting, she demonstrated her ability to make fine distinctions in cultural difference.

> I think it is also because I moved around before I lived abroad. I never lived anywhere more than five years, so even just changing schools in the US, you have sort of learn how to adapt to people, you know, how they act, how the school is different, how they act in the other school, even though you are in the same country. You just might be two states away, it is

completely different so you always have to figure out how people act and what is acceptable and what is not acceptable. (Michelle, personal interview, p. 8).

Her discussion here reflected her stage of adaptation.

Michelle related a story that demonstrated her ability to suspend judgment early on in her life.

[…] I moved to Japan for five years. And I was, in my sixth grade class, I was one of two black people. […] when I walked outside of the school around Japanese people, a lot of them had never seen a black person except for on television or the movie screen, so you had things where people would come and like rub your skin to see if it came off. […] And it was not like they were being impolite—it is a little impolite just to touch somebody, but it was not malicious that they were doing it. They were curious and that was the way to express their curiosity just like with people with blond hair. They were curious to see what blond hair felt like and looked like so it would be like on crowded trains, I think they felt a little bit safer in a bigger group situation rather than like just coming up to you with hardly anybody around. (personal interview, p. 8)

Michelle demonstrated high capacity for intercultural sensitivity in this story by accepting the Japanese behavior and coding it as innocent curiosity. However, she still lost her equanimity when confronted with a stereotype about her race and ethnic group, and she participated in shutting Paige out from the group. In order to understand this wide range of behavior fully, other variables may need to be considered, such as the dynamic of Michelle's ethnicity as the only African American in class.

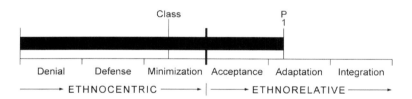

Figure 28. Michelle's (P1) score on the Intercultural Developmental Inventory, version 2 (IDI-2). Author's image.

On the TPI, Michelle gave medium scores for all of the stages of team performance.

Compared to the U.S. average scores on the PCSI, Michelle leaned slightly more toward hierarchy and was more indirect, more group-oriented, more relationship-oriented, and more cautious (see Figure 29). The structure of her curve was very similar to the generic U.S. curve, but more to the right side of the pole on each continuum. This shifting to the right may not come as a surprise considering her background as an African American female. Stereotypically, women in general are coded as more relationship-oriented and more group-oriented, and African American women as more oriented toward hierarchy within their own ethnic group. In addition, Michelle would stereotypically have had to learn to prove herself in the dominant culture—for reasons of safety, therefore, maybe being more cautious, more indirect, and more accepting of social hierarchy. Her PCSI score for task orientation was confirmed and so was her capacity to lead a group through relationship-building.

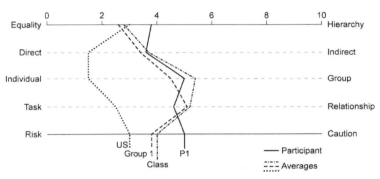

Figure 29. Michelle's (P1) score on the Peterson Cultural Style Inventory (tm) (PCSI), shown with Group 1, class, and U.S. averages. Author's image.

Michelle self-identified as an accommodator on the LS; musical intelligence was her highest preference on the MI, followed by linguistic and visual/spatial intelligence, all of which matched her behavior and performance levels.

Michelle demonstrated high performance abilities and strong leadership skills throughout the semester. Michelle's online participation scores were 96% of the class average for number of hits, 92% for pages read, and 107% for postings. Michelle's overall participation average was 94% of the class average. In her final reflection she wrote,

> I also learned a lot more in terms of how to work in groups both virtually and in face-to-face meetings....Setting up and managing a team has been a challenge throughout the course of the semester. While I find that the lessons I learned about how to work with people who have different motivations, learning styles, and cultures will be something I can use in my career, it was frustrating dealing with the pressures of trying to get the group going and remain focused. There were times when I felt that I was carrying the group, and that if I didn't do the work it wouldn't get done. After the midterm this feeling led me to step back and not lead as much in the second half of the semester, even though I still had to take the lead more times than I wanted to. (Final Reflection, May 19, 2007)

There is an interesting correlation between Carolina's (Group A lead) and Michelle's experience regarding leadership. Leadership came to them naturally but then turned into a burden and was resented—to the extent that they backed off from their teams at about the same time (during the last third of the semester). The teams continued, but the drop in energy could definitely be felt. While a diverse community can be exhilarating and exciting it also can be exhausting all by itself—which was expressed in multiple ways in the feedback from the participants.

Olive confirmed Michelle's capacity to lead a diverse team:

> Michelle was definitely leading, asking the questions and getting us to come up with ideas and thoughts because I really didn't know how to start out and she asked some really good questions. And then things evolved from there when she asked the questions. (personal interview, p. 45)

Michelle's gift in leading the group, especially in the beginning of the group process, was grounded in her ability to consolidate people's comments into a single message in which they all could see themselves reflected—including Paige, the group's antagonist.

Nick

Nick is a 25-year-old male who identifies his nationality as U.S. and his ethnic background as Caucasian. His country of origin is the US. His native language is English, and he also speaks a little bit of Spanish. He has never lived abroad. He has been living in San Francisco for one year. Nick spent his formative years in North America. He is a college graduate. Culturally, he identifies as male, college graduate, returning student, professional, Buddhist, sober, and gay. On data collection day, Nick acted as questioner, supporter, and mediator.

Nick's IDI-2 scores placed him in the DMIS stage of minimization with an overestimation of his intercultural sensitivity by two stages (see Figure 30). Nick showed his stage of minimization in his conclusion to the personality versus culture discussion of Group 1, when he said, "everyone had an idea kind of that they wanted to incorporate and it happened" (class debrief, p. 15). Later in the class debrief, Nick made another statement from minimization about learning that he could trust the team to pull it together even if he couldn't see that happening at first:

> We all kind of were together on that and really had this vision. But for me seeing it up there and having it all make sense to me compared to what we started with it makes sense and just the fact that we could do that and it helps me to like trust more and trust the team. Everyone did have their area that they are stronger in and kind of really utilized those. I think everyone really participated. (p. 14)

Nick used minimization language in this conversation in that he expressed the assumption of uniformity in the group (excluding Paige). However, Nick also demonstrated a high level of self-awareness and ability to recognize that his own culture is just one frame of many possibilities (ethnorelative frame and coordination of meaning) when he described the way the homogeneity of U.S. culture left him "isolated in a bubble" (p. 26). This statement and several others showed that the IDI-2 scores did not fully capture the range of his experience, as his metacognition went beyond an ethnocentric worldview, at times even pushing him toward the edges of ethnorelativity. As with Carolina, Nick defied his stage of minimization as many times as he confirmed it.

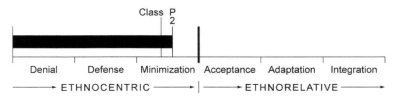

Figure 30. Nick's (P2) score on the Intercultural Developmental Inventory, version 2 (IDI-2). Author's image.

On the TPI, Nick scored every stage of team performance equally in the medium range bordering on high. All key scores were scored positive except for one—explicit assumptions.

Compared to the U.S. average scores on the PCSI, Nick had the lowest possible score in equality orientation and was more oriented toward a direct communication style (see Figure 31). He scored much higher in group orientation and relationship focus and was also the highest risk-taker in the class. With his lowest possible score for equality, very direct communication style, and high score in risk-taking, Nick was very much unlike the U.S. average. His behavior matched his PCSI scores—he watched out for other people on the team, was very direct, and took risks by being very honest when he exposed his feelings.

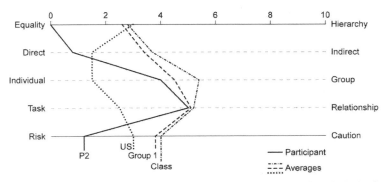

Figure 31. Nick's (P2) score on the Peterson Cultural Style Inventory (tm) (PCSI), shown with Group 1, class, and U.S. averages. Author's image.

Nick's life circumstances as a gay man in a dominantly heterosexual culture and as an addict in recovery may have influenced the constellation of his interior landscape to an extent that allowed him to live with these challenges in a world that supports neither. With this profile it would be natural for Nick to orient himself toward groups and to focus on building solid relationships out of safety concerns. It would also be natural to assume or desire to be the same as everyone else in order to gain the illusion of fitting in. During the class debrief, Nick made profound statements that demonstrated a high degree of self-awareness and metacognition, and indicated intercultural sensitivity beyond the ethnocentric position into which he scored.

Nick self-identified as the only assimilator in class on the LS; visual/spatial intelligence and logical/mathematical intelligence were his highest preferences on the MI, followed by musical and naturalist intelligence.

Nick demonstrated high capacity to engage in academic work even though he did not finish the class (and therefore his participation scores are not available).

Olive

Olive is a 33-year-old female who identifies her nationality as Vietnamese/Chinese American and her ethnic background as Vietnamese/Chinese American. Her country of origin is Vietnam. Her native language is Vietnamese and she also speaks English. She has lived in the US for 27 years, and the San Francisco Bay Area for 22 years (currently in San Francisco). Her formative years were spent in North America. She is a college graduate. Culturally, she identifies as Vietnamese/Chinese American and as a heterosexual. On data collection day, Olive acted as colead (and colead from the back), thought stimulator, timekeeper, and gallery walk presenter.

Olive's IDI-2 scores placed her deeply in the DMIS stage of acceptance with an overestimation of her intercultural sensitivity by one stage (see Figure 32). Olive's contributions to the class debrief discussion generally reflected her DMIS stage of acceptance. Responding to the question of how she felt about the experience, she said, "Yes, it was definitely interesting to see the different groups' way of thinking. I love that most actually about the class is to see how people's thinking are, very interesting" (p. 1). At another moment in the class debrief, Olive asked how their group should have dealt with Paige's very different style so that Paige would not have felt disengaged. Her choice of words reflected acceptance, "How do you find that balance as a group because you want to incorporate everybody and you don't want a person to feel disengaged, so how can you resolve that?" (p. 3). Olive concluded that discussion by saying,

I wonder in actual reality, the business world, whether sometimes we just have to accept that there's going to be a little bit part of such a diverse team and we all have different values and you know sometimes it just has to be that way [...]. (p. 4)

This statement also reflected a position of acceptance.

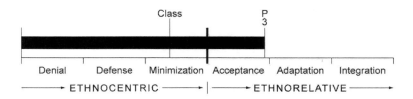

Figure 32. Olive's (P3) score on the Intercultural Developmental Inventory, version 2 (IDI-2). Author's image.

Olive demonstrated high capacity for cultural awareness and an interest in constantly comparing how different cultures showed up in class. However, she also backtracked to defense at times, with one particular instance that shocked most of us (including herself) when she expressed a stereotype about African Americans during the class debrief. This retraction into defense is an unusual case for Olive's stage of development and for the friendship that she had built with Michelle prior to this incident, especially since Olive could identify the injury she had placed— "I'm sorry, I'm stereotyping completely. But..." (p. 24)—yet her system offered it anyway. This incident provided a learning opportunity for some people in class including Olive, while it escaped others, and hurt the one it was addressed to.

On another occasion Olive demonstrated signs of ethnorelativity beyond her stage:

[...] for me I've been here since 1980 but it is still so hard to live and I feel like I am living in two worlds and trying to find a balance trying to straddle the Asian culture and American life because I have my parents' thinking and that they will force upon me, and then I have the American culture thinking. So living in two worlds is very hard actually. I feel that way still. (class debrief, p. 27)

Olive's bicultural experience as described here indicated flexibility in moving between the two worlds, which is beyond her stage of acceptance.

On the TPI, Olive self-identified medium and high scores for all of the stages of team performance.

Olive matched the U.S. average score on the PCSI only in equality (see Figure 33). She was more indirect, more group-oriented, more relationship-oriented, and also more cautious than the average U.S. scores. In fact, several times during the semester Olive hesitated to participate in activities because she was afraid she couldn't do them.

Olive freely expressed thoughts and feelings of insecurity and shyness that were, however, not observable. She shared that she wished she could be assertive consistently, as she acknowledged Michelle having that strength. She didn't like that she relied on others when she felt shy.

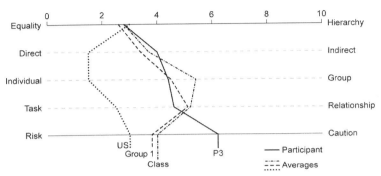

Figure 33. Olive's (P3) score on the Peterson Cultural Style Inventory (tm) (PCSI), shown with Group 1, class, and U.S. averages. Author's image.

> I hate that, I really wish I was consistent in being assertive all the way through and have this strong sense of direction. I notice that's your strength. Michelle's very good, you know, she moves and she sees things. For me I see myself driving and in certain aspect [...] I can't think real well and I rely on others and I don't like relying on others. I hate that and I wish I could change that [...]. (class debrief, p. 12)

> I learned I don't know what caused it but I learned I am not comfortable seeing myself that way and I wish to change it and I wish there was a way like coming to it now, coming up it I am still scared to put an opinion on it. It kind of piss me off actually. I admire them for it and I wish I was more like that. (class debrief, p. 12)

In this conversation Olive again exposed her identity struggle typical of a bicultural. She often framed it as a place of limitation, indicating that she had not quite mastered the coordination of her cultural frames. On the other hand, she also demonstrated capacity to shift between these frames at times rather quickly. In her final reflection she wrote:

> I had more than a breakthrough, and I'm amazed how I'm already changing the way I feel and believe about myself when it comes to creativity....Learning to interact within a dynamic team is an important skill to acquire because these different challenges will reappear in the 'real' world. Each person has different goals, values, and skills coming into this class. When the goals and values are not aligned, it's hard to achieve submitting weekly tasks collectively when an individual are not holding up his/her own part. (final reflection, May 19, 2007)

In this comment she expressed her ability to learn from an experience that she coded as problematic, but was able to manage and improve upon throughout the semester.

Olive had the lowest number of hits in the online participation forum (66% of the class average) and lowest number of pages read (61%), but she had a higher than average number of postings (114%). Her overall participation average was the lowest in the class (66%), but she made up for the lower online scores in her noticeable presence in the face-to-face meetings and the high level of reliability she demonstrated regarding her responsibilities to her team.

Paige

Paige is a 26-year-old female who identifies her nationality as American and her ethnic background as white. Her country of origin is the US. Her native language is English and she speaks no other languages. She has lived in the US, in San Francisco, all her life. She is a college graduate. Culturally, she identifies as American, female, heterosexual, white, and blond/redhead. On data collection day, Paige acted as questioner, outgroup participant, and antagonist.

Paige's IDI-2 scores placed her into the DMIS stage of defense with some issues in reversal and an overestimation of her intercultural sensitivity by approximately two stages (see Figure 34). Paige demonstrated defensive behavior during the data collection activities. While choosing images for the visual map, she commented, "I don't know about the multicultural thing, is that really important to you guys? I mean to me it's not really important" (Group 1 process, p. 10). This statement together with her resistant behavior qualified her into an ethnocentric position, as did the lack of awareness she expressed that she held privilege as a member of the dominant class. Her inability to distinguish the finer nuances of the cultures in the US and in San Francisco (where she has lived all her life) was further confirmed in the class debrief. In addition, the level of her insensitivity as a woman from the dominant culture in the midst of working with three women from nondominant frames (African American, Vietnamese/Chinese American, and Russian-speaking Ukrainian Moldovan) and an openly gay male was rather striking, as in her dismissal of the need to discuss multiculturalism because "it's so much just around" (class debrief, p. 26). On the other hand, Paige did demonstrate capacity for openness and creative expression in her own way at times and encouraged others to allow individual expression throughout the semester, which may be an indication that she did not code differences in creative expression as challenging.

On the TPI, Paige self-identified medium scores for all of the stages of team performance.

163

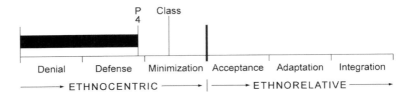

Figure 34. Paige's (P4) score on the Intercultural Developmental Inventory, version 2 (IDI-2). Author's image.

Paige approached the U.S. average score on the PCSI only in equality, and was more indirect, more group-oriented, more relationship-oriented, and more cautious than the average U.S. scores (see Figure 35). In her behavior throughout the semester, Paige was self-absorbed but not task-oriented or relationship-oriented, "moving to the beat of her own drummer."

Paige self-identified as an accommodator on the LS; linguistic intelligence was her highest preference on the MI, followed by naturalist, logical/mathematical, intrapersonal, and interpersonal intelligence. None of these scores showed up noticeably in her performance.

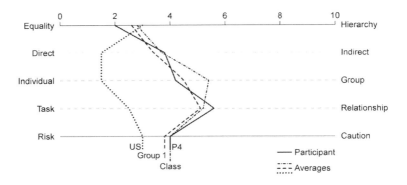

Figure 35. Paige's (P4) score on the Peterson Cultural Style Inventory (tm) (PCSI), shown with Group 1, class, and U.S. average scores. Author's image.

Paige was not willing to compromise her style to that of the group norm and was not well equipped for fulfilling academic tasks of the linear kind, but was consistently highly creative in everything she represented and how she performed. Her personal style was an asset to the class at times, a distraction at other times, and a challenge for her team when her creative ways interfered with the tasks that needed to be performed by the team as a unit. In this struggle to follow the class routine Paige often took the path of resistance and defense when challenged, but this attitude was not taken consistently and was not predictable. At times she was in agreement and clear about her place and responsibilities and demonstrated some flexibility, and at other times she seemed off register and limited in her capacity to perform.

Paige was always active during the face-to-face meetings and interactions. However, she demonstrated low capacity as well as little interest in following and/or little understanding of the outlined agenda of the class and the instructions of the moderators in her online team. Paige had difficulty with keeping up with the classwork, was often confused about her tasks, and submitted tasks and materials late, incomplete, and/or disorganized. Paige's online participation scores were lower than average for hits, pages read, and postings, giving her the second lowest overall participation (68% of the class average) in the online forum.

Paige had trouble attending the face-to-face classes and was often significantly late to arrive. In fact, she only managed to be on time when someone physically picked her up from her house and brought her to school, which others took turns doing for significant meetings such as the midterm, data collection day, and final. She even "forgot" to come to some meetings, seemed very distracted at times, and did not seem to be willing to take responsibility for her own misperceptions about how things were supposed to flow and integrate into the group. On her self-evaluation, Paige wrote

> I know I really failed in turning in my portfolio work, but I still feel that I deserve at least a C in this class because I put A LOT of time and effort into all the course work during the semester, which will not be reflected in the calculation of my points. (self-evaluation, May 19, 2007).

With this comment Paige exposed an attitude of entitlement and privilege she often displayed in a similar manner. For instance, when she arrived late to class (sometimes more than an hour) she assumed it would be acceptable to just burst into the group and be excused for her tardiness, which was often accompanied by having forgotten to do her assignments, not having completed her work, or having completed it incorrectly.

The beginning of class was usually spent with team check-ins giving students a chance to reconnect, clarify, and plan for the next online tasks. Paige's pattern of showing up late to these important rapport-building and planning activities or missing them altogether robbed her of getting tasks clarified and of solving problems with her team. She had a healthy dose of confidence, understanding and accepting herself as unique with valuable contributions to make to the community. Although this was true to some extent, Paige did not demonstrate an ability to own up to her responsibilities as a student in class nor did she develop skills to integrate better with a diverse group during this data collection process, and this struggle consistently showed up throughout the semester and was commented on by her peers in their personal interviews. As already mentioned, this unique way of operating resulted in Paige being marginalized by the group during the group process. In fact, the marginalization emerged more strongly during this process than at any other time during the semester.

Rusena

Rusena is a 25-year-old female who identifies her nationality as Ukrainian and her ethnic background as Russian-speaking Ukrainian Moldovan. Her country of origin is Moldova. Her native language is Russian and she also speaks some English, Ukrainian, and Romanian. She had never lived outside her native culture(s) until she came to the US three months prior to data collection day. Rusena spent her formative years in Eastern Europe. She is a college graduate. Culturally, she identifies as Eastern European and Post Soviet Union. On data collection day, Rusena acted as supporter and independent participant.

Rusena's IDI-2 scores placed her in the middle of the DMIS stage of denial with an overestimation of her intercultural sensitivity by three stages (see Figure 36), an expected outcome given her short time outside her own cultures. Rusena's reaction to Olive's open discussion of Paige's outsider status could be interpreted as reflecting her DMIS stage of denial, "Actually this class started from sunshine, I don't know, for me, from sunshine now we did this exercise, actually, my feeling is the same, sunshine all the time" (class debrief, p. 3), but may also have been caused by expecting a more aggressive negotiation style for her to connote the event as a conflict. In one moment, she observed that the group came up with many different images in the brainstorming activity (during the other group's map cocreation process), but that they also shared at least as many similar images. She found that very interesting vis-à-vis the fact that her group was composed of different cultures.

> [...] When we did that exercise about associations [...] we had a lot of different associations, ideas, about one image, one word but sometimes we had the same images, yeah? It's interesting because we are from different cultures, but I like that. I learned some from that exercise [...]. (class debrief, p. 16)

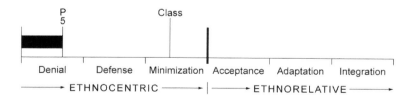

Figure 36. Rusena's (P5) score on the Intercultural Developmental Inventory, version 2 (IDI-2). Author's image.

This awareness and appreciation of different cultures fell beyond Rusena's DMIS stage of denial. Rusena made another statement about what she learned that placed her far outside the DMIS stage identified by her IDI-2 scores, saying that she learned "step by step how to communicate with, how to adapt living here, how to find a common language with people [...] [...RR...] Communication, just communication" (p. 21).

Rusena's understanding of herself and of the diversity within her own country demonstrated cultural sensitivity beyond denial that was not captured by the IDI-2. This meta-awareness about her own cultural background is reflected in a private e-mail where the issue of cultural identity arose and Rusena expressed,

> Here in America I'm considered to be Russian if my native language is Russian. I know it's kind of difficult to understand but I identify myself more with the USSR, which included Moldova (where I was born), the Ukraine (where most of my relatives live and my parents are from), Russia (which language I call my native because I studied in Russian at school and in the university and I speak it with all my friends and relatives), and other countries. So...it's really hard to identify myself with that small country [Moldova] because I feel more connections with more countries and one common culture, which speak Russian. (personal communication, December 17, 2007)

This comment refers to a deep understanding of the complexity her identity presents, and also a capacity to shift into a frame more easily understood in the US—a sign of cultural sensitivity. At other times, however, Rusena missed cultural clues; for example, the stereotyping that happened in the class debrief about African Americans completely escaped her even though she participated in the conversation. This misunderstanding is a form of denial; however, seen from a different communication style this conversation may not have had any signifiers of conflict for her. She could have missed the clues because of her language barrier or possibly because her culture would have carried the conflict out with a more emotionally engaged style. It would not be unusual for Rusena to not understand the dynamic of ethnicity in the US and the sensitive issues around that topic, as much as an American might not be informed about the relationships between USSR, Russia, Ukraine, and Moldova that inform Rusena's complex identity.

On the TPI, Rusena gave medium and high scores for all of the stages of team performance.

Compared to the U.S. average scores on the PCSI, Rusena was more hierarchical; much more indirect, group-oriented, and relationship-oriented; and somewhat more of a risk-taker (see Figure 37). In the research process Rusena worked mostly by herself, off to the side, which would speak to a preference toward individualism in that context (her score falls in the middle of individualism vs. group orientation).

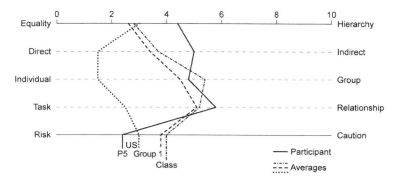

Figure 37. Rusena's (P5) score on the Peterson Cultural Style Inventory (tm) (PCSI), shown with Group 1, class, and U.S. average scores. Author's image.

Rusena self-identified as an accommodator on the LS; visual/spatial intelligence and musical intelligence were her highest preferences on the MI, followed by logical/mathematical, interpersonal, intrapersonal, and naturalist intelligence. She mostly did not demonstrate these preferences on data collection day or in class.

Rusena struggled somewhat with keeping on task and on schedule throughout the semester. However, she always took full responsibility for her results, in contrast to Paige who usually expected the system to bend to her. Compared to the class average, Rusena had significantly high online participation scores in postings, hits on the webpage, and pages read (145%). In her final reflection, she wrote:

> This course was very challenging for me. The challenge itself wasn't in gaining my drawing or computer graphic skills but more in organizing myself to meet deadlines and work as a team member....A hybrid class like this one can help a lot in finding new friends. Thanks to diversity in our team it was very informative and educative to find out how different people (men, women, youth and older people) perceive the same content. It definitely will help me understand nuances of advertising and visual perception of people of different cultures. (final reflection, May 19, 2007)

With this comment, she demonstrated interest in culture to a degree beyond her identified DMIS stage of denial, and also the ability to connote challenging experiences as learning.

168

CHAPTER 8

TRADITIONAL ANALYSIS

This chapter presents the results of the analysis using the selected methods and instruments. The discussion is grouped by research subquestion, beginning with group dynamics and visual map analysis; group-level analysis is provided first in accordance with the focus of this study on group interaction. The next two sections address the individual-level concerns of assessing (a) whether participants acted in alignment with what the IDI-2 and PCSI would have predicted and (b) whether the innate and the cultural can be isolated as they affected participant behavior in this study. The main research question and subquestions are answered based on this analysis and further elaborated upon in the conclusion (Chapter 9).

Group Dynamics

Analyzing group dynamics is more difficult in culturally diverse groups than in homogenous groups. In addition, in polycultural groups there is no ethnic majority, which translates into all frames showing up freely on a more equal footing. Most members of the two polycultural groups in this study held several cultural frames simultaneously. As cultural hybrids they demonstrated a more varied repertoire of cultural frames and more flexibility in applying these various frames creatively, which resulted in complex and rich group dynamics.

In this study I focused on cultural variables (as in intercultural communication) rather than on other coexisting variables—such as age, gender, education, and so on—that are the focus of intergroup communication. In fact, it is common to merge (or confuse) the two categorizations, as the participants did when they named the cultural frames they identify with. For instance, some participants named their professions or political affiliations next to their national or ethnic identity—even the group of "redheads" was listed as a cultural identity. Neither did this study touch upon diversity issues, which are commonly understood as domestic issues related to power dynamics, as in multiculturalism. While all people of all races and ethnicities and from all places are diverse in many ways, it should be kept in mind that this study focused strictly on the cultural variables within polycultural group dynamics that lead to cocreation, and how those cultural variables might be represented visually.

As with the discipline of visual communication, complex cultural dimensions and cultural references are not plentiful in group dynamics theories. Within the group dynamics displayed, some stereotypical cultural patterns and instrument predictions were supported but many were not confirmed.

Some similarities are striking when comparing the group process of Group 1 with Group A. Both groups had five highly diverse participants. Both fell into a calm rhythm at the same time—30 minutes into the process—exactly the time when the structure of the visual map was firmly established on the map itself. After the groups fell into a rhythm, both groups had two people working independently without speaking much while the next tier participants (two in each group) were bonding in their task and self-directing, as the lead and colead had relaxed and no longer made decisions for the group. Both groups had one outsider, and both outsiders occupied the DMIS stage of defense. In Group A, the outsider (Bella) never spoke after she had told her initial story and did not participate actively but rather observed (possibly a flight response). In Group 1, the outsider (Paige) is better described as the antagonist who interfered with the group norm process, trying to deposit her ideas—verbally and visually—without success (possibly a fight response).

Despite these similarities, the groups had different energy that was reflected in their communication patterns. Group A had an easier time reaching and sustaining the flow state, and the energy of Group A was calm and composed with spaces between their conversation acts. Group 1's flow state was harder to establish and maintain, as it was often interrupted by the antagonist. During the coconstruction process, Group 1 expressed emotionally charged communication patterns with overlapping communication that escalated into dissonance at times but never erupted into direct conflict. In the class debrief, the tensions experienced in Group 1 were aired and dealt with openly—Group 1 participants named the issues and let each other talk without interrupting or overlapping communication acts.

The calm rhythm experienced by both groups toward the end of the cocreation process can be understood as the flow state (Sawyer, 2006) that allows groups in creative activities to work without needing to interact much verbally. The *flow state* is an energetic state entered into by participants in a creative activity when intersubjectivity and creative flow is reached (Sawyer, 2006; Purser & Montuori, 1994). In such moments, the group does not need to speak to make decisions, but everyone just knows what to do. In the flow state, group members are not conscious of passing time; Group A did not experience any time pressure, while Group 1 participants were very aware of time running out. Group A described their experience of the flow state beautifully. "It was unspoken, we really just trusted that we knew what we were doing and to let everybody do it" (Carolina, class debrief, p. 4). "We can work without speaking" (Eugene, p. 16). Participants were able to play off each other and build upon the group creation individually but under the consideration of the larger group outcome. Group 1 also reached such moments at times, but was more often interrupted due to the conflict with Paige, a phenomenon described as self-oriented behavior in groups (Purser & Montuori, 1994). In Paige's case there is not enough data to suggest whether, as is often the case, this behavior was driven by fear.

The concept of groupthink (Johnson & Johnson, 2005) played a strong role in the dynamics of both groups; both groups had strong leaders and demonstrated a cohesive group mind with the exception of the outsider in each group. Groupthink analysis shows that the opinions of some members were either not heard or were suppressed in order to maintain the status quo, and both groups avoided controversy in favor of concurrence. The concept of deontic logic in CMM is related to the idea of groupthink, in that it describes participants' underlying feelings of how they ought to act. Comments by both groups reflected strong deontic logic of agreement, trust in the group, inclusion, and the educational nature of the experience—all of which imply that dissenting voices put aside their differences in favor of concurrence.

Group A had a much stronger instance of groupthink, which may have contributed to the group's seemingly docile and compatible nature in comparison to Group 1. Group A described themselves as harmonious and experiencing what amounted to a flow state, working together without needing to speak. The group's illusion of unanimity (Johnson & Johnson, 2005) was reflected in many statements made by Group A participants. "It just kind of all came to everyone put in what they wanted to put in and we felt comfortable with that" (Aiden, class debrief, p. 4). "We got a central idea and then everybody kind of individually contributed to it but we didn't have a group consensus....it was just kind of trusting that we all knew where we were" (Carolina, p. 4).

> I thought that was almost magical. It was, everyone just fell in, even though I felt that Carolina was initiating in most of the areas, we were just organic, coming together and saying, alright, we need to do this, how we do it, and everyone just felt it was falling into place, forming a big structure out of the parts [...] everyone I thought were on their best behavior or something. (Eugene, personal interview, p. 21)

All Group A members enthusiastically described the flow state from a position that sounded like minimization, with the exception of Bella who was silent for most of Group A's process. The other members of Group A talked about how "we were all on the same page" (Aiden, class debrief, p. 9) and "it was unspoken, we really just trusted that we knew what we were doing and to let everybody do it," (Carolina, p. 4). However, it was Bella's silence and the group's assumption that silence indicated agreement that allowed this illusion of unanimity to prevail. In fact, Group A never heard what Bella's thoughts were or whether she was in agreement or not (see Outgroup and Untold Stories). It was named in Group A that the dominant ones would get their ideas on the graphic panel; alluding, indirectly, to the fact that Bella was left out of that process. At the same time, it was the opinion of all Group A participants who spoke during the class debrief that they all cocreated the sketch equally, and that everybody's opinion was heard and fully included. Although there is not enough data to generalize from, it is notable that all members in Group A had intrapersonal intelligence as one of their top preferences, which may have added to their feeling of mutual understanding without needed to speak.

Though Group A did not experience open conflict, controversy was avoided and unheard via self-censorship (Johnson & Johnson, 2005), particularly with Bella and Dianne. When I asked whether or not the process of creating the stories and maps was agreeable to everyone, the supporting members of Group A became mind guards. Dianne replied, "what we were saying was expressed" (class debrief, p. 6), meaning that she did not need to spell out her own thoughts as they were being expressed for her through the group. When the actions did not match what Dianne understood as the plan, she was concerned at first but "learned to work with it and it came out nice in the end" (p. 9). Dianne furthered this position by explaining that she would wait for confirmation from another member before putting an image on the graphic panel. Dianne later alluded to other aspects of self-censorship by suggesting that during the cocreation process, Group A may have been "afraid to cross those boundaries" (p. 28).

Group 1 did not have as many instances of groupthink as Group A, which may have been a factor in their experience of conflict in the group. However, Group 1 also emphasized in their gallery walk presentation that group consensus was important when describing their process of choosing images:

> And when we decide as a group, like if the majority thinks that this is what should be here and what should be left out because we don't wanna put too many stuff and just [...] be agreeable with everybody it has to be a consensus. So we do end up filtering [...] things out that [...] as a group we probably don't like. (Olive, gallery walk, p. 2)

This statement implies that consensus was the desired group norm as Olive reiterated later in the class debrief in her comment, "for even in the team situation, if you don't come together with a certain thing that is common then it's almost like it's going in upward battle to make things work" (class debrief, p. 5).

The conflict in Group 1 centered around Paige's lack of conformation to the group norm, and participants demonstrated several dynamics of groupthink in response to the conflict. Paige was subjected to "direct pressure on dissenters" (Johnson & Johnson, 2005, p. 297). Group 1 also had mind guards (who worked to silence objections), as when members of the group (Olive and Rusena) other than the lead took on the task of monitoring Paige's participation in placing images onto the graphic panel. Rationalization (Johnson & Johnson, 2005) also occurred, in which Paige's image choice was removed from the graphic panel because it did not go along with the groupthink, as witnessed when Michelle said "that space is for CCSF, sorry" (Group 1 process, p. 13) and Olive supported her as a mind guard. Paige continued to put up images in places the group had reserved for other items, often when the lead (Michelle) was not looking. On the other hand, Paige may not have been listening when decisions were made (which would be consistent with her performance in class).

Paige's occasional defense of Group 1's work during the class debrief also demonstrated groupthink; if she were moving in and out of a groupthink mentality, that might help to explain her cycle of fighting and then defending the group. The following exchange exemplifies the avoidance of controversy.

Paige   How 'bout a dog here?

Olive   No, a dog has nothing to do with it.

Paige   How 'bout the rusty sign? No?

Michelle   No.

Paige   (giving in) All right. (Group 1 process, p. 20)

Considering the many incidents of this type of exchange, it is difficult to believe that Paige did not realize that her choices would not meet the group's approval. While she did not escalate the conflict and usually pulled back, she also did not stop offering the same solutions in the same way. Paige expressed in the class debrief that she was trying to help. If so, she demonstrated inflexibility in her behavior; if not, she demonstrated passive aggressive to defensive behavior.

Paige reflected on her inability to be heard during the gallery walk, in a statement that also reflected adherence to groupthink, "At one point I was trying to…have different ideas…and [Michelle] said something like 'Oh no, I want to have the things that go together' […] and it was like okay, fine" (class debrief, p. 4). With this statement, Paige described how she sacrificed her personal preference to allow the group to proceed. Olive mentioned this conflict in the class debrief discussion as a condition of Paige's "distinguished" (p. 3) style, rather than an aspect of the group experience—a statement that may have reflected both groupthink and attribution error.

Olive's classic stereotyping of African Americans was surprising since she scored into the DMIS stage of acceptance. Her framing of criticism as a seemingly positive statement, as she did when stereotyping, was a behavior I observed throughout the semester and other participants noted in their personal interviews. This pattern may be related to an indirect communication style (although her PCSI score shows her as slightly more direct than indirect). Occupying an ethnorelative position may not prevent attribution errors, as Olive's behavior showed.

> People who hold strong stereotypes…attribute negative behavior on the part of a minority-group member to dispositional characteristics. Positive behavior by a minority-group member, on the other hand, is believed to be the result of situational factors. When it comes to judging their own behavior, however, negative behavior is attributed to situational causes and positive behavior is viewed as dispositional. When a minority-group member acts in an undesirable way, the attribution is "That's the way those people are" or "Those people are born like that." (Johnson & Johnson, 2005, p. 454)

Olive, a Vietnamese/Chinese American woman, made exactly that comment to Michelle about Michelle's ethnic group, African Americans.

Role Distribution

Participants who were further along in their DMIS development had more role flexibility. Participants in defense were either supporters or outgroup participants, and all outgroup or antagonist participants were in the DMIS stage of defense. In general, it seems unlikely that a participant in denial or defense would be capable of successfully leading a culturally diverse group. One of the Group A supporters (Dianne) was in defense, but because of her nondominant behavior (possibly attributable to her Filipina cultural background, high on hierarchy and low on individualism, Hofstede, n.d.c), communication style, and personality, she may have been able to blend more with the group process. However, Dianne also demonstrated capacity for intercultural competence that went beyond her designated stage. The Group 1 member in defense (Paige), on the other hand, theoretically held significantly more power with her dominant White American background and personality, which may have led to her being more vocal in her defense stage and acting as an antagonist who was marginalized in her group. These role dynamics provide an interesting example of the potentially complex layering of identity and privilege.

Group A was not well matched in regard to PCSI and IDI-2 scores but did not demonstrate any conflict. Considering PCSI scores, the lead (Carolina) and colead (Aiden) seemed to be balanced between task- and relationship-focus, while the two supporters (Dianne and Eugene) leaned more toward relationship. Carolina occupied the DMIS stage of minimization with occasional movement into ethnorelativity. Dianne and Bella were in defense on one side of Carolina, while Aiden and Eugene occupied the DMIS stage of acceptance on the other side. Both Dianne and Bella demonstrated ethnorelative capacity on several occasions. In her stage of minimization, Carolina probably assumed that everyone had the same needs and desires as she did, which she expressed during the class debrief more than once. From this stage, she would not have been able to interpret dissonance as a sign of dissent but rather as a sign of frustrated desire to join her that would have made her try harder, with the result of not being very helpful in moving people along. The two group members in the DMIS stage of defense were not a challenge to her because one (Bella) was silent and the other (Dianne) had the most indirect communication style of all the participants and the highest scores in group-orientation. Dianne would not have challenged the leader, especially not in a direct way as observed in Group 1 with the antagonist, Paige. The two supporters (Dianne and Eugene) and the outgroup participant (Bella) matched each other in group- and relationship-orientation. Neither Eugene nor Dianne had task-orientation as a preferred mode of operating in their profiles, and this was confirmed in their roles as supporters who glued the group together via relationship-building. The two leads, Aiden and Carolina, matched each other in all categories pretty closely. In addition, behavior beyond the scored DMIS stages was demonstrated at times, which may have helped the group to operate from their strengths and appreciate each other for what they contributed rather than what they lacked.

Group A dynamics both supported and violated cultural stereotypes. Group A had a female lead from the dominant class (U.S. Caucasian) who also happened to be the most senior participant and a male colead from the dominant class (White Irish), and both demonstrated task-orientation as a preference during the event. The other three members were People of Color, two of whom were supporters (of Asian descent: Filipina American and Korean American) and focused on relationship-building. Other Group A dynamics were not predictable based on cultural patterns. The fifth member of the group was an outgroup participant, and her quiet participation, while extreme, could partially be explained by her cultural conditioning. Her Salvadoran culture—which Hofstede (n.d.c) measured as leaning toward hierarchy (66%), toward collectivism (81%), toward femininity (40% masculinity score), and toward uncertainty avoidance (94%)—could indicate that she would lean against speaking up against the group or the leader and toward going with the flow of the group. The two leaders from the dominant culture led in a completely nonlinear and intuitive style, and their visual map exposed this way of processing information holistically and unfolding it organically. Generally speaking, this way of working does not match the usual stereotype of Western culture as predominantly linear and focused on clock time. Group A exposed no conflict that could be observed, and they did not express the experience of time pressure.

Using the lens of the IDI-2 and PCSI illuminates role distribution in Group 1 also. In regard to the PCSI, Group 1's members matched each other somewhat closely in group- and relationship-building, which indicated possibilities for harmony. However, conflict was experienced in this group—both leaders who were in conflict with the antagonist were more oriented toward hierarchy than the antagonist, who was closer to equality. All three matched each other in a more direct communication style, which could explain their verbal communication pattern that seemed aggressive at times. Both leaders (Michelle and Olive) occupied the ethnorelative DMIS stages of acceptance and adaptation, which would indicate more flexibility regarding cultural difference than they demonstrated at times. Rusena, who occupied the ethnocentric DMIS stage of denial was the only one who did not notice any conflict in Group 1, or did not code the interaction pattern as conflictual.

The Group 1 antagonist (Paige) occupied the DMIS stage of defense, which could help to explain her behavior throughout the process and during the class debrief. While it is easy to make a comment in defense of Paige by noting that she was marginalized (an ethnocentric move) by the rest of the group in response to her unique behavior, such characterization oversimplifies the reciprocal dynamic between Paige and the group. Both parties acted from ethnocentricity, and Paige's ethnocentric behavior was even stronger than that of the group—Paige did not demonstrate any desire or capacity to move from her unique position. Neither party chose an ethnorelative response (e.g., voicing the problem or modifying behavior in order to better join with the other side) and Paige took on the role of antagonist for the group. Without Paige's constant interruptions of the flow, Group 1 might have achieved the flow state in a similar manner to Group A. Although Paige's PCSI score indicated her leaning more toward relationship-building than either leader, Paige's behavior did not demonstrate any flexibility (or willingness) in moving from her personal frame in order to meet that of other participants in her group (an individualistic frame).

Nick, in the DMIS stage of minimization (which indicates a general orientation of wanting to get along with everyone), had a natural tendency to act as a mediator and stepped into behavior far beyond his stage at times when he functioned as healer for Group 1 and for the class. Seen through the lens of the CMM concept of coordination, Nick managed the coordination of the social world cocreated in his group. Often, when the other participants burst into dissonance, Nick waited for a silent moment and then stepped in with a calmness that helped the others to find their center again. His compromising suggestions helped the effectiveness of this action, which depended on his timing as much as on his choice of words. This masterful coordination added a calming element to the group process that was accepted by the other participants every time it was offered.

In Group 1, Nick's success as a mediator is an interesting phenomenon to note. On the DMIS, he was positioned right in the middle between two people in early stages of ethnocentricity on one side and two in deep stages of ethnorelativity on the other. Although it is possible to experience states of a developmental stage beyond the one currently occupied, it is generally not assumed that people in ethnocentric positions are able to take the perspective of stages further along on the developmental scales other than the stage adjacent to their current stage. However, Nick demonstrated a metacognition several times that placed him far beyond his stage of the DMIS. Whether or not the gender imbalance (one male and four females) had anything to do with his success as a mediator is highly questionable and problematic in regard to stereotyping, but the fact remains that the other four participants accepted his consolidation of their ideas every time he offered it, helping the group to move forward productively.

The dynamic created by Group 1 fell outside stereotypical cultural frames, and their way of working was not characteristic of their cultural heritage as described by traditional theory generalizing cultures (e.g., Gay, 2000; Diller & Moule, 2005). The conflict between the antagonist and the rest of the group, which was constantly on the verge of breaking out but mostly suppressed, may have been influenced by this—culturally speaking—nontraditional group hierarchy. Group 1 had a female, African American, more task-oriented lead with a female Vietnamese/Chinese American colead who simultaneously played a support role in relationship-building together with the only male in the group (who was a U.S. Caucasian self-identified as gay). The Russian-speaking Ukrainian Moldovan female participant from the former Soviet Union who was new to the US accepted the leadership easily and supported the group norm, but worked mainly individually. Group 1's outgroup antagonist was a White American female who identified herself as heterosexual and a redhead. All participants in Group 1 fell somewhat in the middle between task- and relationship-orientation, and individual- and group-orientation—implying some flexibility but more group- and relationship-orientation than the average U.S. score. The leads worked completely linearly and literally, and the group's map expressed this form of information processing. The only Caucasian male in Group 1 did not lead and the only woman from the dominant class in Group 1 could not establish any authority, in contradiction of cultural stereotyping.

The differences in Group 1's PCSI and IDI-2 scores could have been the cause for some of the conflict in addition to the group dynamic set up by the racial role reversal. It is also interesting that the lead and colead in Group A were the first ones to speak when I gave instructions at the beginning of the process, while in Group 1, the antagonist (Paige) spoke up right away. If speaking up first indicates a claim to leadership in a group, then Paige gave her pitch for leadership early on, and was denied by the group when they accepted Michelle as their lead just a few moments later. This rejection may have been one reason why Paige turned into an antagonist rather than played the role of an outsider. However, while Group 1's conflict scenario is noteworthy, it cannot be completely analyzed with the current data. There is simply not enough information about each participant's different innate and cultural dimensions to draw reliable conclusions.

The leaders in both groups did not have task-orientation as a strong preference and mentioned at several occasions throughout the semester that they did not want to take leadership roles (which they interpreted as task-mastering), but did so anyway when necessary. Michelle spoke about her dislike of leading during the class debrief, and Carolina gave similar responses during various conversations about leadership throughout the semester—she expressed discomfort with taking the leadership role but felt that if she did not, there would be a negative outcome in terms of successful completion of the tasks. With their willingness to act, Michelle and Carolina demonstrated the ability to shift toward more task focus when called for.

Leadership

The leadership dynamic in both groups evoked the famous line, "History is written by the winners" (Orwell, 1944)—there is power in being the one who records the information. I observed that phenomenon in this study, in what I am calling the *power of the marker*—namely, that the graphic facilitator became the lead in both groups. Both leaders established leadership instantly through the power of the marker and thus held the story for the rest of the group. In both groups, the participant who established herself as the lead not only took notes but also stepped, spontaneously, into the role of a graphic facilitator for the entire group, a role accepted by the group and resulting in a mini map/outline used to guide the cocreation of the larger maps. The graphic facilitation procedure became interactive at times, as the leaders made direct attempts to actively engage the other participants in the act of creating the conceptual map. The leader in Group A invited the rest of the group to participate in creating the sketch, both through their input and through their drawing onto the map. The leader in Group 1 consolidated the information given by the group (i.e., found the commonalities among opinions expressed) in verbal notes that served the same function as the sketch in Group A. Both leaders directed the visual map collaboration at times, especially in the beginning. By the time the visual map was in the last stage of completion, both leaders had stepped back from that role so that leadership was shared.

The necessity to consider leadership in both groups a shared responsibility as described in the distributed-action and interaction-process theories of leadership (Johnson & Johnson, 2005) was observed in both groups throughout the process. Shared leadership was also pointed out by the supporters during the member check. As graphic facilitators, the leads solicited information, summarized and consolidated the contributions offered by the group, structured and directed the group's efforts, provided the energy to motivate their peers, and thus coordinated the creation of meaning for the group. In return, the supporters listened, took turns more or less respectfully, assessed and worked with each other's emotional states and built relationship, engaged in the conversation, and offered improvements to the product, and thus assisted in achieving the group's goals through providing leadership of a different kind. Task leaders in both groups gave up power somewhat once the structure of the visual map was laid out and agreed upon, although the groups continued the established power relationships by checking in with the task leaders periodically to make sure they were still on track with the agreed-upon plan.

While the task-oriented leads and coleads in both groups were largely unaware of the complimentary supporters who focused on relationship-building, the supporters themselves were not only aware of their leadership role but also made a conscious effort to build relationships in the background to assure the group's success. In Group A, this effort extended beyond taking care of the group to reaching out specifically to the outgroup participant to pull her into the project. In Group 1, the colead was simultaneously a supporter and colead—she directed from the back as colead and thought stimulator while also watching the group dynamic and building relationship. Had she been up front at the board task-mastering away next to the lead, this duality may not have been possible. The raised tensions in this group, which had an outgroup antagonist, may have caused the colead to take on the additional role of supporter.

Viewed through the lens of the CMM concept of coordination, Group A started off with a mindful multiturn process in which each person was involved equally and was watching out for including everyone else, but then split into task-masters, relationship-builders, and observers. The task-masters demonstrated little awareness of the context in which they operated and the way their actions influenced the other members, while the relationship-builders were highly aware of the intermeshing dynamics and overcompensated for the lack of coordination by the task-masters, maybe even sometimes at the price of the exclusion of their opinions. The one observer (Bella) did not choose to enter the dynamic or could not find a way into it, and thus was also ineffective in coordinating the social world cocreated by Group A. In Group 1, Nick demonstrated masterful coordination of Group 1's overlapping, dissonant conversations through excellent timing and word choice.

Outgroup and Untold Stories

Outgroup members in both groups demonstrated self-oriented behaviors (Purser & Montuori, 1994)—one through withdrawing from the group verbally, the other through fighting the group consistently. I applied the CMM LUUUTT model to investigate the untold stories in each group (including those of the outgroup members).

In Group A, Bella's unheard story finds recognition using the LUUUTT model (Figure 38), as do some untold stories brought to the surface by further investigation. For instance, Dianne mentioned the possibility that participants were holding their boundaries tight during the process but loosened them somewhat during the class debrief (class debrief, p. 28). This confession alluded to untold stories, as did Aiden's comment that people in diverse groups (such as San Francisco) give each other more space rather than argue over things as they would with people from their own culture (p. 25). Dianne tried to include the story of first-time college students, which became an unhighlighted story for Group A.

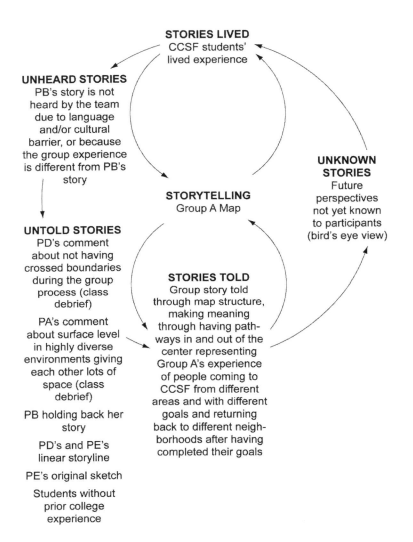

STORIES LIVED
CCSF students'
lived experience

UNHEARD STORIES
PB's story is not
heard by the team
due to language
and/or cultural
barrier, or because
the group experience
is different from PB's
story

**UNKNOWN
STORIES**
Future
perspectives
not yet known
to participants
(bird's eye view)

STORYTELLING
Group A Map

UNTOLD STORIES
PD's comment
about not having
crossed boundaries
during the group
process (class
debrief)

PA's comment
about surface level
in highly diverse
environments giving
each other lots of
space (class
debrief)

PB holding back her
story

PD's and PE's
linear storyline

PE's original sketch

Students without
prior college
experience

STORIES TOLD
Group story told
through map structure,
making meaning
through having path-
ways in and out of the
center representing
Group A's experience
of people coming to
CCSF from different
areas and with different
goals and returning
back to different neigh-
borhoods after having
completed their goals

Figure 38. Group A CMM LUUUTT model. CMM = Coordinated Management of Meaning; LUUUTT = stories Lived, Unknown stories, Untold stories, Unheard stories, stories Told, and storyTelling; PA = Aiden; PB = Bella; PD = Dianne; PE = Eugene. Author's image; the CMM LUUUTT model was developed by B. W. Pearce "The Coordinated Management of Meaning (CMM)", 2005, in W. B. Gudykunst (Ed.), *Theorizing About Intercultural Communication*, Thousand Oaks, CA: Sage, pp. 35–54, and is used here by permission.

The LUUUTT for Group 1 (Figure 39) shows that Paige's story/style was not seen on the visual map. What Paige did share was not expressed in a way that could be understood by the group or was not accepted by the group, and the group chose not to dig deeper into Paige's highly creative offerings. In the member check, Paige did not agree that her story was not told through Group 1's visual map. However, the video records show that Paige struggled in having her voice included. Since the group focused on older college graduates, another set of stories that was not told is that of students without prior college experience (as pointed out by Dianne in Group A as well) (Group 1 gallery walk, Group A episode 3).

The LUUUTT models showed that both groups had an outsider whose story was not heard or told in one form or another. It is expected behavior for groups to delete some stories in their creation of an ingroup mentality. Although reasons for not including these parts may have differed, the result was the same in that the outsiders' perspectives (Bella) or modalities (Paige) in which they would have told the story are largely missing on the visual maps. These untold stories need to be read into what is not there or possibly into the negative space of the map. In this way the LUUUTT model may merge the Western and Asian aspects of the gestalt principle, bringing foreground and background together.

Visual Map Analysis

CMM Serpentine models were used to graphically sequence the coconstruction process for each group, providing clarity and a better understanding of the different modes between the two groups. The area of emphasis in Group A's visual map was the underlying structure that told the story of people coming in and out of CCSF, a story reflective of group members' personal experiences and of the aspect of community to which all group members could relate. As represented on the LUUUTT model (see Figure 38 above), Group A started with their own lived experience, and the shared parts of their story and/or observations built the context and basic structure for telling their story in the form of a visual map. The Serpentine model (Figure 40) reveals that Group A (Carolina) first established a sketch that clearly outlined the structure and movement in and out of the center. They began their visual map in the center, defined the landscape around the center, and then added visual elements. Group A worked visually and nonlinearly with shapes, filled those shapes with words, and then added images, colors, and embellishments.

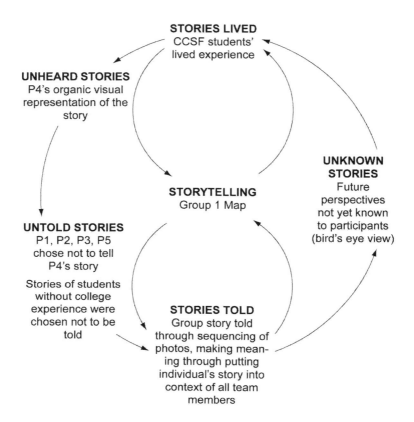

STORIES LIVED
CCSF students'
lived experience

UNHEARD STORIES
P4's organic visual
representation of the
story

UNKNOWN STORIES
Future
perspectives
not yet known
to participants
(bird's eye view)

STORYTELLING
Group 1 Map

UNTOLD STORIES
P1, P2, P3, P5
chose not to tell
P4's story

Stories of students
without college
experience were
chosen not to be
told

STORIES TOLD
Group story told
through sequencing of
photos, making mean-
ing through putting
individual's story into
context of all team
members

Figure 39. Group 1 CMM LUUUTT model. CMM = Coordinated Management of Meaning; LUUUTT = stories Lived, Unknown stories, Untold stories, Unheard stories, stories Told, and storyTelling; P1 = Michelle; P2 = Nick; P3 = Olive; P4 = Paige; P5 = Rusena. Author's image; the CMM LUUUTT model was developed by B. W. Pearce "The Coordinated Management of Meaning (CMM)", 2005, in W. B. Gudykunst (Ed.), *Theorizing About Intercultural Communication*, Thousand Oaks, CA: Sage, pp. 35–54, and is used here by permission.

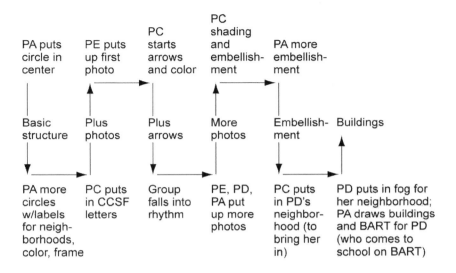

PA puts circle in center	PE puts up first photo	PC starts arrows and color	PC shading and embellishment	PA more embellishment	
Basic structure	Plus photos	Plus arrows	More photos	Embellishment	Buildings
PA more circles w/labels for neighborhoods, color, frame	PC puts in CCSF letters	Group falls into rhythm	PE, PD, PA put up more photos	PC puts in PD's neighborhood (to bring her in)	PD puts in fog for her neighborhood; PA draws buildings and BART for PD (who comes to school on BART)

Figure 40. Group A CMM Serpentine Map outlining visual map coconstruction process. CMM = Coordinated Management of Meaning; PA = Aiden; PB = Bella; PC = Carolina; PD = Dianne; PE = Eugene; BART = Bay Area Rapid Transit, a local light rail system. Author's image; the CMM Serpentine model was developed by B. W. Pearce "The Coordinated Management of Meaning (CMM)", 2005, in W. B. Gudykunst (Ed.), *Theorizing About Intercultural Communication*, Thousand Oaks, CA: Sage, pp. 35–54, and is used here by permission.

During the gallery walk, Group A presented their visual map (Figure 14) creatively with the presenter (the group lead) telling the story and the copresenter (a supporter) playing Vanna White and pointing to various parts of the map. They were not able to describe their strategies very well— for instance, they called their visual map a stream of consciousness piece that was completed intuitively (flow state experience). They had no rationale for the use of colors and they were not very conscious of their choices of images other than their own interpretations of what would best represent the neighborhoods depicted.

In the class debrief, Group A said they were satisfied with their process and their product, and that their visual map would have represented a good start if this had been a client project. They mentioned that it was fun to work together this way and that they probably would have approached the project differently had they worked individually. They also expressed that they would have tried to do it more linearly (like Group 1) if this had been a real client assignment, but their interpretation of the task was also to have fun and do it in the fashion of a free-for-all since the work was not be graded.

From my observations, the visual map fully demonstrated Group A's process as well as their attitudes and beliefs about the purpose of the activity. Their discussions flowed easily and they worked around each other as if they were performing a dance. Both the visual map and their process were completely void of tension, were harmonious, and expressed integration between foreground and background—the composition was even contained in an organic border. Group A's visual map was easily accessed and held the attention of an audience by encouraging the eye to keep wandering through the creation as if one were exploring a garden. The lead is ambidextrous, the colead is a very talented musician and songwriter, and the two supporters were fully focused on establishing and maintaining harmony in the group—all of which is visually noticeable in the visual map by its harmonious flow and balance, rhythmic qualities, and overall cohesive expression. In spite of not contributing directly and leaving little to no trace on the visual map itself, the outgroup member participated in establishing and maintaining group harmony.

The Serpentine model for Group 1 (Figure 41) reveals that Group 1 categorized their images into the events that made up the storyline for their visual map. The images were composed over an underlying invisible grid that structured a flow from left to right across the graphic panel. This grid was visualized and communicated by all participants except for Paige, who kept intervening and asking for a different composition but never communicated what her alternate vision was. The composing of the images took significant negotiation back and forth between Paige and the rest of the group.

Group 1 created a linear visual map that flowed from left to right, up and down, and from black and white to color, and which was not contained (had no outer border). During the gallery walk, Group 1's lead and colead presented the group's visual map in the same straightforward manner as it was created. Group 1 described their process and the elements on the visual map literally, following the logic of the story. They had picked images very carefully for their metaphoric qualities and had been meticulous in representing the parts of the agreed-upon story. They had applied color very rationally in order to emphasize the emotions of each moment. Overall, Group 1 was very literal and methodical in their representation of the CCSF experience, as well as with the execution of the visual map.

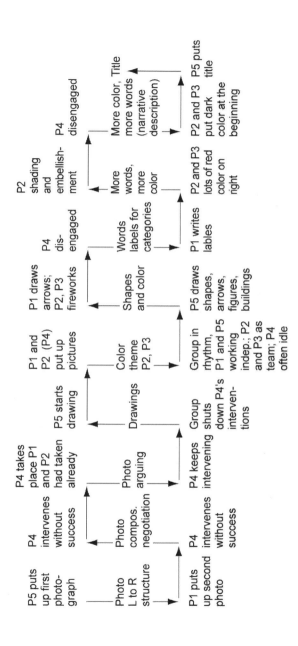

Figure 41. Group 1 CMM Serpentine Map outlining visual map coconstruction process. CMM = Coordinated Management of Meaning; P1 = Michelle; P2 = Nick; P3 = Olive; P4 = Paige; P5 = Rusena. Author's image; the CMM Serpentine model was developed by B. W. Pearce, "The Coordinated Management of Meaning (CMM)", 2005, in W. B. Gudykunst (Ed.), *Theorizing About Intercultural Communication*, Thousand Oaks, CA: Sage, pp. 35–54, and is used here by permission.

Group 1's visual map (see Figure 16) exposed their process as well as their attitudes and beliefs about the purpose of the activity. They were serious about the task, were trying to apply what they had learned in class about design principles, and paid close attention to details. The tension experienced by the participants (in their heated discussions followed by moments of silence) can clearly be felt when looking at this piece. There are highs and lows on the otherwise horizontal movement from left to right. There is intense contrast between foreground and background, and between white background and intense colors, and there are sharp boundaries between the groupings.

Both groups began by sharing their personal stories, and the structure of the visual map was influenced by the sketches or notes taken by the lead. The coconstruction sequence shows the important elements each group chose to use as the underlying theme—Group A organic following Carolina's organic visual sketch, and Group 1 linear following Michelle's linear verbal sketch. Group A's nonlinear visual map might be related to dominance in right-brain thinking; in Group A, the lead had been self-assessed as a right-brain dominant thinker. Group 1's linear visual map might be more related to dominance in left-brain thinking; the Group 1 lead had been self-assessed as a left-brain dominant thinker. (At the beginning of the semester, students performed a very brief self-assessment on right- and left-brain dominant thinking. This self-assessment was not part of the research process, but merely a fun activity to get students started in noticing differences between themselves and others in the class through interactive games.)

Based on the various degrees of coupling of visual elements from very loose to moderate to very tight (Horn, 1998), further meaning could be read in the modality of the elements in the visual maps. For instance, Group 1 had a very tight map expressing the anxiety observed during their process, and Group A's elements were very soft, organic, and fluid—also expressing their communication pattern. In addition, each group could be said to have created their own visual language system (Horn, 1998) that felt foreign to the other group.

Art therapy researchers have found that cocreated group products express "the conscious and unconscious processes operating at the time the mural was created" (Rosen & Mayro, 1995, p. 134) and that any interpretation must include both the observed group dynamics and the evaluation of the product. In the present study, the groups cocreated meaning through their interaction pattern, not by who they were individually. There is a direct correlation in both groups between the cocreated pattern of interaction during the group process (linear and stream of consciousness) and the gestalt of the visual map they cocreated. The participants themselves were aware of and named the difference between the styles of the two groups; however, while Group 1 was aware that their linear visual map matched their communication pattern, Group A was surprised to hear that their "stream of consciousness" (Dianne, class debrief, p. 2) visual map reflected their interaction style as well.

Like a photograph, each visual map captured the group dynamics in a static visual representation—a phenomenon I termed *snapshot 1*. The fact that the graphic facilitation of both leads played such a strong role in influencing the structure of the visual maps was another significant result.

While my results do show that the visual map products were in direct relation to the internal and external processes of the group, I cannot confirm any evidence that the visual expression relates to the cultural norms that the participants represented individually and theoretically (or stereotypically). Culturally speaking, both groups acted differently than could have been expected from a position of generalizations. Visual expressions did not expose any general views of particular cultures.

Observed Behavior and Predicted Behavior

Observations in this study defied the expectations drawn from IDI-2 and PCSI scores as many times as they confirmed them—the diverse groups often acted "out of character" if compared to cultural generalizations (sophisticated stereotypes). While some deviation is always to be expected, there was little evidence of the classic intercultural theory at play, or, at least, less than expected.

The DMIS, the IDI-2, and Worldview Orientations

Regarding the DMIS, participants exposed their worldview structures at times, showed characteristics of the next stage in their development, and in some instances demonstrated capacity far beyond their designated stage or retreated to an earlier stage. Some participant behavior indicated flexibility along the DMIS scales in both directions. The fact that some people could be in denial and also ethnorelative, or in defense and in acceptance simultaneously is confounding given the description of the DMIS and related IDI-2 scores. All participants had a high sense of awareness regarding their own feelings and a rather sophisticated metacognition of cultural differences. Beyond a deep metacognition of their own cultural complexities, they demonstrated authentic interest in other cultures present in the class and elsewhere in their lives, and were inviting of cultural differences—more so than has been described in the DMIS as ethnocentric orientations.

The groups and the class as a whole fell into the DMIS stage of minimization—a rather common score for mixed groups. In the DMIS model, minimization is the last of the three stages in ethnocentricity and represents the opportunity of approaching the threshold where movement into ethnorelativity becomes possible. Considering the behavior displayed by both groups as a whole, Group A fell more toward completing minimization and demonstrated capacity for ethnorelative orientations, and Group 1 fell more toward the middle of minimization with a more ethnocentric orientation. The difference in group experience was the result of certain individuals in each group who allowed or supported movement forward, or held the group back. These individuals' influence on the group may also have been dependent on the composition of the group as a whole at that time in those particular circumstances—a complex matter of group dynamics that is impossible to deconstruct reliably or predict. The particular constellation of cultural competence experienced by a group in that moment may also influence other states a group may or may not experience, such as the flow state.

The striking correlations between the groups' IDI-2 scores could not have been planned for, since participants were randomly accepted as students enrolled in the class during that semester and the forming of the groups followed an organic process rather than conscious organizational efforts. According to the IDI-2 scores, both groups had three participants in ethnocentric stages and two in ethnorelative stages. Both outgroup members inhabited the ethnocentric orientation of defense. Leaders inhabited stages at and above minimization in both groups. It was beneficial to have these similarities in the groups, as they could be better compared and contrasted.

DMIS stages as indicated by the IDI-2 scores were confirmed in many cases by participants' verbal expressions and demonstrated behavior, and denied in others. One participant occupying the stage of denial (Rusena) was culturally aware and carried an understanding and appreciation of cultural difference as was expressed in some conversations, but did not notice the tensions during the stereotyping incident. Three participants (Aiden, Eugene, and Olive) demonstrated their stage of acceptance throughout by being able to acknowledge, invite, and validate other participants' viewpoints, and by making space for other perspectives. Olive, on the other hand, backtracked seriously into defense when she brought up a stereotype—a bit unusual but not unheard of even with highly culturally competent individuals—and when she participated in shutting Paige down for her different style during the group process. Participants in the defense stage, at times, saw the world as a binary phenomenon (us-vs.-them frame) while also demonstrating ethnorelative thinking; participants in the minimization stage referred to all-encompassing assumptions while also holding cultural difference in high regard. In contrast, participants in the ethnorelative stages were able to experience and appreciate differences, which they mentioned in their reflections, but sometimes retreated back to ethnocentricity.

All participants overestimated their own cultural competence (by an average of two stages, see Figure 42). Overestimation is not unusual, but I have never seen such high overestimation with such consistency. While nine participants perceived themselves to be in the stage of adaptation and

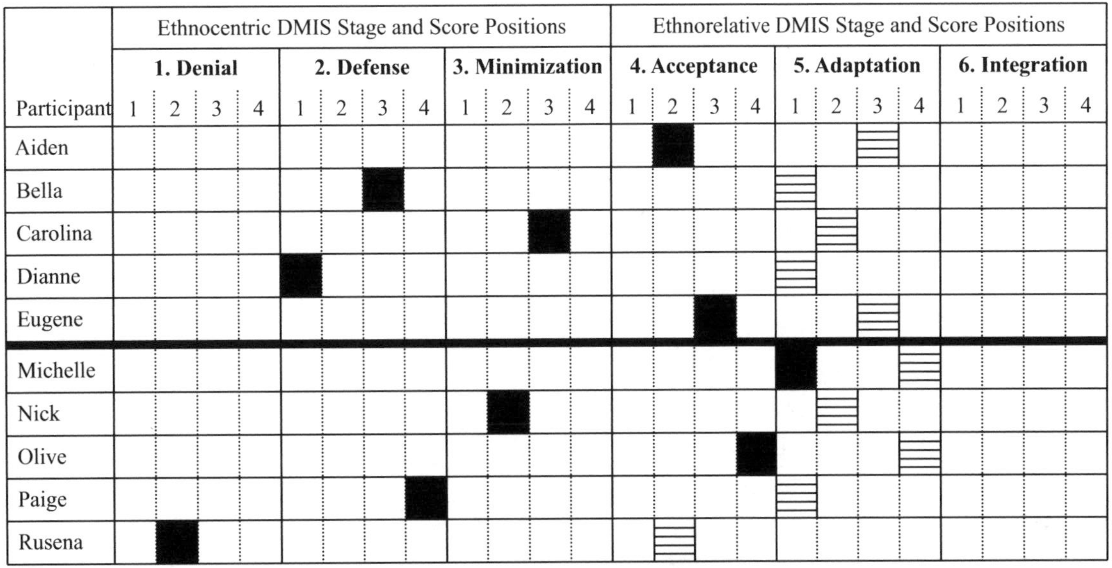

Participant	Ethnocentric DMIS Stage and Score Positions												Ethnorelative DMIS Stage and Score Positions												
	1. Denial				2. Defense				3. Minimization				4. Acceptance				5. Adaptation				6. Integration			
	1	2	3	4	1	2	3	4	1	2	3	4	1	2	3	4	1	2	3	4	1	2	3	4
Aiden													■						▨					
Bella							■										▨							
Carolina											■							▨						
Dianne					■																			
Eugene															■					▨				
Michelle																	■							
Nick									■									▨						
Olive																■								
Paige								■					▨											
Rusena	■																							

Figure 42. Participants' Developmental Model of Intercultural Sensitivity (DMIS) Stages. ■ = Intercultural Developmental Inventory, version 2 (IDI-2) score; ▨ = perceived cultural sensitivity. Author's image; the DMIS model was developed by Bennett (1986b) and the IDI-2 by Bennett and Hammer (2002).

one in acceptance, only Michelle was actually in the stage of adaptation, and she retreated to defense when triggered.

Across the board, these participants were highly cognizant of cultural differences and very interested in other cultures on a deep level, more so than their IDI-2 scores indicated. For example, Carolina exposed sensitivity beyond minimization (which focuses on how everyone is the same) when she tried to distinguish between the different gifts individuals bring to a group. Rusena's metacognition of cultural differences and of her own cultural complexity was far beyond her stage of denial. Paige was rather verbal and more or less (passive) aggressive in her disagreement with the rest of her group and acted as an antagonist; in other ways, she indicated capacity for more acceptance of individuals outside the mainstream. Nick and Carolina confirmed their positions in minimization by pointing toward their level of self-awareness many times around their own perceptions and by expressing universal generalizations, but also demonstrated capacity deep into ethnorelativity. Nick had some epiphanies that were situated far beyond his stage of minimization.

Michelle had the highest scores in adaptation out of all participants and demonstrated much flexibility in her communication and negotiation skills throughout the entire semester. However, during the group process she demonstrated an inability to take the perspective of the antagonist other than suppressing her voice and then blaming the time pressure for her behavior. When restimulated, Michelle retreated, temporarily, into defensiveness due to Olive's stereotyping of her ethnic group. She demonstrated, however, capacity for intercultural competence by quickly returning to adaptation when noticing that her reaction was an emotional one. It is also possible that issues of ethnic and racial oppression may have caused this dynamic. Another possible effect of ethnic/racial oppression may have been observed in the fact that the Caucasian lead in Group A sat at the head of the table, while the African-American lead in Group 1 did not. There is not enough data to draw conclusions about these dynamics; nonetheless, such potential influences deserve mentioning.

Bella's IDI-2 scores indicated that she operated from the ethnocentric DMIS stage of defense with reversal issues. However, in her personal interview Bella indicated a healthy dose of interest in other cultures and well thought-out strategies on how to communicate cross-culturally, which placed her beyond the indicated ethnocentric worldview orientation.

As shown by the results of this study, the IDI-2 did not seem to completely capture the experience of the participants in this particular polycultural environment. In general, predicting people's behavior or capacity for ethnorelativity in mixed-group situations is problematic, especially considering that the DMIS and IDI-2 (and PCSI) were built around individuals in isolation answering questions about hypothetical group interactions.

Likewise, PCSI scores were confirmed in some instances and not in others, and participants demonstrated more flexibility than would be expected from the theory described as underpinning the instrument. The PCSI measures preferences for five cultural styles that are based on values held by particular (national) cultures. Some of the behaviors observed confirmed the accuracy of the PCSI scores—for example, Dianne's indirect communication style, high group orientation, relationship focus, and caution. Her requests for the inclusion of various elements were cautiously placed and in fact had to be repeated several times, because the way she presented her request did not elicit the desired response. Her focus on group harmony was observed in the fact that her ideas were different from the way the visual map was developing, but she stayed with the flow and preserved harmony rather than trying to convince the group to change course. Her caution was demonstrated in that she sought out at least one person's approval before she placed an element.

The class as a whole scored primarily into direct communication and demonstrated this preference in their behavior overall; it caused no conflict issues between direct and indirect styles, but the individuals with the indirect communication preference may not have received equal opportunities to participate. More participants were more risk-friendly than cautious, and this was also observed throughout in their willingness to act. There were some exceptions, however, such as Olive, Bella, and to some extent Dianne, all three of whom shied away from acting or requesting at times.

The data suggested that participants, in general, may have had a wide range of possibilities in their cultural styles, and that their styles might change with different tasks and different contexts; however, the PCSI does not accommodate such variations. For instance, Eugene (who scored high into group-orientation and consciously chose the supporter role) occupied the pole of individual-orientation when constructing the map, while in other instances he was very much aware of and in sync with the rest of the group. Aiden worked independently at times (matching his leaning slightly toward individualism) but also expressed that he was completing this task more successfully because of the group interaction than if he had done it by himself (leaning toward group-orientation).

It is extremely interesting that all 10 participants were significantly more oriented toward the PCSI group- and relationship-orientations than the average U.S. score. Many participants fell closer to the median, and I observed both frames even within the same individual. The significance of this rather high preference for group- and relationship- orientation is still puzzling and may be a complete coincidence, but could possibly also correlate to the LS preference of accommodation (8 of the 10 participants). Group A demonstrated the capacity to work as a harmonious team (confirming group- and relationship-orientations), while Group 1 did not.

Some participants (Eugene, Nick) had radical curves, meaning some of their individual scores were on the extreme left-hand side of some of the continua while others showed up on the extreme right-hand side (within their individual profiles). In monocultural settings, the scores would be more consolidated vertically and place cultures (stereotypically) either more toward the left or more toward the right of the center position. In my experience as an intercultural consultant such radical curves are not unusual in cultural hybrids. While Eugene fit the picture of such a multiple frame structure, Nick did not from the viewpoint of cultural difference but did from the viewpoint of his belonging to an oppressed group.

The PCSI (like the IDI-2 and the TPI) is taken by an individual sitting and thinking alone rather than in context and interaction with others, and ignores the influence of the environmental and social context, which removes the PCSI from the lived experience. Findings in this case study indicate that participants were flexible and shifted positions on the continua of both the IDI-2 and the PCSI, which were not able to capture such flexibility. Therefore, these instruments may not be applicable for accurately measuring the experiences of people with more flexible cultural frames (such as cultural hybrids) inhabiting a polycultural world and demonstrating behaviors in a range outside the traditional charts. The presentation of such scores does provide food for thought and discussion; however, given these inconsistencies and discrepancies observed in the data, the quality of results from such bipolar systems may need to be questioned for their usefulness for the kind of population that participated in this study.

I assumed that the PCSI would be a useful addition to the other tools, and that assumption proved true to some extent. In various cases, however, I received feedback from participants whose intercultural experience made it difficult to answer questions requiring a choice about a scenario that was too generic to be addressed in either one way or another. Typical critical comments have been, "…I couldn't answer the questions with either/or," or "…my reaction totally depends on the specifics of the situation," which matched my own reaction to taking the assessment. Although the PCSI and IDI-2 were useful in this study as background information, it was confirmed that these 10 participants did not act primarily on one end of the spectrum, nor on one point on the continuum. Participants demonstrated more flexibility, which might be described as contextual multipositionality. While the authors of these instruments indicate that context matters, the fact remains that the scores point to unipositionality as a center of gravity but some of the participants swung widely from one end to the other on the continua. Overall, there were as many confirmations as there were discongruencies between the IDI-2 and PCSI profiles and the demonstrated behavior.

Comparing observed behavior to participants' PCSI and IDI-2 scores, it became obvious that the results were, at best, puzzling, if not contradictory. The historic work of creating models like the DMIS and PCSI and their accompanying instruments represented milestones in the development of intercultural communication theory and practice. However, it must be acknowledged that the results of this study point toward the presence of cultural frames that could not be fully captured by the instruments used, instruments originally designed for multicultural environments. Participants were mostly cultural hybrids (i.e., multiple cultural frames were available in their systems, frames that had been built through face-to-face interactions as well as virtual communication across cultures) and demonstrated a high degree of flexibility. In addition, they were highly cognizant of their own cultural complexity and genuinely interested in other cultures. Some of them even demonstrated an astonishing level of metacognition of their own awareness and of multiple perspectives as well as cultural complexity not described in the intercultural communication theories and models upon which this study was based (Bennett, 1986b; Hofstede, 2001; Trompenaars & Hampden-Turner, 1998; Peterson, 2004). Participants considered cultures as autonomous but also saw themselves as part of the larger community in their groups, the class, the institution, the city, and even as world citizens. As Eugene expressed, "I am part of society. I give back what I can. I take back. I am part of this world. [...] I believe that this world is worth saving and so I am going to contribute anything I can" (personal interview, p. 45). These cultural hybrids did not fit a structure identifying them with cultures within boundaries.

The observed behavior and participants' interpretation and understanding of culture approached polyculturalism—a culturism in which cultures are acknowledged as unique and equal to each other but are unified under a larger umbrella. Polyculturalism represents challenges that cannot be solved within the previous worldview structures, thus requiring a paradigm shift in order to move forward as a community. It is possible that polyculturalism might reflect the experience of cultural hybrids better than multiculturalism, where each culture stays autonomous and uniquely positioned in the larger social fabric and where the focus is placed on cultural differences.

All participants in this study considered themselves highly ethnorelative and culturally competent as reflected by their perceived IDI-2 scores (see Figure 42). However, some of them measured into and demonstrated characteristics of ethnocentric stages with occasional capacity for ethnorelativity—a wide range of positions that cannot be explained by the traditional DMIS. All participants including the only participant who scored into the denial stage (Rusena) were highly cognizant of cultural differences and had collected personal experience building refined categories thereof. Their degrees of capacity to create finer differentiations varied, but went off the DMIS and

IDI-2 charts at times. A social structure such as polyculturalism leaves more flexibility for people with diverse backgrounds composed of multiple cultures, and supports their multipositionality on the IDI-2 scales and PCSI continua.

The Innate (Nature) and the Cultural (Nurture)

The instruments were not able to consistently predict or confirm behaviors, and in some cases could not capture the experience of the participants. Culture-specific behavior as described in intercultural communication theory (Hofstede & Hofstede, 2005; Trompenaars & Hampden-Turner, 1998; Peterson, 2004; Bennett, 1993, 2003) was observed, but not necessarily in the representatives of those described cultures. All the PCSI dimensions were acted out including the orientation of hierarchy although no participant identified hierarchy as a preference. For instance, both groups had strong leaders who led through group consensus by majority but nonetheless directed the group and were accepted as the authority figure. The characteristics of all the DMIS stages were acted out including integration (into which nobody scored) and even beyond, which was not captured by the IDI-2. Participants demonstrated capacity for cultural sensitivity and also exposed ethnocentric positions, in some cases within the same person.

Some LS and MI preferences were demonstrated and matched participants' profiles, others did not. While the assessment of learning styles (LS) and intelligences (MI) did not play a major role in this study, it is interesting to notice overlaps in individual behavior and group behavior as compared to the assessment scores, such as the potential correlation between positions of group orientation and accommodator learning style (80% of participants), or a preference for an intrapersonal intelligence and withdrawal in intergroup dynamics (Bella).

The differences the groups displayed in their processes may have related to the different innate traits (inherited), personalities (inherited and learned) in the group composition, flexibility around cultural conditioning (learned), and possibly dynamics related to ethnicity (learned). For example, while Group A's role distribution worked within the norms of dominant culture frames and while this group easily stepped into a peaceful flow state and could hold it once reached, Group 1 reversed those norms and was the group that experienced some conflict and a few interrupted flow state moments. The behavior of these 10 mostly cultural hybrids in this polycultural environment was not predictable, but the data demonstrated that the group dynamics were mirrored in the visual maps.

Overall, participants agreed that the innate and the cultural could not be separated in their experience of the group process and cocreation of the visual maps. Participants were able to easily generate stereotypes of how their culture's monocultural group might behave (Irish would argue,

194

Filipinos would understand each other, San Franciscans would be culturally competent, etc.). However, they were not able to suggest how culture might affect a visual map created by a monocultural group, with the exception of the suggestion that a group of Germans would produce a more linear map (another stereotype). When asked, some individual participants described how a visual map would look created solely by them, but did not feel that culture had much if anything to do with the differences in their hypothetical individual maps. While assumptions about culture-specific behaviors were offered, no distinction could be made by the participants between nature and nurture when it came to discussing personal experiences. While behavior could be observed, sometimes consistently, and could be described specifically, the data of this study suggested that no separation between the innate and the cultural is possible in spite of the assessment tools used.

Bella's case exemplifies the dangers of drawing conclusions about the nature versus nurture discussion. Bella was extremely withdrawn and quiet, and I could easily conclude that her behavior of withdrawal and preferring silence was rather personally motivated. However, we cannot make such determinations and assume that the issue of nature (inherited) or personality (inherited and learned) or cultural conditioning (learned) can be read from behavior. In addition, there are many other mitigating variables to consider, for instance life circumstances, as well as the lens of the observer who is never neutral. Bella identified as Latina and had lived in El Salvador for most of her life after spending her first few years of childhood in the US. The Hofstede (n.d.b) scores for El Salvador (leaning toward hierarchy, strongly leaning toward collectivism, leaning toward femininity, and very strongly leaning toward uncertainty avoidance) may confirm that a female with this cultural background might be rather quiet in group situations. However, we cannot know whether or to what extent Bella's withdrawal was influenced by (a) her personal difference from her cultural stereotype, (b) her language barrier, (c) her personal shyness that she communicated to me in an e-mail (personal communication, September 17, 2006), (d) a possible authority or hierarchy issue, and/or (e) other causes. We also don't know the specifics about her life circumstances and which aspects of those were culturally motivated. In addition, the correlation between values and behavior is not always a positive one (House et al., 2004). However, in order to work with Bella and other cultural hybrids one must wonder what capacities would be necessary for a facilitator to reach her and draw her out.

Cultural Hybridity

As described above, this study's data pointed toward high flexibility in the participants who can potentially be identified as cultural hybrids (multiple cultural frames), and who were possibly operating in what can be called a polycultural environment. In the class debrief, participants determined that the innate could not be teased apart from the cultural, and the data supported that interpretation. In this section, I give a more thorough definition of cultural hybridity in order to initiate a discussion about identity construction.

In this dissertation I offer the term *cultural hybrid* to describe an individual who carries multiple interrelated cultural frames (having become available through face-to-face and virtual interactions across cultures and geographic boundaries) alongside a high degree of flexibility regarding behavior specific to those frames. The contradictory data support the notion that this hybridity showed itself in malleable forms (multipositionality) pointing toward the possibility of unconscious or conscious flexible identity construction. The data also indicated that this flexible behavior may be contextually dependent. For instance, both groups had cultural hybrids in their composition as defined above with similar capacities and characteristics (as measured by the IDI-2 and PCSI), and both groups established a similar intragroup hierarchy formed within the same system (institution). However, their differences in behavior, group dynamics, and artifacts created (visual maps) pointed toward the capacity to contextualize their identities and structure their behavior to the emerging group pattern. This pattern was projected into the artifacts they created, and in which they were also reflected. The totality of the data thus pointed to the possibility that the groups' reality was coconstructed, contextually dependent, and reflected at the same time as it was constructed in a reciprocal relationship. This possibility supports the idea that participants were capable of some flexibility in their identities and constructed them together with the emerging patterns.

Addressing the Research Questions

The groups demonstrated some similarities and differences in how they proceeded through the activities. The striking similarities contain a possible answer to the initial question of how meaning is cocreated by small groups in polycultural environments via interactive graphic facilitation and collaborative visual mapping. Using the discussion above, this section first provides an answer to the main research question and then each subquestion, in order.

The main research question asked how these two polycultural groups of five students each enrolled in a beginning college-level visual literacy class coconstructed meaning when given the task of collaborating on telling a story and representing it visually by assembling a visual map of their own choosing. The answer can be found in the similarities between the processes of the two groups.

Both groups established leadership immediately and through the power of the marker. In other words, both of the individuals who, spontaneously, graphic facilitated the initial group brainstorming activity emerged as strong task-leaders and held that position all the way through the process. In fact, the activity they guided can be considered interactive graphic facilitation because the participant-facilitators consolidated other participants' input verbally as well as visually and invited their group members to participate in that action directly (which many of them did).

Roles were established in the first round of brainstorming and the patterns of interaction within those roles appeared immediately. It is certainly true that the participants had worked with each other before in their teams (which switched around a bit during the first weeks of the semester) and therefore knew each others' strengths and weaknesses, yet the roles they established in this process were more refined, more distinct, and more explicit than the ones they had played prior to data collection day. The expression of their roles and the patterns of interaction between those roles were consistent throughout the process, and held the key to the findings.

Both groups had a similar constellation of roles and shared leadership of the group to some extent. They had one lead, one colead, two supporters, and one outgroup participant. Neither group accepted the outgroup members as equal partners in the cocreation with the exception of some relationship-builders. If leadership is described as the synergy between task-masters and relationship-builders, both groups had shared leadership, a fact of which the relationship-builders in each group were well aware.

In the class debrief, the groups self-arranged their seating constellations and exactly mirrored their roles to each other as though the chairs had been labeled for that purpose (see Figure 43). This arrangement is significant considering that the two groups worked independently from each other and did not experience or observe each other's process; thus, they could not have known what hierarchy had emerged during the process.

Nonetheless, in this frozen moment I termed *snapshot 2*, the groups gave away the entire story—revealing and confirming each group's hierarchy. The leads sat at the head of the table on either end, opposing each other diagonally. To their left and right sat their third-level supporters, and the coleads sat one seat further from the leads. Opposite the colead sat the outgroup member of each group. The outgroup members sat next to each other with an empty chair between them, and so did the coleads. Figure 43 shows the seating arrangements and the participants' roles, with arrows showing the reflection of the roles across the table. When I presented this finding during the member check, participants expressed amazement at what the self-chosen seating arrangement during the class debrief had revealed and confirmed about group dynamics. We also found that there was a noticeable similarity to how participants arranged themselves, again, during the member check meeting.

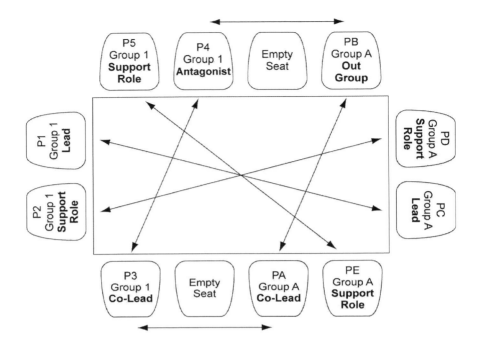

Figure 43. Class debrief seating arrangement (snapshot 2), with arrows showing the reflection of roles between the groups. PA = Aiden; PB = Bella; PC = Carolina; PD = Dianne; PE = Eugene; P1 = Michelle; P2 = Nick; P3 = Olive; P4 = Paige; P5 = Rusena. Author's image.

The relationships that form the gestalt of this seating arrangement metaphorically may signify the internal structure of the system the groups established collectively and then played out individually in the interaction pattern. The internal experience of each participant cannot be replicated in words, but can be shown here in this simple seating chart. This second example of mirroring (the first being the way the groups' interaction patterns reflected into the gestalt of the their visual maps) was an interesting outcome that deserves further investigation (see Epilogue).

The meaning of visual language has been defined as found in the gestalt of the words, shapes, and images (Horn, 1998). Similarly, the meaning of the seating arrangement in the present study was the expression of the internal group hierarchy that the groups mirrored to each other. This meaning only emerged when I looked at the relationships between the roles (visually and semantically) that each member assumed in each group, and then considered the fact that the groups mirrored them in that particular composition to each other. If we examine the seating constellation for its components (the seating location for each individual) and not their relationships to each other (hierarchy as syntax) the meaning of the hierarchy is completely lost.

The narrative in both groups emerged from participants' common experiences and was coconstructed by collecting participants' input. Interactive graphic facilitation as performed by the leads played a key role in collecting input and organizing the comments. The structure of the narrative was influenced by the graphic facilitator in both groups. Once leadership was established, both leaders made sure that the structure from their vision/sketch was transferred to their group's visual map. The personal processing style of the leaders was reflected in the visual structure of the maps in both groups.

Once the structure was established, leaders in both groups relaxed and allowed others to take charge. Leaders highly influenced the building of the structure and supporters filled in the blanks (images). Participants chose many images collectively in both groups but then let the supporters distribute them and add to or delete from the repertoire.

Not everyone's ideas were represented on the visual maps. Dianne had to repeatedly ask to include students who had never been to college before. Dianne and Eugene originally wanted a more linear storyline; Eugene's own sketch was not investigated or adopted by Group A and was completely forgotten by all Group A members by the time of the class debrief. Outgroup members' ideas were largely not included on the visual maps, for different reasons but with the same outcome of missing voices. Both groups were unconscious of the deleted unheard, untold, and unknown stories: Bella's voice was completely missing, and Paige's suggestions for Group 1's map as well as her desire for a more organic representation were not accepted by her group.

One group mastered the flow state beautifully, and the other group also experienced moments of this synergy between group members where very little talking was necessary and where people just knew what to do.

The essence of the group process was completely and fully mirrored back to the groups in their visual maps (snapshot 1). This essence demonstrated not only the patterns of interaction but also the information exchange and its modalities between participants, and thus represented the meaning of the cocreation. This meaning is found not in the individual parts or even in the summation of the parts, but in the gestalt of the entire map which is the same as the gestalt of the group's communication act.

This study found that the experience of the participants interacting with each other led to a certain pattern or rhythm of communication that was replicated in the gestalt of the visual map (the metaphor, snapshots 1) the group created and thus merely was a mirrored image of the previous experience, as suggested by Lakoff and Johnson (1999). In addition, the groups mirrored to each other their group hierarchies by way of a voluntary seating arrangement (snapshot 2), which could be framed as the metaphor for the internalized experience of the hierarchy/role play etched onto neural pathways and acted out unconsciously in seating choices.

In the following chapter, I consider the implications of these findings for the fields under consideration, and make recommendations for future research. The question of cultural hybrids' capacity for contextual multipositionality as an indicator for high flexibility in identity construction—and the potential this possibility holds—is further discussed in the Epilogue.

CHAPTER 9

CONCLUSIONS AND RECOMMENDATIONS

This case study explored the coconstruction of meaning in a polycultural small group environment via interactive graphic facilitation and collaborative visual mapping. I became interested in this topic when I identified a lack of information flow between the disciplines of intercultural communication and visual communication that created a problem for graphic facilitators during international dialogues on issues of global crisis. Having been trained in and participating in both fields, I was inspired to act upon this research opportunity and conducted a transdisciplinary case study at CCSF during the 2007 Spring semester with a total of 10 participants—simulating a situation that would allow me to address the issues identified. Two groups were asked to coconstruct a story and represent it in the form of a collaborative visual map through a largely self-organized process.

It is rare to have the opportunity (as I did in this study) to deeply investigate what is happening in such environments through videography, interviews, member checks, instruments, debriefs, and so on, in order to deliver a thick description of the event. Yet such polycultural dynamics are commonplace in today's world where many classes and events bring diverse participants together. This study represents a close look at exactly such a scenario in order to foreshadow for educators and practitioners the complex dynamics they may face when working with polycultural groups. The results of this small study may contribute to the fields of intercultural communication and visual communication, pointing the way for the former to expand to meet current needs on the global level, and bringing the latter into contact with culture. However, this study may also be of interest to institutions and administrators by providing a glimpse of the actual group dynamics set up by a polycultural environment.

Upon completing my literature review I was highly aware that the two disciplines I reviewed showed a thin record of internal discourse looking critically at the established canon. While the visual world still operates from positions of universal truths, the intercultural field is still organized around the principles of multiculturalism (focusing on the differences in cultures as autonomous units)—neither position seems to support adaptation to current global events. In the present study, I believe that I observed CCSF showing signs of polyculturalism and that the participants carried characteristics of cultural hybridity. The models and instruments currently available in the intercultural communication field and used in this study did not fully capture the experience of these 10 participants, whose range of behavior seemed to fall outside of the established canon (see Contextuality and Multipositionality below).

This chapter begins with a summary of the findings, organized by research question. The issue of contextuality and multipositionality is addressed in its own section, as it was one of the larger findings of the study. Next, the data sources are assessed for their utility for this type of study, so that future studies may benefit from the learnings in this research. After a review of the limitations of the study, recommendations are made for each of the parties and fields of interest: visual communication, intercultural communication, education, practitioners, researchers, and the institution of CCSF. The last section reviews the location of this study in the larger web of published literature pertaining to the topic to remind the reader of the consolidation this study provides due to the transdisciplinary approach taken.

Summary of Findings

A major finding of this case study was that the groups mirrored their interaction patterns into the gestalt of the maps they cocreated (snapshot 1) as well as mirrored the established group hierarchies to each other in the gestalt of their self-chosen seating arrangement during the class debrief (snapshot 2). These gestalt snapshots that are perceptible to the senses are thus the exterior expression of the interior meaning-making produced by the participating individuals on one level and by the group dynamics emerged from interacting participants on another. The main research question was answered on a basic level by this simple insight that the meaning of the cocreation can be extracted from the gestalt of the map (not the content) and the (non)verbal relationship between participants (role acceptance) in the gestalt of the seating arrangement (not the participants themselves). This insight also supports the notion that these participants who inhabited some characteristics of cultural hybridity cocreated meaning flexibly and demonstrated flexibility in their cultural styles and DMIS stages.

The discovery of snapshots 1 and 2 situated this study into the Gudykunst et al. (2005) subcategory of communication networks, which focuses on interrelationships between individuals in communication acts as indicators for behavior rather than focusing on the individuals themselves. Gudykunst et al.'s definition also confirms the present study's findings that the patterns of communication made sense in the context, while the individual behavior of the participants often did not match their profiles.

One aspect of the basic research question was how, specifically, groups cocreate the meaning that we now can describe through the gestalt of the maps or the seating arrangement. The parallels between the processes of both groups dissected this aspect of the research question and gave more granularity to its answer. These 10 participants, inhabiting some characteristics of

202

cultural hybridity in their communication acts within a polycultural environment, cocreated meaning (their story of the CCSF experience) through the following, not necessarily in this order:

1. Establishing leadership via (interactive) graphic facilitation at the onset of the project;
2. Establishing roles and demonstrating their patterns of interaction early in the process—having task-masters, relationship-builders, and outgroup members in their constellations;
3. Soliciting commonalities in their experiences upon which they could build;
4. Having the leaders influence the structure of their (visual) narratives, accepting their leaders' personal processing styles as the group norm, and having other roles filling in the details on the maps;
5. Neglecting unheard, untold, and unknown stories;
6. Replicating their group process (patterns of interactions and modalities of information exchange) in the artifacts they created—the visual representations of their ideas and structure of their maps—thus revealing the meaning of the cocreation in the gestalt of the visual maps (snapshot 1); and
7. Experiencing flow states and intersubjectivity during their creative activities;
8. Having the leaders be involved in presenting the visual maps;
9. Mirroring group hierarchies to each other in a self-organized seating arrangement (snapshot 2), thus confirming the meaning of the cocreation in the gestalt of the arrangements and outside of their awareness;
10. Potentially shifting identity to match/support the context of emerging communication act(s).

Research subquestion one investigated what could be noticed or learned about the group dynamics of this polycultural group engaged in group creativity, through investigation of the data sources. Both groups established a similar composition of roles and were highly (but largely unconsciously) aware of the group hierarchy. Role flexibility varied among participants, and may have been influenced by perceived issues of race and ethnicity. Both groups established leadership in the process itself through the power of the marker, and shared this leadership to some extent. Both groups operated from the underlying assumptions that something ought to be learned in this process and that agreement and inclusion should be reached, but neither fully acted upon the latter. Both groups had trust-building as a high value. Both groups participated in groupthink and flow states. Both groups completely and fully replicated their interaction pattern in the gestalt of their map, and exposed their hierarchy structure in their seating arrangement to each other accurately.

Research subquestion two considered what could be learned about how culture is represented visually in the products of these 10 participants, through analysis of the visual maps cocreated by these two groups of five participants. Since in both cases the map structure directly replicated the group process dynamic, it can be concluded that the composition of the group in that particular moment determined the pattern of interaction and the range of possibilities for the exchange of information. While the individual participants and especially the leaders certainly influenced the group dynamic, the gestalt of the final visual maps did not speak about one particular participant's frame nor that of all the participants together (additive). Rather, the visual map gestalt demonstrated the exchanges that took place in that space, at that time, in that particular constellation, under those particular circumstances, in that particular manner, and within those particular boundaries (transclusive).

Research subquestion three concerned the possibility of using the instruments to account for cultural factors, teasing out the cultural variables, and assessing whether the participants acted in alignment with the cultural values and worldview orientations identified by the instruments. Some participants stayed somewhat true to the profile that could be drawn from the various instruments, others did not, and some occupied contextual multipositionality on the scales and stages. Therefore, it was not possible to tease out the cultural variables consistently from the behavior of this group of cultural hybrids in this class on this day. When comparing values and worldviews to observed behavior, results were as expected as many times as they were contrary to expectations. It was therefore not possible to predict behavior from these instruments for these participants, especially if this judgment is based on (sophisticated stereotypical) cultural framing. In fact, participants demonstrated signs that their worldview structures may have been different (more evolved) than those upon which these instruments were built, which I interpreted as a potential shift in paradigms from multiculturalism to polyculturalism (see Epilogue).

Research subquestion four asked what could be learned about how culture was evoked in these two particular cocreation processes, if the cocreation instructions were designed to elicit participant sharing of values and beliefs and negotiation of such among the group. In addition, the data sources were investigated with regard to what could be learned about participants' conceptions of how the innate (nature) and the cultural (nurture) were at play during the event. The process of collaboration automatically forced participants to expose beliefs and values to each other, and the class debrief process with its carefully planned questions slowly took participants into deeper stages of reflection, which elicited more of the potential dynamic available in the room. Not enough personal or cultural information was collected about each participant to make a reliable statement; however, the investigation of the scores that were obtained and compared to actual behavior and the self-reflection of the participants showed that it was impossible to separate the innate from the cultural.

Contextuality and Multipositionality

The profession of intercultural communication informs its practice through field-specific theories and models. Assessment instruments are commonly used in training situations and in assisting individuals, organizations, and institutions in becoming more effective. Two major veins of cultural issues were investigated in this study: cultural styles and intercultural sensitivity vis-à-vis cultural difference.

In regard to cultural dimensions, two well established theories have been discussed in this study, namely the work of Hofstede (2001) and that of Trompenaars and Hampden-Turner (1998). These scholars have studied, researched, and defined a variety of cultural dimensions that are defined and measured on polarized continua with two opposing orientations. The score received is one point on any of these continua where an individual/culture supposedly resides. All kinds of diagrammatic representations can be drawn from scores on different cultural dimensions to arrive at the profile of an individual/culture, which then can be compared to the profiles of other individuals/cultures. This body of work is similar to the cultural styles that were available for assessment. In the present study, Peterson's (2004) PCSI measured participants' (five) cultural styles. I suspect that the cultural hybrids in this study demonstrated multipositionality on these continua, and their positions may be fluid depending on the context and participants in creative activities (contextuality).

Hofstede (2001) probably performed the largest cultural dimensions research any individual can achieve in a lifetime by measuring IBM employees' cultural dimensions over decades and all over the world. This groundbreaking body of work resulted in a massive and publicly available database providing scores for over 70 countries for five cultural dimensions. While his work is extremely impressive, it must be acknowledged that his sample pool was not diverse enough, as his participants occupied the same organizational dimension. Therefore his participants cannot possibly stand for an entire country—neither can national boundaries be equivalent to cultural ones. In addition, the scores may need to be updated to meet the current status of a globalizing world.

Numerous studies comparing two cultures have led to many books and articles on this subject, which fulfilled the needs of the field for many years while the challenges of a multicultural world were being engaged. Current events on the planet through globalization, however, may have changed how we need to study culture in order to accommodate the experience of cultural hybrids who communicate virtually and face-to-face across the world. Researching many (hybrid) cultures interacting with each other simultaneously may be necessary in this dynamic. The resulting data might then reflect the reality of today's challenges and begin to solve the challenges of polyculturalism.

While the GLOBE project's massive collaboration needs to be applauded for its efforts to address some of the shortcomings of defining cultural dimensions, it did not address one of the main issues found in this study. The GLOBE research addressed each culture independently and studied it in isolation. Massive data were collected for each target culture and are now available for cross-reference and comparison (House et al., 2004). However, nobody knows how individuals and cultures will behave in this new global dynamic upon contact, how their behavior changes in the context of ingroup situations and outgroup experiences, or what relationships the cultural dimensions build to each other under various circumstances.

Participants' intercultural sensitivity levels were measured via the IDI-2, the accompanying instrument to Bennett's DMIS (1986b), which is a developmental model dividing movement from ethnocentric to ethnorelative orientations into six stages. The model is about twenty years old, and the instrument ten (the IDI-3 is still in the process of being refined, Hammer, in press). In the present study, participants' IDI-2 scores compared to their behavior demonstrated that the experience of these 10 potential cultural hybrids may not have been fully captured by the instrument. This discrepancy may be the result of the disconnect between what I needed and what the IDI-2 was designed for; specifically, my focus required models and instruments for studying culturally complex groups (such as cultural hybrids) in polycultural environments during interaction, and the IDI-2 asks individuals in isolation to imagine virtual intercultural interactions in multicultural environments.

Bennett laid important groundwork by researching the development toward ethnorelativity and measuring intercultural sensitivity; Bennett and Hammer spent many years identifying the clusters for the IDI and collecting the appropriate statements/questions for the inventory. While this body of work represents several milestones in the history of intercultural communication that are still widely used in the field, the current versions of the DMIS and the IDI-2 (and the updated IDI-3, which was not available at the time of this study) may no longer be adequate for what needs to be measured given the current state of affairs on the planet and the potential paradigm shift into polyculturalism. What would this model and instrument look like with a thicker record, something other than a questionnaire answered during moments of disconnect from the action being asked about? What would they look like if they matched the current status of a globalizing world with increasing numbers of cultural hybrids who gain their multiple cultural frames during face-to-face interactions as well as from virtual simulations online? What would the stages look like if they included a worldview structure of polyculturalism?

Assessment of Data Sources

A variety of assessment tools were used in this research project—some were more useful than others, and some served multiple purposes. As with all instruments, caution is recommended as their limitations could lead participants and administrators of the instruments to judge from results that may be incomplete at best or even incorrect.

Feedback is crucial when working with assessment tools. While instruments are useful in providing a place to start the discussion about participants' innate and cultural preferences, it must be acknowledged that all instruments are inherently problematic. The results may not be consistent from one day to the next or in changing context—they can only measure a small slice of all we are. In addition, sometimes they cannot capture our experience at all; for example, if they rely on a linguistic mode that does not match the person's personal preferences. Most of the instruments used in this project were also self-administered and thus carry the potential for activating personal blind spots.

The results of any of these instruments automatically also carry the danger of making participants feel categorized into particular positions, or manipulating how they perceive themselves. In an educational context, caution needs to be taken especially if there is a danger of further solidifying stereotypes. Therefore it is important to front-load any discussion about the results of these sorts of assessments with the flaws inherently present in such processes. Instruments should be used as a base for a helpful discussion to learn something about ourselves and those we work with, rather than a base for categorizing or as a measurement of the "truth." With such precautions, taking participants through assessment exercises can be very useful in creating openings to new possibilities rather than shrinking perspectives by accepting the data as absolute coordinates for the experience. In this sense assessments function as tools for an intervention and in this study, the benefits of the discussions were well balanced with the risks listed above.

The video media and transcriptions were the perfect format for collecting and analyzing the primary data, as they could be reviewed multiple times and analyzed from different angles. The observations could be well described due to these records—I would have missed many of them without this method. The insights gained from the possibilities this media provided were deep and rich.

The IDI-2 and PCSI scores provided some valuable background information regarding participants' levels of intercultural competence and the cultural styles expressed by individual participants and/or groups, as well as about the general communication patterns through which the groups interacted. As they were central to the analysis, the IDI-2 and PCSI are discussed in detail in the Contextuality and Multipositionality section above.

The VisualsSpeak(tm) image set provided an efficient way for participants to decide on representative visuals to tell their story. While much of the visual map was coconstructed through a more or less consensus-building process of decisions made by the participants (at least some of which would have depended on rational thinking), the VisualsSpeak(tm) image set allowed for intuition to be included in the process. Ready-made images could be chosen for their emotional qualities as well as their content and aesthetic representations without having participants run them through their rational filter. Discussions around which images to include also revealed some interesting data regarding participants' worldviews and intercultural developmental stages, such as Paige's questioning of the need for multiculturalism.

I had never used the TPI prior to this study, and I used it not as a team-building tool (as it was intended by the developers) but purely as a way to measure the potential for team effectiveness on data collection day. I found the TPI not very useful in the way I applied it. The TPI results confirmed that the groups fell in the necessary threshold of capacity to collaborate on the given tasks together, but had otherwise no bearing on this project.

The TPI scores said more about the individual's orientation in regard to evaluating performance in themselves, which they then may have transferred to how they evaluated other members of their group or the status of team performance as a whole. For example, I was not surprised to find Aiden evaluating lower since he demonstrated tough measurements for himself throughout the semester. Neither was I surprised to find Olive evaluating very high because she demonstrated a healthy dose of optimism most of the time. In this research, Group A had two members with highly divergent TPI scores. Carolina scored rather high in the last three stages, higher than in the earlier stages and much higher than her zero in stage one (orientation). Dianne scored very high in stage one, with the highest score (eight) among the participants. Dianne was always clear on her own goals, so her very high score was not surprising. When comparing Dianne's and Carolina's orientation scores to the performance of their group, it seems unlikely that their TPI evaluations had much to do with the group's actual performance levels; rather, the scores provided a rich foundation for a team-building discussion.

In retrospect, the TPI might have been more useful as a team development tool and as a measurement of the participants' experience of the research process rather than as a prediction of their teamwork issues. Participants mentioned that the research day was a bonding experience that took the groups deeper into their team development. Retaking the TPI at the end of data collection day could have provided a way to measure the effectiveness of this event as an intervention. As a team development tool, the TPM (the model upon which the TPI is based, see Appendix I) also had the potential of being used together with other large-scale graphic templates, such as the Group

Graphics Keyboard (The Grove, 2007a) that would have provided a way for overlapping visual communication and intercultural communication issues.

The secondary data sources did not produce any surprises or controversies; they provided confirmation of and some supporting detail for the primary data. However, they were very useful in corroborating that the conclusions I made from the primary data were not missing anything significant. The informal tools (the LS and MI), interviews, and member check were performed in order to verify some of the data and observations. The personal interviews were minimally used in the final analysis, as my focus was on group interaction and they largely confirmed earlier observations from the primary data sources and thus provided little new information. The member check was useful to enhance the validity of the findings through participant feedback, and also provided some new insights.

The LS and MI assessment tools were used mainly for the purpose of leading a discussion about differences in personality and cultural conditioning, and are a regular addition to this class. All participants acted in accordance with their LS scores, though the lopsided results were surprising. The majority (80%) of the participants self-assessed as accommodators on the LS, which perfectly matched my own preferred style and may have contributed to the deep rapport-building we were able to accomplish as a class. Their scoring as accommodators indicated that they enjoyed learning with each other in a group setting and by doing rather than by theorizing or observing—qualities which were also supported by their PCSI preferences for group orientation and relationship-building. Bella identified as a diverger, which would indicate that she may enjoy observing and considering many viewpoints before acting, and this expectation was confirmed by her observable behavior on data collection day and throughout the semester. Nick identified as an assimilator, which would translate into preferring to learn by pondering content and then dissecting it and putting it back together in the form of theoretical models. Therefore, to some extent Nick would also be more of an observer than a doer, and he was rather quiet and spoke only when he had something important to convey. Nick's score as an assimilator did not show up as a significant aspect for this study, but it may have had something to do with his ability to function as a mediator and healer as he consolidated the group's thinking very cohesively and at the right moments.

The MI scores were varied, confirmed some participants' experiences and surprised others. However, the MI scores did not seem to bear any significance in regard to culture except to confirm some behaviors, such as Bella as an introvert.

Limitations

This study was restricted to 10 participants. While the findings are promising and provide direction regarding content areas and new practices, the results need to be corroborated with larger groups, extended to more research projects in the same or similar contexts, and expanded from student populations to other groups.

The present study was restricted to available theories, models, and instruments in the fields—all of which were heavily influenced by the dominant culture (male) in their conception and development.

In addition, the data were undoubtedly influenced by the way I conducted the activities and asked the questions. For example, I chose to interview only six participants, but in retrospect interviewing all 10 would have provided a more balanced picture. And during the class debrief, I switched my focus from Group A to Group 1 and back again, with the result that I did not get complete answers from both groups for all the questions.

I have a nonlinear bias for information processing because of my strong preference for lateral, creative systems thinking and visual processing. For this research project, I had to diagram information and relationships onto large-scale visual maps to fully comprehend the complexity present in the midst of the creative chaos as it unraveled in front of me. This nonlinear way of learning had the disadvantage of getting lost in too much information that was hard to manage, consolidate, and synthesize, but also had the advantage of producing the many powerful diagrams that revealed significant relationships among the data. A researcher with a less holistic lens may have distilled additional findings that were not perceptible to me.

Part of the transformation I experienced by going through this research process was the recognition of my own bias largely grounded in a Western orientation and conditioned by the cultural frames I occupied. For instance, I entered this project having been colonized by my training in intercultural communication. During the process I crashed into the limitations of this discipline and needed to embark on additional rounds of analysis. This learning assisted me in noticing the same or similar bias built into the theories that had informed my practice previously. In addition, I learned from my participants, who illuminated some of these blind spots. For example, my initial definition of leadership that focused on orchestrating the completion of tasks was revised to consider the inclusion of relationship-building and shared leadership as essential for polycultural groups succeeding in creative activities. I cannot rule out the possibility that my findings, for instance, of leadership and role distribution in the groups, were influenced by the mere fact that I was looking for such concepts.

Further, a repeat of this study might not lead to the same results because even the same participants might react differently on a different day, depending on numerous variables not under the control of the researcher. These variables could be as simple as the mood participants bring to the project that day, which may influence the modality of the interaction patterns and/or the content of coconstructed meaning. However, vis-à-vis the possibility of designer identities in cultural hybrids it must be considered that they might never play the same notes again even if the context were identical.

Future studies of this type would do well to keep these and other limitations in mind. The below listed recommendations emerged from my experience/observation of a potential paradigm shift from multiculturalism to polyculturalism, a possibility that warrants not only further research but also inclusion in the discourse as such a shift would significantly change how we may need to think about culture—that is, in more complex, more dynamic, and integral systems.

Recommendations

Both disciplines, visual communication and intercultural communication, were investigated through the four-quadrant viewfinder, which helped to surface their gaps (both focus on different realms of reality and different aspects of communication). Both disciplines were evoked simultaneously in answering the research question, which facilitated the filling of their gaps to some extent. However, both disciplines were found to be lacking in theories and practices that can address the current paradigm shift from multiculturalism into polyculturalism; therefore, although the data did yield answers to the research questions, a new research dilemma arose from the data analysis for which no answer could be found in either of these two disciplines (see Epilogue). Below is a summary of recommendations that could bring immediate relief to the closing of the gaps between visual and intercultural communication, but more work will be required in order to address the paradigm shift (see Epilogue).

Recommendations for the Field of Visual Communication

The field of visual communication (including graphic design and information design) as a discipline is still operating mainly from the perspective of universalism. Therefore, the discipline is not conceptually in sync with global events or with a potential paradigm shift toward polyculturalism. While the technology-driven interactive design branches are among some of the most advanced fields in regard to transglobal communication techniques, their conceptual frames are still based in the universal ideals taught in design schools that force users into the conceptual frame of the dominant culture.

Visual communication theorists and practitioners are therefore invited to take an active role in infusing cultural aspects to visual communication and to participate in shaping strategies from a more informed theoretical foundation that includes cultural perspectives in design theory and practice. In a globalized world, especially, all communicators would benefit from taking into account the impact of their communication acts upon the intended audiences and practice taking the perspectives of the other and holding flexible delivery frames. At the same time, communicators of all media may be more successful if following a practice of self-reflection as described, for instance, in the concept of cultural humility (Tervalon & Murray-García, 1998) (discussed further in Recommendations for the Field of Education below). Additionally, visual communication scholars would benefit from forming connections with other relevant disciplines so that they all can collaborate on propelling the necessary polycanon forward.

The application-focused branches of visual communication such as fine art and graphic design have historically not engaged in training students for research and doctoral-level work. Since the mid-1990s, a few programs have emerged that offer PhD programs, mostly in an interdisciplinary format that foster cross-fertilization. It would be beneficial for the field to continue this trend and create many more programs to take the discipline to the next level and inform the practice with current and critical information.

However, people participating in transglobal information exchange (such as the cultural hybrids in this study) are much more in touch with current events, as they also shape them in a reciprocal relationship. Such students can thus lead the way for those who are supposed to teach them but are not adequately equipped to bring culture or other contemporary issues to the learning environment. It will take the whole global community to upgrade the discipline to contemporary status in regard to its theoretical underpinning.

This study focused on the cocreation of meaning in polycultural environments, which is why I asked participants to collaborate on constructing the story rather than asking them to individually create stories and then share and negotiate from a pre-existing idea they formulated by themselves. It might, however, be interesting to learn in future research how the results might differ if the process were more individually oriented.

Recommendations for the Field of Intercultural Communication

The intercultural communication field has been continuing to practice and rely on academic sources from within or from closely related disciplines such as organizational effectiveness for advancing the field. Some of this work is cutting-edge, but even then the research is not moving forward fast enough to match the speed of development in the global dynamic. Intercultural communication scholars and practitioners may be more successful in participating in contemporary issues through the pursuit of ways of collecting current data quickly around the globe and the sharing of that data so that everyone has access to updated information. Further, voices from a wide variety of cultures would be an integral part of such community-based hubs and participate directly in exchanging information. Advances in technology can be used to facilitate this transglobal networking.

Methods of researching cultures in this global dynamic need to shift from objective observations of cultures in isolation to objective and subjective research of multiple cultures in interaction. In addition, the field would be best served by including research and researchers from nondominant cultures doing their work in their own languages that can then be translated into a language allowing the results to be shared with most people around the world.

Updating models and instruments would benefit researchers and practitioners greatly. Stepping out of the bipolar frame and considering multipositionality and contextuality in assessment systems to capture the lived experience of cultural hybrids would align the profession with current events in a globalizing world. In addition, models and instruments addressing diverse groups in interaction would be extremely useful.

Visual communication—virtual, interactive, and in print—is part of the information exchange between cultures. Therefore, intercultural communication scholars would benefit from participating in researching visual communication as a major vein of transglobal interaction, and then developing practices that include visual techniques in facilitating exchanges between cultures that can, simultaneously, serve as models back to the discipline of visual communication. Transdisciplinary research and design collaborations would be even more desirable to assure cross-fertilization in the development stages.

The discipline of intercultural communication has been successful in establishing itself in the last century and developing theories, methods, and instruments to engage the challenges of multiculturalism. In this participation, communication moved from intracultural (monocultural groups) to intercultural (multicultural groups). The signs may already be present that we are in the midst of a paradigm shift into polyculturalism on a global level. This shift warrants a rethinking of the discipline and its deepest roots, possibly moving toward developing a new understanding of the field and the contributions it can make in this century. Practitioners of intercultural communication have the opportunity to participate in engaging the challenges of polyculturalism and to align themselves with the new form of communication necessary for this context.

I was not intending to write a manual for educators and facilitators, visual practitioners, or intercultural communication specialists who work with diverse groups. Rather, this study was intended to hint at the complexity of how meaning is cocreated in diverse environments in which learning activities take place via group dialogue, collaborative visual mapping, and interactive graphic facilitation, and to point to the need for advancing each discipline and the practitioners thereof in order to assist in solving the challenging problems the global community is facing at this time.

Although educators have been the subject of much criticism that may be valid, in my experience they have often made heroic efforts to create learning environments and innovate teaching practices that not only include but foster the expression of diverse cultures and learning styles (visual processing included). Many dedicated teachers go above and beyond in supporting the communities they serve, and many schools and programs have taken active steps to grow and nourish cultural diversity across their campuses, some by installing faculty trainings that focus on these issues in particular.

As a faculty developer I am aware of the fact that educators rely on drawing information from other disciplines in the effort to transform their teaching practice to better meet the needs of an increasingly diverse student population. In that process, the current limitations of visual and intercultural communication theory as discussed in this dissertation can be transmitted alongside. It is important that educators become aware of the blind spots they may be inviting into the classroom in their efforts to serve a world in crisis.

The LS and MI materials that are part of the intercultural communication practitioner's toolbox would also serve faculty very well—with the consideration of the tools' limitations. In a training or teaching situation the goal is to bring awareness to participants' personal preferences and to facilitate experimenting with various other positions that may not be present in their daily routine but that would be helpful in learning about how people on other positions process information. Used in this context, these tools are also a form of intervention that may lead to potential self-discovery and more empathy.

It is extremely interesting that all 10 participants were significantly more oriented toward the PCSI group- and relationship-orientations than the average U.S. scores, and that 8 of the 10 scored as accommodators on the LS (which also points toward a group orientation in learning preferences). Whether or not there is a correlation between group- and relationship-orientations and learning styles needs to be left up to future research.

So, while these research results represent important complementary information regarding LS applications, further research is necessary to build a reliable repertoire of culturally influenced learning preferences for practitioners working with culturally diverse learners. Cultural preferences for certain learning phases or intelligences are most strongly observed in the education system, which often has no room for students with nonmainstream preferences. Teachers knowledgeable of the correlations between cultural and learning style preferences would be more able to potentially transform their curriculum to serve all students better.

I recommend that educational institutions develop ways to reward, financially and otherwise, faculty, staff, students, and programs that bring culture to the center of their activities. Diverse learning communities who create best practices and involve students could be established en masse. This collaborative spirit would then foster reciprocal relationships that can be developed and build the trust, flexibility, and skills to engage in critical pedagogy (the sharing of power in the classroom). This sharing of power is necessary to close the growing divide in regard to the wide distribution of much needed resources.

By sharing power I do not mean to suggest leveling all hierarchies but rather building them anew based on the particular gifts and strengths each individual or group of people can bring to solving the global problems at hand. This new type of hierarchy would replace those based on status, race, origin, or material resources. As described by one of the participants in my study, the goal is to "find out what that person's really strong gifts are and what they individually can bring to the group that no one else can and you use them for that" (Carolina, class debrief, p. 4). From an educational standpoint, it would be important to facilitate toward shared leadership in polycultural groups; in fact, sharing leadership may be an excellent way to reduce teacher exhaustion.

Industries are invited to take an active role in participating in education and sponsoring its advancement, as it is in their own best interest to capacitate and empower not only their customers but all who participate in the evolvement of the human race, to foster a healthy economy and society as well as support environmental and social sustainability around the planet.

Educators can take the lead in carving out the path to lived forms of polyculturalism so that a variety of members of the global community feel invited to participate. Educators could provide openings for rapport-building if they began any class with opportunities for sharing values and beliefs via well facilitated and carefully debriefed creative activities that expose the unspeakable and foster the enactment of flexible identities lived and contextualized. Educators are invited to develop their skills in facilitating group rapport, evoking flow state in group activities, and crafting spaces where participants can safely debrief their experiences. Use of these techniques may help culturally diverse groups establish constructive interaction patterns. Debriefing every activity is highly important because much of the (cultural) learning happens during group reflection. These

215

practices can help cultural hybrids dissect their own experiences rather than hiding them if they don't meet the dominant frame. Maximizing cultural hybrids' multiple identities as a resource for problem solving and fostering the cocreation of intersubjectivity may be the next wave of improving teaching practices in a polycultural environment.

This study demonstrated that working in a culturally highly diverse environment can be exhilarating and, at the same time, anxiety-producing. Whether any real work can be done until the group is in sync is highly questionable. Starting each meeting with creative activities would allow the group to (re-)build rapport with each other by facilitating activities that foster the safe and respectful exchange of similarities and differences.

In educational polycultural settings where group dynamics might become more and more fluid, it is interesting to ask whether cultural competence is enough, or whether it might even become a hindering factor if too many assumptions are held? A term used in the health professions, *cultural humility* (Tervalon & Murray-García, 1998), may better describe the humble attitude necessary to approach the subject of interacting with people of all kinds of complex backgrounds. Cultural humility in the context of education would be understood as a "lifelong commitment to self-evaluation and critique, to redressing the power imbalances" (p. 123) in the teacher–student dynamic, rather than assuming that culture can be understood as a set of variables that are predictable and consequently controllable.

Cultural humility translates into developing a high level of self-awareness and openness as a practitioner, and building partnerships that open opportunities for the exchange of commonalities and differences across many areas, culture included. This form of exchange in the overlaps and gaps between self and other produces the potential for respect, curiosity, and humility—in the presence of the mystery of life. This concept of humility—which is really a moral issue—is also referred to as the concept of culture as refinement (Baldwin et al., 2006). This understanding thereby advances the idea of culture as a process and function one step further into the "attainment of higher awareness, with the aid of which one succeeds in understanding one's own historical value, one's own function in life, one's own rights and obligations" (Gramscki, 1981, as quoted by Baldwin et al., 2006, p. 46).

Recommendations for Practitioners

I propose the development of certain internal and external frames as a foundation from which we, individually and as groups, can address global issues with maximum intelligence, capacity, and compassion. Therefore the term *practitioners* is used here to include the fields mentioned above and others beyond. Practitioners working with culturally diverse populations across the disciplines would benefit from practicing cultural humility (Tervalon & Murray-García, 1998)—a lifelong practice of "self-reflection and self-critique" (Hunt, 2001). This attitude of cultural humility would allow practitioners to create partnerships that foster the respectful exchange of similarities and differences in the gap of intersecting with each other. It may be important for all practitioners to seek cultural information from a variety of critical sources, particularly those that discuss culture and identity as flexible.

Recommendations for Researchers

Based on the findings of this study, more research is needed that puts multiple cultures into direct contact and interaction with each other. Research design should include objective and subjective approaches as suggested by Gudykunst et al. (2005), and cover the phenomena from various angles, possibly even from various disciplines or from the perspective of the gaps within disciplines. As the findings in the present study show, the two disciplines involved demonstrated a real need to complement the research with each other's strengths and perspectives and each other's gaps. Neither of the disciplines could have answered the research question by itself or even as a pair until a wider research frame was applied that could address and consolidate their gaps, namely integral theory applied through the lens of transdisciplinary methods.

Given the finding of this study regarding the limitations of the instruments used, I highly recommend adding intuitive, creative, visual methods into the research design and process, allowing for the invisible portion of the iceberg to surface organically. Visual methods, integrated with more traditional "objective" methods, may offer a richer investigation. One possible such visual, integral tool is described in the Epilogue.

It would be useful (although not always practical) to collaborate across disciplines, cultures, and geographical boundaries in order to advance the fields. In addition, it is important to invent new, more immediate forms of research that can include automatic updating of data input to keep information current.

Many other case studies of this kind investigating the concept of interacting cultural hybrids in a polycultural context are needed to generalize the findings of this study. Researchers interested in this kind of research may be well advised to collaborate generously so that issues of data bloat and cognitive overload can be managed. Visual mapping in the process of analyzing the data led to significant insights in this study that I may not have had otherwise. I therefore highly recommend the inclusion of nonlinear tools such as visual diagramming to manage the complexity inherent in transdisciplinary research.

Participants' demographic data was difficult to consolidate because of the inherent complexity cultural hybrids bring to flatlander forms. I recommend that any forms designed to collect demographic data are collaboratively developed together with the participants in order to find clarity about their needs for communicating the information. In addition, I recommend adding white space for documenting any excluded parts not considered on the form, as well as interviewing participants individually to clarify the information given. These recommendations would also be useful for CCSF to follow as the complexity of cultural hybrids cannot be captured on the standard forms, but is necessary to know about if the institution is to serve cultural hybrids—which may increasingly be the norm.

Recommendations for CCSF

The fact that CCSF represents the most diverse community college population in the country places an extra dose of responsibility on all participants to operate from positions of cultural humility. Due to this highly unique context, the CCSF administration also has the rare opportunity to lead other institutions and the field of education in engaging polycultural challenges by undertaking additional qualitative studies of the kind presented here. Because this study was small, the observations of potentially flexible cultural frames and the possibility of culture as an available design need to be further researched at CCSF. Diverse students interacting with each other during creative activities need to be studied to further generalize the findings of this study.

Special attention is needed as to how rapport can be built and facilitated in the polycultural classroom, and how cultural humility and flexibility can be taught and nurtured (collaboratively). I recommend that methods be developed to maximize creative engagement as a form of exposing values and beliefs to each other in a safe environment that fosters respectful and transformative communication practices. In addition, CCSF has the infrastructure and offers the ecology for transformative teaching practices, and might therefore consider taking the opportunity and responsibility to establish an institute where educators from all corners of the world can learn together by immersing themselves in this rich environment. Attendees could then participate in further research to coconstruct knowledge and develop teaching methods for polycultural environments. It takes a global village to solve the global problems humanity is now facing, and CCSF is a thriving institution uniquely positioned to face this challenge, and poised for fulfilling such research needs.

Location of This Research Project

The viewfinder was a useful tool to examine the location of the disciplines involved in this study and surface the reasons why I needed all of them to address the research questions completely. These disciplines have their center of gravity located in different quadrants. For instance, the field of visual communication, which has a special link to psychology, focuses on the exterior quadrants (upper right as objective meaning/reality and as in visual elements or signifiers, and lower right as in visual grammar or syntax). The field of intercultural communication, which has a special link to anthropology, focuses on the interior quadrants (upper left as in subjective meaning/reality or signifieds, and lower left as in collective meaning/reality/cultural exchanges or semantics). However, investigation of the collective interior is almost entirely by means of asking individuals about their personal experience of the collective; it is questionable whether the subjective experience of the individual removed from the action can accurately represent the collective meaning-making process.

Thus, the inclusion of both disciplines addresses three of the aspects of communication, and this study adds the fourth (cultural exchange on the collective level) in the meaning-creation act where the gaps of intercultural communication and visual communication perspectives are activated. Evaluating the usefulness of the viewfinder in this way also indicates how the disciplines participating in this case study can complement each other in order to investigate the full spectrum of a phenomenon.

This research project was one small-scale extension of Gudykunst et al. (2005) through the application of both objectivist and subjectivist approaches to intercultural communication research. In addition, the present study was composed of all three categories as defined by Gudykunst et al.: constructivist theories, variations in communication across cultures, and communication patterns.

The first category includes constructivist theories and was covered by introducing Bennett's (1986b) theory of the DMIS (construction of worldviews) and using its accompanying instrument, the IDI-2. Also in the first category, Pearce's (2004) CMM theory and process concerning the social construction of reality and its accompanying CMM tools were used in the analysis.

The second category of intercultural theories, those that concern cultural differences, was covered by introducing models and research for cultural dimensions by Hofstede (2001), Trompenaars and Hampden-Turner (1998), the GLOBE study (House et al., 2004), and Peterson's (2004) cultural styles, the instrument of which (the PCSI) was used in the present study.

The third category of theories, those that concern communication between people from different cultures, formed the core of this study. In particular, this study investigated the subcategory of communication networks, where it is assumed that the behavior largely depends on the relationships between the participants in the communication act, rather than on the individuals themselves. This relationship dynamic was directly observed, and I concluded that the cocreation of meaning was readable from the communication patterns rather than from the profiles or behavior of the individuals, because communication patterns shift depending on the situation and the flexibility of the participants. This conclusion was also confirmed in that the meaning was located in the gestalt of their collaborative artifact, the visual map, and not in the components thereof. In addition, the importance of the group dynamic to the meaning created was also observed in the roles participants took on and then reflected in the relationships exposed in their self-organized seating constellation. The subcategory of communication networks included the visual communication aspects of the study, as the visual maps were investigated for patterns equivalent to the interaction patterns of the groups.

The present study also offers extensions of theories about cultural dimensions and styles (Hofstede, 2001; House et al., 2004; Trompenaars & Hampden-Turner, 1998; Peterson, 2004) through the suggestion that these theories be developed to include capacities for multipositionality and contextuality. This study had a focus in researching interacting cultural hybrids and is thus an extension of one aspect of the GLOBE study, which identified the lack of research on cultures in interaction (House et al., 2004). Essentially, the many angles this study used to investigate the phenomenon represent an integral approach, further elaborated on in the Epilogue.

The field of visual communication has largely ignored culture as a variable in its pursuits to communicate to a variety of audiences via visual language systems. Horn (1998), who developed a visual language system widely referred to by graphic facilitators, claims that visual language exposes subconscious frames such as worldviews or basic assumptions and thus facilitates communication across cultures. However, no research has been done to confirm this assumption and inform the practice. This study extended Horn's work in that it researched the meaning-making process of polycultural participants collaborating on visual maps. Group visual mapping was also demonstrated as a successful way to overlap the two disciplines and allow them to inform each other. The results of this study support Horn's assertion that visual language would be useful for intercultural communication. In this study, visual language was an excellent means of analyzing aspects of polycultural group dynamics, in that visual language (the visual maps, objective reality) offered an observable indicator of subjective collective reality.

This study was also an intervention by default (Wagner, 1997), as it brought the participants into a deeper relationship with each other and we developed a richer relationship as a class community throughout the process. Some instruments were additionally used as another form of intervention by discussing results in order to allow self-awareness to grow and to expand cultural competence. In addition, participants learned something new about the institution, the researcher role, and the teacher role due to the discussions we led about the project at various times.

This chapter ends the traditional dissertation process; in the following Epilogue, parts of this study are reopened for reinvestigation from a more creative and innovative perspective that is typical of transdisciplinary studies.

EPILOGUE

Here in part two of the dissertation, I open the doors of knowledge freely and invite insights from nontraditional paths. I began this research project colonized into the disciplines I have been a member of for years—intercultural communication, visual communication, and interdisciplinary studies. Diving deeper into the connections that arose in the research process and through the data, I crashed into the limitations not only of those disciplines but also of the standard dissertation format, which naturally did not lend itself to investigations outside the canon. These limitations led me to reinvestigate the entire study from a transdisciplinary perspective and arrive at the conclusions provided here.

Part one of this dissertation (Chapters 1–9) answered the research question and fulfilled the expectations of a traditional dissertation format, as an offering to readers looking for the information organized in its usual sequence. However, after drawing conclusions and making recommendations from that traditional space, I was still dissatisfied because I had accumulated more and more interesting questions. I therefore approached the topic repeatedly after the initial analysis phase was complete, focusing on the investigation from a meta position and letting go of disciplinary boundaries and expectations completely. With this approach I addressed the new research dilemma (described in the following section), which had emerged from the findings but could not be answered within the established canon of the disciplines and the traditional dissertation format.

This epilogue presents an analysis of the data and findings from this meta position. The chapter begins with a short summary of the newly emerged research dilemma (investigated in this chapter), followed by a discussion of the nature of transdisciplinary research. The challenges of culture are then considered in terms of the possibility of a current paradigm shift from multiculturalism to polyculturalism and from intercultural communication to transcultural communication forms. Next, two new models are presented that addressed the synergetic relationship between the innate, the cultural, and situational in individuals and the relationship of the four aspects of communication as emerged from the mirroring effect discussed in Chapter 9. The Epilogue ends with a synthesis inclusive of the new possibilities entertained herein, recommendations for future research, and an overview of the next steps (arising from this new position) for the three fields under consideration (intercultural communication, visual communication, and education). It is this part two of the dissertation that will be interesting to readers looking for the kind of innovative thinkering that is characteristic of California Institute of Integral Studies graduates and also inherent in transdisciplinary research—interrelational, complex, and creative (Morin, 2005).

The research findings from part one opened up new questions about cultural hybrids and shifting identities. While the specifics of cultural hybridity cannot be determined by this small study, the literature review, my own observations and learning, and the findings of this study provided enough questions to hint at the possibility that the world is changing in significant ways. It seems possible that we are at the doorway of a major paradigm shift, warranting redefining the concept of culture itself. With such a redefinition, traditional theories and practices may become less reliable—which parallels the findings of this study.

Although the findings did answer the research questions on the surface level, they did not satisfy my curiosity because so much of the behavior demonstrated could not be explained with the theories underpinning this study nor was it captured by the instruments used. I was left with three significant issues: (a) cultural hybridity in polycultural environments; (b) the interrelationship between the innate, the cultural, and the situational; and (c) the interrelationship between snapshots 1 and 2 (the pattern of communication/interaction projected into the gestalt of the visual map, and role availability/acceptance projected into the hierarchy of the seating arrangement). As the use of both subjectivist and objectivist approaches often leads to the need for more research (Gudykunst et al., 2005), the need to explore the newly emerged questions further should not be surprising.

Within the established disciplines addressed in part one, I had no theory or model to use to illuminate the powerful relationships to which the snapshots alluded, and I had observed that the DMIS and accompanying IDI-2 scores and the PCSI styles did not completely capture the experience of the participants. Neither was the behavior of these cultural hybrids described in the theories underpinning this research. I believe that these discrepancies were caused by a mismatch of developmental stages between the available theories/models and where these participants actually were in their development. The delineation of which elements may have originated from which level (innate, cultural, or situational) was ultimately not possible. An alternative explanatory framework based on ethnographic and integral research has been proposed that may address this gap, described below.

The expansion to a transdisciplinary frame and inclusion of integral theory enabled me to make recommendations I felt would contribute to the fields in question and provided me with a response to the meaningful questions the 2004 CPWR graphic facilitators asked of me as an interculturalist. As is true of transdisciplinary methodology, this widened research space was not merely an additive formula of the participating disciplines but also presented a development of the integral frames used by further exploring, hypothetically, the unexplainable data and integrating them into a comprehensive whole. The methods used in part two are characteristic of the transdisciplinary researcher who composts data multiple times and follows the questions back to theory (in this case, integral theory); interesting results pointed to new possibilities from which the whole could be re-constructed.

Transdisciplinary Approaches and Methods

Transdisciplinary research challenges the traditional Cartesian organization of knowledge for its fragmented and limiting perspectives, where the boundaries of disciplinary thinking structure and organize knowledge in one particular way. Transdisciplinary researchers focus on the inquiry instead and their process is defined as highly creative, positioning the inquirer's subjectivity at its core and pulling from any discipline that can illuminate the phenomenon under investigation. The interdisciplinary approach, on the other hand, is additive; researchers in this genre investigate phenomena by establishing a dialogue between the disciplines under investigation, most likely inclusive of their blind spots. Transdisciplinary researchers investigate the gaps of the disciplines instead—turning the usual inquiry approaches upside down and inside out while acknowledging that their own personal lens highly influences what they can notice. Integral theory provided a very useful frame, the four-quadrant AQAL model, that served the transdisciplinary approach in this study and allowed me to identify the gaps and reconcile various shifting perspectives.

This study fits into transdisciplinary inquiry in a number of ways. The inquiry emerged from my personal experience and observations while consulting on an international project—transdisciplinary research is inquiry-driven and the focus emerges from the "inquirer's agenda...experience and passion, the subject of the inquiry, and the bodies of knowledge available" (Montuori, 2005, p. 154). A self-reflective process, transdisciplinary research fosters the exploration, assessment, and contextualization of the inquirer's subjectivity, and thus not only exposes the inquirer's underlying assumptions but often transforms her in the process. The data were composted creatively several times, raising new questions that ushered me as well as the found matter into transformation more than once, a multiple turn event. Transdisciplinary research is also a "creative process that combines...rigor and imagination" (p. 154) and acknowledges, distinguishes, and reconciles multiple ways of knowing. In this study, I searched back and forth through the underlying web of connecting roots between the (gaps of the) disciplines, the phenomenon investigated, and my personal experience with this matter. I worked myself through the data in a highly creative and intuitive manner to see what could emerge; the many diagrams are the result of this kind of search for comprehension, which led me from drawing to thinking to understanding.

The diagrams illuminated the interconnected relationships that emerged from the data. Due to the complexity of the many compounded tenets involved, this creative process was also reiterative with an ongoing self-reflective dialogue, stepping in and out of my own experience with this material, and back and forth between the various bodies of knowledge evoked in this project.

This creative process resulted in several rounds of analysis representative of open and evolving systems that revealed solutions, one at a time, to the dilemmas in the complex data constellations. The initial round concerned itself with *theoretical transdisciplinarity,* defined as a "methodology…which corresponds to a great number of different methods" (Nicolescu, 2007, p. 4). Subsequent rounds addressed the data via *phenomenological transdisciplinarity,* or the building of new models. The entire inquiry as a whole "connected the theoretical principles with the already observed experimental data" (p. 4)—an aspect of transdisciplinary thinking called *experimental transdisciplinarity,* which refers to repeatable procedures leading to similar but more refined results.

The Inquirer's Lens

As is essential to the transdisciplinary approach, the inquirer's lens is acknowledged as highly influential of what can be noticed from the researcher's position. The following discussion focuses on those aspects of my system that make transdisciplinary thinking possible and that influenced the outcomes of this dissertation. My formal intellectual background includes undergraduate and graduate studies in several disciplines: fine art (two- and three-dimensional), interactive installation and performance art, graphic design, business administration, multidisciplinary studies, interpretation and translation (German/English/French), and intercultural communication. My professional practices reach from teaching and facilitating to designing processes, products, and programs for organizational effectiveness across cultural boundaries, leadership development, teambuilding, and personal excellence. My neurolinguistic programming (NLP) background continues to find application in coaching activities, and my visual art background merges with all other knowledge areas and skills in activities such as graphic facilitation and strategic visioning. My personal background includes living and working in different places around the world, experiences that continue to grow my cultural sensitivity and interest in global affairs; my personal development, although asymmetrical at times, spans the entire spectrum of body, mind, and spirit. Although spiritual development has been an important part of my personal path, this study is largely aligned with the two disciplines it addresses (neither of which acknowledge spirituality as an aspect in the human core), and spirituality therefore is purposefully omitted from the discussion in spite of playing a major role in integral theory.

I am grounded in the belief that the essence of life is in the process not in the outcome, in the same way that transdisciplinary thinkering may be more about the process of the discovery rather than the end product. The ability to let go of the outcome and the desire to explore the mystery of the "rabbit hole" in depth are characteristic of transdisciplinary researchers, who take pleasure in pulling on all the threads of a complex system and in watching beautiful patterns emerging from creative chaos.

These and other aspects of my system influenced the way I designed and conducted this study, and analyzed the data. Some specifics of how my personal system may have limited the outcomes are discussed in Limitations in Chapter 9; Appendix L provides a thorough background summary of my personal history as it relates to this study.

Integral Theory as a Tool for Transdisciplinary Inquiry

Integral theory provided well articulated tools for achieving the transdisciplinary approach needed to reconcile the otherwise disconnected disciplinary fragments involved in this investigation. In particular, integral theory concepts were used and developed as cognitive organizing tools and maps to simultaneously investigate macro and micro perspectives, interior and exterior locations, individual and collective experiences and expressions, and interrelationships between everything that emerged in the data. Integral theory thus brought a useful frame to the traditional part one of this dissertation with the viewfinder, and more granularity to the phenomenon in part two of this dissertation after the traditional analysis had been completed. The integral theory tools of Spiral Dynamics Integral (SD*i*) and All Quadrants All Levels (AQAL) (see Appendix O) were used to propose a set of new models. These new models, described below, are potentially useful tools for investigating the challenges brought up by this research that could not be solved in the traditional frames of the disciplines involved.

The metaphor of the viewfinder used throughout this dissertation is an appropriate description for the function of integral theory in this project. Integral theorists strive to understand the human condition and evolution contextually and interrelationally, as experienced and described through subjective and objective realities and on the individual and the collective planes. Integral theory aims to reconcile body, mind, and spirit and reintegrate the true, the good, and the beautiful (also called science, morals, and art, or "self, culture, and nature" [Integral Institute, 2005]). As is the case with transdisciplinary research, integral theory has been embraced only by marginal but growing groups of theorists and practitioners, those who understand the current need on the planet for the integration of all bodies of knowledge and who seek integration and solutions to problems through connected and complex thinking.

Integral theory as applied in this transdisciplinary study added to the layers of investigation of the two approaches and three categories of intercultural communication theory (Gudykunst et al., 2005). Selecting AQAL as the viewfinder bridges objective and subjective approaches by having all quadrants engaged, in order to fully understand intercultural dynamics through the communication acts. SD*i*, which forms the base of each AQAL quadrant, describes the differences between cultural value systems, called vMEME structures (see Appendix O), and is thus a theory of the second category that addresses variances in communication across cultures (gravitating toward certain vMEME structures). SD*i* also belongs to the first category because it is a developmental model of constructivist nature for the individual and the collective consciousness. In addition, the collective interior quadrant of AQAL addresses the third category by discussing the cocreation of meaning via (inter)cultural exchanges in the realm of the lower left quadrant (subjective reality on the collective plane)—equivalent to the realm of semantics of the four aspects of communication).

Further Investigation of the Instrument Results

Participants demonstrated flexibility in their cultural frames beyond what might have been expected given the data collected. In addition, their performance levels were rather high and reached beyond the capacity levels individuals may have experienced working by themselves. Theorizing about possible reasons for these outcomes brings up interesting hypotheses that may be useful to consider in future research of this kind.

Insights from the Zone of Proximal Development

Some additional insight into the surprisingly wide ranges of capacities demonstrated in the data emerged from considering Vygotsky's *zone of proximal development* (ZPD) theory (Vygotsky, 1978) as a form that stretched participants' capacities beyond their preexisting conditions. The zone of proximal development is "the distance between the actual development level as determined by independent problem solving and the level of potential development as determined through problem solving…in collaboration with more capable peers" (p. 86). In the present study, each group developed its own group mind and collective group IQ that was higher than any individual's capacity and motivation. Observed behavior indicated that, through the group mind and its collective IQ, most participants may have excelled by continually being pushed beyond their comfort zone into the zone of proximal development.

Group alignment, the creation of rapport across cultures, and the scaffolding of affordances may be necessary presuppositions for individuals to be able to perform on that level (M. C. Bronson, personal communication, March 15, 2008). This high-performance state seemed to parallel flow state moments. Whenever the interaction between an individual and the group mind interrupted the flow, the energy of the group and its capacity to perform in the zone of proximal development dropped significantly. In Group 1, the antagonist's inability to step parallel with the group mind had a debilitating effect upon group performance until the rest of the group decided to ignore her and continue with the task. The antagonist continued to recreate the individual experience and was therefore never really part of the group conversation. She missed the experience of flow and of the zone of proximal development, as well as the embodiment of the group mind. In addition, her actions created anxiety for other members and discontent in her group. As she communicated in the class debrief, she was the only one who did not learn anything in the process. This observation supports the importance of reaching group rapport and the flow state for the transcendence of the individual profile to occur.

When a group is in rapport and group members parallel the group mind, individuals can excel and move beyond their previous levels of performance, as Group A demonstrated. When, on the other hand, the flow and rapport are broken by an individual's inability to follow the group mind, participants may operate on the lowest denominator of the group mind. The group mind of Group 1 managed to keep rapport with itself by ignoring the antagonist and thereby allowing the system to succeed in spite of the interruptions. Thus it seems that the individual needed to be sacrificed for the group to succeed in this case.

The range of participant behaviors demonstrated capacity beyond the highest DMIS stage reflected by any participant's IDI-2 score, implying that a group working together can attain a zone of proximal development that would be out of reach for any of the individuals working on their own. The zone of proximal development theory is relevant to explain some of the data; other perspectives discussed below bring additional insights.

Cultural Hybridity and Shifting Identity

The idea of flexible identity construction (suggested by the data and discussed briefly in Chapters 8 and 9) is not new; in fact, it has been described and discussed in other disciplines (Chandra, 2006; Kulick, 2000; Derrida, 1972; Howard, 2000; Podur, interviewed by Albert, 2003). Due to globalization efforts, the world has been continuously changing at a rapid pace. In addition, the world is becoming more complex and cultures are interacting and collaborating in unprecedented ways across the planet, which presents new and unmet challenges for intercultural communication research. Even the traditional concept of the "global village" has been transcended by new hybrid forms of communication such as interactive virtual communication combined with face-to-face meeting formats and networks.

The term *transglobal terrain* may better describe the platform for current modes of intertwined human connections and interactions across cultures and geographic boundaries. This new term was chosen to indicate the capacity for flexible communication patterns and strength through diversity, and it is my assumption that subsequent generations will grow into this capacity more easily. This terrain houses loosely grouped individuals (cultural hybrids) brought together temporarily by common interests and to solve common problems of global significance, thereby mixing and intermingling their cultural aspects in the process (face-to-face and virtually). I expect that this type of cultural hybridity will increase under the current circumstances and likely become the norm on the transglobal terrain.

The changing life conditions of cultural hybrids in the transglobal terrain may support a new metaphor for the core of culture—*the sand is always shifting*. What can be observed, defined, and described, at best, is this shifting pattern created anew in each moment of communication. In this shifting sand model of the cultural core, the pattern constantly increases in complexity due to the learning involved in mastering various challenges in the process of recombining and readjusting. The system (i.e., the "rules" of cultural interaction) under these circumstances may require its participants to learn from their own actions and continually adjust to the changing context, and may therefore never repeat the same pattern twice (which is why this research project may be easy to repeat but hard to replicate, even with the same participants).

Given contextual multipositionality (as demonstrated by at least some of the participants in this study) and the possibility that cultural aspects can be exchanged between cultural hybrids during group interaction, then culture may have become an *available design*. This new concept brings choice into the equation and brings creativity and openness to the forefront of needed skills in a global society on the move. A similar design problem has been discussed in critical literacy (Kern, 2000), which defines literacy as "a dynamic set of linguistic, social, and cognitive processes that are culturally-motivated" (p. 39) and fundamental to meaning-making by "designing meaning through texts within a community" (p. 187). Reading, writing, and speaking are not held separately, but rather as overlapping parts of the whole. This description evokes the concept of the intertwined aspects of the human core (innate, cultural, situational) that form a person's identity flexibly. In the case of the present study, these three elements of identity (or human core) were found to be overlapping and working together with some degree of flexibility in order to create meaning in the individual through interaction within a community. This concept of culture as an available design is termed here *designer identity*. From my experience as an NLP Master Practitioner working with individuals on their personal change, I know that the potential for flexibility exists in identity construction, the sense of choice can be evoked, and choices about the experiences one would like to have can be practiced in order to achieve a defined outcome—a concept I term *designer experience*. With the emerged hypothesis that culture may be available to construct designer experiences and identities in the gaps of transcultural interactions, this research extended The New London Group's work on designing social futures through literacy (The New London Group, 1996).

The interaction in the groups in this research took place in the intersection between flexible identities who may have been oscillating between those of the others in the group, constantly adjusting until a common meaning emerged. This common meaning then may have been more or less unconsciously engineered by the participants who may have readjusted the three elements (innate, cultural, situational) that made up their identity in that moment until the group settled into a rhythm to which all participants could dance. This rhythm may have been created by the relationships that were available in each group's constellation, expressed in a flexible formation during the initial period, a more stable reliable capacity in the flow state, and a tangible form expressed in the cocreated artifacts.

The group's collective meaning may thus have been coconstructed in this intersection of overlapping identities. Some participants noticed when the overlap was dense enough ("We can work without speaking," Eugene, class debrief, p. 16) or when there were gaps still to be worked out (Olive's discussion of how people with a different style get disengaged, p. 3). Depending on the individuals' interior structures, some participants may have probed for the overlap (towards metaprogram or a habitual perceptual filter) and others may have calibrated the gaps (away from metaprogram) (O'Connor & Seymour, 1993). All participants focused on the common goal (the story on the visual map) even during moments of conflict (Paige, "I tried to just sort of stop [creating a problem]," class debrief, p. 4). The shifting context may itself have been the learning space (Olive, "I learn from my team," p. 12) where epiphanies could happen, as expressed during the class debrief.

In such a dynamic context, all available parts can be acknowledged as important, which translates into appreciation of the diverse aspects each participant brings to the scenario. This appreciation was expressed by Carolina's desire to "find out what that person's really strong gifts are and…use them for that" (class debrief, p. 4). These appreciated aspects (cultural included) thus become the design elements for the meaning-making process, and the interaction patterns (exchange of those aspects) form the gestalt for any tangible expression emerging from that interaction. The design process has been defined as a "productive process of recycling old materials in fresh ways—establishing new relationships among stock elements" (Kern, 2000, p. 54). This definition matches descriptions of the creative process as a recombining of known elements (Epstein, 1996).

We know a lot about the creative process and the design process, and methods can be adjusted to meet this new goal of becoming competent *identity designers* in polycultural contexts. Some of the principles might be (a) knowing and experiencing oneself as a flexible structure of available design elements implying possibilities of choice, (b) staying open to learning about other possible structures and collecting a rich repertoire of usable design elements (found aspects), thereby increasing design sophistication and complexity, and (c) managing the coordination between one's own elements in motion interacting with others.

The last element brings us back to the maxims of CMM (Pearce, 2005) describing a set of skills that build better social worlds. Coordination is the awareness that our actions are "intermeshed with the interpretations and actions of other people" (p. 50). The management of meaning is accomplished through coherence and mystery. Coherence refers to the need to pay attention to the "stories that we tell ourselves to make our lives meaningful" (p. 50). Mystery refers to the endless complexity of the universe that, by far, surpasses any stories we could possibly tell. In this sense life is interpreted not as a "riddle to be solved but a mystery to explore" (p. 50).

The concept of designer identity also has similarities to the DMIS stages of adaptation and integration, but would include even more flexibility and more ways of building capacity in the moment by consulting a bank of available designs (either in the room, in one's system, or virtually). Bennett's DMIS is a developmental model and therefore inherently includes the concept of growth through reciprocal relationships, as he describes. However, at the time the DMIS was developed, it may not have been recognized that the model itself may only be part of a much larger system of nested value systems, systems that are also dynamic and evolve in a similar manner but span across more layers. Since different groups of people around the planet may live in different layers of human value systems (in SD*i*, at least two tiers of such systems have been defined), the DMIS is likely not applicable universally, as has been assumed by users of the DMIS and the IDI. The concept of designer identity can only be conceptualized after the last stage of the DMIS (integration) has been completed—a stage that has been completely removed as unmeasurable in the IDI-3. If the DMIS (and instruments measuring the stages) could be extended to include the current global developments (i.e., leaping into SD*i* Second Tier, see Appendix O), culture as an available design may need to be included as a major aspect of the emerging stages of the new paradigm.

Nick pulled the class together at the end of the class debrief and demonstrated masterful management of the cocreated meaning when he shared with the class, "As soon as I start trying to define things, is when I stop looking at them for what they really are" (p. 28). His statement reflected his recognizing the need for flexibility and contextuality. While Nick only scored into the DMIS stage of minimization, the metacognition he demonstrated at various times during the event indicated capacity for ethnorelativity and even beyond. Eugene also demonstrated this capacity when he answered my question of whether or not he would participate in such a research project again:

Probably....I would do it again, because I believe research is important for anything and if done ethically and correctly, I think it can lead to a lot of problem solving that we are having in globalization? Especially in studies between intercultural affairs of meanings and semantics behind different symbols that different cultures have, I think that would help a lot in easing of the globalization because we are having too many problems right now with miscommunication culturally and that leads to war.... (personal interview, p. 45)

This is not the only occasion where Eugene demonstrated his capacity to see himself as one unit intermeshed with others collaborating toward solving a global challenge.

Placing this concept of designer identity as a central element in learning situations would also produce the benefit of welcoming all cultural aspects to participate—the more the merrier. The more cultural designs are available in the group, the more learning can take place. The traditional education system and training world were originally built by the dominant culture, with well known limitations in teaching/facilitation styles and methods and one-dimensional content—participants who did not meet the established canon were penalized or marginalized. An education system where culture is made available for designing flexible identities would not only be completely open, it also would presuppose a deep appreciation of the richness of diversity, an essential ingredient for engaging the challenges of a world in crisis.

The Challenges of Culture

Because we now find ourselves in a world of crisis with many global issues that must be solved collaboratively, the global community might be better off in these tasks if cultural groups were supported as autonomous units that feel, at the same time, also part of this larger global community (Podur, 2003; Kelley, 1999; Kureishi, 2005; Prashad, in Frontlist Books, n.d.). The traditional hierarchies of the dominant culture occupying the leadership roles cannot be sustained under the pressure of having to solve problems that span across the planet collaboratively.

Thus, a move is appropriate toward redefining the concept of culture to what has been named a polycultural worldview with a social structure of unique but interrelated and collaborating cultures (Podur, 2003; Kelley, 1999; Kureishi, 2005; Prashad, in Frontlist Books, n.d.). This new polycultural worldview and collaborative structure may be carried by cultural hybrids who gain their multiple viewpoints from face-to-face and virtual interactions (Goodfellow & Hewling, 2005) with other cultures, and where hierarchies are no longer built based on origin or status but by the importance of gifts that can be brought to the larger community.

A global community collaborating on solving global problems would need to move beyond ethnorelativity to a new paradigm that would be ushered in by the worldview of *worldcentricity*—a worldcentric orientation toward a complex, cultural, globally connected fabric that has enough commonality to form the next level of development in human evolution. A worldcentric worldview (which has been discussed widely within the integral theory community, e.g., Wilber, 2000, 2005) is open to the mystery of what is not known, with an understanding of one's own filters as circumscribing one particular worldview among many others. This basis for thinking avoids the dichotomizing right/wrong thinking of an ethnocentric stage, and was beautifully expressed by Nick when he closed the class debrief by saying:

> ...having those feelings of security and comfort I've really come to find that those aren't really real that it's kind of false. Inherently. There's always going to be this unknowing. As soon as I start trying to define things, is when I stop looking at them for what they really are....Yeah, it is uncomfortable at first but I feel like then everyone has a fair say on what is actually going on instead of [my] viewpoint, which is only my viewpoint. (p. 28)

With this closing statement, Nick also expressed the characteristics of cultural humility (Tervalon & Murray-García, 1998) and culture as refinement (Baldwin et al., 2006).

I believe that in this research project, I observed cultural hybrids who may have been pushing against the boundaries of SD*i*'s First Tier (see Appendix O) and thus were in the process of engaging the challenges of the last stage of development (Human Bond). In other words, they were close to reconciling the differences of cultures and experiencing them as interrelated—these participants at times seemed to approach worldcentricity (or the beginning of SD*i*'s Second Tier, see Appendix O) in both their speech and behavior.

The hierarchies in the groups were constructed based on strengths and skills participants brought to the communication act, rather than through their positions in society (which might otherwise be based on status and origin). For instance in Group A, the most educated person did not take the lead, nor did the white male—the oldest female was the lead. In Group 1, the only white male took the role of relationship-builder, and the only white female (antagonist) could not establish any authority—the lead was an African American well educated female with an Asian American female colead. The demonstrated hierarchy structures overlap with polyculturalism and the worldview orientation of worldcentricity, where hierarchies are not based upon culture, race, or origin, but rather on the leadership skills needed to solve certain problems collaboratively in the transglobal terrain.

The difference between a worldcentric stage and the ethnocentric DMIS stage called minimization (which may look similar at first glance) would be a form of metacognition, which was exposed by some participants in this study. In a worldcentric worldview, cultural differences are the norm and appreciated, as people would understand that a certain sense of commonality is necessary to engage the challenges of polyculturalism, challenges that require the merging of many diverse ideas. In the DMIS stage of denial, on the other hand, there is little to no concept of difference available in the system. For instance, Rusena acted at times from a position of denial but also inhabited a metacognition that is not possible in the ethnocentric DMIS stage of denial in the way it is currently described in the theory, but which could be explained through a first new stage in worldcentricity. Since the DMIS is a developmental model, expanding it to include these experiences that cannot be captured with the current DMIS system would not be a far stretch, and seems timely given the current events on the planet.

In order to better describe this development, the challenges of culture need to be reinvestigated. SD*i* theory offers one useful framework for discussing broad issues of human development. In SD*i*, multiculturalism in its resolved form occupies the last stage of the First Tier, where the human bond is experienced by striving for equality and leveling all hierarchies. Once problems are solved in one stage of development, new problems arise that require new structures and push humanity into the next stage of evolution. At times, a bigger push happens—a leap, such as is described by SD*i* in the move to the Second Tier, which is predicted to be preceded by overwhelming and unprecedented multifaceted and complex problems that require an entire paradigm shift in order to be solved (Beck, n.d.; Beck & Cowan, 2006) (see Appendix O for a more detailed description of SD*i* theory).

Applying the additional developmental perspective provided by integral theory (and SD*i* in particular), it follows that the DMIS and IDI stages would be experienced and expressed differently in each of the cultural value systems, according to the frames possible in each tier (or paradigm) for each individual. Large discrepancies (even paradoxes) could potentially be found between IDI scores/DMIS stages in their traditional description (looking at the stages universally) and observed behavior, if the participants were leaping from First Tier to Second Tier. This possibility fits the data and would explain why the DMIS descriptions and IDI-2 assessment were not adequate for these participants and their circumstances. Even without the consideration of integral theory (SD*i*), one would have to wonder whether the descriptions and concepts of each DMIS stage and the IDI scoring system are still accurate vis à vis the current state and opportunities of cultural exchanges in the midst of globalization. It is quite likely that any developmental models would need to be expanded to accommodate the new developments toward a globally networked terrain that has already significantly changed how we interact in the world.

This new Second Tier paradigm we are shifting to may express itself in its beginning stages with the concept of worldcentricity and, logically, might lead to the concept of worldrelativity (utopian, but logical in its sequencing). From this study's data, it cannot be conclusively determined whether the cultural hybrids who participated in this study were located in the end stages of ethnorelativity (engaging the challenges of multiculturalism) and/or moving toward the beginning stages of worldcentricity (opening the challenges of polyculturalism and moving toward transcultural communication and nation-states). However, it is not inconceivable to think of the participants as simultaneously inhabiting worldCENTRIC positions, which would have some similarities to ethnocentricity, and ethnoRELATIVE positions. For example, when Carolina exposed sensitivity beyond minimization in her effort to distinguish between the different gifts individuals bring to a group for the good of all, her behavior could be captured by a worldcentric stage. At other times, Carolina clearly expressed positions in minimization by assuming other participants were having the same experience as she. Another example was given when Rusena clearly referred to several layers within her own cultural hybridity on a sophisticated level that could not be noticed, much less articulated, by an individual in the denial stage (ethnocentricity), yet she may have demonstrated stages of denial when not coding a critical incident during the debrief as a conflict.

Spinning this thread further, then, the data from this study suggest the potential for transcending cultural differences without losing the concept of cultures as unique and distinguishable units but considering them, on a sophisticated level, as interrelated groups. Such groups would thrive on their power of diversity but move toward a common goal, that of creating sustainable cohabitation on this tiny planet—not because they have become "better" people but because they "must" in order to survive vis à vis the new global challenges resulting from engaging the challenges inherent in the development through the previous paradigm.

Forms of communication would then change to fit the new circumstances in the new paradigm. During monoculturalism, the form of communication was sufficient as intracultural and other cultures were ignored through dominance. In multiculturalism it was intercultural communication and the focus was on cultural difference through autonomy. In a system that can be described as polyculturalism, we may be developing transcultural communication skills with a focus on strength through cultural, interrelated diversity. The focus in the Second Tier in the form of a worldcentric worldview would be on freedom without cultural boundaries and would also represent a return to some form of cultural ignorance, but on a more sophisticated and informed level that facilitates contextual multipositionality and invites authentic expression.

A name change to *transcultural communication* may better reflect the efforts of creating socially sustainable ways of collaborating across the planet on global issues that only the entire global community can solve, together. In these efforts the discipline of transcultural communication needs to include all forms of communication as they are evoked on the transglobal terrain. Transcultural communication could even potentially merge with disciplines that have traditionally focused on other forms of communication, such as visual communication, or with other disciplines that include wider perspectives. Transcultural communication practitioners could, for instance, learn much from the research social and cultural anthropologists have conducted for many years as they have already laid the foundations for the concept of flexible identity development. Their view of culture is nicely summarized in this definition:

Culture is a complex set of relationships, responses, and interpretations that must be understood, not as a body of discrete traits, but as an integrated system of orientations and practices generated within a specific socioeconomic context. Culture is ever changing and always being revised within the dynamic context of its enactment. (Hunt, 2001)

In this understanding of the world as a transglobal terrain, individuals with multiple cultural frames would grow their capacity for transcultural communication not only in face-to-face interactions, but also virtually and in hybrid forms (such as the one we used for this class).

Transcultural is here defined as integrating various cultural frames and transcending them—not abolishing culture altogether but making the adoption of cultural aspects a matter of choice (designer identity). The word *trans* implies transcendence as in moving beyond culture. In this sense, transcultural communication concerns the integration of various cultures into a meta position that implies choice and moving beyond cultural boundaries (rather than moving beyond culture itself). Transcendence here means going beyond the usual limits of cultural boundaries (the ones described in intercultural communication theory through the cultural dimensions and styles defined for various cultures). Integration is then an opportunity for folding in various available cultural aspects that an interacting community of cultural hybrids exchanges during communication acts. These various aspects are then formed into a whole that is greater than the differences among the cultural hybrids (a universal theme that distinguishes itself from minimization by a metacognition about one's own possibilities for cultural frames and implies a flexibility not possible in ethnocentric orientations). Polyculturalism with a transcultural communication form here represents an attitude of non-attachment to any particular cultural frame and a capacity to adopt any one cultural aspect as an available design in the moment.

In a flexible transglobal world in which culture is constantly changing, the human core has to be shifting, too, and consequently, it must be concluded that identity cannot be fixed and behavior cannot be predicted even if all the variables are known. If identity is flexible and the variables can be known, it must also be concluded that identity as a whole and culture as a component of identity in the human core are/have become available designs. Consequently, those who choose transcultural communication as a new discipline have the opportunity to collaborate with anthropology and other disciplines to develop theories, models, and practices to usher in the new paradigm of polyculturalism with the establishment of design principles and elements for the designer identity. These principles could then be formally taught in order to foster the full integration of cultural aspects as available designs and the transcendence of culture as a system of differences—at will.

If one were to assume that these findings show that CCSF is on the verge of moving beyond the challenges of multiculturalism, CCSF could be considered a microcosm on the forefront of this potentially momentous worldwide event of shifting paradigm. Such a context would provide opportunity to move vertically to the next stage on the Second Tier (Beck, 2007), a move that is only possible if enough density has been reached in previous stages. A move to the Second Tier would mean a full integration of all First Tier stages and transcendence thereof (not leaving them behind, but folding them in and moving to a new chapter all together), making the previous issues obsolete. The CCSF community strives for the flattening of hierarchies in a multicultural sense—a portion of the CCSF community already demonstrates, at times, the emergence of Second Tier worldviews and behavior by acknowledging and integrating diverse groups into a larger community matching the characteristics of polyculturalism. Hierarchies in polycultural communities are re-established but not based on status or origin; rather, leadership is shared depending on the needs of the larger community and who can best fulfill those needs at any given time. This concept was directly proposed by a participant of this study as a solution to a conflict situation about cultural and/or innate styles (Carolina, class debrief, p. 4), and was practiced in the class through the acceptance and rotation of the voluntary role of moderator in the virtual space.

Integral Theory Applied: New Models

The interwoven complexities noticed in the analysis phase supported the need to reintegrate the disparate aspects of the findings. Integral theory offered one tool for this task, and AQAL was applied and adjusted specifically to these data. In the course of this analysis process, aspects of SD*i* and the four-quadrant frame were further developed into new models. The resulting models led to some interesting ways of reanalyzing the findings from these new perspectives, and may offer potentially useful tools for similar research projects. These integral-theory-based tools offer one possible way to expose the gaps of the disciplines and put diverse professions into holistic dialogues through these gaps. It may be possible to create theories based on these tools, to address the current developments of cultural hybrids in polycultural environments underpinned by the worldview orientation of worldcentricity. In addition, these tools offer one additional avenue of investigation for research questions such as the one addressed in this case study.

The Layers of Complexity

The new research dilemma that emerged from the traditional analysis raised the issue of the interrelationship between the innate, the cultural, and the situational in the human core. Two of the research subquestions (3 and 4) and the pilot study all came to the same conclusion—that nature and nurture cannot be isolated. The model described in this section allows the inclusion of intercultural communication theories discussing motivation for cultural frames, while offering an explanation for why the results of an instrument taken by an individual in a room alone do not necessarily reflect that individual's lived behavior or even the potential thereof.

The Layers of Complexity (see Figure 44) is inspired by the concentric circles describing the relationships between the inner and outer layers of culture, as described by Hofstede and Hofstede (2005) and Trompenaars and Hampden-Turner (1998), by CMM sequencing in the Serpentine model, and by the human core as described by SD*i* (C. Beck & R. Rowland, personal communication, November 20, 2007; Beck & Cowan, 2006). This new model explains the interdependence between the innate and cultural aspects of the self and the life conditions an individual is exposed to or participates in at any time, and why it is nearly impossible to separate this trinity. This interdependence between culture and the lived experience has been well described by Bennett (2000).

> Culture is a result of the lived experience (praxis) of participating in social action....culture is a construction, but culture is not purely a cognitive invention. It is both the explanation and the essence of our lived social experience. Our cultural behavior is an "enactment" of our collective experience, and, through this enactment, becomes yet more experience. (p. 2)

The lenses not included in this statement are the view that culture can be understood as highly dynamic through this enactment, and the interdependence between all three aspects of the trinity. The innate cannot be left off in this equation as it is an inherent element in the dynamic and as such participates in the construction of identity, or what is available for constructing identities.

The Layers of Complexity model also provides a simple map for how the human core forms the base from which the act of meaning-making emerges for the individual. At the center of the Layers of Complexity's spiral formation (see Figure 44 above) lies the human core, which comprises the basic elements of SD*i*—gDNA, mDNA, and life conditions (discussed further below). Out of this human core grows a person's *worldview*. Worldview can be considered the set of available criteria for making distinctions, partially influenced by language structures (Bennett, 1998, p. 16; Pearce, 2005), which create meaning from our previous conditioning and previous and current experiences. The worldview then provides the foundation for *ways of thinking*. As these ways of thinking are confirmed through more of similar or same experiences, *basic assumptions* are formed out of which emerge *beliefs* (through the repetition of certain experiences). Out of beliefs and cultural conditioning then grow *values* (value judgments*), all of which then are building blocks to the *structures* we build to confirm and uphold our values, and the *systems* in which these

---

*Value judgments are largely dependent on the available mDNA structures. For instance, values can be judged on whether or not they are right or wrong, whether something can be scientifically proven, whether something is based on equality or a hierarchical structure, and so on.

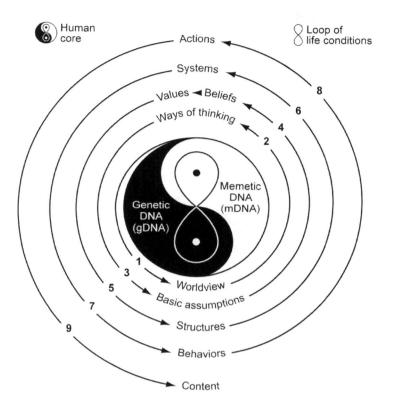

Figure 44. The Layers of Complexity model: an interpretation of Don Beck's concept of the human core with the addition of sequencing of the steps from the most fundamental building blocks of meaning-making to the establishment of social systems out of which behavior and content emerge, providing a map to locate entry points of various scholars to the culture discussion. Author's image, based on the understanding provided by Spiral Dynamics Integral (C. Beck & R. Rowland, personal communication, November 20, 2007; Beck & Cowan, 1996) and various intercultural communication models.

structures can grow and reach density. Our *behaviors* then emerge out of these systems within which we restrict ourselves and which lead, eventually, to *actions* that match, confirm, and sometimes stretch the basic structures of the system. Our actions determine which *content* we can grow as individuals, social and cultural groups, nations, and a global community. Content is the totality of all knowledge in the world that we construct and then have access to including access to information itself and advancements in technology and science (C. Beck & R. Rowland, personal communication, November 20, 2007, based on D. E. Beck's interpretation of SD*i*).

In the human core as explained by SD*i*, the *genetic DNA* (gDNA, i.e., the human biological system with its basic elements of genes) and the *memetic DNA* (mDNA, i.e., the "biopsychosocial" system with its basic elements of memes, Beck, n.d.) interface with each other through one's *life conditions,* which permeate both. This interplay is composed of three interlacing and interdependent forces in a dynamic play—the formula for the *human core*. Life conditions are a combination of historic times, geographic place, existential problems, and societal circumstances, and determine whether or to what extent the genes in the gDNA and the memes in the biopsychosocial mDNA will be available for expression (theoretical background derived from Beck & Cowan, 1996).

Such a human core system would then hold DNA as the available design elements within a system of circumstances; having certain DNA structures in place does not guarantee expression. Likewise, culture as an available design within the temporarily constructed system (established by interacting cultures in an event such as this case study) would not guarantee a certain outcome. Assuming that the design elements are available and flexible under certain circumstances creates the potential for transcultural communication to occur. The development into transcultural forms of communication within the worldview structure of polyculturalism is thus a consequence of the circumstances of the paradigm shift, not a requirement. As the system (in this case based in multiculturalism) approaches the bifurcation point, new challenges are predicted to occur that cannot be successfully engaged by adhering to the old structures. The presence of signs of polycultural worldview structures in connection with global challenges needing to be engaged collaboratively would serve as evidence that we are approaching or are already in the midst of this paradigm shift.

The major determining factor for any evaluation of personality traits or cultural orientations may be found in the gestalt that results from the relationship between the three basic components of the human core. Culture is a main fiber in the human condition as a whole, but it cannot be separated from the gestalt of the human core; as an element of life conditions, culture is only one of the factors that determine which genes and/or memes get expressed from the many possibilities of the gDNA and mDNA pools. Personality traits are not considered the same as genetic dispositions. Personality traits are inherited (gDNA) and learned (mDNA) (Hofstede & Hofstede, 2005). Life conditions (already containing culture in their fibers) interface with gDNA and mDNA simultaneously. Therefore it is nearly impossible to separate the innate (gDNA), the cultural (mDNA), and the situational (life conditions).

SD*i*'s conception of the human core is supported by the writing of social and cultural anthropologists on the topic of shifting identity. For example, Howard (2000) writes, "[the] details of our larger cultural environments may be markedly more unsettled and shifting. Both contexts are part of our experiences of identities" (p. 388). In addition, "the postmodern element is that authenticity is no longer a question of being true to self for all time, but rather of being true to self in context or self in relationship" (p. 385). As individuals or groups experience vertical development (moving up in SD*i* stages and/or leaping into Second Tier), complexity increases on an interior and exterior level. This increase goes hand in hand with movement inside the human core where its three elements (the innate, the cultural, and the situational) shift according to the changed life conditions in order to match the new circumstances, thereby supporting the emergence of new challenges. In both of these concepts identity is recognized as malleable and alive, in contrast to existing intercultural communication theories describing the deep core of culture as changing slowly or not changing at all.

The significance of the Layers of Complexity to this study lies in the interdependent trinity at the center, which demonstrates that the innate cannot be separated from the cultural, and that neither develops independent from the other nor from one's life circumstances. An expression of this triple helix can be found in the role acceptance each individual exposed throughout the process and in the seating constellation, which also carried the meaning each individual made of herself in this context. As discussed previously, the cultural hybrids in this research study carried multiple cultural frames and demonstrated high flexibility on various levels that may have indicated the capacity for contextual identity design. Observations in this case study led me to believe that individual meaning shifted as the context was cocreated anew by all participants until they fell into the flow state, at which point the constructed identities could remain stable.

The Layers of Complexity model is also useful to mark the location through which different intercultural communication scholars enter the discussion. For instance, Beck (SD*i*, 2006) and Hofstede and Hofstede (the social game and mental programming, 2005) enter it at the human core level (deepest). Bennett (construing meaning through language, 1986b) enters it at the level of worldview. Trompenaars and Hampden Turner (model of culture, 1998) enter at the level of basic assumptions, and Hofstede continues at the level of values (onion diagram, 2001), where he is joined by Pearce (deontic logic, 2005). This realization clarifies the difference between terminology, supports the utility of all of these models, and allows one to choose the model most useful to solve a particular problem.

By looking at culture as a construct of the lived experience, the Layers of Complexity model lays the foundation for more flexibility in cultural identity. Cultural aspects of one's identity may shift if the lived experience changes or is expanded in significant ways, possibilities that are not

241

acknowledged in other models discussing culture as a fixed point of departure. The Layers of Complexity model thus merges the understanding of the core of culture from the field of intercultural communication with the various perspectives on meaning-making explored in Chapter 4, using SD*i* integral theory as the container.

The Layers of Complexity model is a two-dimensional, static representation of a dynamic energetic sculpture that manifests only a fraction of itself in the physical observable realm. It is my assumption that individuals who have developed into cultural hybrids in a worldcentric worldview carry a more complex and flexible energetic sculpture of their Layers of Complexity, or at least the potential for deeper understandings, than do those who still operate from ethnocentric worldviews as originally defined by Bennett (also defined by Beck as First Tier).

Since the Layers of Complexity diagram is a dynamic matter, it will only reveal what can be recognized by the observer (D. Beck, personal communication, December 31, 2007); the observer's own SD*i* stage of development, innate and cultural filters, and biases will enhance certain aspects of the diagram and hide others. This is an important aspect of how to use this model, as a two-dimensional and static representation cannot possibly imply how things will shift on one person's map when put into the context of other maps, nor can it consider the state of the viewer.

The Layers of Complexity represent one individual's interior landscape, and suggestions can then be made for measuring the human core (innate, cultural, and situational) by a variety of personality assessment tools including some instruments used in this study (e.g. the LS and MI) as well as others (the Ennegram, Strengthfinder, Reiss Profile of Core Desires, Myers-Briggs Type Indicator, Big Five Personality Test, iWAM Metapropgrams, etc.). There is also an assessment instrument for the mDNA structure developed by the Spiral Dynamics Group, named the Values Test "which reflects assumptions about living and how people establish priorities" (Beck, n.d., p. 141). In addition, an accompanying tool, the Change State Indicator (CSI) (p. 159), measures different change states and individuals' capacity to move between stability and chaos. The results drawn from an array of these assessment tools would have provided a much better definition of the expressed personality of each participant. It can be assumed that each of these assessment tools focuses on a certain aspect in the human core; however, no measurement can be unaltered by the other two remaining components of the human core trinity, because of their interrelated dynamic.

Map of Complexity

The comparison of the challenges of culture helped to clarify what I believe is the current paradigm shift from multiculturalism (intercultural communication) into polyculturalism (transcultural communication), and from ethnorelative into worldcentric worldviews. This paradigm shift may hold the potential characteristics of cultural hybrids who (like the participants in my study) occupy multipositionality and contextuality and can work with cultural aspects as design elements for their flexible identity construction. Creating the Layers of Complexity model addressed the interrelationship between innate dimensions, cultural dimensions, and changing life conditions in the transglobal terrain, and further defined for me the base of the meaning-making process for the individual participants.

However, the data relating to the cocreation of meaning-making as performed by the groups in this study still was not completely addressed. My study concerned group dynamics and group cocreation of meaning, so, I wanted to overlay the individual maps (Layers of Complexity) with each other to learn something about the dynamics of the group interaction. I also wanted to put the group interaction pattern into dialogue with snapshots 1 and 2, in order to address the mirroring effect that ethnographic studies describe as the micro and macro perspectives. I wanted a method for plotting the event of this study onto an elegant map that could carry enough coordinates to offer information about the cocreation of meaning in diverse groups in spite of possible data gaps for some of the specifics.

In answer to these concerns I developed the Map of Complexity, which builds from the Layers of Complexity of an individual and considers individuals' relationships and interactions with what lies outside the self. The Map of Complexity is an extension of the four-quadrant viewfinder, and the Layers of Complexity permeate all four quadrants, with a different focus in each.

The four-quadrant system of the AQAL model (Wilber, 2000, 2005) was used in this study as the literal viewfinder through which subjective and objective realities on the individual and collective levels could be investigated. In the traditional dissertation (part one), the viewfinder was used to consider the foci of each discipline separately as well as to facilitate the integration of all the perspectives into a whole. (Only the aspect of AQAL used in this study is discussed, rather than the entire sophisticated and complex model—for an overview of AQAL, see Appendix O.) It is important to consider that the observer's lens provides another variable affecting what can be noticed on the AQAL map (D. Beck, personal communication, December 31, 2007), an issue not addressed by Wilber. In this study, attention is brought to this issue through the inclusion of the inquirer's vanishing point in the research space diagrams and in Appendix L.

AQAL provides a playing field in the form of a conceptual map to pull apart the interior structures from their exterior expressions, as well as to provide windows into individual and collective meaning-making processes. The idea, though, is not to separate internal and external phenomena, or individual and collective experiences and processes, but to provide temporary lenses under which different aspects of the same phenomenon can be investigated and then reintegrated. In this study, the four aspects of communication (signifier, signified, syntax, and semantics) were incorporated into the AQAL viewfinder, which can be used to connect this model to the various fields studying communication.

In the Map of Complexity model (see Figure 45), each quadrant contains simplified representations of one (or more) individual's Layers of Complexity and their extensions into the world (structures and systems, content). In the upper left quadrant, the interior landscape of an individual (the human core) is marked by the solid black area on the individual's Layers of Complexity graphic. In the lower left quadrant, the collective interior (culture and worldview) depicts the exchange of information between the participants and each of their human cores. In the upper right quadrant, the exterior individual/singularity (brain and organism/physical thing) focuses on the exterior offerings that express the interior processes, as reflected by the black outer ring. In the lower right quadrant of the exterior collective (social system and environment), the black ring points to the perspective layer which is activated here and represents the institution itself as well as the structure of the groups.

Of course, this is an abstract model that of necessity simplifies the difficulty (and sometimes impossibility) of teasing these layers apart. However, for the purpose of investigating the phenomenon from various angles, this model is useful in eliciting a deeper understanding of the observations.

The arrows of exchange between the various quadrants of the Map of Complexity represent the interplay between these various layers, areas, and foci. The visual diagram reflects the tight fit between the horizontal and vertical opposites, between interior and exterior on the individual plane and the collective plane, and between individual and collective interior and exterior. There is a creative tension between the elements diagonally opposite each other that holds the quadrants together, and elements have the potential of being mirrored from one quadrant diagonally across to the other. This reflection implies then that one can learn much about the diagonally opposite quadrant even without extensive data present by merely looking into its mirror. As reflected by the findings of this study, this mirroring effect offers a means of investigating the subjective quadrants through the objective quadrants, and the individual quadrants through the collective quadrants, and vice versa. Establishing data coordinates on all four quadrants would address the need for combining subjective and objective approaches to intercultural communication research, as suggested by Gudykunst et al. (2005) and extended here to the concept of transcultural research.

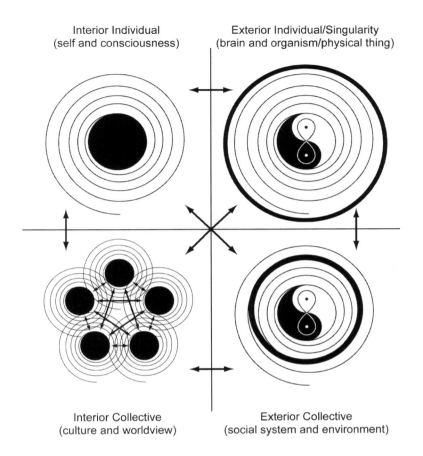

Interior Individual
(self and consciousness)

Exterior Individual/Singularity
(brain and organism/physical thing)

Interior Collective
(culture and worldview)

Exterior Collective
(social system and environment)

Figure 45. The Map of Complexity model: each spiral represents either one individual's Layers of Complexity (see Figure 44) and/or the areas that connect each individual to the exterior world (structures and systems, content)—the thick black area marks that quadrant's area of focus inside the graphic of the Layers of Complexity. Author's image, with quadrant system drawn from the work of Wilber (2000, 2005) as discussed in Beck (n.d.).

The diagonal mirroring effect in the AQAL frame is a finding of this study that had not been previously mentioned, to my knowledge, by Wilber himself or in other applications of his AQAL model, but it is a natural consequence of investigating the very same phenomenon from a variety of angles. As already mentioned, this mutually disclosing mirroring effect has been practiced and relied upon by anthropologists for many years in their work of investigating a phenomenon through triangulating the macro and micro perspectives. Anthropologists generate thick cases of the individuals they research over long periods of time, as well as of the context in which those individuals live, and thoroughly investigate the inter-relationships between macro and micro positions. The Map of Complexity model then also offers an extension of the work of anthropologists by providing a graphic representation of this mirroring effect, and potentially a graphic tool to demonstrate anthropological data in a visual medium.

The advantage of the Map of Complexity lies in its potential to refer to the tight relationships of data spread over all four quadrants without the need to collect data for each coordinate point in all its completeness (which is, in most cases, impossible). Even with gaps in the data grid on one quadrant, information can be filled in by referring to the existing data in the other three quadrants.

In this case study, meaning was constructed collectively and contextually in the exchange of information and communication patterns (lower left) within the structure of the institution (lower right). This coconstructed meaning could be observed in the gestalt of the map (upper right) and gestalt of seating arrangement (lower right) reflective of interrelationships, but was influenced by individuals' human cores (upper left) that reacted and shifted as necessary until the groups had found their flow states.

Deconstructing the Research Question

Embedded in the main research question was the consideration of who was cocreating the meaning. Participants in this study were examined mainly through a cultural lens, yet their probable cultural hybridity (a relatively new concept that is still being defined) warrants the need for a much deeper investigation of their interior landscapes. Such an investigation of what anthropology would call the micro perspective would include life circumstances, cultural and social conditioning, and innate aspects of individuals' identity.

The location of the cocreation must also be considered. Information about the institution and the class itself was considered in framing the circumstances of this case study. However, a wider scope that allows for recognizing the relationships between framework and participants would provide more depth to the understanding of the entire research space (the macro perspective of anthropology). This would mean a full investigation of the core of the institution (attained by interviewing administrators, faculty, staff, and other students) and a comparison of that data to the history of CCSF and its context (state, nation, Western world). This would be termed a thicker macro-record in a standard ethnographic approach. The results would then be put into context with the observed phenomenon and individual participants of the present study—an undertaking that would require a fleet of collaborators.

This complexity thus explodes the scope of this study; however, the findings show a need to investigate at least four aspects of the communication acts:

1. Core element—participants (life circumstances, innate aspects of identity, and cultural and social conditioning = human core);
2. Essence—the act of exchanging information between participants (communication/ interaction patterns);
3. Expression—cocreated artifacts = maps (snapshot 1 or gestalt of the maps); and
4. Structure—the boundaries of and reciprocal relationships in the system in which the communication acts took place (snapshot 2 in the constellation of group hierarchy, structure of institution).

The Map of Complexity provided a tool to address these areas identified as required components of the expanded research space. As already mentioned, the complexity of the investigation is amplified when adding the lenses of the various observers (inquirer and readers) who bring their own interpretations into what can be noticed. Most likely, they will (and are invited to) interpret from their centers of gravity (or SDi stage) and thus it is possible that they will come to different conclusions—all of which have validity.

Applying the Map of Complexity to This Study

Once these tools were designed, I worked my way through the key aspects of the data and plotted them onto the Map of Complexity. What emerged from this exercise provided the last missing pieces to consider the aspects of the data and of current events in the transglobal terrain that could not be captured using the existing theories, models, and tools. Further, laying the data out visually as a diagram allowed me to notice certain relationships between all the aspects of the data that I had noticed in the traditional analysis but could not adequately explain—in particular, the mirroring effect of communication patterns in snapshot 1 and group hierarchies in snapshot 2. First, I plotted each snapshot separately, and then I considered the interrelationship between the snapshots by mapping them both on one map.

On the Map of Complexity, snapshot 1 would be a reflection from the lower left quadrant (the group's communication pattern dynamic or semantics) to the upper right quadrant (the gestalt of the map as a whole single element or signifier/denoted objective reality) (see Figure 46).

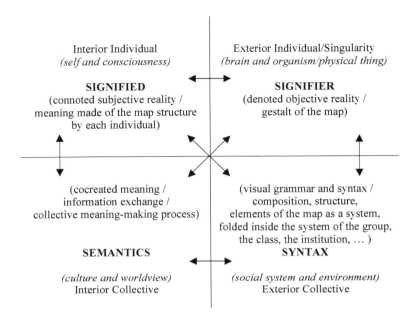

Interior Individual
(self and consciousness)

Exterior Individual/Singularity
(brain and organism/physical thing)

SIGNIFIED
(connoted subjective reality /
meaning made of the map structure
by each individual)

SIGNIFIER
(denoted objective reality /
gestalt of the map)

(cocreated meaning /
information exchange /
collective meaning-making process)

(visual grammar and syntax /
composition, structure,
elements of the map as a system,
folded inside the system of the group,
the class, the institution, …)

SEMANTICS

SYNTAX

(culture and worldview)
Interior Collective

(social system and environment)
Exterior Collective

Figure 46. Map of Complexity depicting snapshot 1, the visual map gestalt. Author's image.

I noticed the mirroring because the exposed behavior expressed in the group communication pattern was identical to the gestalt and overall feeling of the visual map. The mirroring effect exposed the reciprocal relationship between the participants' patterns of interaction with the products that emerged from their exchange of information (cocreated artifact) and was a perfect reflection, in this case, of the meaning the groups cocreated in their communication act.

Although less significant to answering my research question, the other two quadrants in Figure 46 complete the deconstruction of snapshot 1. In the upper left quadrant (interior individual or signified/connoted subjective reality), the meaning each participant made of the gestalt of their group's visual map appears as their personal connotation of their group's snapshot. On the lower right quadrant (exterior collective, or visual grammar and syntax), the structure and composition of the map appears as the group system that they cocreated during the event. This group system is also nested in the wider context in which this event took place (system and structure of the class, institution, city, state, country, etc.).

Examining snapshot 2 on the Map of Complexity (see Figure 47) also adds to the findings. In the signified (upper left) we consider the meaning that each participant made in their seat selections at the table, which correlates to their individual role acceptance in their group. In the syntax (lower right) we consider the seating diagram with the participant roles labeled, thus exposing the relationships between different roles that were reflective of the group's system/hierarchy and that the groups subconsciously mirrored to each other. As with snapshot 1, the seating constellation was a frozen moment reflecting the hierarchies at play and revealing the groups' cocreation of meaning in the relationships participants had formed and exposed to the other group. The meaning was not found in the individuals themselves, but in the roles they played in that context; the meaning was not found in the details of the simple seating chart but in the relationships between the roles aligned across the table.

Although less significant to investigating the new research dilemma, the other two quadrants complete the deconstruction of snapshot 2. The signifier (objective reality in the upper right quadrant of the Map of Complexity) is the diagram of the seating arrangement itself without labeling the roles, another gestalt frozen in time. The semantics of the lower left quadrant contain the collective meaning that the group made by cocreating this hierarchy, which correlates to group role-play.

The mirroring effect between the upper left and lower right quadrants in the analysis of this event exposed the reciprocal relationship between individuals and the roles they accepted within the system they cocreated. Because the system of the group was nested within other systems (class, institution, etc.), it is likely that the social system to which the participants were drawn (the institution) must have mirrored their interior landscape to some extent or they would not have been able to sustain themselves in it (center of gravity). In addition, the structure and system of the institution and the group hierarchy shared some similarities, which then created the availability of certain roles that individuals could play within these structures.

When both snapshots are mapped together, the final pieces of the research dilemma puzzle fall into place (see Figure 48). Snapshot 1 falls into the upper right quadrant (signifier) and snapshot 2 into the lower right (syntax). The following discussion moves through each of the four quadrants, first presenting necessary concepts or background information and then investigating the contents of that quadrant. My investigation of this particular map of complexity highlighted certain additional limitations of the study, descriptions of which are incorporated into the following discussion.

The human core on the upper left quadrant, the signified, is folded into each individual's Layers of Complexity. In those layers, the elements that form the base of individual behavior are, to some extent, definable or assessable. In this study, I used several assessment tools and observation and analysis methods, but because of the lens I applied when I started this project, I focused on the cultural realm (housed in mDNA) and thus missed many of the coordinates I could have collected.

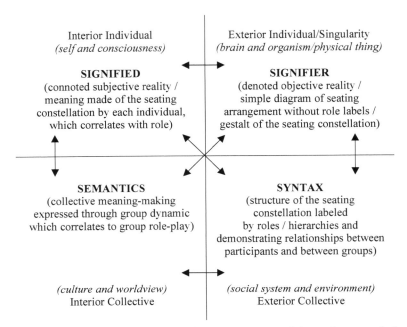

Interior Individual
(self and consciousness)

Exterior Individual/Singularity
(brain and organism/physical thing)

SIGNIFIED
(connoted subjective reality /
meaning made of the seating
constellation by each individual,
which correlates with role)

SIGNIFIER
(denoted objective reality /
simple diagram of seating
arrangement without role labels /
gestalt of the seating constellation)

SEMANTICS
(collective meaning-making
expressed through group dynamic
which correlates to group role-play)

SYNTAX
(structure of the seating
constellation labeled
by roles / hierarchies and
demonstrating relationships between
participants and between groups)

(culture and worldview)
Interior Collective

(social system and environment)
Exterior Collective

Figure 47. Map of Complexity depicting snapshot 2, the moment of the seating constellation at the class debrief. Author's image.

The syntax of the communication acts is located diagonally across from the human core; here on the lower right quadrant reside the nested systems with their structures, hierarchies, and rules in which this event took place. The closest system to each participating individual was that of the group in which they played their role(s), and the groups' internal hierarchies were spontaneously exposed in the seating constellation (snapshot 2).

A fuller investigation of all the nested hierarchies would bring more information to the essence of the structures but also to the individuals participating in shaping them. Thus information can be reflected back and forth between the human cores and the systems in which they operate. The core and the system live in a symbiotic relationship and inform each other through reciprocity, and once this dynamic has been exhausted with the available tools and methods any remaining gaps can be filled by checking the opposite quadrant to see if it might offer additional information in its mirror image. This approach echoes a traditional ethnographic approach in which the micro-scale perspective on human-scale events is juxtaposed with the macro-scale perspective of societies, institutions, and cultures. Tools and methods are available to explore the mystery of the system(s), some of which were used in this case study. However, because of the lens I used when I started this project, I focused on the groups and not on the institution.

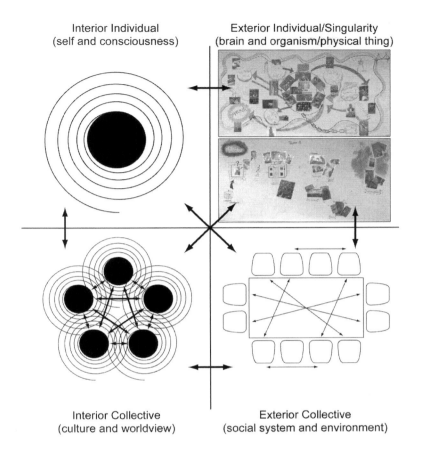

Interior Individual
(self and consciousness)

Exterior Individual/Singularity
(brain and organism/physical thing)

Interior Collective
(culture and worldview)

Exterior Collective
(social system and environment)

Figure 48. Completed research puzzle: this Map of Complexity shows the groups' artifacts called snapshot 1 (upper right), the diagrammatic representation of seating constellation for class debrief called snapshot 2 (lower right), a Layers of Complexity diagram for one individual participant's human core (upper left), and graphic representation of five interacting human cores equal to the number of participants in one group (lower left). Author's image.

The semantics of the event lie on the lower left quadrant, which holds the cocreated collective meaning formed through the information exchange between group members and expressed in emerging communication patterns. Both groups were very diverse in every aspect and occupied various positions on the coordinates taken for their individual innate and cultural backgrounds, and group performance. Each group exposed a very different communication pattern and described, consequently, a very different experience of the cocreation act.

Given that both groups in this study were embedded in the same systems (class and institution) and had similar profiles for cultural competence, the difference in outcomes between the two groups was noteworthy. Based on the exposed flexibility of the individual group members and on the discrepancies between participants' personal and cultural scores as compared to their behavior, I concluded that the specific meaning and context cocreated by participants in the group was dependent on the group's composition and which aspects of each individual's layers of complexity were engaged at any time (i.e., which cultural aspects were available designs). If participants did (as I believe I observed) cocreate both meaning and context in this flexible way, behavior would then have been impossible to predict even if all the variables had been known.

Another important observation is the hypothesis that cultural hybrids may be cocreating context anew at any given moment and shift the context, themselves, and the whole group as needed at the time and required by the task in context. Theories and methods are available for analyzing group dynamics, some of which were used in this case study. Further investigating other aspects of group dynamics might have given more granularity and coordinates in explaining the nature of the dynamic relationships at play. However, because of the realization that the meaning lies in the pattern of the information exchange (analog), such investigation (with its focus on the elements rather than the modalities of the pattern) was deemed unnecessary.

The signifier is located diagonally opposite the collective interior (the cultural exchanges); here we find the symbolic representation of these exchanges in the upper right quadrant, in the form of an artifact of the cocreated meaning. In this event the group's pattern of communication was directly projected into the gestalt of the cocreated visual map and could be read from it like a book. Theories and methods are available for reading and analyzing artifacts (usually not including all quadrants), and some of them were used in this study to construct the whole, but it should be noted that an analysis like the one executed here—that is, based on the four quadrants—yields significantly more information and provides multidimensionality to telling the story of an artifact. As with its mirror image on the lower left quadrant (the cultural information exchange), the key observation lies in the recognition that the communication pattern was visible in the gestalt of the map as a snapshot temporarily holding the threads to the cultural exchanges. The cocreated meaning is not to be found in the deconstructed map, the elements (or individual participants), or in the summation of the whole (the laundry list of elements or the group itself as an entity), but in the gestalt of the whole that they cocreated and contextualized to the situation.

This full analysis of the event in detail and across all four quadrants of this map found the mirroring effect in the creative tension between the quadrants that hold them together.

Metaphorically, therefore, it became clear that not all possible coordinates were needed to arrive at a fuller picture of the event that completely satisfied my curiosity. Inferences could be made between quadrants diagonally across, but also horizontally and vertically.

Researching With the Map of Complexity

While the complete data analysis for this study was of massive proportion, the outcome solidified into a tangible product in the Map of Complexity, which is a flexible frame that may be useful for other investigations, other disciplines, and other research questions. At the very least, it provides opportunity for discussion about the dynamics in the gaps between the fields of visual communication and intercultural communication.

Conceptual maps and diagrams are powerful and wonderfully simplified two-dimensional objects that can display incredibly complex ideas in relationship to each other. Such a map is this Map of Complexity—simple and elegant, thus approachable and decipherable. However, the map is not the territory, and readers of the map are not neutral; the effects of researcher and observer biases on the meaning made from the map must be kept in mind.

For example, the Map of Complexity offers a useful perspective on how Western perceptual biases affect research. As has been discussed, scholars (Hayashi & Jolley, 2002; Nisbett, 2003) have noticed a certain preference in Western thinking for digital perception (focusing on objects), and a certain preference for analog/holistic perception in Asian orientations (objects dependent on field, or synesthesia). While one orientation leads to a focus on details, the other leads to seeing the whole together with the negative space; while a Westerner might be waiting for words in a conversation, a Japanese (for instance) might be listening for pauses between the words, instead of or in addition to registering the words. Figure 49 shows how the Western/digital frame preference for figure–ground relationships affects how visual communication and intercultural communication theorists and practitioners perceive the four quadrants of the Map of Complexity.

In Figure 49, Western visual communication and intercultural communication assumptions are presented in each quadrant in the manner of digital perception. Visual communication theory lists design elements as denoted shapes (neutral, objective reality, signifier) moving into connoted (interpreted, decoded by a receiver, subjective reality), but no references are made about how the decoding occurs—cultural references are largely missing in visual communication literature. On the plane of syntax, visual communication literature refers to relationships between denoted shapes and ignores any tight relationship between ground and figure, focusing instead on the positive space and ignoring any relationship between foreground and background other than giving the background a subordinate role. Intercultural communication theory follows this pattern by acknowledging a figure–ground distinction in the quadrant of the signified, which translates into concepts of

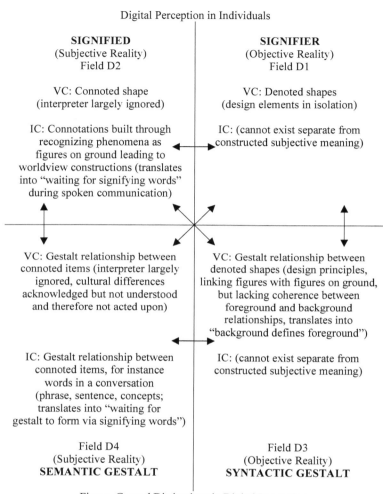

Digital Perception in Individuals

SIGNIFIED	**SIGNIFIER**
(Subjective Reality)	(Objective Reality)
Field D2	Field D1

VC: Connoted shape
(interpreter largely ignored)

VC: Denoted shapes
(design elements in isolation)

IC: Connotations built through recognizing phenomena as figures on ground leading to worldview constructions (translates into "waiting for signifying words" during spoken communication)

IC: (cannot exist separate from constructed subjective meaning)

VC: Gestalt relationship between connoted items (interpreter largely ignored, cultural differences acknowledged but not understood and therefore not acted upon)

VC: Gestalt relationship between denoted shapes (design principles, linking figures with figures on ground, but lacking coherence between foreground and background relationships, translates into "background defines foreground")

IC: Gestalt relationship between connoted items, for instance words in a conversation (phrase, sentence, concepts; translates into "waiting for gestalt to form via signifying words")

IC: (cannot exist separate from constructed subjective meaning)

Field D4	Field D3
(Subjective Reality)	(Objective Reality)
SEMANTIC GESTALT	**SYNTACTIC GESTALT**

Figure–Ground Distinctions in Digital Perception

Figure 49. Meaning-making in the digital frame and as figure–ground distinctions, analyzed through the Map of Complexity, providing an example of differences in observer lenses when applying the Map of Complexity. VC = visual communication; IC = intercultural communication. Author's image.

language where phenomena are only noticed if recognized as figures distinguished (carved out of) from the (back-)ground. This dynamic leads to expectations of a Westerner waiting for words to appear (sound distinguished from the silence in the background), and becoming uncomfortable with too much silence between words.

Figure 50, on the other hand, demonstrates how analog perception (e.g., characteristic of a Japanese frame) allows observers to perceive the same structures differently. On the level of visual communication, an observer with an analog lens would perceive reality in a form of synesthesia (senses merged, foreground and background melted together with individual elements not noticed in detail but only as part of the whole). Instead of figure–ground distinction, an analog perceiver would notice a figure–ground relationship on the individual as well as the collective level. In intercultural communication theory from the perspective of an analog processor, words would be merged with silence and be perceived as a unit; thus, silence carries meaning that gets translated through duration.

These different ways of making meaning have significance in the fields of intercultural communication and visual communication, and to me as the observer of the research phenomenon in the present study. For instance, Bennett (1998) describes perceptual relativity as a process of "figure/ground distinction" (p. 16):

From the "kaleidoscopic flux" (ground) of undifferentiated phenomena, we create a boundary that distinguishes some object (figure) from the ground. These figures may literally be objects, or they may be concepts or feelings. Collections of figures are "categories." What we think exists—what is real—depends on whether we have distinguished the phenomenon as figure. And since culture through language guides us in making these distinctions, culture is actually operating directly on perception. (p. 16)

With this statement Bennett identified his work as digitally focused.

As a transdisciplinary researcher with a heavy preference for synesthesia, I made an effort to pool from both ways of perceiving when interpreting the data, but I relied more heavily on analog perception. My personal bias in this interpretation of the data thus led me to seeing snapshot 1 from the holistic perspective of field A1 (foreground and background merged through synesthesia/field-dependence), and to perceiving the group interactions as a semantic gestalt described in field A4 (figure–ground relationship leading to holistic pattern that can be felt rather than focusing on acts of individuals that can be described). Snapshot 2 was analyzed through the lens described in field D3 (digital perception of figure–ground distinction), which exposed individuals' role acceptance as perceived through the lens of field A2 (individual participants accepting their roles in relationship to each other and the system they created during the group process, again of an amorphous nature).

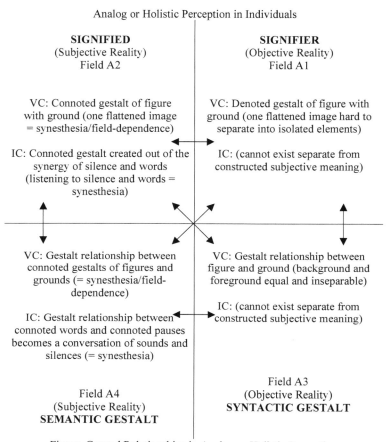

Analog or Holistic Perception in Individuals

SIGNIFIED
(Subjective Reality)
Field A2

SIGNIFIER
(Objective Reality)
Field A1

VC: Connoted gestalt of figure
with ground (one flattened image
= synesthesia/field-dependence)

VC: Denoted gestalt of figure with
ground (one flattened image hard to
separate into isolated elements)

IC: Connoted gestalt created out of the
synergy of silence and words
(listening to silence and words =
synesthesia)

IC: (cannot exist separate from
constructed subjective meaning)

VC: Gestalt relationship between
connoted gestalts of figures and
grounds (= synesthesia/field-
dependence)

VC: Gestalt relationship between
figure and ground (background and
foreground equal and inseparable)

IC: (cannot exist separate from
constructed subjective meaning)

IC: Gestalt relationship between
connoted words and connoted pauses
becomes a conversation of sounds and
silences (= synesthesia)

Field A4
(Subjective Reality)
SEMANTIC GESTALT

Field A3
(Objective Reality)
SYNTACTIC GESTALT

Figure–Ground Relationships in Analog or Holistic Perception

Figure 50. Meaning-making in the analog holistic frame and as figure–ground relationships, analyzed through the Map of Complexity, providing an example of differences in observer lenses when applying the Map of Complexity. VC = visual communication; IC = intercultural communication. Author's image.

Perception, mine included, may be largely more complex than the description of this conceptual frame, but this frame explains the choices I made that led me to recognize the phenomena in this particular way.

Digital perception seems to be more related to scientific evidence—a shape or a sound that can be distinguished from the background is either there or not. Analog perception, on the other hand, seems to be more related to a feeling space that is hard to describe and translate back into words—a shape or a sound are not defined by the background they sit upon but by the relationship they engage in with the other elements *and* the background. Other metaphors to explain this difference are that of notes played individually and picked out by an audience versus a symphony that envelops the audience, or of someone who looks at the object as an observer from a distance rather than feels the object from inside. My perceptual choices also distinguish my results from the traditional Western intercultural communication frame as described, for instance, by Bennett (1998). This is an important distinction to be made because my experience is influential in my role as the inquirer and observer (as described by Japanese intercultural communication scholar Hayashi in Hayashi & Jolley, 2002) even if it's not described in the mainstream (Western) literature and even if I am not Japanese.

An Overview of the Utility of the New Models for This Study

With these new models and tools, I had identified potential resolutions to all three of the issues that remained at the end of part one. First, the flexibility demonstrated by the participants in this study supported the possibility of designer identity. Cultural hybrids may (co)develop systems through which aspects of culture become available designs for identity construction in the moment, with the cultural aspects available in that particular situation, by exchange among the group members. Second, the Layers of Complexity model contained and offered an explanation for the question of innate versus cultural or nature versus nurture in the context of lived experience, through the interrelationship between the innate, the cultural, and the situational. Third, the Map of Complexity model proved a useful tool to explain and demonstrate the relationship between the snapshots and group dynamics observed in this study. In addition, through the mirroring effect, the Map of Complexity model suggests that conclusions can be made about the subjective realm even when some data are not available.

Synthesis

Culture was scanned as a product in this study through the comparison of the behavior of the participants to the product they created. This study thus encompasses both the essence of culture (a process definition) and the creation of products (a functional definition) (Baldwin et al., 2006). These layers of perspectives (culture as process, function, and theory) were then forged into a metaphorical holographic representation (Baldwin & Hecht, 2003, and Hecht & Baldwin, 1998, both as discussed in Baldwin et al., 2006) composed of interpenetrated parts, defining the complexity of culture as "constitutive" (Baldwin et al., 2006, p. 64). Culture as constitutive requires that the complex social phenomena be investigated from many perspectives to reconstruct a full expression of the whole, which brings us back to the reasons why the present study could only be successful as a transdisciplinary inquiry applying the viewfinder of integral theory as a frame that could hold all the pieces together.

This study used both objectivist and subjectivist approaches to the topic, as recommended by Gudykunst et al. (2005) and as necessary to understand transcultural communication dynamics fully. In this study participants exposed their own personal and shared experience through the group processes and interviews. Their collaborative visual maps also offered a direct window not only into how reality was experienced but how it was coconstructed. All of these data were thoroughly described, and fall into the subjectivist approach. In addition, I analyzed and compared individual and group profiles to behavior and attempted to explain the observed communication acts and group dynamics, and came to the conclusion that behavior may be largely contextual in the case of cultural hybrids. This investigation of observable behavior places this study into the objectivist realm as well.

In this study, using a transdisciplinary approach led me to develop two potentially useful models. The Layers of Complexity and the Map of Complexity allowed me to consolidate the objective reality of the individual and the system, as well as the subjective reality of the individual and the collective onto one plane. My own lens was more fully investigated in the process, providing a window into my interpretive reality (see Appendix L). Both models are conceptual in nature and offer the practical application of their use as graphic tools to help compare and contrast various aspects of a phenomenon similar to the one investigated in this study, to reconstruct the whole and represent it visually. Even if coordinates are missing, inferences may be made through the mirroring effect.

The present study stands on the solid ground of intercultural communication theory (see Location of This Research Project in Chapter 9). The additional analysis presented in this Epilogue adds to the discussion of the third category of Gudykunst et al.'s (2005) theories (those that concern communication between people from different cultures) the possibility that cultural hybrids may design their identities in the moment with the available cultural aspects of the group as a whole. In addition, integral theory offered one approach to define a larger research space where all these coordinates could be put into dialogue with each other and meta-analysis could be performed, aligned with the practices of standard ethnographic studies. In this analysis, I found the gestalt of the entire event by mapping the cocreation of meaning onto the Map of Complexity, including the mirroring effect.

As a transdisciplinarian I feel that my search to find ways for the disciplines of visual communication and intercultural communication to complement each other through their areas of strength has been successful. Although my study is small, the findings have contributed to both fields by suggesting promising avenues for future, similar case studies, and the theoretical rethinking of existing data. I found that both disciplines would benefit from updating and expanding their theoretical underpinning, and investing in research that matches the current needs in the globalization era and the potential paradigm shift toward worldcentricity.

As an educator I found the study to be successful not only for the results in the research arena, but for the transformative experiences it generated for all participants, myself included, a value that was communicated by the student–participants in the class debrief and beyond. Researching systems (such as groups within this class set into larger frames such as the institution) changes them, and my research project was thus also a successful intervention.

This dissertation took a rare and unique opportunity to investigate a group activity (one day in a visual design class) in great detail—the thorough documentation methods applied during the event, the instruments used to address confounding variables, the group debrief, a member check, and personal interviews—which led to the construction of a thick case from subjective and objective viewpoints (event and participants). Much could be observed that confirmed some of the theoretical frames underlying this research project, but new phenomena emerged that could not be explained by the traditional theoretical underpinnings. In addition, some aspects of the data could not be measured with the traditional methods and instruments available. Many participants were cultural hybrids who demonstrated a high degree of flexibility and multipositionality regarding their cultural sensibilities and styles. They also showed the promise for capacities to design cultural identities contextually, and to coconstruct the context (in which they were also reflected) from which flexible identities could be accessed—designer identity.

Based on these results, I believe I observed the first signs of a shift in consciousness and consequently a potential paradigm shift out of multiculturalism into polyculturalism, which may result in finding that cultural hybrids in such polycultural environments lean toward worldcentric worldviews. This potential shift may overlap with the predicted movement into the first stages of the SD*i* Second Tier (Beck & Cowan, 2006). From this perspective, I offer the following recommendations for future research.

Recommendations for Future Research

This was a small case study and future research is necessary to support the generalizeability of my findings and explore some of the hypotheses discussed in this Epilogue. For other researchers interested in investigating similar questions, I offer the suggestions below. First of all, I suggest that researchers question the frame they come from early on so as to not fall into the trap of their own colonization gained through belonging to and participating in their discipline(s). A transdisciplinary approach would allow more flexibility in engaging with virgin territory and unknowable circumstances, and an integral frame would encourage a consolidation of the findings in the gaps of the known spaces participating in the study.

Many more similar studies would be necessary to establish a theory and practice of how creative activities (such as interactive graphic facilitation and collaborative visual mapping) build group rapport, facilitate flow states, and expand zones of proximal development in groups across cultures, and for cultural hybrids in particular.

In individuals, it would be interesting to study whether people who naturally may fall on a performance level of N as their normal competence level, display differing levels of competence in different groups (competence here refers to any competence brought in by the group to solve a problem they are working on). For example, someone might increase their capacity to $N + 1$ in one group, $N + 3$ in another, and so forth, and end up increasing their personal individual performance to a higher level permanently. I suggest that participating in collaborative creative work in polycultural groups may stretch participants to levels beyond what they would have been capable of by themselves, and that exposure over time may help to grow capacity.

Given the findings of this study regarding the limitations of the instruments used, I highly recommend adding intuitive, creative, visual tools into research design and the research process. Such tools would allow the invisible portion of the iceberg to surface without having to be measured by a tool that imposes its limitations upon the data. The Map of Complexity is one such tool that can be used to hold the findings graphically so that different realities can be compared and contrasted directly and visually, and can complement each other for the purpose of reconstructing the whole.

The intercultural communication field is lacking studies of interacting groups. Along the same lines, what is needed are studies of cultural hybrids collaborating in polycultural situations.

Future studies are necessary to learn more about cultural hybridity and how it is formed and maintained through face-to-face and virtual experiences. Flexible frames were observable in this study, and it would be interesting to find out whether there is a correlation to the potential shift in consciousness hinted at in this study. In particular, the potential of multipositionality and contextuality is of special interest in regard to developing proper assessment tools that can capture the experience of cultural hybrids.

The idea of culture as an available design is very interesting and could be very useful for a globalizing world. Future research is necessary to learn more about the possibilities of designing (cultural) identity, the mechanics of such flexibility, and whether or how designer identity can be taught. In addition, if educators recognize the current state of affairs, collect the appropriate resources, and draw upon the necessary community, they also may be able to assist in developing the concept of culture as an available design. In this way educators can help define, nurture, and teach transcultural communication practices infused into teaching content, thereby including the fostering of flexibility in constructing culturally appropriate and contextually dependent/adjusted identities. This would be a huge gift to the world.

One important finding of this study was the possibility that cultural hybrids may be cocreating context anew at any given moment and shift the context, themselves, and the whole group as needed at the time and as required by the task in context. If this hypothesis proves true, then the important aspects to pay attention to are not the individuals themselves but the pattern that emerges from their interactions. Like the gestalt of the map, this pattern can be read in its modalities—more so in its analog expressions and missing parts, and less in the digital information.

I entertained the possibility that the participants in this study were moving back and forth between multicultural ethnorelative and polycultural worldcentric worldview structures. This bold hypothesis offers interesting research opportunities that may lead to reframing the discipline of intercultural communication to transcultural communication and thus an updating of the current theories and models to include the events of globalization and its consequences. Future research is necessary to further explore the potential paradigm shift from multiculturalism and intercultural communication forms to polyculturalism and transcultural communication forms. It would also be interesting to investigate whether there might be a relationship between preferences for the collective experience in polycultural worldview structures.

The new models proposed here have potential in assisting studies of this kind. In addition, the models could be useful to anthropologists as graphic tools to map their findings and notice even more correlates. Further investigation of their validity and usefulness in similar contexts would be helpful to develop their potential as analysis tools for scholars and researchers.

The Layers of Complexity may be useful in further research to graphically map various aspects of identity in the human core. Mapping the various coordinates for the innate (gDNA plus individual nature), the cultural (mDNA), and the situational (life conditions) may present a pattern of certain shapes for possible designer identities. This graphic tool could thus be helpful in future research for developing the concept of designer identities.

The Map of Complexity could be useful in defining and graphically representing the interrelationships between subjective and objectives realities on the individual (micro) and collective (macro) levels. The power of such visual diagrams lies in the fact that they add another dimension for comprehending the information and offer the possible recognition of relationships more obvious in visual form. In addition, the use of visual diagrams closes, at least conceptually, the gap between objective and subjective realities.

It may not be practical to integrate objective and subjective realities on individual and collective levels in all research, but it is important to clarify which quadrant of the AQAL viewfinder any theorist or theory is occupying. This clarification would automatically expose the excluded parts that carry meaning—a much more informed position from which to begin research. The viewfinder provides a complimentary perspective and encourages communication between intercultural and visual communication scholars, which was one of the goals of my study. The scholars and their theories and practices can be more complete without having to totally reinvent themselves, through an understanding of which quadrant they are working in, and through communication or inquiry into those fields looking at the same thing from other quadrants.

Future research for the development of transcultural communication theories and practices should include the investigation of the relationships between actual and conceptual figure–ground relationships (not only figure–ground distinctions) in order to merge thinking (the latter) and feeling (the former) for the benefit of synthesizing ways of knowing and constructing greater wholes. This integration of foreground and background and the inclusion of the gaps would provide more granularity in the investigation of the meaning-making process and inform our understanding of how meaning is coconstructed collaboratively and negotiated across cultures. Additional insight would also be generated into how this process of coconstructing reality creates complex and flexible structures and also reflects them. For this reason, I strongly recommend that any future research meant to illuminate the coconstruction of social worlds reconcile in its methodologies the frames offered by Western, Asian, and other non-Western orientations in order to address the blind spots held by each. The necessary research would then be of transdisciplinary, transcultural, and, naturally, collaborative nature including multiple ways and modalities of communicating.

The transdisciplinary approach was successful in holding all the various aspects of the disparate disciplines at play in this study, and integral theory provided ways to consolidate them back into a whole. Both approaches led to observing and analyzing the phenomenon from a meta position and through the gaps of the disciplines. I highly recommend this approach when studying culture and how cultural frames interact in collaborative meaning-making processes where traditional frames sometimes fail to explain the data and the traditional instruments cannot always capture the experience.

A Note About Research Methods in the Era of Globalization

The way research is conducted is problematic for the needs of the transglobal terrain. In this complex world it is no longer sufficient to work independently; rather, researchers need to work collaboratively across disciplines, cultures, languages, and geographical boundaries to solve complex problems that expand beyond the boundaries of one or more disciplines. The gaps in the disciplines are a potent space of knowledge construction (Kern, 2000) that have not been adequately addressed in traditional Western-oriented research.

The speed at which knowledge is doubling and being shared around the globe is another problem for researchers. Postdisciplinary research models (Wolmark & Gates-Stuart, 2004) foster collaborations and immediacy in sharing information. The new media art/design worlds depend heavily on technology and have made contributions in innovating postdisciplinary ways of researching; postdisciplinary research does not focus on providing definite answers, and instead provides opportunity to enrich research with flexibility, creativity, and self-reflection. Ongoing research that is constantly and possibly even automatically updated on an interactive space would be extremely helpful to researchers and practitioners alike so that they can build their work upon current data.

Response to CPWR Graphic Facilitators

It was my original intention to look for specific cultural patterns expressed in visual form so that I could generate recommendations for graphic facilitators working in polycultural environments. Many pages and four years later, I am ready to return to the CPWR graphic facilitators who inspired the conception of this research project with their curiosity about visual communication concepts in support of polycultural dialogues. Given the findings of this study, I encourage a reframing of the question "How can we visually address various cultural styles and dimensions and represent them authentically in our graphic panels?" The more appropriate question to ask is: How can we support transcultural communication aided by creative methods (visual communication included) appropriate for the context of polycultural dialogues? With many thanks to the community of graphic facilitators for their support in searching for answers to their dilemmas and for asking these significant questions, I offer the following thoughts and concepts for their consideration.

First, practicing cultural humility to support events on the transglobal terrain may be more useful than striving for cultural competence. Cultural humility is a practice of constant personal evaluation and reflection in order to show up in any place as neutral as possible without any assumptions about other people's human cores and expected behaviors. Cultural competence, on the other hand, is a frame that includes the assumption that behaviors can be predicted and that one can learn how to step into particular cultural patterns authentically in accordance with the expected behavior. If the transglobal terrain includes a growing number of cultural hybrids as participants, one may need to expect shifting identities; in order to be of service to those participants, a neutral position may be more helpful than one that is full of assumptions.

Second, considering the Map of Complexity, a culturally sensitive graphic facilitator would be able to work in all four quadrants and evoke each of them at different times during the construction of a graphic panel. Keeping the Map of Complexity in mind might be useful so that practitioners do not get stuck in any one quadrant.

Third, in such a malleable space it is comforting to know that interaction patterns are noticeable in a tangible way, for instance in cocreated visual maps as this study has demonstrated. Thus it may be helpful to develop and offer creative activities (visual mapping included) that involve the participants directly and early in the process of dialoguing so that their interaction patterns can be known in a visual representation and then be supported by graphic facilitators in that very manner.

Fourth, providing opportunities for participants to build rapport with each other through creative engagement early in the process may foster the respectful sharing of beliefs and values, commonalities and differences—especially if task-orientation is required for the subsequent processes. Setting the context this way may prepare the participants for a transformative experience and may support the emergence of an effective process. If visuals are involved in this rapport-building process they may provide valuable information to graphic facilitators who then could better support the process by matching the emerged styles.

Fifth, evoking the imagination to more easily close the gaps between outer and inner realities—in other words, encouraging the gestalting of different realities and thereby the meaning-making process—may facilitate group rapport. Collaborative visual mapping may be an excellent way to engage participants' imagination. Facilitating collaborative mapping activities and interactive graphic facilitation with the participants may be more useful, at times, than creating the graphic panels for them. Along these lines it also may need to be considered that the most effective collaborative activities may not be visual techniques; staying open to other forms of creativity that could accomplish the goal of exposing interaction patterns to the participants themselves and to facilitators of the process may be a useful frame to hold.

In this research project I found that public information about the nature and benefits of graphic facilitation is very thin to nonexistent. Developing, publishing, and teaching theories and practices of graphic facilitation is highly important in order to develop the profession and establish it as a discipline. Likely partners could be found in the disciplines of organizational effectiveness, transcultural communication, and visual communication.

Shifting the practice and scope of graphic facilitation in this way would facilitate the embracing of the ambiguity and complexity inherent in events such as the CPWR Assemblies and Parliaments. This shift would result in deep rapport-building across cultures and nations, and the opportunity to continuously circle back to the shared meaning and interests necessary to hold effective transglobal dialogues.

Next Steps

With this research project I hope to contribute to the development of the disciplines of intercultural communication and visual communication, as well as education. While the contributions in both communication fields have to be honored for their importance at the time, substantial but appreciative criticism of the current state of the disciplines is necessary in order to point to the possibilities of and necessity for growth.

Intercultural communication scholars and practitioners have made tremendous contributions to engaging the challenges of multiculturalism. We are now poised to step into the next phase of evolving the discipline to assist with managing social sustainability across the planet. This next step may include moving from the concepts of multiculturalism (with a focus on cultural differences) to the concepts of polyculturalism (with a focus on cultural interrelatedness and strength through diversity), and therefore moving from intercultural communication to transcultural communication.

Visual communication is in the forefront of global connectivity, and innovated a framework for a visual language system from the position of the dominant culture. We are now ready to diversify from that limited perspective to better serve a world that is in need of communication tools matching the complexity level of current global events.

Despite the energy often brought to "diversity issues," traditional teaching frames were originally created for and by the dominant culture; therefore institutions, administrators, and instructors are often at a loss when faced with the necessity to build capacity in polycultural groups to collaborate productively in creating learning communities. This is especially true as teaching increasingly incorporates both traditional face-to-face and contemporary virtual formats. The insight offered by this study into polycultural group dynamics and meaning-making lights a path toward effective teaching in vital institutions populated by polycultural individuals. The possibility of including identity design in the curriculum in polycultural contexts is an important issue to be taken up by educators. It would be extremely helpful in readjusting hierarchies as a whole to teach participants in polycultural environments flexible construction of identity by making culture an available design via creative activities. Such teaching would also help to diminish any dichotomies between dominant and nondominant cultures in the room. In such a flexible environment all frames would be welcome and interesting to try on—a true collaborative effort that then has a chance to be replicated outside the school context.

It is my hope that the findings of this study will be of interest to many disciplines, as scholars, theorists, and practitioners seek more appropriate conceptual frameworks in order to meet the needs created by globalization.

REFERENCES

Across Cultures. (2007a). *Across cultures.* Retrieved December 27, 2007, from http://acrosscultures.com/pcsidescription.html

Across Cultures. (2007b). *Across cultures FAQ.* Retrieved December 27, 2007, from http://acrosscultures.com/faq.html

AIGA. (2008). *What is graphic design?: Graphic design, a career guide.* Retrieved June 8, 2008, from http://www.aiga.org/content.cfm/guide-whatisgraphicdesign

Albert, M. (2003, July 15). *Revolutionizing culture part one: Michael Albert interviews Justin Podur.* Retrieved December 25, 2007, from http://www.zmag.org/content/showarticle.cfm?SectionID=30&ItemID=3914

Alford, D. M. (n.d.). *Manifesting worldviews in language.* Retrieved March 10, 2007, from http://www.enformy.com/dma-wv.htm

Auyeung, P. K., & Sands, J. S. (2003). The learning styles of accounting students in vertical and horizontal collectivist cultures. *Journal of Accounting and Finance, 2*, 31–45.

Baldwin, J. R., Faulkner, S. L., Hecht, M. L., & Lindsley, S. L., (Eds.). (2006). *Redefining culture: Perspectives across the disciplines.* Mahwah, NJ: Erbaum.

Ball, J. (1998, April). Graphic facilitation focuses a group's thoughts. *Consensus*, [volume & page nos. unavailable]. Retrieved January 8, 2008, from http://www.mediate.com/articles/ball.cfm

Barry, A. M. (1997). *Visual intelligence.* Albany: State University of New York Press.

Barthes, R. (1977). *Image music text.* New York: Hill & Wang.

Beck, D. E. (n.d.). *Spiral Dynamics Integral level one certification course manual.* Denton, TX: Spiral Dynamics Group.

Beck, D. E. (2007, October). *Spiral Dynamics 1 & 2 training.* Training session, Boulder, CO.

Beck, D. E. & Cowan, C. (2006). *Spiral dynamics: Mastering values, leadership, and change: Exploring the new science of memetics.* Cambridge, MA: Blackwell Business.

Bennett, M. J. (n.d.). *Radical constructivism: The assumptive base of intercultural communication.* (Available from the Intercultural Communication Institute, 8835 SW Canyon Lane, Suite 238, Portland, OR 97225)

Bennett, M. J. (1986a). A developmental approach to training for intercultural sensitivity. *International Journal of Intercultural Relations, 10*(2), 179–196.

Bennett, M. J. (1986b). Towards ethnorelativism: A developmental model of intercultural sensitivity. In R. Michael Paige (Ed.), *Cross-cultural orientation: New conceptualizations and applications* (pp. 21–72). New York: University Press of America.

Bennett, M. J. (1993). Towards ethnorelativism: A developmental model of intercultural sensitivity. In M. Paige (Ed.), *Education for the intercultural experience* (pp. 21–71). Yarmouth, ME: Intercultural Press.

Bennett, M. J. (Ed.). (1998). *Basic concepts of intercultural communication.* Yarmouth, ME: Intercultural Press.

Bennett, M. J. (2000). *Radical constructivism* [Course materials for the Summer Institute of Intercultural Communication]. Portland, OR: Intercultural Communication Institute.

Bennett, M. J. (2003). *Developing intercultural competence: A reader.* Portland, OR: Intercultural Communication Institute.

Bennett, M. J. (2004). Becoming interculturally competent. In J. Wurzel (Ed.), *Toward multiculturalism: A reader in multicultural education* (2nd ed., pp. 62–77). Newton, MA: Intercultural Resource.

Bennett J. & Bennett M. (2003, August). Becoming a skillful intercultural facilitator. Handout packet presented at the Intercultural Communication Institute's Summer Institute for Intercultural Communication in Portland. OR.

Bennett, M. J., & Hammer, M. R. (2002). *The intercultural development inventory: Administrator's manual.* Portland, OR: IDI.

Bleicher, S. (2005). *Contemporary color.* Clifton Park, NY: Thomson Delmar.

Center for Studies in Higher Education. (2007, October 10). *A new generation of students: They are unlike those of the past according to a census survey at the nation's largest research university.* Retrieved December 20, 2007, from http://cshe.berkeley.edu/news/index.php?id=38

Chandra, K. (2006). What is ethnic identity and does it matter? *Annual Review of Political Science, 9,* 397–424.

Christison, M. A. (2005). *Multiple intelligences and language learning.* San Francisco: Alta Book Center.

Clark, D. (1999). *Kolb's learning styles.* Retrieved November 18, 2007, from http://www.nwlink.com/~donclark/hrd/history/kolb.html

City College of San Francisco. (n.d.). *Our vision.* Retrieved December 22, 2007, from www.ccsf.edu/Catalog/Admin/mission.html

City College of San Francisco. (2005). *Graphic communications: About us: Vision statement.* Retrieved December 27, 2007, from http://www.ccsf.edu/Departments/ Graphic_Communications/About_Us/ Vision.htm

City College of San Francisco. (2006). *Institutional self study for reaffirmation of accreditation.* San Francisco: Author.

City College of San Francisco. (2007, November 29). *CCSF tuition and fees office.* Retrieved December 22, 2007, from http://www.ccsf.edu/Services/Admissions_Records/ Tuition_and_Fees.html

Cronen, V. E. (Ed.). (1995). *Social approaches to communication.* New York: Guilford.

Csikszentmihalyi. M. (1990). *Flow: The psychology of optimal experience.* New York: HarperCollins.

Diller, J. V., & Moule, J. (2005). *Cultural competence.* Belmont, CA: Thomson Wadsworth.

Drexler, A., & Sibbet, D. (2004). *10.1 TP Model.* San Francisco: Grove Consultants.

Eagleton, T. (2000). *The idea of culture.* Oxford: Blackwell.

Epstein, R. (1996). *Cognition, creativity, and behavior.* Westport, CT: Praeger.

Evans, P., & Thomas, M. A. (2008). *Exploring the elements of design* (2nd ed.). New York: Thomson Delmar Learning.

Forrester, R. & Drexler, A. (2005). *Forrest/Drexler Team Performance Indicator guide to interpreting the results.* San Francisco: Grove Consultants.

Friedman, T. L. (2005). *The world is flat.* New York: Farrar, Straus, & Giroux.

Frontlist Books. (n.d.). *Interview with Vijay Prashad.* Retrieved December 25, 2007, from http://www.frontlist.com/interview/PrashadInterview

Gardner, H. (1999). *Intelligence reframed.* New York: Basic Books.

Gay, G. (2000). *Culturally responsive teaching.* New York: Teachers College Press.

Goodfellow, R., & Hewling, A. (2005). Reconceptualising culture in virtual learning environments: From an "essentialist" to a "negotiated" perspective. *E-Learning, 2*(4), 355–367.

The Grove Consultants International. (1999). *Drexler/Sibbet team performance model* [Brochure]. San Francisco: Author.

The Grove Consultants International. (2003). *The team performance model abstract* [Brochure]. San Francisco: Author.

The Grove Consultants International. (2007a). *Group graphics keyboard.* Retrieved December 27, 2007, from http://store.grove.com/site/method_pm_ggk.html

The Grove Consultants International. (2007b). *Graphic facilitation retrospective:Charting what we learned.* Retrieved January 2, 2008, from http://www.grove.com/site/ resources_articles_gfr.html

Gudykunst, W. B., Lee, C. M., Nishida, T., & Ogawa, N. (2005). Theorizing about intercultural communication. In W. B. Gudykunst (Ed.), *Theorizing about intercultural communication* (pp. 3–22). Thousand Oaks, CA: Sage.

Hall, E. T. (1976). *Beyond culture.* New York: Doubleday.

Hall, E. T. (1998). The power of hidden differences. In M. J. Bennett (Ed.), *Basic concepts of intercultural communication* (pp. 53–67). Yarmouth, ME: Intercultural Press.

Hammer, M. R. (in press). The Intercultural Development Inventory (IDI): An approach for assessing and building intercultural competence. In M. A. Moodian (Ed.), *Contemporary leadership and intercultural competence: Understanding and utilizing cultural diversity to build successful organizations.*

Hammer, M. R., & Bennett, M. J. (1998). *Intercultural Development Inventory (IDI) manual.* Portland, OR: Intercultural Communication Institute.

Hammer, M. R., & Bennett, M. J. (2001). *Intercultural Development Inventory (IDI) manual* (2nd ed.). Portland, OR: Intercultural Communication Institute.

Hayashi, K., & Jolley, G. (2002, October). "Two" thoughts on analog and digital language. *The Aoyama Journal of International Politics, Economics and Business, 58* [page numbers unavailable].

Hay Group. (2005). *The Kolb Learning Style Inventory (LSI), version 3/1.*

Hofstede, G. (n.d.a). *Geert Hofstede cultural dimensions.* Retrieved November 22, 2007, from http://www.geert-hofstede.com

Hofstede, G. (n.d.b). *Geert Hofstede cultural dimensions.* Retrieved November 6, 2007, from http://www.geert-hofstede.com/hofstede_dimensions.php

Hofstede, G. (n.d.c). *Philippines Geert Hofstede cultural dimensions.* Retrieved November 19, 2007, from http://www.geert-hofstede.com/hofstede_philippines.shtml

Hofstede, G. (2001). *Culture's consequences* (2nd ed.). Thousand Oaks, CA: Sage.

Hofstede, G., & Hofstede, G. J. (2005). *Cultures and organizations.* New York: McGraw-Hill.

Horn, R. E. (1998). *Visual language.* Bainbridge Island, WA: MacroVU.

House, R. J., Hanges, P. J., Mansour, J., Dorfman, P. W., & Gupta, V. (Eds.) (2004). *Culture, leadership, and organizations: The GLOBE study of 62 societies.* Thousand Oaks, CA: Sage.

Howard, J. A. (2000). Social psychology of identities. *Annual Review of Sociology, 26,* 367–393.

Hunt, L. M. (2001, December). Up front: Beyond cultural competence. *Religiously Informed Cultural Competence, 24.* Retrieved March 10, 2008, from http://www.parkridgecenter.org/Page1882.html

Intercultural Communication Institute. (2008). *About ICI.* Retrieved July 5, 2008, from http://www.intercultural.org/about.php

Integral Institute. (2005). *About integral: Facts.* Retrieved March 25, 2008, from http://in.integralinstitute.org/faq-pdf.aspx?id=2

International Forum of Visual Practitioners. (2003). *Visual Practitioner.* Retrieved February 21, 2007, from http://www.visualpractitioner.org/education

Johnson, D., & Johnson, F. (2005*). Joining together.* Boston, MA: Pearson Education.

Kayes, A. B., Kayes, D. C., Kolb, A., & Kolb, D. A. (2004). *The Kolb team learning experience: Improving team effectiveness through structured learning experiences.* [Location unknown]: Hay Resources Direct. (Latest version available from http://www.haygroup.com/)

Kelley, R. (1999, winter). People in me "So, what are you?". *ColorLines Magazine.* Retrieved December 25, 2007, from http://www.zmag.org/content/showarticle.cfm?SectionID=30&ItemID=3865

Kern, R. (2000). *Literacy and language teaching.* New York: Oxford University Press.

Kolb, D. A. (1984). *Experiential learning: Experience as the source of learning and development.* Upper Saddle River, NJ: Prentice Hall.

Kureishi, H. (2005, August 4). The carnival of culture: Multiculturalism has to be a robust exchange of ideas, rather than of festivals and food. *The Guardian.* Retrieved March 8, 2008, from http://www.guardian.co.uk/world/2005/aug/ 04/religion.uk

Lakoff, G., & Johnson, M. (1999). *Philosophy in the flesh.* New York: Basic Books.

Lee, L. (1999). Going beyond classroom learning: Acquiring cultural knowledge via on-line newspapers and intercultural exchanges via on-line chatrooms. *CALICO Journal, 16*(2), 101–120.

Levine, R. (1997). *Geography of time.* New York: Basic Books.

Lewis, J. (2002). From culturalism to transculturalism [Electronic version]. *Iowa Journal of Cultural Studies, 1.* Retrieved January 15, 2008, from http://www.uiowa.edu/~ijcs/issueone/lewis.htm

Making Meaning. (2005). *Making meaning: 15 meanings.* Retrieved January 8, 2008, from http://www.makingmeaning.org/meanings.html

Margulies, N., & Maal, N. (2002). *Mapping inner space* (2nd ed.). Tucson, AZ: Zephyr Press.

Margulies, N., & Valenza, C. (2005). *Visual thinking.* Norwalk, CT: Crown House.

Mayall, K., Humphreys, G. W., & Olson, A. (1997). Disruption to word or letter processing? The origins of case-mixing effects. *Journal of Experimental Psychology: Learning, Memory, and Cognition, 23,* 1275–1286.

Meggs, P. B. (1989). *Type & image.* New York: Wiley.

Montuori, A. (2005). Gregory Bateson and the promise of transdisciplinarity. *Cybernetics and Human Knowing, 12*(1–2), 147–158.

Morgan, J., & Welton, P. (1992). *See what I mean?* London: Hodder & Stoughton.

Morin, E. (2005). *On complexity.* Cresskill, NJ: Hampton Press.

The New London Group. (1996, Spring). A pedagogy of multiliteracies: Designing social futures. *Harvard Educational Review, 66*(1), 60–92.

Nicolescu, B. (2007). *Transdisciplinarity as methodological framework for going beyond the science-religion debate.* Paper presented at the 2007 Metanexus Conference on Transdisciplinarity and the Unity of Knowledge: Beyond the "Science and Religion Dialogue".

Nisbett, R. E. (2003). *Geography of thought.* New York: Free Press.

O'Connor, J. & Seymour, J. (1993). *Introducing neuro-linguistic programming* (Rev. ed.). London: Thorsons.

Orwell, G. (1944). *As I please.* Retrieved June 10, 2008, from http://www.orwelltoday.com/ orwellwarwritten.shtml

Osland, J. S., & Bird, A. (2000). Beyond sophisticated stereotyping: Cultural sensemaking in context. *Academy of Management Executive, 14*(1), 65–79.

Pearce, B. W. (1999). *Research reports and theory development.* Retrieved November 14, 2006, from http://www.pearceassociates.com/essays/research_menu.htm

Pearce, B. W. (2005). The Coordinated Management of Meaning (CMM). In W. B. Gudykunst (Ed.), *Theorizing about intercultural communication* (pp. 35–54). Thousand Oaks, CA: Sage.

Pelli, D. G., Farell, B., & Moore, D. C. (2003). The remarkable inefficiency of word recognition. *Nature, 423,* 752–756.

Perea, M., & Lupker, S. J. (2003). Transposed-letter confusability effects in masked form priming. In S. Kinoshita & S. J. Lupker (Eds.), *Masked priming: State of the art* (pp. 97–120). Hove, UK: Psychology Press.

Peterson, B. (2004). *Cultural intelligence.* Yarmouth, ME: Intercultural Press.

Purser, R. E., & Montuori, A. (1994). Miles Davis in the classroom: Using the jazz ensemble metaphor for enhancing team learning. *Journal of Management Education 18*(1), 21–31.

Reicher, G. M. (1969). Perceptual recognition as a function of meaningfulness of stimulus material. *Journal of Experimental Psychology, 81*(2), 275–280.

Rosinski, P. (2008). *COF assessment questionnaire.* Retrieved March 25, 2008, from http://www.philrosinski.com/cof/

Rowland, R., & Valek, L. (2005, July). *Graphic facilitation: A new genre in information design.* Paper written for the International Institute for Information Design and American Institute of Graphic Arts, Vision Plus Symposium 11, Vienna, Austria. (Available from http://www. iiid-visionplus.net/Login.aspx?ReturnUrl= %2fPresentations -VP11%2fSurvey.aspx)

Sawyer, R. K. (2006). Group creativity: Musical performance and collaboration. *Psychology of Music 34*(2), 148–165.

Shaughnessy, A. (2005). *How to be a graphic designer without losing your soul.* New York: Princeton Architectural Press.

Sticks and Stones. (2006). *Sticks + stones: A collaborative exchange exploring labeling and stereotyping in graphic design* [Catalog of the exhibit with the same title, Birmingham Civil Rights Institute, Birmingham, AL, July 5–August 27, 2007]. Birmingham, AL: Author.

Stiller, D., Shedroff, N., & Rhea, D. (2005). *Making meaning: How successful businesses deliver meaningful customer experiences.* [Location unknown]: New Riders Press.

Swales, J. (1990). *Genre analysis: English in academic and research settings.* Cambridge, UK: Cambridge University Press.

Tervalon, M., & Murray-García, J. (1998). Cultural humility versus cultural competence: A critical distinction in defining physician training outcomes in multicultural education. *Journal of Health Care for the Poor and Underserved, 9*(2), 117–125.

Trompenaars, F., & Hampden-Turner, C. (1998). *Riding the waves of culture.* New York: McGraw-Hill.

Tseng, T. (2003, January). *Transculturalism and the future of ethnic marketing.* Retrieved January 15, 2008, from http://www.newamericandimensions.com/transculturalism.html

Tuan, Y. (1974). *Topophilia.* New York: Columbia University Press.

Tufte, E. R. (1990). *Envisioning information.* Cheshire, CT: Graphics Press.

Tufte, E. R. (2001). *Visual display of quantitative information* (2nd ed.). Cheshire, CT: Graphics Press.

Tyler, C., Valek, L., & Rowland, R. (2006). *Graphic facilitation and large-scale interventions.* In Alban B. T. & Bunker B. B. (Eds.), *The handbook of large group methods* (pp. 394–406). San Francisco: Jossey-Bass.

VisualsSpeak. (2006). *VisualsSpeak image set* [Brochure]. Portland, OR: Author.

Vygotsky, L. S. (1978). *Mind in society: The development of higher psychological processes.* Cambridge, MA: Harvard University Press.

Wagner, J. (1997, October). The unavoidable intervention of educational research: A framework for reconsidering researcher–practitioner cooperation. *Educational Researcher 26*(7), 13–22.

Whorf, L. B. (1956). Science and linguistics. In J. B. Carroll's (Ed.), *Language, thought, and reality.* Cambridge, MA: MIT Press.

Wilber, K. (2000). *A theory of everything.* Boston: Shambhala.

Wilber, K. (2005). *The integral operating system* [compact disc set and booklet]. Boulder, CO: Sounds True.

Wolmark, J. & Gates-Stuart, E. (2004). *Cultural hybrids, post-disciplinary digital practices and new research frameworks: Testing the limits.* Retrieved December 2, 2007, from http://dspace.anu.edu.au/bitstream/1885/41954/1/ GCWPixel_Raiders.pdf

Yamazaki, Y. (2005). Learning styles and topologies of cultural differences: A theoretical and empirical comparison. *International Journal of Intercultural Relations, 29*, 521–548.

Young, A. M. (1976a). *Reflexive universe.* Cambria, CA: Anodos.

Young, A. M. (1976b). *Geometry of meaning.* Novato, CA: Briggs.

APPENDIX A
GLOSSARY OF ACRONYMS

CCSF—City College of San Francisco

CMM—Coordinated Management of Meaning

CPWR—Pre-Parliaments, Assembly, and Parliament of the World's Religions in East Africa, the Middle East, and Southern Europe

DMIS—Developmental Model of Intercultural Sensitivity

IDI—Intercultural Development Inventory

IDI-2—Intercultural Development Inventory, version 2

IDI-3—Intercultural Development Inventory, version 3

MI—Gardner Multiple Intelligences

LS—Kolb Learning Phases and Learning Styles

LUUUTT—stories Lived, Unknown stories, Untold stories, Unheard stories, stories Told, and PCSI – Peterson Cultural Styles Indicator (tm)

PCSI—Peterson Cultural Styles Indicator (tm)

SD*i*—Spiral Dynamics Integral

TPI—Forrester/Drexler Team Performance Indicator

TPM—Team Performance Model

APPENDIX B

DATA TABLES

Table 8

Participants' Self-Identified Kolb Learning Styles (LS)

Learning style	Group A					Group 1				
	PA	PB	PC	PD	PE	P1	P2	P3	P4	P5
Diverging		X								
Assimilating							X			
Converging										
Accommodating	X		X	X	X	X		X	X	X

Note. LS scores are measured on two axes: the vertical axis measures an orientation between Abstract Conceptualization and Concrete Experience, and the horizontal axis measures an orientation between Reflective Observation and Active Experimentation. One point is then plotted onto the quadrant where the two orientation scores meet. Each quadrant represents a certain learning style that lies between two learning phases (Kayes, Kayes, Kolb, & Kolb, 1984). Often these learning phases are shown on a circle, called the Kolb Wheel, with the learning styles occupying the space between two phases next to each other; styles are listed in clockwise order starting at the 12:00 position. PA = Aiden; PB = Bella; PC = Carolina; PD = Dianne; PE = Eugene; P1 = Michelle; P2 = Nick; P3 = Olive; P4 = Paige; P5 = Rusena.

Table 9

Participants' Peterson Cultural Styles Inventory (tm) (PCSI) Scores with Class and U.S. Average Scores

Continuum	Group A					Averages		Group 1				
	PA	PB	PC	PD	PE	Class	U.S.	P1	P2	P3	P4	P5
Equality vs. hierarchy	2.6	4.2	2.6	4.2	1.0	2.8	3.0	3.8	0.0	2.8	2.0	4.4
Direct vs. indirect	3.4	3.8	4.0	7.0	1.2	3.7	1.5	3.6	0.8	4.0	3.8	5.0
Individual vs. group	5.6	6.8	4.0	8.0	6.8	5.4	1.5	5.0	4.0	4.4	4.2	4.8
Task vs. relationship	4.0	3.6	5.2	6.0	7.2	5.2	2.5	4.6	5.0	4.6	5.6	5.8
Risk vs. caution	4.0	4.8	3.8	6.6	1.6	4.0	3.0	5.0	1.2	6.2	4.0	2.4

Note. The PCSI is scored on a scale of 0-10. PA = Aiden; PB = Bella; PC = Carolina; PD = Dianne; PE = Eugene; P1 = Michelle; P2 = Nick; P3 = Olive; P4 = Paige; P5 = Rusena.

Table 10

Participant Scores on the Forrester/Drexler Team Performance Indicator (TPI)

Stage	Group A					Group 1				
	PA	PB	PC	PD	PE	P1	P2	P3	P4	P5
1. Orientation	-1	+1	0	+8	+3	+1	+3	+5	+3	+2
2. Trust building	+1	+1	+2	+1	+3	+1	+3	+4	+1	+7
3. Goal clarification	-3	+1	+2	+2	+3	-1	+2	+3	+1	+4
4. Commitment	-2	+3	+3	+1	+3	-1	+3	+4	-1	+3
5. Implementation	-4	+3	+5	+1	+3	-1	+3	+1	-3	0
6. High performance	-3	-1	+5	0	+3	+1	+3	+4	-1	+5
7. Renewal	-1	+2	+4	-1	+3	-1	+3	+2	+1	+1

Note. The TPI is scored from +9 to -9. PA = Aiden; PB = Bella; PC = Carolina; PD = Dianne; PE = Eugene; P1 = Michelle; P2 = Nick; P3 = Olive; P4 = Paige; P5 = Rusena.

Table 11

Participant Scores on Gardner's Multiple Intelligences (MI)

Intelligence	Group A					Group 1				
	PA	PB	PC	PD	PE	P1	P2	P3	P4	P5
Linguistic	17	17	10	18	17	15	8	11	17	9
Logical/mathematical	16	2	8	11	20	7	19	11	15	15
Visual/spatial	12	7	16	19	9	14	19	11	14	18
Bodily/kinesthetic	16	3	15	12	15	13	15	17	11	12
Interpersonal	9	2	13	17	14	13	14	14	15	15
Intrapersonal	18	16	15	19	18	11	13	11	15	15
Musical	17	10	16	16	14	17	17	9	13	18
Naturalist	14	5	9	12	17	13	17	11	16	15

Note. The MI is scored from 0 to 20. PA = Aiden; PB = Bella; PC = Carolina; PD = Dianne; PE = Eugene; P1 = Michelle; P2 = Nick; P3 = Olive; P4 = Paige; P5 = Rusena.

Table 12

Online Class Participation at Final Grading

Participant	Hits	Read	Posted	Average[a]
Group A				
Aiden	3666	2883	163	108%
Bella	3853	3091	155	114%
Carolina	2838	1832	388	82%
Dianne	3982	3180	342	121%
Eugene	4110	3187	608	127%
Group 1				
Michelle	3160	2393	300	94%
Nick	—	—	—	—
Olive	2194	1592	320	66%
Paige	2304	1694	247	68%
Rusena	4704	4072	216	145%
Class Average	3305	2613	280	6198

Note. Dash indicates that data were not available, as Nick dropped the class in the second half of the semester. [a]Each participant's total score (Hits + Read + Posted) was measured against the class average total score (6198).

SYLLABUS AND OTHER COURSE INFORMATION

Syllabus

Course title: Visual Literacy
Course number: GRPH 21
Course discipline: Graphic Communication
Course description: A beginning level course assisting students in developing visual literacy via learning about theories discussed in graphic design (design elements & principles, Gestalt); practical applications in sketching and perspective drawings; color theory as it applies to printing; analysis of found graphic design pieces via message deconstruction and critique of design principles and elements applied; introduction to typography, imagery, branding & identity systems, and advertising.
Course date: Saturday, January 20, 2007 through Saturday, May 19, 2007
Location: Phelan Campus, Health Center 207 and Visual Arts V143 (computer lab visits as necessary)
Face-to-Face meetings—following Saturdays: January 20 Orientation, January 27, February 10, February 24, March 3, March 17, March 24 with Nathan at the Mission Campus on Alabama Street, April 14, May 5, May 19
Meeting time(s): 10:00 AM–2:00 PM
Prerequisite(s): There are no prerequisites for this course.
Textbook(s)/Required Reading:
Basics of Design by Lisa Graham, Delmar/Thomson Learning, second edition ISBN 1-4018-7952-7;
Design Yourself by Kurt Hanks, Larry Belliston, and Dave Edwards, Crisp Publications, ISBN 1-56052-046-9;
Perspective Drawing by Raymond Holbert, Self-Published, available in the CCSF Bookstore;
All three available in the CCSF Bookstore (Ray Holbert's book can only be bought in the CCSF Bookstore)

Course Content

- Sketching as a means of communication
- Sketching systems—isometric, oblique, perspective
- Drawing 3D objects on 2D surfaces
- Basic presentation skills—materials and techniques
- Vocabulary and principles of visual information organization
- Design process: steps to problem-solving
- Vocabulary and fundamentals of type
- Imagery and its use in visual communication
- Color models and terminology used in visual communication (primarily print), cultural implications and psychology of color
- Discussion and analysis of various types of communication media including visual identities (logotypes, marks, systems), advertising, periodicals (magazines, newspapers), corporate communication (brochures, annual reports), and electronic media (TV, web, kiosks, CD-ROM, internet)
- Stimulating creativity
- Collaborating in teams

Procedure

Online
- Team discussions of readings, exercises, visual assignments, and quizzes
- Submissions of synthesis of readings and discussions
- Sharing of additional information relating to class topics
- Posting imagery
- Developing and managing team

Face-to-Face (F2F)
- Regular check in, review of readings, tasks and submissions
- In-class activities (hands-on, discussions, lectures, assignments, team-building, activities)
- Demos
- Midterm and final exams

Tests
- Midterm and final exams conducted as interactive team activities during F2F meetings
- Quizzes throughout

Evaluation
- Midterm and Final Grading is accumulative
- Visit Grading Policy on course menu

Materials
- Ruler (with metal edge at least 12 inches long)
- Type gauge (optional!!! clear plastic, with E-gauge) can be bought in **art/design supply stores**
- 3 Pencils (a soft graphite one: 4B, a medium one: HB, and a hard graphite one: 4H) and pencil sharpener
- Eraser, preferably a soft kind like a kneadable or white one
- Bristol Board, bright white, 11x14 inches or larger
- A roll of tracing paper (white)
- Small, portable sketchbook that can be carried along and pulled out at any time to sketch out ideas
- Glue stick
- X-acto knife with extra blades and scissors
- A 10x Loupe (that's a stand magnifier that has pre-focused dual lenses to examine printed items close-up; available in a good camera or art store, cost is around $10–15)
- Binder with dividers and protective plastic sheets
- A sturdy cardboard box to collect magazines, business cards, junk mail and other printed materials to be used for design examples during the second half of the course
- Portfolios for midterm and final submissions (11 x 17)

Attendance/Participation

Saturday F2F meetings are mandatory. It will be impossible to complete the class successfully without being present during these class meetings. Please bring food and drinks in order to stay energized and well nourished.

Attendance during F2F meetings counts for 15% of your grade which is collected via a point system. We will start class promptly at 10:00am and will usually not leave until 2:00pm. If you are not present by 10:15am you are considered late which will result in a 50% reduction in points for attendance for that day. Leaving class early will also result in a 50% reduction in attendance points.

Attendance/participation online is just as or even more important, and counts for 25% of your grade. You are expected to check in daily and post, at the very least, three times a week (postings may include: reading comments, insights/imagery, questions, and responses to team members' postings). You are also expected to function as online team moderator several times during the semester and collaborate with your team on tasks.

Sorry, no excuses for difficulties with attending and/or participation. In case of illness or emergencies proper documentation is needed in order to deviate from the above outlined attendance/performance policy.

Policies

- All online tasks, assignments, and submissions need to be completed by the due dates (late submissions will result in lower grades).
- Saturday F2F meetings are required.
- Prompt and full attendance is required, especially during midterm and final exams (which are designed as group activities and cannot be made up at another time).
- It is the full responsibility of each student who misses class or comes to class late or leaves early to obtain the missing information from his/her peers and come caught up and fully prepared the following class period.
- Participation in class critiques, class activities, and online discussion board are required.
- Craftsmanship is critical.
- Clean up after class is required.
- Textbook and materials are required.
- In case of withdrawal from class, students will need to take care of any withdrawals themselves through the proper channels.

Course Objectives by Week

Week 1, 1/20 F2F
Get acquainted with **WebCT**
Develop **team**
Learn and practice **mind-mapping**
Learn about **left brain/right brain activities**
Prepare for this **semester's work**

Week 2, 1/27 F2F
Continue to **develop team**
Continue practicing **mind-mapping**
Learn about **gestalt**
Practice **drawing**
Learn about **copying techniques**
Learn about **perspective**
Learn about **values and shading**
Learn about **basic shapes**
Define **areas of design**
Learn about how to begin the **design process**
Become familiar with **design principles**
Learn how to create **hierarchies in print media**
Become familiar with various **drawing techniques**

Week 3, 2/3 Online
Continue to **develop team**
Continue practicing **mind-mapping**
Learn about **copying techniques**
Learn about **perspective**
Learn about **values and shading**
Learn about **basic shapes**
Learn about **optimizing design approaches**
Learn about various **design disciplines**
Learn about various **design process**
Learn about **contrast** in design

Week 4, 2/10 F2F
Continue to **develop team**
Continue practicing **mind-mapping**
Learn about **perspective drawings**
Learn about **visual thinking**
Learn about **balance**

Week 5, 2/17 Online
Continue to **develop team**
Continue practicing **mind-mapping**
Continue to learn about **perspective drawing**
Learn about **problem solving & ideation**
Learn about **alignment, repetition, and flow**

Week 6, 2/24 F2F
Continue to **develop team**
Continue practicing **mind-mapping**
Continue to learn about **perspective drawing**
Learn about an ancient Asian game of wisdom , the **Tangram**
Learn about **different types of images** (photographs, illustrations, type)
Learn about **color in design**

Week 7, 3/3 F2F
Complete **midterm portfolio**
Prepare for **midterm exam**

Week 8 | 3/10 Online Assemblage of Midterm Submissions

Week 9, 3/17 F2F
Closure of introductory **2D visual assignments** & **readings**
Moving into **analysis** and **application** of concepts and vocabulary learned in 1st half of semester
Gestalt Theory

Week 10, 3/24 F2F
Learn about various **design formats and tools**
Going deeper with **color theory and application in print**
Reviewing and deepening some principles in preparation for **scrapfiles**

Week 11, 4/14 F2F
Explore and apply the **creative process used in graphic design**
Become familiar with **scrapfile tasks**
Become familiar with **process** of analysis (evaluating application of design principles and elements, creation of composition, meaning and application of color, type treatment, choice and quality of imagery, encoding, transmitting and decoding messages, consideration of context, overall effectiveness)
Reach a deeper understanding of topics at hand: **type, imagery, color, branding/identity systems/logos, advertising**
Become comfortable with the **process of critiquing**

Week 12, 4/21 Online
Become familiar with **process** of analysis (evaluating application of design principles and elements, creation of composition, meaning and application of color, type treatment, choice and quality of imagery, encoding, transmitting and decoding messages, consideration of context, overall effectiveness).
Reach a deeper understanding of topics at hand: **type, imagery, color, branding/identity systems/logos, advertising**
Become comfortable with the **process of critiquing**

Week 13, 4/28 Online
Become familiar with **process** of analysis (evaluating application of design principles and elements, creation of composition, meaning and application of color, type treatment, choice and quality of imagery, encoding, transmitting and decoding messages, consideration of context, overall effectiveness)
Reach a deeper understanding of topics at hand: **type, imagery, color, branding/identity systems/logos, advertising**
Become comfortable with the **process of critiquing**

Week 14, 5/5 F2F
Refine skills and strategies for **formal analysis and critique**
Refine and perfect **teamwork**

Week 15 | 5/12 Online Complete Case Study Complete Final Submissions

Week 16 | 5/19 F2F We will meet in class at our usual hour 10:00am . Teams will collaborate on Final Exam starting at 10:00am (Case Study in Fish Bowl Format). Be prepared to submit Final Submissions at 10:00am, and Case Study Package at the end of the Final.

Weekly Content

All weeks of instruction start on a Saturday and end on a Friday (midnight due date for assignments). Dates listed below refer to the beginning of the week, and list the tasks that begin on Saturday. F2F refers to face to face meetings.

week 1 | 1/20 F2F
Orientation
Left/Right Brain
Introductory Readings
Team-building

week 2 | 1/27 F2F
Team-building
Introductory Readings and Activities
Gestalt
Face-Vase & Picasso Assignments
Drawing & Copying Assignments
Value Scale
Values, Shapes, Shadings

week 3 | 2/3 Online
Design Principles & Perspective
Perspective Sketches from Book
Readings
Continue all projects

week 4 | 2/10 F2F
Bring all projects for in-class feedback
More Demos: Perspective Drawings, What's My Point, Cubes and Ellipses
Readings

week 5 | 2/17 Online
Continue projects
Readings

week 6 | 2/24 F2F
Bring all projects for feedback
More Demos: Now There Is Two
Tangram
Readings

week 7 | 3/3 F2F
Bring all your projects for feedback plus your materials
Readings

week 8 | 3/10 Online
Assemblage of Midterm Submissions
Review Theory for Midterm Exam
Collaborate with team as necessary and appropriate

week 9 | 3/17 F2F
Midterm Activities & Exam
Midterm Submissions
Scrapfiles and Case Study Show & Tell
Readings

week 10 | 3/24 F2F
Color in Print Guest Lecture at Temporary Mission Campus
374 Alabama at 17th Street, classroom/lab 101 at the back of the garage
Readings

Spring Break | 3/31-4/7 Site Closed
Suggestion: get midterm submissions up-to-date and start building the final submissions package
(do this regularly every week)

week 11 | 4/9 Online
Scrapfile #1
Typographic Self-Portrait
Readings

week 12 | 4/14 F2F
Creative Process
Scrapfiles #2, #3
Readings

week 13 | 4/21 Online
Scrapfiles #4, #5
Readings
week xx in the Tenth Dimension | 4/28 Online
Begin working on final submissions
Begin discussing Case Study

week 14 | 5/5 F2F
Scrapfiles Critique
Case Study
Collaborate on Case Study
Continue working on final submissions

week 15 | 5/12 Online
Complete Case Study
Complete Final Submissions

week 16 | 5/19 F2F
We will meet in class at our usual hour 10:00am
Teams will collaborate on Final Exam starting at 10:00am (Case Study in Fish Bowl Format)
Be prepared to submit Final Submissions at 10:00am, and Case Study Package at the end of the
Final

Midterm Submission Items

Congratulations! You've made to the mid-point, and you have worked hard to create the
items listed below.
Please assemble the below items exactly in the below listed order. Practice good
organization, and please label everything. If we can't find your items in the place where they are
supposed to be we will not hunt for them somewhere else, you will simply miss points in such a
case.

A. Portfolio with Visual Assignments
Cover
- Name
- Class
- Semester

- Table of Contents

Visual Assignments (total of 12)

Divider page and learning analysis
- Gestalt: Creative Assignments (Face-Vase/Picasso)
- Copying Assignment (Visual)
- Copying Assignment (Type)
- Value Scale
- Basic Shapes & Shading
- Perspective Sketches
- Perspective Drawings
- 20 Cubes & Ellipses
- What's My Point
- Now There Is Two
- Tangram

B. Sketchbook/Journal

Submit your sketchbook for review. You may submit copies from your sketchbook instead in case you don't want to leave your sketchbook with us. What we are looking for in this item is a representation of the development of your assignments and peripheral sketching activity. I will not grade the quality of your sketches, but will look for quantity.

If you submit copies instead of a book, please create a section in your binder (see *C. Binder with Peripheral Items* below)
- Sketches

C. Binder with Peripheral Items

Cover
- Name
- Class
- Semester
- Table of Contents

Note on Divider Pages

Each section below needs a divider page and a learning analysis
****

Midterm Reflection

Divider page and learning analysis

Answer questions as outlined
- Midterm Reflection
****

All Class Synthesis

Divider page and learning analysis

Submit the below listed items. All items must be clearly labeled (you may want to copy and paste these into a template that you create rather than just print out the original posting)
- Week 1
- Week 2
- Week 3
- Week 4
- Week 5
- Week 6
- Weeks 7 & 8 none
****

Quizzes
Divider page and learning analysis
     All items must be clearly labeled by week and quiz number (you may want to copy and paste these into a template that you create rather than just print out the original posting)
- Week 1: WebCT Quiz
- Weeks 2: Basics of Design, page 20, Mini Quiz #1 Basics of Design, page 38, Mini Quiz #2
- Week 3: Basics of Design, page 56, Mini Quiz #3
- Week 4: Basics of Design, page 84, Mini Quiz #4
- Week 5: Basics of Design, page 118, Mini Quiz #5 Basics of Design, page 144, Mini Quiz #6 Basics of Design, page 162, Mini Quiz #7
- Week 6: Basics of Design, page 186, Mini Quiz #8 Basics of Design, page 198, Mini Quiz #9
- Weeks 7 & 8 None

****

Exercises
Divider page and learning analysis
     All items must be submitted in the below listed order and clearly labeled by week and exercise number!
- Week 1: None
- Week 2: Basics of Design, pages 39-40, Exercises #1, #2, #3, #4
- Week 3: Basics of Design, pages 59-61, Exercises #1, #2, #3
- Week 4: Basics of Design, pages 85-86, Exercises #1, #2
- Week 5: Basics of Design, pages 119-120, Exercises #1, #2 Basics of Design, page 145, Exercises #1, #2 Basics of Design, page 163, Exercise (no number mentioned)
- Week 6: Basics of Design, pages 186-188, Exercises #1, #2 Basics of Design, pages 198-200, Exercises #1, #2, #3, #4
- Weeks 7 & 8 None

****

Mind-Maps
Divider page and learning analysis
     Please put all your mindmaps in chronological order which makes it convenient for your audience. You should have one mindmap for each reading. These can be created by hand or electronically rendered.

     If your mindmaps are too large to fit into this binder, please create an empty section (divider page and your learning analysis) and then clearly communicate where I can find the mindmaps, i.e. end of portfolio.

****

Final Submission Items

     Congratulations! You've made it to the end, and you have worked hard to create the items listed below.

     Please assemble the below items exactly in the below listed order. As we have discussed with you, feel free to improve some of your visual assignments for a better grade (if you submit new work, please mark it with a sticky note drawing our attention to it).

     Practice good organization, and please label everything. If we can't find your items in the place where they are supposed to be we will not hunt for them somewhere else, you will simply miss points in such a case.

A. Portfolio with Visual Assignments
Cover
- Name
- Class
- Semester
- Table of Contents

Visual Assignments (total of 13)

Divider page and learning analysis
- Gestalt: Creative Assignments (Face-Vase/Picasso)
- Copying Assignment (Visual)
- Copying Assignment (Type)
- Value Scale
- Basic Shapes & Shading
- Perspective Sketches
- Perspective Drawings
- 20 Cubes & Ellipses
- What's My Point
- Now There Is Two
- Tangram
- Typographic Self-Portrait (instructions: Week 11 Tasks)

B. Sketchbook/Journal
Submit your sketchbook for review. You may submit copies from your sketchbook instead in case you don't want to leave your sketchbook with us during the summer break. What we are looking for in this item is a representation of the development of your assignments and peripheral sketching activity. We will not grade the quality of your sketches, but will look for quantity.

If you submit copies instead of a book, please create a section in your binder (see *D. Binder with Peripheral Items* below).
- Sketches

C. Case Study (Sample 1, Sample 2, Sample 3)
As a group you will only submit ONE case study package. This will be a separate item that does not live in your portfolio. The case study and its representation on our final day of class is your final exam. If you miss the final exam you will have to miss the points given for the presentation, but you will still collect points for the case study itself.
- Case Study Package

D. Binder with Peripheral Items (Sample)
Cover
- Name
- Class
- Semester
- Table of Contents

Note on Divider Pages
Each section below needs a divider page and a learning analysis

****

Final Reflection
Divider page and learning analysis
- Final Reflection

****

All Class Synthesis
Divider page and learning analysis
Submit the below listed items

All items must be clearly labeled (you may want to copy and paste these into a template that you create rather than just print out the original posting)

- Week 1
- Week 2
- Week 3
- Week 4
- Week 5
- Week 6
- Weeks 7 & 8 None (Prep for Midterm)
- Week 9
- Week 10
- Week 11
- Week 12
- Week 13
- Weeks 14-18 None (Prep for Final)

****

Quizzes
Divider page and learning analysis

All items must be clearly labeled by week and quiz number (you may want to copy and paste these into a template that you create rather than just print out the original posting)

- Week 1:
  WebCT Quiz
- Week 2:
  Basics of Design, page 20, Mini Quiz #1
  Basics of Design, page 38, Mini Quiz #2
- Week 3:
  Basics of Design, page 56, Mini Quiz #3
- Week 4:
  Basics of Design, page 84, Mini Quiz #4
- Week 5:
  Basics of Design, page 118, Mini Quiz #5
  Basics of Design, page 144, Mini Quiz #6
  Basics of Design, page 162, Mini Quiz #7
- Week 6:
  Basics of Design, page 186, Mini Quiz #8
  Basics of Design, page 198, Mini Quiz #9
- Weeks 7 & 8 None (Midterm prep)
- Week 9:
  Basics of Design, pages 226–227, Mini Quiz #10
  Basics of Design, page 250, Mini Quiz #11
- Done!!!

****

Exercises
Divider page and learning analysis

All items must be submitted in the below listed order and clearly labeled by week and exercise number!

- Week 1: None
- Week 2:

Basics of Design, pages 39-40, Exercises #1, #2, #3, #4
- Week 3:
  Basics of Design, pages 59-61, Exercises #1, #2, #3
- Week 4:
  Basics of Design, pages 85-86, Exercises #1, #2
- Week 5:
  Basics of Design, pages 119-120, Exercises #1, #2
  Basics of Design, page 145, Exercises #1, #2
  Basics of Design, page 163, Exercise (no number mentioned)
- Week 6:
  Basics of Design, pages 186-188, Exercises #1, #2
  Basics of Design, pages 198-200, Exercises #1, #2, #3, #4
- Weeks 7 & 8 None (Midterm prep)
- Week 9:
  Basics of Design, page 228, Exercise #1
  Basics of Design, page 228, Exercise #2
  Basics of Design, page 251, Exercise #1
  Basics of Design, page 252, Exercise #2
  Basics of Design, page 252, Exercise #3
  Basics of Design, page 252, Exercise #4
- Week 10:
  Basics of Design, page 282, Exercises #1–14
- Done!!!

****

Mind-Maps (total of 25)
Divider page and learning analysis

Including the reading assignments for the recent review there should be at least 25 mindmaps in this section. Please put them in chronological order so we can see how you have improved your techniques throughout the semester.

If your mindmaps are too large to fit into this binder, please create an empty section (divider page and your learning analysis) and then clearly communicate where we can find the mindmaps themselves.

****

Scrapfiles (total of 5)
Divider page and learning analysis

Please label each of the scrapfiles clearly.

Team members will each have the same content in this section. Make copies for each other so each of you has a representation of the original print sample in her/his portfolio.

- Scrapfile #1 Type (1-3 samples, we'll discuss quantity as a class)
- Scrapfile #2 Imagery (1-3 samples, we'll discuss quantity as a class)
- Scrapfile #3 Color (1-3 samples, we'll discuss quantity as a class)
- Scrapfile #4 Branding/Identity/Logo (1-4 samples, we'll discuss quantity as a class)
- Scrapfile #5 Advertising (1-4 samples, we'll discuss quantity as a class)

Family

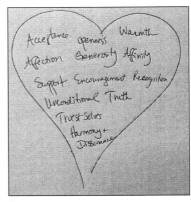

Love

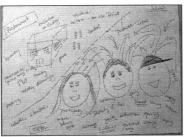

School

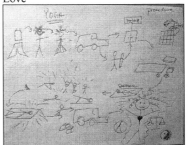

Procedure

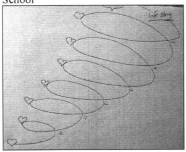

Life Story/Critical Moment

Woman, 33
Nationality: USA
Country of origin: USA
Native language: English
Foreign language: Spanish, German
Lived in Germany for 1 year
Current residence: Long Beach, CA
Identifies as:
Biracial, cultural bridge, queer, activist,
advocate, athlete, dancer, family
member
Profile

Family

Love

School

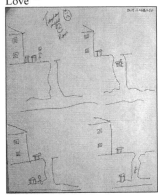

Procedure

Life Story/Critical Moment

Man, 43
Nationality: USA
Country of origin: India
Native language: Kannada, Tamil, Telugu, Hindi
Foreign language: English
Current residence: USA
Identifies as:
Indian, US American, male, interculturalist

Profile

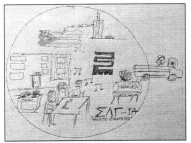

Family

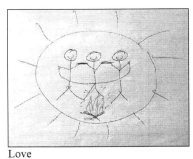

Love

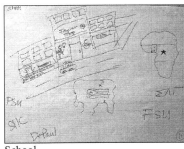

School

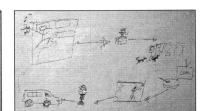

Procedure

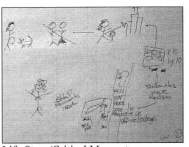

Life Story/Critical Moment

Woman, 27
Nationality: USA
Country of origin: Puerto Rice
Native language: English & Spanish
Foreign language: Portuguese
Current residence: Pennsylvania
Identifies as:
Caribbean, Puerto Rican, female,
educator, interculturalist, social justice
activist, educational equity activist

Profile

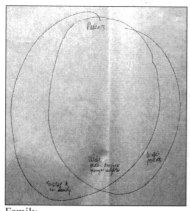

Family

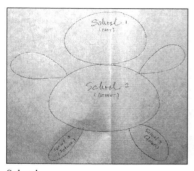

School

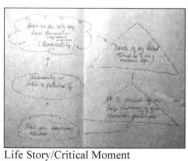

Life Story/Critical Moment

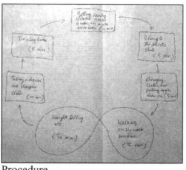

Love

Procedure

Man, 68
Nationality: Japanese
Country of origin: Japan
Native language: Japanese
Foreign language: English, French, Spanish
Lived in USA, Canada
Current residence: Japan
Identifies as:
Japanese but internationalized

Profile

297

Family

Love

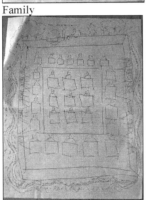

School

Procedure

Life Story/Critical Moment

Profile

Woman, 55
Nationality: Japanese
Country of origin: USA
Native language: English
Current residence: Oregon
Identifies as:
Middle class white fringe

298

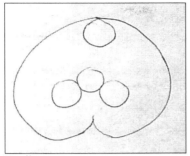

Family

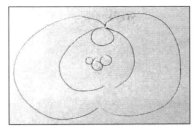

Love

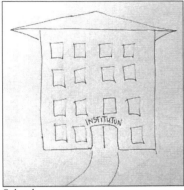

School

Procedure

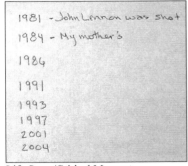

Life Story/Critical Moment

Woman, 48
Nationality: USA
Country of origin: USA
Native language: English
Foreign language: Spanish
Lived in Japan for 3 years
Current residence: USA
Identifies as:
Working class, feminist, lesbian,
hippie, mother, student

Profile

Regina Rowland, Doctoral Student
California Institute of Integral Studies
Summer 2005

Purpose for collecting data:
This study's purpose is to solicit information about various ways of structuring information. It is the assumption that individuals might structure information differently depending on personal and/or cultural preferences. In addition, this pilot study allows for testing the used methodology.

Samples from:
SIIC participants and other volunteers.

Time frame:
Summer/Fall 2005

Application:
Data from this study will be used in Regina Rowland's preliminary dissertation research—which is about developing integrated visual language systems. Data from this study may also be used in potential articles and publications.

Procedure:
Participants will be fully informed of the nature of the project and the steps to completing participation. Before fulfilling any of the tasks participants will receive a copy of the consent form and will be asked to sign an attached consent form as well as give permission to the researcher to collect and use the data in the described formats. Thereafter participants will engage in representing five ideas/scenarios by using words, images, and symbols.

Confidentiality:
Participants' names or any other critical identity information will not be disclosed in any form when the data is presented. However, to make the study useful in regard to cultural frames, information which identifies the data as belonging to particular cultural groups will be subject to disclosure.

Time:
Up to 30 minutes.

Instructions:
"You will be asked to represent five ideas and/or scenarios with words, images, and symbols . The facilitator will be available to draw for you if you prefer, following your detailed instructions. In this research project we are interested in observing what kinds of imagery you come up with and how the elements on the page relate to each other. The activity will be followed by a debrief which will be taped with a tape recorder.

With this study we are not interested in evaluating the quality of the drawings in any way, only in the structure that you build, and how you represent ideas in a visual language. There is no right or wrong way of doing this. All solutions are informative and useful for this research. Thank you for your participation."

You have the right to have enough time to decide whether or not to be in the research study and to make that decision without any pressure from the researcher.

Your participation is voluntary with no obvious benefits to you, and without compensation.

You have the right to refuse to be in the study at all, to refuse to answer particular questions, to refuse to perform particular tasks and/or to discontinue at any time without needing to give an explanation.

You have the right to be informed about the nature and procedure of the study. With your signature you confirm that you understand the purpose of the study, your involvement, and how the data will be used. Your signature also represents your full consent as outlined below unless indicated otherwise.

Strict confidentiality in regard to names and critical identifying information about you and all participants will be held by Regina Rowland who will keep all project packages and tapes in her possession. However, data collected (anonymous drawings) may be used in research papers, dissertation, and publications with the potential disclosure of participants' age, gender, nationality, country of origin, countries of residence, culture, native and other spoken language(s).

You may request final outcome of this research project from the researcher:

Regina Rowland **[contact information withheld**
105 Carlotta Circle **for privacy]**
Mill Valley, CA 94941

If you have concerns or are dissatisfied at any time with any part of the study, please contact Regina Rowland's academic advisor—anonymously, if you wish:

Matthew Bronson **[contact information withheld**
California Institute of Integral Studies **for privacy]**
1453 Mission Street
San Francisco, CA 94103

You may also report your concerns—anonymously, if you wish—to:

Chair of the Human Research Review Committee **[contact information withheld**
California Institute of Integral Studies **for privacy]**
1453 Mission Street
San Francisco, CA 94103

Print Participant's Name: _____

Participant's Age: _____

Participant's Gender: _____

Participant's Nationality: _____

Participant's Country of Origin: _____

Additional Countries in which Participant has lived for a number of years:

_____

Participant's Native Language(s): _____

Participant's Foreign Language(s):_____

Participant's Current Domicile: _____

Participant's Cultural Frame(s) s/he identifies with:

_____

With the below given signature I consent to participate in the study of visual language conducted by Regina Rowland, doctoral student at the California Institute of Integral Studies. I have received a copy of this consent form, and I fully understand that my confidentiality will be protected within the limits of the law and as described above.

Signature of Participant: _____

Date: _____

With the below signature I give permission to Regina Rowland to publish the data collected. I understand that my name and other critical identifying information will be kept confidential in such circumstances.

Signature of Participant: _____

Date: _____

With the below signature I also give permission to Regina Rowland to tape the debrief and use the taped information to clarify research results.

Signature of Participant: _____

Date: _____

Please represent the following five ideas/scenarios on the supplied sheets.
You may use words, images, and/or symbols to do this.
If you don't want to draw feel free to ask the facilitator to draw for you.

1. Family

2. Love

3. School

4. Familiar Procedure
a). Choose something that you do on a regular basis, such as taking a shower,
b). baking a cake, washing a car, buying a flight ticket.
c). Generate a diagram of your chosen scenario (using words, images, and symbols).
d). Indicate below which procedure you chose to work with:

_____

5. Life Story
What have been critical moments or turning points in your life

APPENDIX E

RESEARCH INSTRUCTIONS FOR THIS STUDY

Research Project Participant Package

Title of Research Project:
The Co-Construction of Meaning
In The Multicultural Context
Via Group Dialogue and Visual Mapping Processes

Researcher:
Regina Rowland
Doctoral Student, California Institute of Integral Studies
Professor of Graphic Communications, City College of San Francisco
Senior Lecturer, California College of Arts
Intercultural Communication Practitioner • NLP Master Practitioner

This package includes:
Project Description & Procedure, Confidentiality & Data Storage
Participant Consent Form
Participant Release Form
Bill of Rights

Project Description & Procedure
This case study makes contributions to the disciplines of visual communication, intercultural communication, organizational development, and communication theories and practices at large, by attempting to address the question of the co-construction of meaning in the multicultural context via group dialogue and visual mapping processes. The intended audiences for this study include educators, instructional designers, trainers, organizational development professionals and communication practitioners. Specifically, this study speaks to audience members who are interested in learning how meaning is co-created in multicultural groups which is an important aspect for the design and facilitation of effective collaborative learning across cultures through group dialogue and visual mapping processes.

This case study involves human research subjects from a beginning level design class at City College of San Francisco (Department of Graphic Communications), in particular GRPH21 Visual Literacy Online/Hybrid. The main data will be collected on April 14, 2007, which is a regular face-to-face class day with the topic of Creativity and Ideation Processes for Designers. There are several aspects to data collection as listed below. Data will be handled and used as described in the consent form.

Prior to Data Collection Day
Inventories taken by individual participants
a) The Hammer Bennett Intercultural Developmental Inventory, version 2 (IDI-2)
measuring the position of participants' developmental stage from ethnocentricity (denial, defense, minimization) to ethnorelativity (acceptance, adaptation, integration) PS: This inventory will be taken during any face-to-face class time prior to data collection day
b) The Peterson Cultural Style Indicator (PCSI)
measuring participants cultural styles locating themselves compared to other cultures (equality/hierarchy preferences, direct/indirect communication style, individual/group orientation,

risk/caution preferences) PS: This inventory will be taken during any face-to-face class time prior to data collection day

c) The Forrester/Drexler Team Performance Indicator
measuring the participants' perception in regard to the perceived stage of their team development (orientation, trust building, goal clarification, commitment, implementation, high performance, renewal) PS: This inventory will be taken during the face-to-face class meeting directly prior to data collection day

On Data Collection Day

Participants will work in small groups (preferably in the teams in which they have been working in class so far). The groups will be asked to co-construct a story with provided materials to be placed on a large wall space four by eight feet. The major theme for the story will be prompted by a question. Materials for construction will be provided as components of a visual language system (images, symbols, opportunities to create words such as press-0n type and markers). This collaborative activity and the concluding large group debrief will be videotaped. This part of the process is considered the group dialogue and will be analyzed with Barnett Pearce's Coordinated Management of Meaning (CMM).* The visual representations created by the teams will be considered visual maps and will be analyzed for form and content/syntax and semantics. This project fully aligns with the class content for that particular day.

Groups will work in rotation so that the researcher can focus on each team's process. A research assistant will videotape each team's process. The rest of the class will be engaged in other similar creative activities that align with the topic of the class content and will be facilitated by another faculty member (Amy Conger).

*CMM is a theory and method that is used to understand, describe and critique the co-construction of social realities of people in dialogue.

After Data Collection Day

Some participants will be individually interviewed (videotaped) to further describe and clarify their personal experiences participating in this group process.

Field notes will supplement all data throughout the semester and on data collection day (journals written by researcher and research assistant).

Confidentiality & Data Storage

The outcome of this project will be summarized in the researcher's dissertation, potential publications, and a video documentary. While names will be changed in all materials in order to protect participants' privacy, cultural information is crucial for this study and may be disclosed unless otherwise requested.

Throughout the study the researcher will use a lockable cabinet to store data in her home. Only she will have a key to the cabinet. Names of participants will be changed in the data interpretation with a master list that will be stored in a safety deposit box at Wells Fargo Bank. Eventually, all data and peripheral materials will be stored in a safety deposit box at Wells Fargo Bank until one year after the research process is complete which ends with the completion of Regina Rowland's dissertation. All materials and data will be properly destroyed.

Group dialogues and individual interviews will be videotaped and handled by the research assistant, Julie Gieseke, for purposes of digitizing video footage, and by professionals for transcription purposes. After working with the materials, video footage will be kept in a safety deposit box at Wells Fargo Bank and destroyed one year after the project is complete.

The researcher would also like to obtain permission to produce a documentary about this research project and its outcomes to be used for instructional purposes. A separate release form will give permission to have participants featured in this documentary video. Confidentiality will be handled as described above. All video documentary materials will be stored for ten years in a safety deposit box and properly destroyed thereafter.

Participant Consent Form

You have the right to have enough time to decide whether or not to be in this research study and to make that decision without any pressure from the researcher, Regina Rowland, who is also your instructor in this introductory design class GRPH21 Visual Literacy. If you decide not to participate in this study, you can still fully participate in this class and engage in similar creativity activities during the day of data collection, April 14. You will receive a complete Research Project Participant Package (the one that you are reading now) which you may keep for your personal use.

Your participation is voluntary with no benefits to you and without compensation. Participation will not be rewarded in any way or form. Likewise non-participation will not be punished in any way or form.

You have the right to refuse to be in the study at all, to refuse to answer particular questions, to refuse to perform particular tasks and/or to discontinue at any time without needing to give an explanation.

You have the right to be informed about the nature and procedure of the study, how data is handled, and how confidentiality is promised. These issues are covered in this package.

With your signature you confirm that you understand the purpose of the study, your involvement, and how the data will be used and stored. Your signature also represents your full consent as outlined below unless indicated otherwise.

You may request final outcome of this research project from the researcher:
Regina Rowland
[contact information withheld for privacy]

If you have concerns or are dissatisfied at any time with any part of the study, please contact Regina Rowland's academic advisor—anonymously, if you wish:
Matthew Bronson
California Institute of Integral Studies
1453 Mission Street
San Francisco, CA 94103

You may also report your concerns—anonymously, if you wish—to:
Chair of the Human Research Review Committee
California Institute of Integral Studies
1453 Mission Street
San Francisco, CA 94103

You may also report your concerns—anonymously, if you wish—to:
Vice Chancellor of Institutional Advancement
City College of San Francisco
50 Phelan Ave
San Francisco, CA 94112

Although it is not the intent of this case study to cause discomfort, albeit, if you experience any discomfort that arises from participation in this study and in the case this discomfort requires the attention of a healthcare professional, please make an appointment with a licensed healthcare professional at City College of San Francisco Student Health Services/Psychological Services. As a student currently enrolled at CCSF, this service is free of charge to you:

Student Health Services   **415 239 3148**
City College of San Francisco   **HC100 (location)**
50 Phelan Ave
San Francisco, CA 94112

Print Participant's Name: _____

Participant's Age _____

Participant's Gender _____

Participant's Nationality(ies): _____

Participant's Country of Origin _____

Additional Countries in which Participant has lived for a number of years (how many?):

_____

_____

_____

_____

Participant's Native Language(s): _____

Participant's Foreign Language(s): _____

Participant's Current Residence (City/Country):

_____

How much time at the Current Residence: _____ (months, years)

Participant's Cultural Frame(s) s/he identifies with: _____

Participant's current contact (address, e-mail, phone number):

_____

_____

_____

_____

With the below given signature I consent to participate in the study of the Co-Construction of Meaning conducted by Regina Rowland during the Spring Semester 2007 at City College of San Francisco in the GRPH 21 Visual Literacy class. I understand that this research project is Regina Rowland's doctoral work at the California Institute of Integral Studies. I understand that my confidentiality will be protected within the limits of the law and as described above.

I have received a copy of this Research Project Participant Package which includes both the consent and release forms, and the Bill of Rights. I understand that I can choose to withdraw from my participation at any time without having to give reasons and without any repercussions whatsoever.

Signature of Participant: _____

Date: _____

With the below signature I give permission to Regina Rowland to publish the data collected. I understand that my name and other critical identifying information will be kept confidential in such circumstances.

Signature of Participant: _____

Date: _____

With the below signature I also give permission to Regina Rowland to videotape or audiotape all activities relating to this research and to use the taped information to clarify research results.

Signature of Participant: _____

Date: _____

Model Release Form

Date:_____

Videographers/Photographers: Regina Rowland (researcher) and Julie Gieseke (research assistant)
Address at City College of San Francisco:
Department of Graphic Communications
50 Phelan Avenue
Mailbox: V52
San Francisco, CA 94112

For valuable consideration, I hereby irrevocably consent to and authorize the use and reproduction by you, or anyone authorized by you, of any and all video footage and photographs which you have this day taken of me, for any purpose whatsoever without further compensation to me. All video footage and photographs together with the prints shall constitute your property, solely and completely.

I am over 18 years of age Yes _____ No _____

Name of Model: _____

Signature of Model: _____

Address of Model: _____

Witnessed by:

Name _____

Signature_____

Bill of Rights for Participants in Research

You have the right to...

- be treated with dignity and respect;

- be given a clear description of the purpose of the study and what is expected of you as a participant;

- be told of any benefits or risks to you that can be expected from participating in the study;

- know the researcher's training and experience;

- ask any questions you may have about the study;

- decide to participate or not without any pressure from the researcher or his or her assistants;

- have your privacy protected within the limits of the law;

- refuse to answer any research question, refuse to participate in any part of the study, or withdraw from the study at any time without any negative effects to you;

- be given a description of the overall results of the study with the Human Research Review Committee, California Institute of Integral Studies, 1453 Mission Street, San Francisco, CA 94103.

April 14, Saturday, 10:00 AM – 2:00 PM — Data Collection Day
Sample Instruction Sheet

Time, Duration, Facilitators:
Data collection will take 4 hours maximum as part of the class events. This is a regular class day with the topic *Creativity and Ideation Processes for Designers.* Students will be engaged in a variety of creative activities that are co-facilitated by Regina Rowland and Amy Conger, City College of San Francisco professors in the Graphic Communications Department. The group activity subject to this research will be facilitated by Regina Rowland who will work with each team separately in rotation. A research assistant, Julie Gieseke, will be videotaping the sessions. All students (including those who choose not to participate in the research project) will be engaged in all other creative activities on a rotating basis (work stations) which will be facilitated by Amy Conger.

Data Collection Procedure
At the beginning of class the research project details and participants' rights are reviewed by re-reading this packet aloud with the students present. Signatures will be collected. (This is the same packet that has been handed out previously).

Teams will then be working on creative activities in rotation and throughout the class. Relating to the research project following procedures will be repeated with each team:

Step 1:
For the next five minutes please reflect on your decision to study at City College and consider:
What is your story?
Why are you here?
And what is your experience of being part of the CCSF community?

Step 2:
Please collaborate with your team on generating a story that captures the City College experience
(narrative structure, could be true or not, could have imaginary characters or real persons).

Step 3:
Represent your team's story on a large-scale visual map.
You have at your disposal a large wall space (4 x 6 feet), large paper panel, the elements of visual
language (images, shapes, words), and a time frame of 30 minutes total to construct your story
visually.

After both teams have constructed their visual maps we will come together as a class and have each
team present their story. We will call this the "gallery walk". Following the gallery walk we will
have an all-class discussion about the process. We will call this class discussion "large group
debrief", and we will be using a format called the "Six-Step Debrief Frame".

Step 4 (Each Team):
Spend five minutes and decide as a team how you will perform this task:
Take us through your visual map and tell your team story in ten minutes or less.

INSTRUCTIONS FOR DATA COLLECTION

Instructions
Data Collection on April 14, Saturday, 10:00am-2:00pm

Research Project:
The Co-Construction of Meaning in the Multicultural Context Via Group Dialogue and Visual Mapping Processes

Researcher:
Regina Rowland
Doctoral Student, California Institute of International Studies
Professor of Graphic Communications, City College of San Francisco
Senior Lecturer, California College of Arts
Intercultural Communication Practitioner • NLP Master Practitioner

Subjects:
Students in GRPH 21 Visual Literacy class at CCSF

Step 1:
For the next five minutes please reflect on your decision to study at City College and consider:
What is your story?
Why are you here?
And what is your experience of being part of the CCSF community?

Step 2:
Please collaborate with your team on generating a story that captures the City College experience (narrative structure, could be true or not, could have imaginary characters or real persons).

Step 3:
Represent your team's story on a large-scale visual map.
You have at your disposal a large wall space (4 x 6 feet), large paper panel, the elements of visual language (images, shapes, words), and a time frame of 30 minutes total to construct your story visually.

After both teams have constructed their visual maps we will come together as a class and have each team present their story. We will call this the "gallery walk". Following the gallery walk we will have an all-class discussion about the process. We will call this class discussion "large group debrief", and we will be using a format called the "Six-Step Debrief Frame".

Step 4 (Each Team):
Spend five minutes and decide as a team how you will perform this task:
Take us through your visual map and tell your team story in ten minutes or less.

SIX STEP DEBRIEF FRAME

The Six Step Debrief Frame:

1. How do you feel?
2. What happened?
3. What did you learn?
4. How does what you learned relate to real life?
5. What if?
6. What next?

The Six Step Debrief Frame with prompts:

How do you feel?
> Potential prompts:
> How do you feel after having worked with your team on this task?
> Was this a fun process?
> Are you satisfied with your team's work?
> How do you feel about the collaborative aspect?

What happened?
> Potential prompts:
> How did you decide on a particular story line?
> How did you decide which visual language elements to use?
> How did you decide which composition to construct for your story?
> Where did you start with your story on the blank map space?

What did you learn?
> Potential prompts:
> What was confirmed/revealed to you about yourself and your teammates in this process?
> What significant group dynamics did you notice in your team?
> Do you think that working in homogenous rather than multicultural groups would have been different?
> If so, how different specifically?
> If at all, which parts/events of this teamwork would you classify as "culturally conditioned"?
> What is the story behind your or your team's story?
> Did you find any commonalities between your own personal story and those of your teammates?
> What else did you notice/learn that might be of interest?

How does what you learned relate to real life?
> Potential prompts:
> Are there any particularly interesting aspects of the group dynamics that you observed during this process? If so where else in your personal or professional life would they also apply and/or be important to remember?

What if?

      Potential prompts:

      What difference would it have made to have you draw your elements rather than provide the materials to be used to construct your visual map?

      What difference would it have made to have other people on the team?

      What would have been different if we had had larger or smaller groups?

      How would it have turned out differently if you had worked alone ?

What next?

      Potential prompts:

      How will what you learned today (about the process, the group dynamics, yourself, or your teammates) make a difference in your personal or professional life?

SAMPLE INTERVIEW QUESTIONS FOR PERSONAL INTERVIEWS

Time, Duration, Facilitators:

After data collection day (April 14), the researcher will decide who to interview personally to further clarify group dynamics. If necessary all participants will be interviewed. Sessions will be videotaped or audio recorded. Some personal information will already be known to the researcher from the inventories and signed consent forms (e.g. nationality, languages, age, gender, etc.).

Potential Interview Questions:

Please tell your personal story about deciding to study at City College.

What is your experience as a student at City College?

What is your experience working with different cultures?

How do you identify culturally?

How did you feel after the in-class group process?

In your opinion, what happened during that process?

Are you satisfied with your own participation?

Are you satisfied with the team collaboration?

What significant group dynamics did you notice in your team?

What was confirmed/revealed to you about yourself and your team mates in this process?

How did your team decide on a particular story line?

How is this story the same and/or different than what you personally would have told?

Did you find any commonalities between your own personal story and those of your teammates?

What does your team's story mean?

What is the story behind your team's story?

How did your team decide which visual language elements to use?

How did your team decide which visual structure/composition to use for your story?

Where did you start with your story on the blank map space?

If at all, which parts/events of this teamwork would you classify as "culturally conditioned"?

What else did you notice that might be of interest?

How would you describe this process to a friend who was not present?

Would you participate in such a research project again?

APPENDIX I

THE TEAM PERFORMANCE MODEL (TPM)

The TPM and its accompanying instrument, the TPI, are based on the theory of process, which is an integral theory/hypothesis about human evolution merging scientific findings with the spiritual realm (Young, 1976a, 1976b). The TPM also developed out of the four interdependent concerns of team development tasks: acceptance, data, goal formation, and control (Bradford, Gibb, & Benne, 1964, as discussed by Drexler & Sibbet, 2004).

Visually and conceptually, the TPM follows the theory of process arc describing the development of teams from freedom to constraint and back toward freedom as issues are dissolved and constraints are mastered (see Figure 51). In the TPM arc, the movement goes down to the bottom line (action) and up to the top line (awareness). Freedom is gained through learning and developing consciousness of the process via creativity and via building and overcoming constraints through discipline and practice. The freedom/constraint pattern moves through the four different aspects of reality identified by the theory of process (The Grove, 1999). *Process* is an eternal dance between freedom and constraint, order and disorder, and entropy and negentropy. Process is basically an interrelationship between certainty and uncertainty that each team has to master in order to perform well (The Grove, 2003).

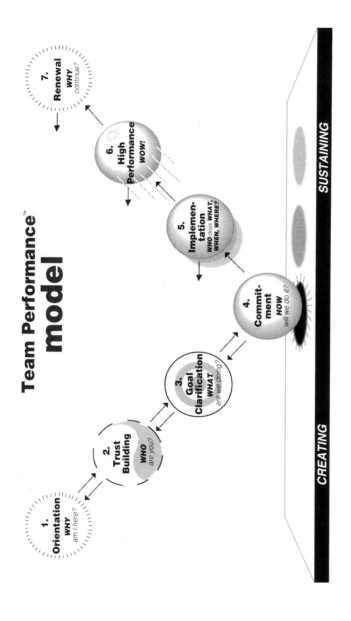

Figure 51. The Drexler/Sibbet team performance model (TPM). From *Drexler/Sibbet Team Performance Model* [Brochure], by The Grove Consultants International, 1999, San Francisco: Author. Reprinted with permission of the author.

THE LEARNING STYLES (LS) INVENTORY

"IT'S NOT HOW SMART YOU ARE…IT'S *HOW* YOU'RE SMART" (LeFabre)

Learning Styles Inventory

What is a preferred learning style? Learning styles are simply different approaches to learning. If your learning style and the professor's teaching style are vastly different it could mean the difference how much you learn in a class and/or in the grade you receive. Below is a short learning styles inventory. There are many other learning style survey instruments on the internet as well as good information on multiple intelligences.

****

Read each statement carefully. To the left of each statement, write the code that best describes how each statement applies to you.

Answer honestly as there are no correct or incorrect answers. It is best if you do not think about each question too long, as this could lead you to the wrong conclusion.

SECTION 1

PLACE EITHER AN AE OR A RO NEXT TO THE STATEMENT BELOW, DEPENDING UPON WHICH PART OF THE STATEMENT MOST CLOSELY DESCRIBES YOU.

1. _____ (AE) — I often produce off-the-cuff ideas that at first might seem silly or half-baked.
   (RO) — I am thorough and methodical.

2. _____ (AE) — I am normally the one who initiates conversations.
   (RO) — I enjoy watching people.

3. _____ (AE) — I am flexible and open-minded.
   (RO) — I am careful and cautious.

4. _____ (AE) — I like to try new and different things without too much preparation.
   (RO) — I investigate a new topic or process in depth before trying it.

5. _____ (AE) — I am happy to have a go at new things.
   (RO) — I draw up lists up possible courses of actions when starting a new project.

6. _____ (AE) — I like to get involved and to participate.
   (RO) — I like to read and observe.

7. _____ (AE) — I am loud and outgoing.
   (RO) — I and quite and somewhat shy.

8. _____ (AE) — I make quick and bold decisions.
   (RO) — I make cautious and logical decisions.

9. _____ (AE) — I speak slowly, after thinking.
        (RO) — I speak fast, while thinking.

        TOTAL OF AES: _____.
        TOTAL OF ROS: _____.

        THE ONE THAT HAS THE LARGER NUMBER IS YOUR TASK PREFERENCE.

SECTION 2

PLACE EITHER AN AC OR A CE NEXT TO THE STATEMENT BELOW, DEPENDING UPON WHICH PART OF THE STATEMENT MOST CLOSELY DESCRIBES YOU.

1. _____ (AC) — I ask probing questions when learning a new subject.
        (CE) — I am good at picking up hints and techniques from other people.

2. _____ (AC) — I am rational and logical.
        (CE) — I am practical and down to earth.

3. _____ (AC) — I plan events down to the last detail.
        (CE) — I like realistic, but flexible plans.

4. _____ (AC) — I like to know the right answers before trying something new.
        (CE) — I try things out by practicing to see if they work.

5. _____ (AC) — I analyze reports to find the basic assumptions and inconsistencies.
        (CE) — I rely upon others to give me the basic gist of reports.

6. _____ (AC) — I prefer working alone.
        (CE) — I enjoy working with others.

7. _____ (AC) — Others would describe me as serious, reserved, and formal.
        (CE) — Others would describe me as verbal, expressive, and informal.

8. _____ (AC) — I use facts to make decisions.
        (CE) — I use feelings to make decisions.

9. _____ (AC) — I am difficult to get to know.
        (CE) — I am easy to get to know.

        TOTAL OF ACS: _____.
        TOTAL OF CES: _____.

        THE ONE THAT HAS THE LARGER NUMBER IS YOUR THOUGHT OR EMOTIONAL PREFERENCE.
        SCORING PROCEDURES

EACH PREFERENCE (HIGH SCORE) FROM THE TWO ABOVE SECTIONS ARE USED TO DETERMING YOUR LEARNING STYLE:
        _____ AE   _____ CE   _____ RO   _____ AC

319

If you are an **AE** and **CE** then you are a	If you are a **RO** and **CE** then you are a	If you are a **RO** and **AC** then you are a	If you are an **AE** and **AC** then you are a
Doer/Planer	**Watcher**	**Thinker**	**"Sensor"/Feeler**
Concrete Experience and Active Experimentation	*Reflective Observation and Concrete Experience*	*Abstract Conceptualization and Reflective Observation*	*Abstract Conceptualization and Active Experimentation*

Remember:
EVERYONE LEARNS IN ALL FOUR STYLES!
YOU NORMALLY LEARN BEST BY STARTING IN AND USING ONE STYLE THE MOST!
THIS INVENTORY IS MEANT AS A SNAPSHOT IN TIME – IT CAN & WILL CHANGE OVER TIME!

Self-Assessment Form from Dr. Jackie Rezza, CCSF Multicultural Infusion Project Consultant. Reprinted with permission of the author.

THE MULTIPLE INTELLIGENCES (MI) QUESTIONNAIRE

Read each statement. Write 0 if you disagree. Write 2 if you agree. Write 1 if you are somewhere in between. Total the number of points you have in each intelligence. Compare your scores. Which score is the highest (strongest intelligence)? Which is the lowest (weakest intelligence)?

```
0 = disagree
1 = somewhere in between
2 = agree
```

Linguistic Intelligence
___ 1. I like to write papers and articles.
___ 2. Almost everyday, I read something just for pleasure.
___ 3. I often listen to the news on the radio or to cassettes of lectures, books, etc.
___ 4. I read billboards and advertisements.
___ 5. When I read stories, I create clear images about the characters and places in my mind.
___ 6. I use illustrations, charts, posters, and quotations frequently to add information to the papers I write.
___ 7. If I hear a song or a commercial jingle a few times, I can usually remember the words.
___ 8. I am a good letter writer.
___ 9. I encourage others to spend time reading and writing.
___ 10. I have written something that I like.

Logical/Mathematical Intelligence
___ 1. I feel more comfortable believing an answer is correct when it has been measured, calculated, or demonstrated in some way.
___ 2. I can calculate numbers easily in my head.
___ 3. I like my classes to be consistent with rules, routines, assignments, and other expectations clearly stated.
___ 4. I like playing games such as hearts, bridge, gin rummy, chess, or checkers.
___ 5. I like or have liked math classes in school
___ 6. I believe that most things have logical and rational explanations.
___ 7. I like brainteaser games.
___ 8. I am interested in new developments in the sciences.
___ 9. I am good a solving problems.
___ 10. I like to measure things exactly.

Visual/Spatial Intelligence

___ 1. I pay attention to the colors I wear.

___ 2. I pay attention to the colors others wear.

___ 3. I like to use visual aids in the classes I teach.

___ 4. I like to draw.

___ 5. I like to read articles containing many charts and illustrations.

___ 6. I prefer textbooks with illustrations, graphs, charts, and pictures.

___ 7. I like doing puzzles and mazes.

___ 8. I notice the seating arrangement in a room almost immediately.

___ 9. It is easy for me to find my way around unfamiliar cities.

___ 10. I like to take photographs on trips and vacations.

Bodily/Kinesthetic Intelligence

___ 1. Many of my hobbies involve some form of physical activity.

___ 2. I like to use activities in my classes that require students to get out of their seats and move around.

___ 3. I find it difficult to sit for long periods of time.

___ 4. I like to be involved in many forms of outdoor activities.

___ 5. I often get my best ideas when I am jogging, walking, or doing other physical activities.

___ 6. When learning a new skill, I have to actually try it out in order to absorb it.

___ 7. I like doing things that involve working with my hands.

___ 8. I participate or have participated in one or more sports.

___ 9. I like to dance.

___ 10. I like to go on rides at amusement and theme parks.

Interpersonal Intelligence

___ 1. I like to listen to other people's ideas.

___ 2. I try to incorporate others' ideas into my own thinking.

___ 3. I would prefer going to a party with strangers over spending the evening alone.

___ 4. I like to discuss my problems with my friends.

___ 5. My friends often seek help from me in solving their problems.

___ 6. I like to entertain friends and give parties.

___ 7. I like to meet new people.

___ 8. I like to teach others how to do things.

___ 9. I consider myself to have strong leadership qualities.

___ 10. I frequently assume leadership roles and related positions.

Intrapersonal Intelligence

___ 1. I often spend time reflecting on things that have happened in my life.

___ 2. I plan for quiet time in my life.

___ 3. I consider myself to be independent and not necessarily swayed by the opinions of others.

___ 4. I keep a personal journal and record my thoughts and activities.

___ 5. I prefer to study and learn new material on my own.

___ 6. When hurt or disappointed, I find that I bounce back quickly.

___ 7. I can articulate the primary values that govern my life.

___ 8. I prefer to generate my own methods and procedures for learning new materials.

___ 9. I often create new activities and materials to supplement my classes.

___ 10. I have hobbies and interests that I enjoy doing on my own.

Musical Intelligence

___ 1. I have a very expressive voice when I am in front of a class or in other groups.

___ 2. I often incorporate music or chants into my lesson plans.

___ 3. I can tell if someone is singing off-key.

___ 4. I know the melodies to many different songs.

___ 5. When I listen to music, I have no difficulty identifying or following the rhythm.

___ 6. If I hear a new song a couple of times, I can usually remember the melody.

___ 7. I often sing in the shower.

___ 8. I frequently listen to music.

___ 9. Listening to music makes me feel good.

___ 10. When I hear a piece of music, I can harmonize with it easily.

Naturalist Intelligence

___ 1. I like to be outdoors.

___ 2. I like to observe what is happening around me when I am outdoors.

___ 3. I like to hike and camp outdoors.

___ 4. I know the names of many different plants.

___ 5. I know the names of and can describe most of the plants and animals in my neighborhood.

___ 6. I like or have liked biological and life science courses in school.

___ 7. I support ecologists' efforts to preserve our environment.

___ 8. Knowledge of the world and how it works is important to me.

___ 9. I often look at the sky and can recognize different types of clouds and the weather they bring.

___ 10. I believe that all natural phenomena can be studied and explained.

From M. A. Christison, *Multiple Intelligences and Language Learning*, 2005, pp. 349–350, San Francisco: Alta Book Center. Reprinted with permission of the publisher.

APPENDIX L

THE INQUIRER

As the particulars of my own layers of complexity inevitably inform my research, in this appendix I provide background information on myself and my bias, so that my results may be viewed from a more complete perspective—as is customary for transdisciplinary research. As can be seen from Figure 52, my lens provided the third vanishing point to the construction of the metaphorical research space.

Half of my life I spent in Europe, Austria in particular, with some work and study experience in France, England, and Italy. For the other half I have been living in the United States, about equally split between the east and west coasts. I have always enjoyed working with cultures other than my own, a passion that grew out of my living in a mixed neighborhood in Vienna during my childhood years. I was fascinated by the many different colors, languages, customs, sounds, and smells that surrounded and enriched my life. As an only child of parents who both worked very hard to make a living, I often had to entertain myself and did so by creating my own fantasy world and by making things that one could appreciate as art—a form of meaning-making.

My mother worked at a factory where they produced film cameras, the only ones in all of Austria, and she often brought the equipment home to try something out. This put me in touch with moving images, the sound of film running through the projector, the smell of burned plastic when it melted on its way through, the feel of cutting and gluing filmstrips together to recreate new stories, and the idea of observing the world in frames. I still see life this way, as a pastiche of framed opportunities that can be cut and pasted at will, recombined, restructured, and viewed through a kaleidoscopic looking glass—thus my fascination with diagrams and frozen moments on complex maps. One can be the artist of one's fate as well as simply observe it running by in motion, occasionally stopping at particular frames to take score. This belief keeps me flexible, optimistic, creatively engaged in life, and interested in ever-new combinations and shifting patterns, an ideal backdrop to the contributions I am interested in making to the world.

My education includes several disciplines and occurred in a nonlinear but intuitively connected sequence. I followed what I was most interested in at the time without thinking of the consequences of not following a more traditional (linear) career path, such as not fitting a prescribed setting or having to explain my path to the world for the rest of my life. Examining my professional development through the four-quadrant viewfinder reveals different aspects of the circular journey I experienced (see Figure 53).

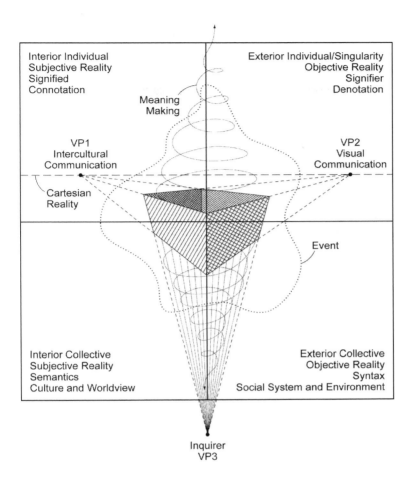

Interior Individual
Subjective Reality
Signified
Connotation

Exterior Individual/Singularity
Objective Reality
Signifier
Denotation

Meaning
Making

VP1
Intercultural
Communication

VP2
Visual
Communication

Cartesian
Reality

Event

Interior Collective
Subjective Reality
Semantics
Culture and Worldview

Exterior Collective
Objective Reality
Syntax
Social System and Environment

Inquirer
VP3

Figure 52. The metaphorical research space seen through the four-quadrant viewfinder, with the focus on the inquirer at vanishing point (VP) three. Author's image; four-quadrant grid based partly on concepts from *The Integral Operating System* [compact disc set and booklet], by K. Wilber, 2005, Boulder, CO: Sounds True.

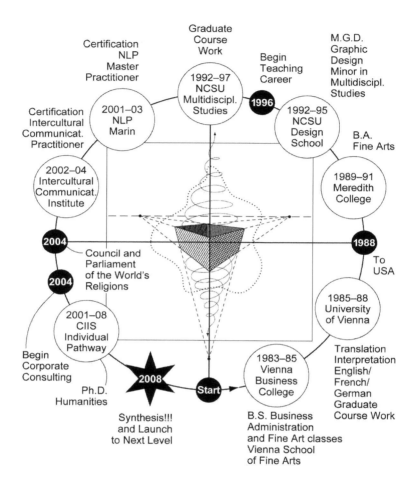

Figure 53. My educational path, seen through the four-quadrant viewfinder, showing how the different facets of my professional development led me to the investigation of this particular metaphorical research space. NCSU = North Carolina State University; MGD = M.A. in Graphic Design; NLP = neurolinguistic programming; CIIS = California Institute of Integral Studies. Author's image.

I started in the lower right quadrant (objective reality, systems) with a very structured education that focused also on building relationships between areas of study, as is the case in a classic European education. In Vienna, I studied fine art, languages, and business, and I came to the US with a B.S. in Business Administration, half an M.A. in interpretation and translation (English, French, German), and some fine art credits.

Once in the US, my focus turned to art and design and I moved through the upper right quadrant (objective reality) learning concepts and acquiring skills in a very focused manner while looking at disciplines in isolation, one step at a time. I acquired a B.A. in Fine Arts and an M.A. in Graphic Design. Being an immigrant to the US and surviving two years of culture shock highlighted my interest in culture and increased my sensitivity and desire to connect across cultures. I became familiar with the outgroup experience, and because of this I began seeing things from an observer position that I would certainly have missed had I been central to the action (which would have matched my personality better). My love for art-making and for creatively building concepts from complex ideas also intensified in the US because of the absence of intellectual engagement with the general US public. In Europe, I was comfortable with bars and coffeehouses as intellectual hothouses, which satisfied much of my curiosity. But in the US, initially, I had a hard time finding people and thought partners (university included) who were interested in thinking about thinking or creating for the fun of it. My European education had been more rigorous and was broader than what I found to be true in the US, which led me to become an educator.

Next, I added graduate level multidisciplinary studies to my repertoire, to fill a void I noticed in my intellectual realm. Opening my lens to other disciplines pushed me over the threshold into the area of subjective reality of the individual (upper left quadrant), in particular psychology and philosophy. These new disciplines nicely complemented my teaching and my design practice by adding new capacities to understand myself and others. When I moved to California, a whole new world opened up, and I felt that I was missing the intercultural and interpersonal communication skills to be fully effective in this new world of many cultures.

Beginning my doctoral level work introduced me to new concepts and ideas that caused me to seek additional training and certification paralleling my Ph.D. studies, all of which transformed my teaching practice to the benefit of my students and my own personal growth. I studied to become a certified intercultural communication practitioner and a certified NLP master practitioner. My increased awareness and understanding of cultural differences encouraged me to transform my teaching practice to that of critical pedagogy. Various other coursework brought me to graphic facilitation, coaching, and consulting.

I became a facilitator of learning experiences in the business world as well. Once I stepped into corporate and organizational consulting, my capacities and experiences started to synergize in a magical way, and I fully explored the lower left quadrant (subjective collective, cultural), which my Ph.D. work wonderfully enriched. My university education culminated with the Ph.D. this project completed.

Thus all my previous academic and professional endeavors came full circle, also nicely wrapping around the metaphorical research space I explored in my doctoral work. Drawing this map confirmed that I am currently closing an entire tier of development, poised for the next level (which is really a leap toward full integration and, consequently, transcendence of my previous self). Different layers of spiritual development opened at various points during the last twenty years, and doors to several spiritual practices revolved. However, this study is largely aligned with the two disciplines it addresses, neither of which acknowledges spirituality as an aspect in the human core, and spirituality therefore is purposefully omitted from the discussion in spite of playing a major role in integral theory.

I participate in various professions and I like this pastiche of activities—in fact, it is what feeds my intellect and enthusiasm. I teach, make art and create, facilitate, consult, train, design processes, work with people one on one and in groups, am a social activist, and am a visual thought partner. For example, I collaborate with writers to help them see what they mean by conceptualizing and transforming their concepts into visual form. I love to travel and will hop to Bangkok on an assignment in a heartbeat, which makes me a flexible and accommodating partner for any organic endeavor but can present a challenge to people who prefer a structured, more linear approach.

To me, the connections are crystal clear between all I am involved in among my areas of expertise and passion. My work has taken me to different urban settings in the US, as well as to Europe, Africa, the Middle East, and Asia. Being immersed in different places and cultures around the world is not unlike the film clips I remember from my childhood—sometimes more immersed emotionally, other times taking the observer role, but all of it falling together into one beautiful pattern of expressions of life. At my core, however, I am solidly grounded in a European frame with some flexibility in stepping in and out of it as needed and desirable.

In this research I was looking for communication patterns emerging from observed group dynamics and visual maps. In particular, I was paying special attention to cultural patterns expressed in visual form. It needs to be acknowledged that my lens most certainly was Western, more specifically Middle European and Viennese (a center of immigrants streaming from all directions). In addition, the theories, analytical methods, tools, and instruments for interpreting and analyzing the data all used Western lenses (and were, for the most part, developed by male members of the dominant culture) as is the norm in the fields relative to this study. These Western approaches thus controlled, to some extent, what I was able to pay attention to beyond my own lens.

Other blind spots and assumptions such as those inherent in the disciplines and professions in which I participate certainly all have had influence upon my interpretations. For instance, I consider creative engagement—any creative activity—worthwhile even if the outcome is not clear or the activity not lucrative. The blind spots from my focus on art and creativity would thus be couched in assuming that all people are creative and want to exercise their creativity, and that it is my job to facilitate it.

I am sensitive to cultural and social justice issues, and because of my experience and culture training will tend to pay close attention to the basic underlying assumptions that drive behavior, often resulting in uncovering issues of dominance. Politically I fall on the left, and my idea of how to run a business is focused on the wellbeing of the human race at large rather than on having certain groups' interests at the center of the enterprise. Therefore, I may not consider valuable options if they look suspicious to me as benefiting certain groups over others and/or if they don't serve the larger purpose of assisting the evolution of humanity. This does not mean that I do not want to make money, or that I have a problem with people making money, but I personally prefer to do so by keeping my larger goal on target. In change work, I believe the responsibility falls upon both the individual and the system, which translates into exposing multiple points of view rather than walking down one path.

As an experienced NLP Master Practitioner, it is hard for me not to reframe negative experiences when they are expressed, and I instinctively offer a reframe often not noticeable by the receiver. In this sense I follow a positivist approach, which causes me to deny or choose to ignore negativity and usually to find an upside to focus on. With this issue I deviate from my European frame, which tends to focus on the critical aspects.

As the teacher for the participants in this study, it is possible that I may have contaminated the data interpretation with assumptions I built about participants and teams throughout the semester. Students often surprise me. I have experienced more than once that a student exposed capacities I did not know she had until she arrived at a certain point of understanding and then took off from there like a rocket—when I might already have given up on her. Likewise, I have caught myself in stereotyping about a certain learning style or behavior that I considered cultural, which then was revised by getting to know the student better. I have become aware that my preferred experiential teaching style matches my information processing and preference for ambiguity, and that this approach is not comfortable for people who like more clarity and structure before they begin a task. I consciously attempt to walk around the Kolb Wheel in my teaching to address all learning styles, sometimes more successfully than other times.

When I began this study, I was aligned with intercultural communication theories and practices (and their blind spots), and this inquiry involved to a great extent a rethinking of those frames. I now believe that a new generation of transculturalists is emerging who will lead a rethinking of all disciplines. This rethinking would be well supported by transdisciplinary methods. Although visual communication does have its blind spots, as discussed above, I do not believe I shared them at the time of this inquiry, having been aware of them for many years.

My perception is that of synesthesia and leads to holistic, lateral thinking. I tend to experience my world as one interconnected and interrelated unit, and I find it difficult to separate the whole into its parts. I am a big-picture visionary who gets excited very easily about opportunities and possibilities, but I have little tolerance or patience for the details. The California Institute of Integral Studies (CIIS) provided a perfect home for my divergent thinking style, which resulted in noticing the threads between disciplinary gaps, as well as for my preference for active experimentation. Given the fact that CIIS is an institution of integral education it is not surprising that my research project became a transdisciplinary study applying integral theory as a frame to hold it all together. The individual pathway program at CIIS provided much freedom for the collection of coursework that prepared me for this project, and for the structure of this dissertation. In addition, my preference for social constructivist viewpoints was greatly supported and nurtured through the philosophy prevalent at CIIS.

The transdisciplinary approach to this research project perfectly matched my thinking style and who I have become. I learned through the process and was changed because of it, which further altered the process and set me on another learning curve, and so forth. I turned the content of this project upside down several times and approached the subject from various angles in a nonlinear fashion. I am comfortable with the creative chaos of this methodology, with the ambiguity that many things remain unknown. In fact, I believe that the gap of the unknown or unknowable—the mystery—is also an area of knowledge that needs to be acknowledged in the disciplines. All these personal qualities contributed to my design and execution of this transdisciplinary inquiry.

As I ended this dissertation, I became highly aware of the potent transformative quality of this process for the researcher. As a transdisciplinarian, I feel pleasantly saturated with the disciplines I have visited, and feel excited to turn over a new leaf, integrating and maybe even transcending these disciplines in order to approach new territory yet to be built and create new stories yet to be told. With this excitement in mind I rush to the top of the mountain I have just finished climbing, and while looking around and enjoying the view I find myself—unexpectedly—reframing my life question from "What do I want to do in life?" to "What does life want from me?" (James Flaherty, personal communication, January 6, 2008). What a surprise!

California Institute of Integral Studies
Human Research Review Committee

March 5, 2007

Dear Regina Rowland,

Congratulations, the Human Research Review Committee (HRRC) has approved your research proposal.

This approval is in effect for one year from the date of this letter. Any changes to your proposal from this point forward must be approved by the Committee in advance. It is understood that HRRC approval of your research does not imply endorsement by CIIS of any treatments, products, or theories associated with your research.

If you need more than one year to complete your research, you will need to apply for an extension to the HRRC before your one year expiration date. If this is needed, please submit in writing a statement of your request for extension and the reasons. You must also include a statement that no changes to your research have been made since this initial approval.

We wish you success with your research.

Sincerely,

Robert Duchmann
HRRC Member

cc: M. Bronson

OFFICE OF INSTITUTIONAL ADVANCEMENT

50 PHELAN AVENUE • CLOUD 306 • SAN FRANCISCO, CA 94112 • 415.239.3014 • FAX 415.239.3010

Memo

To: Regina Rowland

From: Robert Gabriner, Vice Chancellor of Institutional Advancement

Date: February 9, 2007

Re: Your research project

The Office of Institutional Advancement has reviewed the proposed research project entitled "Co-Creation of Meaning in the Multicultural Context Via Group Dialogue and Visual Mapping Processes". We are agreeable to having the research proceed at CCSF as long as the proposal and its related materials (e.g., consent form) receive the approval of the California Institute of Integral Studies' Human Research Review Committee.

Upon completion of the project, please submit a copy of your final findings to our office for our reference.

FINAL REFLECTION FORM

Address the below listed questions (no essay please, simply restate the questions and provide your answers).

You get most out of this assignment...

* if you follow the below listed sequence
* if you write this reflection after you have completed all other tasks
* and if you leave yourself plenty of time to enjoy completing this assignment.

1. How do you feel?

This is a chance for you to reflect on how the semester has been for you personally. What rewards and challenges have you experienced?

2. What happened?

Reflect on some significant moments of your learning experience in the class (face-to-face and online).

3. What did you learn?

Think about all the activities you participated in and the tasks you performed either individually and/or in your team.

Revisit "objectives" listed in each week (weekly content) to see if you accomplished the class goals.

Reflect on some objectives that provided significant insights for you personally and/or professionally.

List different aspects of your learning. What worked? What didn't work?

4. How does this relate to the real world?

Reflect on how the learnings you take away from this class assist you in your personal and professional life.

What knowledge base did we tap into and/or build that ads to your professional repertoire?

What skill sets did we practice that you consider important for your professional/personal growth?

What did you learn that assists your personal growth beyond the classwork?

5. What if?

Reflect on various aspects of your participation (face-to-face, online, team, assignments, etc...)

If this was a traditional face-to-face class what would you do differently?

If this was a full online class with no face-to-face meetings what would you do differently?

How would your experience of learning be different in these three scenarios: a) traditional, b) hybrid, c) 100% online

6. What next?

Now since you've been through the entire semester, and you are working on assembling your portfolio, what new strategies might you put in place in regard to work habits for future classes?

Has your real-world perspective/behavior changed due to your learnings in this class?

What classes might you want to take next?

Will you consider taking an online class again? Why? Why not?

What advice might you have for me teaching this class again next spring?

INTEGRAL TOOLS: SPIRAL DYNAMICS INTEGRAL (SD*i*)
AND ALL QUADRANTS, ALL LEVELS (AQAL)

The current version of SD*i* (Beck & Cowan, 2006) represents the development of a 50-year research effort initiated in the 1960s by Clare. W. Graves, a U.S. professor of psychology. Graves' Spiral Dynamics research was continued by Don Beck and Chris Cowan, who have successfully performed transformative practical applications of this theory in corporate management and governments in North America and South Africa. Beck is currently involved in solving the Middle East crisis. The two developers, Beck and Cowan, have since gone separate ways. In spite of the successful application of SD*i* in organizations and governments, the theory remains a hypothesis that is hard to prove; Cowan himself—while still working with Spiral Dynamics as a foundation for his consulting business—no longer supports the integral branch of SD*i* (used in this dissertation) as it emerges from Beck and other integral theorists such as Ken Wilber.

Beck's SD*i* together with the work of some other developmental scientists and Wilber's AQAL have, at times, been presented as one merged set of theories, with small variations in terminology. Wilber incorporated SD*i* concepts into AQAL but renamed them with a rainbow color system; Beck adjusted SD*i* to incorporate some AQAL concepts. Each AQAL quadrant's fundamental structure also interfaces with SD*i*, and Figure 54 shows how the terminology of SD*i* has been adjusted to address the issues pertinent to each AQAL quadrant.

This appendix presents a brief and somewhat simplistic summary of Beck's SD*i*, the aspect of Spiral Dynamics theory used in this dissertation. In SD*i* theory, cultures evolve through a series of values-attracting meta-meme (vMEME) systems (Beck & Cowan, 2006) that form a spiral of evolution. vMEMEs are similar to genes in the human DNA, in that they belong to the psychosocial and organizational DNA that holds the code for the "dynamics of change, leadership, complexity, alignment and integration" (p. 4). Each vMEME

> represents, firstly then, a *core intelligence* that forms systems and directs human behavior. Secondly, it *impacts upon all life choices* as a decision-making framework. Thirdly, each vMEME can manifest itself in both *healthy and unhealthy forms*. Fourthly, such a vMEME is a discrete *structure* for thinking, not just a set of ideas, values or cause....it can *brighten and dim* (p. 4)

as life conditions change. A vMEME structure is thus engrained deeply into the human system where it interacts with a person's genetic makeup and participates in forming identity.

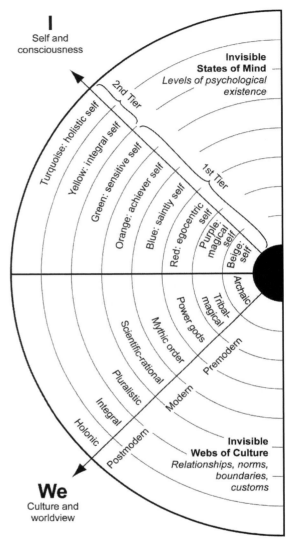

Figure 54. Spiral Dynamics Integral (SD*i*) applied to All Quadrants All Levels (AQAL). Author's Quadrants: All Levels: All Lines Schematic). From *Spiral Dynamics Integral Level One* Reprinted with permission of the author.

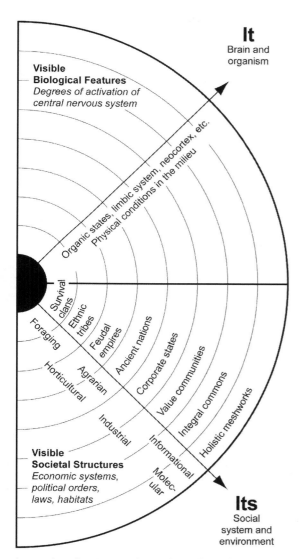

It
Brain and
organism

Visible
Biological Features
*Degrees of activation of
central nervous system*

Organic states, limbic system, neocortex, etc.
Physical conditions in the milieu

Survival
clans
Foraging
Ethnic
tribes
Horticultural
Feudal
empires
Agrarian
Ancient nations
Corporate states
Industrial
Value communities
Integral commons
Informational
Holistic meshworks
Molec-
ular

Visible
Societal Structures
*Economic systems,
political orders,
laws, habitats*

Its
Social
system and
environment

image, based on Don Beck's 4Q/8L: All Quadrants All Levels (based on Ken Wilber's All

Certification Course Manual, by D. E. Beck, n.d., Denton, TX: Spiral Dynamics Group, pp. 6–7.

Each vMEME stage of SD*i* has a distinct structure of experiencing the world and making meaning, and presents particular dilemmas (cultural, social, environmental, personal, political, economic, technological, medical, financial, etc.) that need to be solved in order to resolve the stage. Once those dilemmas are solved, the qualities of the next stage naturally evolve to solve the new dilemmas that cannot be solved with the previous stage's qualities (Beck & Cowan, 2006).

Evolution through the vMEME stages involves vertical movement up a spiral. Life conditions "consisting of historic times, geographic place, existential problems, and societal circumstances" (Beck & Cowan, 2006, p. 5) change and in this process activate vMEMEs "which may merge, surge, regress or fade in response" (p. 5) as the individual or society evolves up the spiral. This evolutionary spiral is "forged by a pendulum-like alteration" (p. 5) between focus on "me"-vMEMES and focus on "we"-vMEMES. In the me or individual phase, individuals acquire new ideas and perspectives. When many individuals have integrated the new perspective, new problems manifest on a societal level and the focus naturally shifts to the we or collective phase. This evolutionary process is cyclical, and vMEMEs come in phases "like waves on a beach, ENTERing as a surge, dominating the scene as strong PEAK, and then EXITing from prominence to be replaced by another" (p. 5).

The spiral grows upward from "lesser to greater complexity" (Beck & Cowan, 2006, p. 5). The movement into more complexity cannot be avoided; in other words, the development is unidirectional up the spiral and cannot be undone once completed. However, it is horizontal development, growing density in each vMEME system, that provides the upward movement. Vertical development happens gradually. A person or a group usually spends most of their time in a particular vMEME system where they have their center of gravity, but they are also influenced by the systems on either side of the one they are currently occupying. vMEMEs "coexist as mixtures" (p. 5), with a center of gravity in a particular vMEME but with aspects of other vMEMEs awakened under certain circumstances. There is always the opportunity to project forward in the form of a peak experience that achieves a state that is characteristic of the next stage, outlining a path to follow later as more density is achieved in the qualities of the current stage. In addition, completed evolutionary stages do not disappear but are integrated into the whole and are always available when a problem calls for awakening various integrated parts of earlier structures. The simplified visual depiction in Figure 55, showing the eight vMEME structures that have been defined so far, implies nested hierarchies (Beck & Cowan, 2006). Each vMEME is represented by a color and its name (code) expresses the essence of that stage (p. 5). In addition, each vMEME is directed by a certain principle through a motivational form and a system focus.

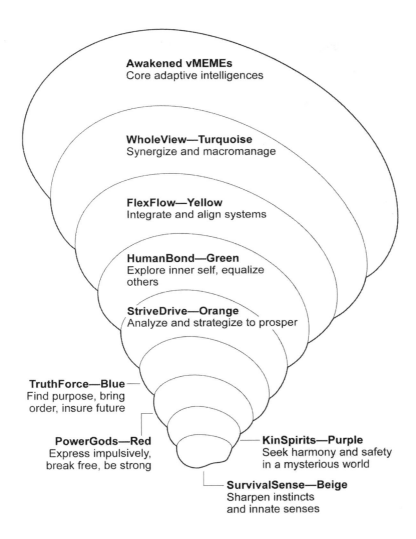

Figure 55. The holonic cone of Spiral Dynamics Integral (SD*i*) vMEMEs. vMEME = values-attracting meta-meme. Author's image, based on the figure from *Spiral Dynamics Integral Level One Certification Course Manual*, by D. E. Beck, n.d., Denton, TX: Spiral Dynamics Group, pp. 6–7. Reprinted with permission of the author.

As in other developmental models, vMEMEs "cluster in tiers of six" (Beck & Cowan, 2006, p. 5), with the shift from First Tier to Second Tier occurring when the quality and quantity of new dilemmas is so overwhelming that an entire paradigm shift and leap is necessary to create solutions. The first six vMEMEs form the current paradigm and the First Tier, and have in common "subsistence-level concerns with starvation (beige), of magical spirits (purple), of aggressors (red), of disruption to law and order (blue), of loss of autonomy (orange), and of social disapproval (green)" (p. 5). The Second Tier, a newer and emerging paradigm, deals with a different set of basic interests:

> [The] being series recontextualizes the old in terms of an information rich, highly mobile, "Global village" where all the vMEMEs are active at once (yellow) and (turquoise) as they resonate with compassionate strength for the enhancement of both one and all. (p. 5)

Qualities manifest differently in the Second Tier. For example, SD*i* has been critiqued for its proposal of hierarchy, but it is not the same kind of hierarchy we are accustomed to presently on the First Tier. In the Second Tier, hierarchies are expected to be redefined or redesigned to serve the good of all in a self-organizing manner (Beck & Cowan, 2006).

The following tables present brief descriptions of the various SD*i* vMEMEs and their associated code, color, principle, motivational form, system focus, start date, and characteristics. First Tier vMEMEs are shown in Table 13, and Second Tier vMEMEs in Table 14.

Table 13

Spiral Dynamics Integral (SDi) First Tier vMEMES and Their Qualities

Quality					First Tier vMEMES	
Code	SurvivalSense	KinSpirits	PowerGods	TruthForce	StriveDrive	HumanBond
Color	Beige	Purple	Red	Blue	Orange	Green
Principle	Survival band	Tribal order	Exploitive empire	Authority structure	Strategic enterprise	Social network
Motivational form	Instinct-driven	Safety-driven	Power-driven	Order-driven	Success-driven	People-driven
System focus	Individual/elites	Communal/collective	Individual/elites	Communal/collective	Individual/elites	Communal/collective
Started	100,000 years ago	50,000 years ago	10,000 years ago	5,000 years ago	300 years ago	150 years ago
Characteristics	Automatic/instinctive—sharpen instincts and innate senses (biology-driven, sensory, humans as smartest of animal species)	Animistic/tribalistic—seek harmony and safety in a mysterious world (mystical spirits, signs, and nests for safety, individual subsumed in group, powerful shaman chieftains)	Egocentric/exploitive—express impulsively, break free, be strong (power impulses, and displays, hedonism and immediate sensory satisfaction, spontaneous guilt-free, daring)	Absolutistic/saintly—find purpose, bring order, insure future (only one right way to think/be, finds purpose in causes and dedication to crusades, guilt-based obedience to higher authority)	Materialist/achiever—analyze and strategize to prosper (success-driven search for best, goal-oriented planning and strategies to do better; economic focus of competition)	Relativistic/sociocentric—explore inner self, equalize others (consensus-seeking spirituality, egalitarian and humanitarian, tolerance/acceptance of a range of differences)

Quality	First Tier vMEMES					
	SurvivalSense	KinSpirits	PowerGods	TruthForce	StriveDrive	HumanBond
Code	SurvivalSense	KinSpirits	PowerGods	TruthForce	StriveDrive	HumanBond
Color	Beige	Purple	Red	Blue	Orange	Green
Basic orientation	"I survive"	"We are safe"	"I control"	"We are saved"	"I improve"	"We become"
Deep concerns	Basic survival	Clan wellbeing and custom	Dominance and control	Obedience and stability	Autonomy and improvement	Equality and community
Political system and power distribution ratio	Survival clans	Tribal orders (e.g. Haiti)	Feudal empires, confederal (e.g. Taliban, Iraq)	Authoritarian democracy, unitary (e.g. Cuba)	Multiparty democracy, federal (e.g. US, UK, Singapore)	Multiparty/social democracy, unitary, (e.g. Scandinavia)
Economic system/resource distribution	Eat when hungry	Mutual reciprocity and kinship	To victors belong the spoils	The just earn of the rewards	Each acts on own behalf to prosper	All should benefit equally
Transitional factors leading to next vMEME	Awareness of distinct self, awakening of cause and effect, concerns with threats/fears, survival requires group effort	Emergence of dominant ego, self more powerful than group, confronts adversaries and dangerous forces to control, niches are limited	Recognition of mortality, quest for meaning and purpose in life, extended time-frame/structures, consequential thinking arises	Aspires to better life now for self, challenges higher authority to produce tangible results, seeks one best way among many options	Discovers material wealth does not bring happiness or peace, renewed need for community, sharing, and richer inner life, sensitivity to have, have-not gap	Overwhelmed by economic and emotional costs of caring, confronted by chaos/disorder, need for tangible results and functionality, knowing moves above feeling

Note. vMEME = values-attracting meta-meme. Author's table; data from Beck (n.d.).

Table 14

Spiral Dynamics Integral (SDi) Second Tier vMEMES and Their Qualities

	Quality	Second Tier vMEMES	
Code	FlexFlow or Integral Commons	WholeView or Holistic Meshworks	Not defined yet but stands as symbol for continuous motion
Color	Yellow	Turquoise	Coral
Principle	Systemic flow	Holistic organism	
Motivational form	Process-oriented	Synthesis-oriented	
System focus	Individual/elites	Communal/collectives	Individual/elites
Started	50 years ago	30 years ago	
Characteristics	Systemic/integrative—integrate and align systems (big-picture views of living systems, integrative structures and forms in evolutionary flows, understands that chaos and change are natural)	Globalist/renewalist—synergize and macromanage (synergy of all life forms/forces, planetary concerns rank above narrow group interests, recorded world for new meanings and good of the commons)	
Basic orientation	"I learn"	"We experience"	
Deep concerns	Flexibility and natural flows	Living systems and harmonies	
Political system and power distribution ratio	Stratified democracy, integral	Holonic democracy	
Economic system and resource distribution	All formulas contribute to spiritual health	Resources focus on all life	
Transitional factors leading to next vMEME	Senses order within chaos, search for guiding principles, while earth problems arise as technology connects everybody, spirituality back with physics	The next system will be a new form of expressiveness, extended to the planetary level, global problems will appear to require unified control, a new way of being to fit a world where collective living has changed the milieu	

Note. vMEME = values-attracting meta-meme. Author's table; data from Beck (n.d.)

VDM publishing house ltd.

Scientific Publishing House

offers

free of charge publication

of current academic research papers, Bachelor´s Theses, Master's Theses, Dissertations or Scientific Monographs

If you have written a thesis which satisfies high content as well as formal demands, and you are interested in a remunerated publication of your work, please send an e-mail with some initial information about yourself and your work to *info@vdm-publishing-house.com.*

Our editorial office will get in touch with you shortly.

VDM Publishing House Ltd.
Meldrum Court 17.
Beau Bassin
Mauritius
www.vdm-publishing-house.com